THE LIFE OF
ST. MARGARET MARY
ALACOQUE

*"I am come to cast fire on the earth: and what
will I, but that it be kindled?"*—Luke 12:49

GW00566610

Apparition of the Sacred Heart of Jesus to
St. Margaret Mary Alacoque.

The Life of St. Margaret Mary Alacoque

By
Most Rev. Émile Bougaud, D.D.
Bishop of Laval

Translated by
A Visitandine of Baltimore, Maryland

"The thoughts of his heart [are] to all generations. . . . To deliver their souls from death; and feed them in famine."
—Psalm 32:11, 19

TAN Books
An Imprint of Saint Benedict Press, LLC
Charlotte, North Carolina

Nihil Obstat: Arthur J. Scanlon, S.T.D.
                Censor Librorum

Imprimatur: ✠ Patrick J. Hayes, D.D.
                Archbishop of New York
                August 5, 1920

Library of Congress Catalog Card No.: 86-80329

ISBN: 978-089555-297-6

Printed and bound in the United States of America.

TAN Books
An Imprint of Saint Benedict Press, LLC
Charlotte, North Carolina

2012

PUBLISHER'S NOTE

Bishop Bougaud's biography of St. Margaret Mary Alacoque has been recommended to us by several knowledgeable people as the best, most authentic and most inspirational life of the Saint in English, for which reason we have chosen to reproduce this work rather than any number of others that are available.

The reader may easily omit reading Chapter I (beginning on page 17), which gives the historical background against which the story occurred. This chapter will be of interest to those who enjoy history and/or are interested in the theological context in which St. Margaret Mary lived, particularly with regard to the spread of Jansenism and Protestantism. But one can skip over this chapter without missing any vital facts connected with St. Margaret Mary's life and the message entrusted to her.

—The Publisher, 1990

CONTENTS.

PAGE

DEDICATION 5

INTRODUCTION 9

CHAPTER

I. State of the Church in France at the Birth of
Saint Margaret Mary. 1647 17

II. Birth of Saint Margaret Mary—First Years—
Childhood and Youth. 1647-1662 34

III. Margaret's Vocation—She Enters the Visitation
of Paray. 1662-1671 54

IV. The Convent of Paray. 1671 71

V. Margaret Mary's Novitiate—God Prepares her for
the Great Mission about to be intrusted to her
—Her Profession. May 26, 1671-November 6,
1672. 92

VI. Final Exterior Preparations—Last Finishing
Stroke within. November 6, 1672-December
27, 1673 110

VII. The Aurora of the Devotion to the Sacred Heart 126

VIII. The Visitation Established to be the Sanctuary of
the Sacred Heart 142

IX. The Revelations of the Sacred Heart. 1673-1675 160

X. Almighty God Prepares the Convent of Paray to
become the Sanctuary of the Sacred Heart.
1675-1678. 180

XI. Mother Greyfié submits Margaret's Extraordinary
Ways to a New Examination—Her Severity and
her Fearlessness—Father de la Colombière
Returns to Paray—His Death. 1678-1684 . . 194

XII. The Saintly Sister among her Novices—The
Secret of the Sublime Revelations Escapes her
in Spite of herself—First Public Adoration of
the Sacred Heart. 1684-1685 220

7

CHAPTER   PAGE

XIII. The Apostolate of the Sacred Heart Begun—With what Modesty and Zeal Margaret Mary begins to Spread Devotion to the Sacred Heart. 1686–1689 244

XIV. The Last Grand Revelation—The King and France. 1689 263

XV. Margaret Mary's Mission Ended—She is Consumed in the Flames of Divine Love—Her Holy Death. 1690 274

XVI. Devotion to the Heart of Jesus Begins in the World—Anger of Some, Enthusiasm of Others 290

XVII. The First-fruits of Devotion to the Sacred Heart —The Church of France Vivified in the Rays of the Sacred Heart—Beatification of Saint Margaret Mary 315

XVIII. Unexpected and Marvellous Spread of Devotion to the Heart of Jesus amid the Misfortunes of France—The Second Part of the Mission confided to Saint Margaret Mary Approaches its Accomplishment. 1870–1874 334

XIX. Montmartre—The Wish of St. Francis de Sales —The Visitation Order and Jansenism—The Visitandines as Reformers and Founders— The Visitandines in the Revolution—the Scapu‧lar of the Sacred Heart in the Reign of Terror —The Guard of Honor of the Sacred Heart— The Consecration of the World to the Sacred Heart 356

XX. Enthronement of the Sacred Heart—Some American Associations—The Words of Pope Benedict XV., and the Decree of Canonization of Saint Margaret Mary Alacoque, Professed Religious of the Order of the Visitation of the Blessed Virgin Mary of the diocese of Autun 378

INTRODUCTION.

In the two volumes devoted to the telling of St. de Chantal's story and the origin of the Visitation, I thought I had finished my task. But a pure, sweet voice called me, that of the first of St. Chantal's daughters raised to the altar, Saint Margaret Mary. She it was who was chosen by God to finish the work of St. Francis de Sales and his great co-operatrix. Both had labored together in the construction of the edifice. They dug the foundations, drew the grand plans. But the crown was wanting. It was Margaret Mary, that saintly and humble virgin, who was deputed to place it on its brow. In some way, then, the Life of our saintly Sister is a necessary sequel to the history of St. Chantal. The biography of the one illumines and perfects that of the other.

But if Saint Margaret Mary interests us as the first beatified daughter of the holy founders of the Visitation, we hesitate not to say that she awakens our sympathy from still another point of view. Hidden in the depths of her cloister, in the seclusion of a little town far from Paris, she received a first-class mission. She was deputed by Almighty God to come to the assistance of the Church in the fulfilment of a work the greatest and, at the same time, the most formidable ever accomplished in this world.

This work, we well know, is not to remain inactive in the midst of the instability of human things, of dynasties, empires, and even whole nations, which shall sooner or later crumble into dust. Nor is it to impose on man's proud reason a collection of dogmas whose titles he has,

9

indeed, the right to study, but which can regenerate him
only by humbling him. This work, still more elevated,
so luminous and yet so obscure, is to persuade man that
God loves him.

Yes, one day, from the depths of His eternity, God
looked upon man ; and like some great king, some
powerful genius, who falls a victim to the charms of a
little lisping child, that child his own, God was capti-
vated. He loved man. He loved him even to passion,
even to folly. He loved him so far as to make Himself
man, in order to bridge those distances which, of whatever nature they may be, are insupportable to love.
God loved man even to suffer and to die for him.

Yes, He who hangs there on that gibbet, His hands
and feet pierced, His Heart opened, is God ! And what
is He doing there ? He is suffering, He is dying, through
love ; yea, He is dying of love !

This is what the Church is commissioned to teach to
man. This is the price of his regeneration. Outside
this we find only feebleness of heart, shipwreck of morals.
A man may indeed be an honest man ; but the folly of
sacrifice, of virginity, of devotedness, of martyrdom,
arises only from faith in the folly of the Cross.

This love of God for man is so great, so prodigious,
that it has become a scandal to the world. It is the old
and universal stumbling-block, the final reason of all
schisms and all unbelief. If Arius, for example, separated from the Church, it was because he could not believe that that Man who had one day appeared in Judea
could, without certain equivocal expressions, without
exaggeration, be truly styled the Only Son of God.
There was in such abasement a grandeur of love revolting to the heresiarch. Nor could Nestorius admit that
the Eternal Son of God had reposed in the womb of an
humble virgin, that he had been nourished with her
milk, and that He had called her mother ! Luther and
Calvin,—why did they break anew the unity of the

Church ? Because they could not believe either in the
tribunal of reconciliation, that is, in mercy that makes
no account of ingratitude; or in indulgences, that is,
in one of the most tender industries of the Saviour to
supply for our ever-recurring insufficiencies ; or in the
Holy Eucharist, that is, in His constant abiding with
those whom He loves. Narrow hearts, which know not
what it is to love ! And if in our day there are so many
men that pass before the Cross wagging their head, who
gaze at our altars with a smile of contempt, it is because
the folly of the Cross disgusts them. Man's egotism,
incapable of loving, sinks under the weight of such
mysteries ; and the Church cannot draw from him this
cry that would transfigure him : *Et nos credidimus cha-
ritati quam habet Deus in nobis:* " Yes, we believe that God
has love for us." [1]

But precisely because the work is formidable, because
the Church seems at some moments to bend under the
weight, God comes to her aid by some master-strokes.
As, when sophists multiplied, He made a sign, and we
saw appear those whom we shall call volunteers, extraordinary agents of the truth, a St. Augustine, a St.
Thomas, a Bossuet : in like manner, when the world
grew cold, and God's love was no longer credited ;
when we saw degenerate purity, sacrifice, apostleship,
devotedness, and martyrdom,—all those qualities that
derive their origin from the heart, but from the heart
transfigured by divine love,—God made a sign, and we
saw arise those whom we shall call volunteers, the
extraordinary agents of love. Thus, for example, when
Constantine ascended the imperial throne, the early
persecutions passed ; when he extended over the Church
his imperial purple, he introduced with those honors,
though unknown to himself and without willing it, the
seeds of lukewarmness. When arise those cold-hearted
doctors whom we have already cited, Arius, Nestorius,

[1] I. John iv. 16.

Eutyches, whose doctrine was at best only the denial of infinite love ; when old pagan sensualism was slowly penetrating into the Church,—at that moment the earth opened, and from her bosom came forth the instruments of the Passion of Jesus Christ : the cross on which He died, the nails that pierced His feet and hands, the crown that wounded His brow, the lance that opened His Heart.   The world was providentially roused to new life by contact with those sacred trophies of the Passion.

And who was the privileged creature to whom God gave this great mission of reviving the world in the fourth century ?   A woman—the pious Helena, the mother of Constantine, the imperial Liberator of the Church.   It was a woman, and we can divine the cause. Ordinarily inferior to man in gifts of intellect, woman is his superior in those of the heart.   She loves more, she loves better.   Even in thought she never separates love from sacrifice.   To love is for her self-immolation.   It was, then, a woman ; and, moreover, it was a mother. That, too, we can understand.

Before the Cross, before the folly of love, man may sometimes pass wagging his head ; but the mother, never !   She takes her child in her arms, she raises her eyes to the Cross, and she says to herself : " What is there so astonishing in Jesus Christ's dying for His children ?   Would *I* not do the same for mine ?"

It was, then, a woman, a wife, a mother, who, in the fourth century, received the mission to revivify the world by holding up to it the Cross of Jesus Christ ; and, in fact, she succeeded.   The great devotion of those barbarous nations of the Middle Ages was devotion to the Cross.   They even fought battles for its restitution when it had passed out of their hands.   The West rose to a man to get possession of the Saviour's empty tomb. When arrived in Jerusalem, those hardy warriors, a God-frey de Bouillon, a Tancred, a Baldwin, were seen mak-ing the circuit of the Holy City, barefoot and shedding

,bundant tears. Some of them even expired of love
and sorrow when kissing the rocks of Calvary. France
trembled one day with the purest emotion that had
ever thrilled her soul, when St. Louis re-entered his capital, bearing in his royal hands the crown of thorns that
had steeped in blood the brow of Jesus Christ. During
five centuries, from St. Helena to St. Louis, the world,
rewarmed by contact with the holy cross on which
Jesus Christ had died, could utter the conquering cry :
Yes, we believe in God's infinite love for man !

But it was not difficult for an observer to see that this
devotion, owing to human infirmity, would soon be insufficient to support a flame that had evidently begun
to flicker. The Crusades became more and more an im-
possibility ; in vain did the Sovereign Pontiffs urge the
Faithful to rescue the profaned tomb of Jesus Christ.
A symbol more touching than even the Cross had become
a necessity, something that would sink more deeply into
hearts. Then, in the solitude of a Belgian convent, God
appeared to a privileged soul, and gave her the mission
to turn all eyes and hearts to the Holy Eucharist, and to
ask from the Church some new manifestations of homage
for this august mystery.

And who was the favored creature predestined to
revive the world in the thirteenth century, and to be
what we shall call an extraordinary agent of love?
Again a woman, and this time a virgin! However
pure, however clear-sighted the heart of the mother,
there is something more beautiful, more crystalline still,
and that is the heart of a virgin ! And besides, the
mystery of the Eucharist being the mystery of the
angels, it was fitting to reserve to virginity the honors
of that revelation and of that apostolate.

As nothing happens in the Church but by the breath-
ings of God's Spirit, whilst the new pomps of Corpus
Christi were being displayed, an unknown monk sent
forth the *Book of the " Imitation,"* the most beautiful

pages that have ever fallen from the pen of man, especially Book IV., so calculated to inflame hearts with love
for the Holy Eucharist. At the same time St. Thomas
composed his incomparable hymns, "*Lauda Sion*" and
"*Adoro Te Supplex.*" Then Gothic cathedrals rose as if
to be triumphal arches in honor of the Holy Eucharist.
From their hallowed precincts came solemnly forth
those beautiful processions of the Blessed Sacrament of
which we know ; and the world, reanimated and transformed by the warmth of the devotion, began its march
anew, the cry of victory upon its lips : *We believe in
God's infinite love for us.*

Three centuries rolled by ! Suddenly there sweeps
over the Church a current icy cold, freezing. Luther
appeared, and denied infinite love in its most tender
manifestations. Calvin followed, and suppressed the
Eucharist. Jansenius arose, and, though not denying
the Holy Eucharist, taught the Faithful to abstain from
it with *the most profound respect.* Books on, or, as we
should say, against, frequent Communion were written,
and treasures of learning were called into play, in order
to teach the Faithful that Jesus Christ established the
Divine Sacrament that they might receive it as seldom
as possible. Faith in infinite love grew weak throughout the world ; coldness was everywhere felt.

O my God, my God ! what art Thou now going to
do ? By what ingenious device art Thou going to reanimate souls ? What secret remedy hast Thou in reserve for times so sad ? And to what privileged soul
art Thou now going to confide it ?

To reanimate faith and piety, God again chose a
woman, a virgin. Evidently, He wished to make none
other the extraordinary agent of His love !

With divine art He prepared the chosen virgin for
her mission. When her heart had become like that of
an angel ; when one night she was plunged in ecstasy,
immovable, recollected, her arms crossed on her breast,

her face strangely lighted, all aglow with interior fire, a celestial radiance, visible to her alone, arose above the altar. In it she perceived, as she tremblingly glanced through the grate, the adorable person of our Lord Jesus Christ! When, at last, she ventured to fix upon Him her eyes moist with tears, she saw the Saviour's breast resplendent, and His Heart sparkling like a sun in the midst of flames. And hark, a voice addressed her : " *Behold the Heart that has so loved men, even to consume itself for them !*" Several times were these visions repeated, and in them were the adorable designs of God revealed to her. She saw the wounds of society healed by degrees through contact with this Divine Heart ; and the Church, rewarmed, reanimated by the rays of this furnace of love, resume her triumphant, benevolent march through the world.

To add one more charm to this devotion, that is for the French heart, God gave it to His Church by the hands of France. It was to a French religious, member of a French Order, in a town of France, that He made known what He wished her to promulgate to the universal Church. And not only is it *to* France that the revelation is made, it is made *for* France. So well does it correspond on the one hand to her most noble aspirations, her most elevated sentiments ; so sweetly and efficaciously does it touch on the other her saddest wounds, that it is evident God thought of France in giving to the world the grand revelation of the Sacred Heart. Yes, He not only thought, He expressed His thought in words ; He announced it with a precision truly miraculous. In fact, in proportion as France plunged into the Sacred Heart, has she been regenerated.

Behold of what we shall treat in the following pages, though for it we should borrow the tongues of angels or of saints. We shall, however, try what we can do ; for not to try would be in us the blackest ingratitude.

Before beginning, we shall, however, premise one observation. Just as we might say to a youth about entering upon the study of mathematics, "This book treats of infinitesimal calculus. Do not open it, for you will understand nothing in it:" in like manner, if any one believes not in the infinite love of God for man displayed from His crib to His cross, and still shown in the Holy Eucharist, let him not open this book! Should he do so, he will be amazed and scandalized. I am going to recount the strangest things, facts the most extraordinary, the most inconceivable, and yet the most certain, as well as the most touching: a God loving man to folly, yes, even to passion! This God, forgotten, despised, betrayed, ignored by man, has not despaired of man. Instead of punishing him, of crushing him, as He might have done, He resolved to conquer him by force of love. And this is the story that I am now going to tell.

O Jesus, from my mother's arms to the ardent years of my youth, I never ceased to believe in that infinite love which is the sap, the divine sustenance, of Christianity; and now, at the age that brings to man experience of the world, and, if he has been faithful, opens to him the splendors of heaven, I feel that same infinite love shining on my head with undimmed brilliancy. It is true to say, I now scarcely believe in man's love, for I believe much more in God's love! Help me, then, O Christ, O Saviour, O Friend, and may these my last words, if they are to be my last, bear to the very depths of souls the knowledge of that love whose charm I have tasted, but of whose sweetness I shall never be able to speak!

ORLEANS, May 24, 1874.

LIFE OF
SAINT MARGARET MARY ALACOQUE.

CHAPTER I.

STATE OF THE CHURCH IN FRANCE AT THE BIRTH OF SAINT MARGARET MARY.

1647.

"Mane nobiscum, Domine, quoniam advesperascit, et inclinata est jam dies."

" Stay with us, O Lord, because it is towards evening, and the day is now far spent."—*St. Luke* xxiv. 29.

IN 1647, the year in which Margaret Mary was born at Vérosvres, a small Burgundian village seven leagues from Paray, Catholic France had just achieved a great victory. The latter part of the sixteenth century had been spent in expelling schism and heresy from her bosom. Freed from the bad leaven, she flourished in the seventeenth.

Joy was great in Christian homes; for never, perhaps, had France known so fearful a danger. With its doctrine of reason's absolute independence, its contempt of authority, and its hatred of ecclesiastical rule, Protestantism was calculated to please a nation in love with equality, naturally rebellious, and quickly wearied of that authority of which it had so much need. On the other hand, enervated and corrupted under the frivolous reigns of Francis I., Henry II., Charles IX., and Henry III., she was only too well prepared by her depraved morality to curtail her ancient doctrines. She hesitated a moment; and heresy, which had seduced a part of the high nobility, mounted the steps of the throne. It was

)ne of those solemn hours that deride the future of a
world. Let us suppose that, after the defection of all
England, of a part of Germany, Prussia, Sweden, Nor-
way, and Switzerland, France, too, had proved recreant:
humanly speaking, the Catholic Church in Europe
would have succumbed.

Happily, if under certain forms Protestantism exercised a charm over France, under others it inspired invincible repugnance. France is a thoroughly religious
nation, though led rather by the heart than the head.
Into religion, as into all things else, she carries her
ardent and lively nature, her love of being led rather than
convinced; and in the love she bestows she conceives no
limit other than that which she exacts. In this respect,
Protestantism was radically incapable of satisfying
France.

Protestantism is not a spontaneous growth. It only
ingrafted itself on the old trunk of the Gospel as a so-
called development and improvement. It established
itself in a manner entirely contradictory; that is, by
lopping off, by retrenching. Now, what it suppressed
was precisely that which had charms for France, that
which had, from the first, so completely, so lastingly,
attached her to the Catholic faith.

The first dogma of Protestantism, or rather its first
curtailment, was that Jesus Christ did not become incarnate for all men ; He suffered and died only for
some; His Heart is not large enough to embrace all
humanity.

The second dogma of Protestantism is that, even in
this narrow circle of the predestined, the mercy of Jesus
Christ has limits. It does not pardon sins, it does not
remit debts. One cannot weep at His feet the misfortune of having offended Him, nor rise up, his eyes
glistening with tears, in the assurance that the love of
Jesus has consumed all, purified all, forgotten all.

The third dogma of Protestantism is that the Lord

does not remain among us in the Holy Eucharist. According to the Lutheran doctrine, He passes like a flash of lightning; whilst the Calvinists teach that He is not present at all. Neither the one nor the other believes God sufficiently loving " to make it His delight to be with the children of men." [1]

Viewed in the light of faith and in relation to God, Protestantism is only a half-gift, a half-love. Hence, how could it captivate a nation in which the heart predominates; a nation moved more by feeling (with which in vivacity none other can compare) than by principle? France, believing or infidel, virtuous or depraved, is never anything by halves. She is, according to the love that sways her, always in the extreme of good or evil.

The consequences of Protestantism are, besides, worthy of its principles. When Protestants admit in God only a half-love, how require of man a whole love? Thus, scarcely had Luther and Calvin formulated their doctrine, than one sees the spirit of heroic self-sacrifice die out like a wind suddenly lulled. Holy enthusiasm is extinguished ; no more consecrated vestals and apostles; souls that despise all for God are no longer to be found. To the rapture that produced wonders succeeds the morality that is limited to the avoidance of faults. Soon it was necessary to mask this sterility. That to which these innovators could no longer attain was despised; the religious state was suppressed, penance abolished. Fearing lest man should surpass God in proofs of love, those proofs are forbidden him.

This was the finishing stroke of Protestantism in France. What ! no more religious? Can we no longer give apostles to God? We are forbidden voluntary sacrifice, the outward expression of love's passion and folly . What ! shall we have no more tabernacles in our churches? Shall the living Christ go forth?

[1] Prov. viii. 31.

Shall we have of Him but a shadowy remembrance as of one belonging to far-off ages? France felt to the core the stroke aimed at her deepest religious interests, and she rejected Protestantism as one would a restless, troubled dream.

Other reasons, political and national, were added to these. Owing to circumstances in which it is permitted us to see the hand of God, France was the first-born of Catholic nations; and in consequence of circumstances still more marvellous, she found herself from her crib endowed with a genius so like that of the Church that, from the very first, their union was perfect. Time, which destroys all that is artificial, has only developed and confirmed this harmony. All the grand enterprises of France have had a religious as well as a national character. Her greatest men, Clovis, Charlemagne, St. Louis, have had a double aureola on their brow. They are as celebrated in the history of the Church as in that of France. The only hours in which our prosperity appeared for a moment to decline, were those in which we seemed desirous of separation from God. Our glorious epochs, on the contrary, are contemporary with our greatest services rendered the Church. So true is this, that the idea now possesses all minds that we are a privileged race, a sort of royal priesthood, charged to protect and defend truth, justice, and virtue, and gain for them the world's respect. Protestantism would drag us down from our unique rank. This mission that we believe to have received at Tolbiac; this title of Eldest Sons of the Church, gratefully decreed us by the Papacy; this distinctive feature of a nation the most Catholic, the freest, the most devoted, and the most independent, in which we find soldiers, apostles, Sisters of Charity; in fine, the watch we have kept as sentinels for twelve long centuries at the door of Rome,—must we renounce? Must we sheathe Charlemagne's trusty sword? France shuddered at the thought; and, with characteristic ardor, turned once more to the old religion of her fathers!

I do not think history records a more acute, a more general emotion than that which seized upon France in 1589, at the death of Henry III. He had no children, and his only heir was a Huguenot. We have had in our hands a number of manuscripts of the sixteenth century: deliberations of parliament, municipal acts, private papers never intended for publicity; and we should never be able to recount the expressions of consternation therein recorded at the thought of an heretical king. The ardent emotion that then burst forth was subdued by the cool determination to suffer everything rather than accept him. What happened in Paris at the announcement of Henry III.'s death was renewed throughout France. "In place of the acclamations of '*Vive le roi!*' usual on such occasions, hats were slouched over eyes by some, or thrown to the ground by others; whilst others again, unwilling to have a Huguenot king, clinched their fists, or grasped hands in pledge of their vow: Rather death a thousand times!" [1]

Then began those public prayers, those solemn pilgrimages; those processions, too noisy, if you will, but so expressive and, on the part of the people, so sincere; in fine, all those manifestations that, far better than the *League*, made Henry IV. understand how true were the dying words of Henry III.: "Cousin, you will never be king of France if you do not become a Catholic." The sincerity of the conversion of Henry IV. has been questioned. But were it even true, which we do not believe, that he yielded to human views in the accomplishment of that great act, what better proof could we wish of the depth and invincible force of the religious current that then bore France along?

Two-and-twenty years of the most reparative of reigns had passed, when France, after the unlooked-for good

[1] Histoire universelle de d'Aubigné, t. iii. liv ii. ch. xxii.

fortune of finding so great a man in the midst of such
a storm, saw him fall under the implacable dagger of
the malcontents. A new cry of anguish escaped her
lips, and she felt for the second time that she was about
to be ingulfed, that she had no longer any hope but in
God. Men's passions were but lightly slumbering, and
there were no barriers to restrain them. The hostile
parties were so irreconcilable that the hand of Richelieu
could with difficulty subdue them, and so unpatriotic
that they were ever ready to call in foreign aid. The
powerful house of Austria surrounded France with a
band of iron, menacing at the time her frontiers; and
when, after a stormy minority, Louis XIII. reached manhood, by one of those strokes in which Richelieu's policy
was revealed, he married Anne of Austria. This was a
brilliant but sterile union. No children—hence, no future! France, full of alarm, again asked herself, in the
event of the king's death, into whose hands the most
Christian kingdom was to fall. Prayers were offered, pilgrimages revived. The king and the queen implored the
intercession of the most saintly persons—the venerable
Mother de Chantal, Blessed Mary of the Incarnation,
the humble Sister Margaret of the Blessed Sacrament, M.
Olier, curé of St. Sulpice, and a host of others—that God
would be pleased to send an heir to the race of St.
Louis. Finally, as individual prayers did not suffice to
avert perils so great, King Louis XIII. descended from
his throne, went to Notre Dame, and there solemnly
consecrated to the Blessed Virgin his person and his
kingdom. All France joined enthusiastically in this
consecration.

Contemporaries have left us long and curious details
of that solemn action; painters and engravers have represented it in a thousand ways. But what is most important to note is its astonishing result. The self-same
year in which France was consecrated to Mary, 1637,
the child was born who was to be called Louis XIV.,

and who was to reign for two-and-seventy years of the most eventful epoch of our history. Six years later, in 1643, a young captain, like Clovis of old, received on the battle-field one of those sudden lights that change the face of the world. Rocroy, realizing at last the dream so patiently pursued by Henry IV., Louis XIII., and Richelieu, snatched from Austria the preponderance of European power, and transferred it to France. At the same time was seen arise a phalanx of geniuses: statesmen, warriors, orators, poets, and first-class prose writers, a single one of whom would suffice for the glory of an age. Their numbers were so great, their variety so rich, that no nation, not even Greece in her palmiest days, could offer anything comparable to it. To this powerful sixteenth century, so agitated, so troubled, so devoured by detestable passions, in which grand national unity, as well as national grandeur, was at every hour jeopardized, succeeded that calm and magnificent period which saw France become the envy and admiration of the world; that period in which Bossuet spoke, Pascal thought, Fénelon wrote, Corneille and Racine sang, Fontaine smiled. Every year produced a masterpiece. Enthusiastic France looked on in rapturous surprise and amazement. She produced for herself and the world a spectacle of the most magnificent intellectual development, moral and religious, that the world had yet witnessed. This was the result of the vow of Louis XIII., the smile of the Mother of God on the people consecrated to her honor.

But gifts, even the rarest, do not dispense a people from energetically rejecting the last dregs of poison, nor from vigilance against relapses into error. Whilst Europe contemplated with astonishment this nation, at one time fallen so low and agitated by convulsions so terrible, then raised so suddenly to the pinnacle of greatness, the year 1675 saw her visibly decline, and succeeding years beheld her prosperity gradually diminish.

Like the patriarch who, after wrestling all night with the angel, rose up in the morning victorious though wounded; so France, from her fearful contest against Protestantism, rose indeed, but not without marks of her struggle.

The violent attacks of Protestantism against the Papacy, its calumnies so manifest, the odious caricatures it scattered abroad, had undoubtedly inspired France with horror; nevertheless the sad impression remained. In such accusations all, perhaps, was not false. Mistrust was excited, and, instead of drawing closer to the insulted and outraged Papacy, France stood on her guard against it. In vain did Fénelon, who felt the danger, write his treatise on the " Power of the Pope," and, to remind France of her sublime mission and true rôle in the world, compose his " History of Charlemagne." [1] In vain did Bossuet majestically rise in the midst of that agitated assembly of 1682, convened to dictate laws to the Holy See, and there, in most touching accents, give vent to professions of fidelity and devotedness toward the Chair of St. Peter. We already notice in his discourse mention no longer made of the "Sovereign Pontiff." The " Holy See," the " Chair of St. Peter," the " Roman Church," were alone alluded to. First and, alas! too manifest signs of coldness in the eyes of him who knew the nature and character of France! Others might obey through duty, might allow themselves to be governed by principle—France, never! She must be ruled by an individual, she must love him that governs her, else she can never obey.

These weaknesses should at least have been hidden in the shadow of the sanctuary, to await the time in which some sincere and honest solution of the misunderstanding could be given. But no! parliaments took hold of it, national vanity identified itself with it. A strange spectacle was now seen. A people the most

[1] This history is, unfortunately, lost.

Catholic in the world; kings who called themselves the
Eldest Sons of the Church and who were really such at
heart; grave and profoundly Christian magistrates,
bishops, and priests, though in the depths of their heart
attached to Catholic unity,—all busied in barricading
themselves against the head of the Church; all digging trenches and building ramparts, that His words
might not reach the Faithful before being handled and
examined, and the laics convinced that they contained
nothing false, hostile, or dangerous.

God keep me from saying any harm of the old French
Church! We have not forgotten that, only a century
before, the bishops of England apostatized at the command of Henry VIII. ; whilst, in 1793, even after the
enervating effects of the eighteenth century, the French
bishops and priests ascended the scaffold, or went into
exile, rather than separate from Catholic unity. It is
not less true that the Church of France at that period
was no longer closely united with the Pope. That
great luminary of the Church, as St. Francis de Sales
calls His Holiness, met in France too much that was
opposed to the benign influence of its rays ; consequently there resulted a diminution of life-giving
warmth, of sap, and of fecundity. This was the first
wound dealt us by Protestantism, and from it the
Church of France bled for two centuries.

There was at the same time a second, perhaps a more
dangerous, wound. The blasphemies uttered by Protestants against the Blessed Sacrament could not be
heard without a thrill of horror. Was there not, however, some truth in what the reformers said ? Was it
not the light and irreverent conduct of Catholics toward
the Holy Eucharist that gave rise to those blasphemies ?
Would it not be better to abstain from holy Communion, or henceforth to make use of it with more reserve ?
Vainly did Fénelon, whose intuitive perception told
him all, write his famous letter on " Frequent Commun-

ion." Vainly did Bossuet pour out his great soul in his admirable " Meditations on the Discourse after the Last Supper." Naught availed. Arnauld's book on " Frequent Communion," or rather *against it*, received universal approbation, and began to direct the conscience of many.

Such writers did unquestionably reject with fear the blind predestination of Protestantism ; but under the pretext of a reaction against the softness of Catholic morals, they led souls to despair. Massillon unconsciously headed the crusade against the mercy of God by his famous discourse *on the small number of the elect ;* and Pascal followed with his biting irony on the Society of Jesus, guilty only of the crime of maintaining and defending the goodness, tenderness, and mercy of God in His relations toward sinners.

All these tendencies were floating, so to say, in the air, vague and undecided, when Jansenism appeared, seized upon them, and reduced them to definitive shape. Jansenism is the most astonishing heresy that has afflicted the Church. Its doctrine is, after all, only a shameful form of Protestantism, for their fundamental principle is the same. It is the doctrine of a God whose love is half-hearted ; who came upon earth, but who had not the heart to die for all men ; who dwells, it is true, in the Holy Eucharist, though one does not precisely know why, for He wishes that we receive Him therein as seldom as possible ; who has established the tribunal of mercy and pardon, but has hedged it round with such conditions as to render it unapproachable.

In order to get a hold on the mind of the people and make these ideas familiar to them, Jansenism concealed the beautiful crucifixes of Christian ages, on which the Saviour is represented with arms widely extended to embrace all mankind, and eyes tenderly lowered to the earth to attract all souls to Himself. They replaced them by the hideous little images still found in some houses, poverty-stricken and ugly, the hands of the Saviour fastened perpendicularly above His head, to enclose within them as few souls as possible, and His eyes so raised toward heaven as no longer to behold the earth. Instead of these words, so sweet to faith, engraven above tabernacles in which the God of love resides : *Quam dilecta tabernacula tua Domine !* (" How lovely are Thy tabernacles, O Lord of hosts !" [1]) they substituted such words as these : " Keep my Sabbaths, and reverence my sanctuary. I am the Lord." [2] Jansenius wrote treatises on frequent Communion, that is to say, against it ; and he made lavish use of his erudition to teach the Faithful to absent themselves from it as much as possible. Toward the Sovereign Pontiff this serpent-like heresy pursued the same policy. It did not deny His power, as do Protestants, but it worked with incredible skill. It knew how to do without Him, and even to disobey Him with profound respect. That is to say, wherever Protestantism denied, Jansenism was hypocritical. Both aimed, though by different means, at the same result, namely, the diminution of divine love in souls.

There was no hope of escaping such dangers except by an energetic reaction of faith and piety. The infinite love of God should have been boldly affirmed ; souls should have been urged to approach the holy table, to frequent Communion ; they should have been cast into the arms of the Sovereign Pontiff, as children more obedient, more tenderly devoted, than ever. But this was not the case. Some allowed themselves to be frightened by simulated austerity, and others were seduced by these grand words : " Return to the discipline of the primitive Church." Sentinels did not perform their duty, some were traitors ; and little by little Jansenism penetrated everywhere, not as a doctrine in which souls believed, but as an influence to which they yielded. The most fervent communities, the most austere cloisters, were not preserved from it. They

[1] Ps. lxxxiii. I. [2] Levit. xxvi. 2.

inhaled it, almost unsuspectingly, like those subtle poisons floating in the air, which bear with them death sometimes, disease always.

From these combined influences there resulted in France, at the end of the seventeenth century and during the whole of the eighteenth, a corruption of the true spirit of the Gospel, a kind of semi-Christianity, commonplace and cold, utterly incapable of captivating souls. The conquering charm of Christianity, the principle of its eternal fruitfulness, is the dogma of God's infinite love for man, that grand doctrine, at once so full of mystery and yet so luminous, of a God who loves man unto passion. In the same measure as one approaches it, whether entirely to deny or merely to diminish this infinite love, one sees die out or sensibly decrease that sublime inebriation which makes virgins, apostles, and martyrs, that folly of man responding to the folly of God. The world had had a first example in the absolute sterility of Protestantism ; and France was about to offer a second, which, though less perfect, was none the less striking ; since, without absolutely denying infinite love, it was content with an unintelligible conception of it.

In proportion as this quasi-Christianity spread over France, the sublime inspirations of faith and piety became weaker. During the whole of the eighteenth century there was but one new institution, that of de la Salle, a tardy scion of the great tree of which some years before it was impossible to number the new shoots. The old institutions languished, and some literally died out. In France, virgins and apostles, souls consecrated to God, became fewer and fewer. The old abbeys were too spacious for their inmates daily diminishing in numbers; and in revenge at not being able to people them, they pulled them down. The riches no longer necessary, since the monasteries were now deserted, were used in demolishing the old cloisters of the twelfth and the thirteenth centuries, so interesting in point of art, which had been erected by saints, and embalmed with the still living traces of their footsteps. They replaced them by magnificent abbeys in the style of Versailles, that is to say, as destitute of style as of reminiscences. The same spectacle was witnessed in the ranks of the clergy, among whom were found some zealous priests, some men of duty, but no saints. All was mediocre, no enthusiasm, no fire. Missions died out, and a sensible diminution of warmth and life was everywhere felt. As one sometimes sees a grand old tree no longer shooting its huge branches toward heaven, no longer clothed in luxuriant foliage, because of the wound at the root, so the Church of France gave signs of deep-seated disease.

This was, however, only the beginning of the trouble. Whilst within the Church pious souls grew cold, the breath of irreligion was blowing without. This half-Christianity, which had not sufficient beauty to enrapture souls, was still less capable of opposing the detestable effects of Protestantism. They filtered through, if we may dare so to speak, the swaying and disjointed dikes. In the same way as Luther and Calvin tore the Creed to pieces and scoffed at the Church, Voltaire and Rousseau cut up the Gospel and mocked at Jesus Christ. By virtue of the same right, also, and supported on the same principles, Diderot, d'Holbach, Helvétius, Lamettrie, denied the immortality of the soul, and jeered at a future life. Nothing in the intellectual, moral, or religious order was respected. A spirit of universal revolt agitated France, till then so devoted to her kings. Never had there been so much said of tenderness, benevolence, philanthropy; yet never had hearts been harder. Intense egotism dried them up. Never had men been more gracious, more amiable, more frizzed and powdered, more fascinating; but never had men so heartily despised one another. The one step between contempt and hatred was cleared at a single bound toward the

close of the eighteenth century. A hatred till then unknown, universal and ferocious, filled souls. The day
came on which that hatred, no longer able to restrain
itself, burst forth. Then fearful scenes were witnessed.
Scaffolds were erected, and to them were dragged the
king, the queen, the royal family, the nobles, clergy,
parliament, all kinds of people. Men were drunk with
blood. They massacred one another without being
able to satisfy the madness that dishonored them.

But if this hatred of man for man was at the time
inexplicable, if it pointed to some prodigious derange-
ment in the French nature, what shall we say of the
hatred of men for God ? Everything that recalled His
memory was odious. They cut priests' throats; burnt
monasteries, broke crucifixes, riddled statues at the
church doors ; profaned altars by the most revolting ob-
scenities; rolled consecrated Hosts in the dust, then
cast them into the flames, and performed around them
lascivious dances. Never before had the like shocked
Heaven. During the early part of the nineteenth century, there were seen in our cities and villages wander-
ers whom the sight of such horrors had crazed.

Behold what the French nation, so noble, so generous,
had become! That old Frankish race which had contracted with Jesus Christ so beautiful an alliance; which
had received from Heaven incomparable gifts; which,
magnificent in gratitude, had cast on the religion of Jesus
Christ the greatest human glory ever received from any
nation; whose kings esteemed themselves honored in
being called the Eldest Sons of the Church,—behold how
it has fallen ! Love grew cold, and then, as often happens, we see it totally extinguished in hatred against
self and God. We behold the descendants of those
sturdy Franks with cries of fury tearing out their own
intestines, if we may use the expression, and France become an enduring example of a nation straying from its
course and unfaithful to its mission.

Still this ebullition of hatred was not the saddest symptom. Coldness soon entered into its hatred, as once before into its love. For that Christ whom it had loved so much, it now felt only indifference. We behold France during the first fifty years of the nineteenth century coolly effacing His name from her laws and constitutions. Even His memory she could no longer tolerate in her official life. She banished Him from her soil; but being forced to let Him return, she inclosed Him in His churches, or, as she said disdainfully, in His sacristies, and forbade Him to appear in public. Thus unfaithful and adulterous, after an explosion of rage against Him who had so much loved her, she sought even to efface Him from her memory.

What a misfortune could such things be done with impunity ! But God does not permit that. The woman who has once freely given her heart may desert the object of her choice, may throw herself into the arms of her guilty love, may be intoxicated for the moment ; but happiness has fled from her forever. Never again can she taste the peaceful charm of innocent affection; never again can she know the dignity of the wife, the honor of the mother, and those other joys so unmixed because blessed by God. Thus it is with France in her sad nineteenth century, now drawing to a close. Unfaithful to her mission, she has lived to behold her grandest gifts turned against herself. Vainly has she called science and genius to her aid. France is no longer the same. She no longer exerts a world-wide influence. She no longer rests on the same elevated plain; each day sees a new step toward the abyss. Yesterday, in the name of pretended political rights, she banished her kings and tore her constitutions into shreds. To-day, there is question as to whether she will guard the family tie, the right of property; whether, in fact, society itself shall remain standing. One catastrophe evokes another. France is quaking to her very foundations; and we may confidently look forward to the time in which an honest man will not find on the once generous soil of France a stone whereon to rest his head.

And yet she pursues her follies. She sows impiety broadcast. She makes use of her beautiful language, that ideal tongue, to propagate the brutalities of atheism and materialism. Impious and voluptuous, she dances on Vesuvius in flames. The world looks on alarmed, and asks what would become of the remnant of faith, of religion and morality, in Europe, if France were still queen of the nations.

One might have thought that, after such an abandonment of her sacred vocation, God would have indignantly rejected France, that He would have withdrawn her mission, and with it the gifts received for its accomplishment, but which have now become useless to her. But in those pitiable divorces in which man sunders what God had united, something very wonderful occasionally happens, and that is, the abandoned, the betrayed, the unloved, continues to love. He pursues the unfaithful one with a love from which love never dies. He multiplies benefits in his eagerness to reach the heart from which he cannot sever his own. He says with the poet:

> " I have lavished them upon thee,
> I wish to lavish them upon thee."

This was what was seen here. Knowing France, knowing that no nation is so capable of excesses so sad; but knowing, also, that none can compare with her in fervor of repentance, none in ardor of love, God resolved to conquer her by the force of His own tenderness. One day He appeared and, laying bare His breast, showed her His Heart, and demanded hers in return. Eighteen hundred years have rolled away since Jesus Christ died on the Cross, and no genius has yet succeeded in representing Him to us in His ideal beauty. After Raphael and Leonardo da Vinci, even after Blessed Angelico, the crucifix is still a piece of art greater than any painting. And so it will be with this second revelation of infinite love. No one will succeed in portraying the apparition of Jesus to France and to the world: that look in which reproach was drowned in tenderness; that gesture of unrecognized love; that breast glowing like a furnace; that Heart shining like the sun! All this will reach the ideal of beauty only in the ecstatic contemplations of the saints; and the ages as they roll on will learn from astonished humanity the grandeur of this stupendous event. Two hundred years since the apparition took place, and we are yet too near to measure its majestic proportions. It was born at a time in which France deemed herself at the pinnacle of her glory; but in which God, who sounds the heart and reins of man, already perceived the worm about to touch the flower and blight it on its stem. Unknown, or vaguely understood, in the eighteenth century, which was too sceptical and too sensual for emotions so pure; not shown upon our altars till the nineteenth century; having need of overwhelming misfortunes to be welcomed by society in its distress,—the devotion to the Heart of Jesus will probably not reach the sublime acme of its expansion until the twentieth century, when will be drawn the last consequences of the fatal principles that are now ruining us, and when shall occur misfortunes more frightful than those we have yet experienced. Then, in that storm of consummate evil, shall arise the perfect remedy. France shall lift her despairing eyes to that Heart " which has so loved men." She will consecrate herself to its infinite love, and thus arise from the abyss.

In expectation of this glorious event, we must study the genesis of the great devotion. For this we must transport ourselves to Paray-le-Monial, where it was revealed, stopping on our way at Vérosvres, where was born the lowly virgin to whom it was first confided—its first apostle, the humble Margaret.

CHAPTER II.

BIRTH OF SAINT MARGARET MARY. FIRST YEARS. CHILDHOOD AND YOUTH.

1647—1662.

" Sicut lilium!"
" As the lily among thorns, so is my love among the daughters."
—*Cant.* ii. 2.
" Tota pulchra es, amica mea, et macula non est in te."
" Thou art all fair, O my love, and there is not a spot in thee."
—*Cant.* iv. 7.

N setting out from Paray for Vérosvres, one leaves on his right the little town of Charolles. He admires as he passes along the sweet and tranquil beauty of the horizon's broad lines imperceptibly lost in the distance, and, at a turn of a high, wooded mountain, comes suddenly upon a landscape whose novelty strikes him with surprise. It is a vast amphitheatre of granite rocks, four leagues, perhaps, by five. One might think them moulded from the molten mass of earth's first formation, and then suddenly cooled. They form against the horizon a chain of jagged mountain-peaks, rising one above the other like the tiers of an amphitheatre. In vain has ever-fruitful nature scattered amidst these deeply embedded rocks and on their lofty summits clusters of tall oaks, and even some sombre forest pines. At every turn the granite surface displaces the verdure, and immense blocks rising through the trees produce the effect of gigantic ruins.

If one looks back from the distant horizon, a similar scene presents itself. Deep, narrow valleys, sudden projections; ponds that seem to occupy the place of extinct craters; streams of clear, sparkling spring-water,

the happy privilege of granite soil; and here and there
in the fields enormous blocks, framed in wild broom
and heath rising to the sun.   Now we have the picture;
and it would be sombre were it not so varied.   There
is in it something sublime and austere that invites one
to silence and recollection.   The vast horizon, the lofty
mountains, the massive rocks that defy man's power to
move; the sterile soil that exacts abundant sweat,
and gives but poor harvests in return,—all these make
felt the grandeur of God and the littleness of man.   We
might say that this corner of the world was created expressly to awaken the desire for heaven.

   In the centre of the amphitheatre and on its highest
peak, rises a church, rebuilt unhappily, and now dedi
cated to the Sacred Heart.   This is the church of Vérosvres. [1]   The village, instead of grouping around
the church, is scattered in all directions.   We noticed
on different sides groups of houses forming little hamlets, inhabited by husbandmen and farmers.   Each of
these hamlets has its name.   It was in that of Lhautecour,

   [1] The new church has been rebuilt some years.   Although we grant
that the old one in which Margaret was baptized, in which she prayed,
received holy Communion so frequently, and was ravished into ecstasy,
needed rebuilding, yet an intelligent and Christian architect like those
of the Middle Ages would have found means to enclose the most precious parts of the old edifice in the new.   For example, the apse with
its altar and Communion-table he would have made a chapel.   Instead
of this, everything was destroyed, razed to the ground, not a stone
preserved.   Even the altar was demolished; even the baptismal font
was not spared.   At Assisi is shown the font in which St. Francis was
baptized; in Spain, that of St. Dominic; at Siena, the spot upon which
St. Catharine knelt: but here in Vérosvres is found nothing suggestive
of sweet reminiscences.   A huge, cold church without souvenir or
legend.   Alas! God grant that what has been done here be not soon
repeated at Ars!   There, too, has been begun an immense church, which
threatens the destruction of the poor old one of the venerable curé.
Even a short time after his death we approached the confessional in
which he passed his life, and which ought to be held sacred as a relic, and
we found a missionary of Ars installed in it!   Oh, how frivolous is our
age!   Nothing now commands respect!

running in a right line behind the apse of the church and within a quarter of an hour's distance from it, that Margaret Mary was born.[1]

Her father was Claude Alacoque. He belonged to that portion of the French nation which, in 1647, was nothing and yet was preparing to be everything; which, while waiting, was silently amassing fortune and influence; which had not yet lost, thanks to God, either faith or morals. His dwelling, which is still standing, possesses a certain degree of style with its two large main buildings, separated by a courtyard. The first served as a family residence. It was commonly called the "cabinet house," because in it was the office of Mr. Alacoque, royal notary of Lhautecour. There is also to be seen the room in which Margaret was born, now transformed into a chapel and dedicated to the Sacred Heart. The beams and rafters of the ceiling are covered with allegorical pictures in the Renaissance style. In the middle of them is a cartouch, supported by two cupids, on which are inscribed the Alacoque arms; for this family, already ancient, had its arms. "It bore on a field of gold a red cock at the summit, and a lion, also red, at the base of the shield."[2] This building was consumed by fire, traces of which are yet seen. It was rebuilt later on, but all that now remains of it is the square tower at the end of the edifice, in which Margaret Mary was born.[3]

[1] One or two documents lightly studied and only partly understood have, in these latter times, cast a shade of obscurity on this point. We shall see in a note at the end of the volume that the fact is not even to be questioned, and that a contemporaneous tradition, uninterrupted and unanimous, permits no doubt on the birth of Margaret at the hamlet of Lhautecour in the village of **Vérosvres.**

[2] "The coat-of-arms of Chrysostom Alacoque, mayor for life of Bois-Marie, bears on a field of gold a red cock at the summit, and a lion, also red, at the base of the shield" (Tome ii. p. 205).

[3] The tradition of the country is that the residence of Mr. Ala-

The other building is in front, perfect and entire, the entrance through an arched gateway now closed. It is probable that it also served as a dwelling for the Alacoque family, either after the fire had consumed part of the adjoining house, or when their increase in numbers rendered the first too small. On the ground-floor were three large rooms, with large chimney-places and planks and beams black from age. An exterior gallery, the stairs to which were formed of large blocks of granite, now disjointed and broken, led to the second story, which consisted of two spacious apartments opening on the gallery. In the first, in a corner to the east, is found a small room which is still called the "Chamber of the Venerable." The ceiling is covered with pictures representing a hunt, in which figure a lion, a tiger, an ostrich, an elephant, etc. These pictures are of the same style and appear to be by the same hand as that which ornamented the other parts of the building. There are no paintings in the second room, but it is beautifully floored with oak carefully joined, which sufficiently indicates that the dwelling was not a mere farm-house.

A court separates the two buildings. The old walls may still be seen, and, strange sight! the roofs are formed of granite flags of a single piece. The whole is surrounded by gardens terminating in a little wood, which clothes the rapid descent into a narrow valley. This was the whole extent of the property. In the cen-

coque, at least that portion of it which they called the "cabinet house," was destroyed by fire. M. l'abbé Beauchamps testified to this fact in 1831, on the assurance of the oldest inhabitants of the country. Even before learning this tradition, it was evident to us. By a careful study of the first building, we discovered traces of fire, and saw that the repairs had been made with inferior materials. The square tower, in which was the saint's chamber, had been converted into a chapel. It alone escaped the flames, and it alone presents an appearance of age. It was from not having proved this fact that M. l'abbé Beauchamps and M. l'abbé Deverchères blundered in their researches. They sought, we know not where, traces of a burned house, but sought in vain!

tre of the little valley darts up one of those immense
blocks of granite with which, as we have seen above,
the whole country is sown. It formed for twenty years
Margaret's chosen solitude, her refuge in hours of trial,
the scene of her prayer, the witness of her first ecstasies.

The spacious dwelling had passed into the Alacoque
family in consequence of the marriage of the grandfather
of the saint with Jane Delaroche,[1] whose patrimony it
was. Claude had received the title of eldest son, or
perhaps, as was the custom, that of co-heir. He had an
unmarried sister named Catharine, who lived with him.
Another sister, named Benedicta, married Toussaint
Delaroche, and became the mother of four children.
In accordance with the custom of these patriarchal families, she, too, dwelt with her brother. Lastly, he had
a brother named Antoine. He was in Holy Orders and,
at this time, curé of Vérosvres. Besides the care of his
domain, the charge of which rested particularly on his
brother-in-law Toussaint Delaroche, Mr. Claude Alacoque held the office of royal notary of Lhautecour.
Later on he joined thereto the title of judge for the
seigniories of la Roche, Terreau, Corcheval, and Pressy.
All this, together with the highest reputation for honor
and integrity, had made Claude a man of consideration
scarcely a degree below the neighboring nobility, and
very much superior to the common people.

Hence we find his name on every page of the parish
register of Vérosvres. There is not a marriage at Lhautecour in which he does not figure as witness, and,
what is more extraordinary, scarcely a baptism in which
he is not godfather. In the latter case, whether owing
to his title of royal notary or on account of his beauti-

---

[1] According to the archives found in the Chateau D'Audour,
see that they were originally of the hamlet of Audour, parish of
Dompierre-les-Ormes, and that this grandfather of Margaret,
who married Jane Delaroche, came to reside at Lhautecour.

ful penmanship, his brother Antoine, curé of Vérosvres, invariably handed him the pen, and it was he who registered the proceeding.

In 1639, M. Claude Alacoque, hardly five-and-twenty years old, married Mlle. Philiberte Lamyn, then nineteen. Both were pious and worthy of giving birth to a saint. Of this union, blessed by God, were born seven children, four sons and three daughters.[1] Margaret was the fifth child. She was born on July 22, 1647, feast of St. Magdalen, and was not baptized, we know not why, until three days after, the 25th, in the church of Vérosvres. Her own uncle, her father's brother, M. Antoine Alacoque, curé of Vérosvres, was her godfather. The godmother was Madame Marguerite de Saint-Amour, wife of M. de Fautrières, lord of Corcheval.[2] The noble family wished to give this public proof of the high esteem in which they held M. Alacoque.

God, who destined this holy child to rekindle in the world the fire of His divine love, wished that she herself should first be consumed in it. As a little one, she breathed only for Jesus Christ, she feared only to dis-

[1] In the archives of the Chateau D'Audour we find the records of the birth of Margaret's brothers, sisters, uncles, and aunts. We are indebted to the kindness of M. l'abbé Dessolin, curé of Vérosvres, who searched up and copied these precious parish registers. He thus helped us to solve some of the very delicate problems one meets in the early part of Saint Margaret Mary's life ; though we are unable to do more, as the necessary data are wanting.

[2] Here is the baptismal register :

"Margaret, daughter of M. Claude Alacoque, royal notary, and of Lady Philiberte la Main, was baptized by the undersigned, curé of Vérosvres, Wednesday, July 25, 1647. I, Rev. Antoine Alacoque, was her godfather (*en surcharge*), and Toussaint de la Roche held her over the baptismal font. Her godmother was Mademoiselle Marguerite de St. Amour, wife of Mons. de Corcheval, who are subscribed.

"C. DE FAUTRIÉRES. M. DE ST. AMOUR.
 CORCHEVAL. ANT. ALACOQUE."

The original is preserved in the presbytery of Vérosvres.

please Him. " From the age of two or three years," writes her first historian, " she had so great horror of even the least shadow of sin, that to curb her childish inclinations it was sufficient to tell her that it was offensive to God. Nothing more was necessary ; she yielded at once." [1]

" O my only Love," exclaims Margaret, " how indebted I am to Thee for having prevented me from my tenderest youth, for having made Thyself Master of my heart ! As soon as I came to the use of reason, Thou didst display before my soul the deformity of sin, and this impressed me with such horror for it that the least stain was to me insupportable torment. To restrain the vivacity of my childhood, my friends had only to say that what I wished was perhaps displeasing to God. This put an end to my childish pranks." [2]

[1] " Abridgment of the Life of Sister Margaret M. Alacoque, Religious of the Visitation of Holy Mary, of whom God made use to establish devotion to the Sacred Heart of Jesus Christ, and who died in the odor of sanctity, October 17, 1690." Published at Lyons by Antoine and Horace Molin, 1691, the year following the death of Margaret Mary. It has been republished in our times by Rev. C. Daniel, in one vol. 12mo (Paris, Douniol, 1865).

[2] "Mémoire " written by the saint by order of Rev. Father Rollin, her director. Autographic MSS. belonging to the Visitation of Paray. Of the different Mémoires written by the saint in obedience to her directors, this is the only one that has escaped the flames, the same power forbidding its destruction. It was never finished. But as it begins with her birth and includes the revelations of the Sacred Heart, it is of inestimable value, as well for the relation itself, as for the manner in which her story is told. One feels impressed at every instant with the sublimity of a Teresa and the heart-felt and touching utterances of an Augustine. It alone suffices to prove the truth of the revelations, whilst demonstrating the beauty, sincerity, purity, and humility of the soul to whom they were made. We shall copy from it as often as possible, thus giving it to our readers almost entire. It was first edited by Père de Gallifet, at the end of his beautiful treatise on " The Excellence of Devotion to the Adorable Heart of Jesus Christ." Père Charles Daniel republished it in 1865. Many other editions appeared in the mean time, but in all were detected numerous faults. In 1867

Her brother Chrysostom relates a charming example in this connection. "Whilst still a child," said he, "she evinced singular marks of sanctity, fervor, and horror of sin. Once at carnival-time when I was seven years old and my little sister five, I proposed to exchange dress with her. Mine was a soldier's suit, and I had a sword with which I was going to sally forth against the farmers whom I espied approaching. Margaret replied that it would perhaps offend God and that she did not wish to do anything displeasing to Him. She had no desire either to imitate or to accompany the maskers. The child was then only five years old." [1]

To this delicacy of conscience was added such a love of prayer, with instincts for penance so precocious and so astonishing, that there is no room to doubt, say her first historians, that for several centuries her like was never seen. [2]

the Visitation of Paray determined to publish a carefully collated edition of the original. It formed part of the work entitled "Life and Works of Blessed Margaret Mary Alacoque," 2 vols. 8vo (Paris, Poussielgue, 1867). This is the edition from which we shall cite.

[1] "Process of Beatification and Canonization of the Venerable Servant of God, Margaret Mary Alacoque, Religious of the Visitation, B. V. M., of the Convent of Paray in Burgundy," published by authority of the ordinary in 1715 ; 1 vol. in folio MS. belonging to the Visitation of Paray, approved and signed by the ecclesiastical commissaries. We have carefully studied it, and all our citations are made from the original.

[2] "Life of the Blessed by Contemporaries." They call this a "Mémoire" written by two of the religious of Paray contemporary with Margaret Mary: Sister Frances Rosalie Verchère and Sister Péronne Rosalie de Farges. This "Mémoire ' had been compiled for Mgr. Languet, Archbishop of Sens, Vicar-General of Autun, when he was preparing to write the "Life of the Blessed." After using it, and the "Life" had appeared (1 vol. 4to, 1719), he returned to the Visitation of Paray this "Mémoire," which formed the basis of his work. Considered henceforth useless, it remained among the MSS. in the archives of the convent. Finally, the religious of Paray published a first edition carefully collated from the original and even increased from documents preserved in their archives. It forms the first volume of the work

At the age of four and a half years, Margaret left her father's house to reside with her godmother, Mme. de Fautrières de Corcheval, who greatly desired to have the child with her. Perhaps the increasing number of M. Alacoque's children, already seven, had inspired this noble lady with the thought of relieving the burden of so excellent a family. Perhaps, too, having no children, a privation always regretted by her, she proposed to adopt her little godchild. M. and Mme. Alacoque, having their child's interest at heart, consented. This they did all the more readily, as the castle of Corcheval was only a league from Lhautecour, and, as M. Claude was judge of that manor, as well as of Terreau, he was frequently obliged to go thither. Mme. Alacoque prepared her dear little daughter, and took her herself to Corcheval. Built in the far-off past, stripped of its towers by Coligny, who demolished them during the religious wars when he held possession, and restored under the reign of Louis XIII., the château de Corcheval still stands, joining to the massive architecture of the feudal ages the imposing appearance of the magnificent castles of the seventeenth century. A high mountain covered with forests overshadows it, and the most beautiful trees in the world, a clump of young hornbeams three centuries old, wave their verdant branches under the very windows. The whole place breathes solitude, and here our holy child developed the rare beauty of her innocent soul. The deep shadows of the groves and forest attracted her. "My greatest desire," said she, "was to bury myself in some wood; and nothing prevented me from gratifying it but the fear of meeting men." [1]

Just outside the gate of the castle, and on the very same terrace, stood the chapel, shaded also by horn-

entitled "Life and Works of the Blessed," of which we are now speaking.

[1] *Mémoire,* p. 290.

oeam-trees. Here the little girl often retired. " Here
she passed long hours kneeling, her little hands joined.
Far from growing weary, she esteemed no pleasure in life
equal to that tasted in those moments of silent prayer,
which was never discontinued but with regret." [1]

" I was constantly urged," she says, " to repeat these
words, the sense of which I did not understand: ' My
God, I consecrate to Thee my purity! My God, I make
to Thee a vow of perpetual chastity!' Once I repeated
them between the two elevations of holy Mass, which I
generally heard on my bare knees however cold the
weather might be. I did not know what I had done,
nor what the words *vow* and *chastity* signified." [2] She
understood but one thing, and that was that these
mysterious words, which hovered constantly on her
lips at the most solemn moments, meant the complete
gift of herself to a God whom she esteemed worthy of
all gifts.

At the same time there was born in her that attraction for prayer which was to make her one of the greatest contemplatives ever known in the Church. " From
this early age," says Père Croiset, " the Holy Ghost
Himself wished to teach her the fundamental point of
the interior life, and bestow upon her the spirit of
prayer. Whenever she could not be found on her knees
in some part of the house, her friends were accustomed
to look for her in the church; and there she was sure to
be discovered immovable before the Blessed Sacrament."

The weak health of Mme. de Corcheval did not permit her to superintend, as she wished, Margaret's education; therefore she remitted that charge to two of
her lady companions, who taught the child to pray, to
read and write, and to study the catechism. One of
these ladies was gracious and amiable, but Margaret

[1] Croiset. *Abrégé*, p. 3.   [2] Mémoire, p. 290.

fled from her. The other, though harsh and severe, failed not to attract the little pupil, who preferred the rebuffs of the one to the caresses of the other. The sequel will show that this surprising conduct was owing to one of those secret instincts which God implants in pure hearts; for later on it was discovered that she who appeared so gracious was not all that she seemed.

Horror of evil, desire of solitude, flight from men, love of purity,—behold the first impressions engraven by God in the soul of this holy child, now in her sixth year! To perfect the picture here given, we must add that from her cradle she united to all other graces a most tender devotion to the Blessed Virgin. "I had recourse to her," she says, "in all my needs, and she warded off great dangers from me. I ventured not to address myself to her Son, but I feared not to go to her. I offered her the little crown of the Rosary on my bare knees on the ground, or else I made as many genuflections as there are Ave Marias, or I kissed the ground at each." [1] The Blessed Virgin never lets herself be outdone in love; and, from her earliest childhood, the dear little one received most signal graces.

There was no cure for Mme. de Fautrière's malady. After suffering a long time, she died in 1655, and little Margaret, then only eight years old, returned to her family. Hardly had she entered Lhautecour than to this first misfortune was added a second, though of a far more serious nature. Her father died at the close of the same year. [2] Still young, scarcely forty-one years old, bearing the unblemished reputation of an honest man and a good Christian, he left a young widow and five little children, the youngest not yet six years old, a very moderate fortune, and embarrassed affairs. It appears that this excellent man knew neither how to pay his

[1] Mémoire, p. 290.

[2] Mémoire of Chrysostom Alacoque: "the said M. Alacoque having died in 1655," etc.

debts nor to collect his dues.[1] His debts were few, his
creditors many. The poor widow accepted courageously
the care of her five children, and resolved to retrieve
her embarrassed fortune. But as this necessitated frequent journeys, which allowed her no leisure to devote
herself to her children's education, she placed the two
eldest sons for a time at Cluny; the other two with
their uncle, M. Antoine Alacoque, curé of Vérosvres;
and our holy child was sent to the Poor Clares of
Charolles.

The silence of this sacred cloister, the austerity and
continual prayer of the religious, their nocturnal devotions, their modesty and recollection, made an extraordinary impression upon Margaret. She became conscious that this was the kind of life God desired of her.
"I thought," she said, "were I a religious, I should become holy like those around me. I conceived so great
a longing for the life that I breathed but for it. I did
not find the convent in which I was, retired enough for
my taste; but not knowing any other, I thought I must
remain there."[2] Let us note this new feature. This
convent of Poor Clares, enclosed by austere grates,
shrouded in silence and fervor, was not sufficiently retired to satisfy the craving after a hidden life already
experienced by this young child. From the cradle to
the tomb, that desire of hers was to go on increasing.

Hardly had she entered with the Poor Clares, when
they prepared her to make her first Communion. She
was only nine years old; but her angelic dispositions
supplied the defect of age. The results were extraordinary. Margaret was gay, lively, naturally given to
play and amusement; but from this day, she no longer
found in them the same attraction. "This first Com-

[1] We judge of this from the fact of the physician's bill sent the widow
at this time. It comprised the accounts of the entire family for ter
years. These accounts are at the Visitation convent of Paray.

[2] Mémoire, p. 291.

munion," she said, "infused so much bitterness into all the little pleasures and amusements of my age that I could find no relish in them, though I still sought them eagerly. When I desired to share my companions' games, I always felt something restraining me, something that called me apart; and I had no peace until I obeyed. The same impulse made me begin to pray, almost always, provided I was not seen, on my bare knees, or making genuflections. To be observed was for me inconceivable torment." [1]

A very serious illness at this time endangered the child's life, and obliged her family to withdraw her from the Poor Clares. She returned to Lhautecour, where she was surrounded with the tenderest care by her mother and brothers, who loved her dearly. They did everything to promote her cure, but in vain. " They could," said she, " find no cure for my malady till they gave me to the Blessed Virgin. They promised her, if I were cured, I should some day be one of her daughters. I had no sooner made the vow than I was cured. I ever after experienced the Blessed Virgin's protection in a manner altogether marked, as of one belonging entirely to her." This was the first public sign of the special love of God for the holy child. She was deeply moved by it, and resolved more firmly than ever to belong to Him without reserve.

During the solitary hours of this long illness, Margaret's thoughts were centred in God. She says: " I felt strongly attracted to prayer. But this attraction gave me much suffering, as I was unable to satisfy it. I knew not how to make prayer, and I had no one to teach me. I knew nothing more of it than the name, but that name itself ravished my heart."

Margaret then turned to God, and with tears conjured Him to teach her the secret. He did it with admirable goodness. " The Sovereign Master taught me how He wished me to pray, and that lesson has served me all

[1] Mémorie n. 201

my life. He made me prostrate humbly before Him to ask pardon for everything by which I had offended Him. After having adored Him, I offered Him my prayer without knowing how I was going to make it. Then He presented Himself to me in the mystery in which He wished me to consider Him. He applied my mind to it so forcibly, ingulfing my soul and all my powers in Himself, that I felt no distraction. My heart was consumed with the desire of loving Him, and that gave me an insatiable hunger after holy Communion and sufferings." [1]

God was about to hear both these desires. When Margaret was brought back ill to Lhautecour, she did not notice the great change that had come over it. The efforts of her mother to retrieve the fortune of the family had not been successful. A new lease of the land had been made in the name of the minors. It was concluded not with their mother, but with Toussaint Delaroche, their uncle, who had summarily enough taken the management of affairs. His wife was installed absolute mistress at Lhautecour, where were already her grandmother, Mme. Alacoque, *née* Delaroche, and her daughter Catharine, who was not married. Little by little, the poor widow had been pushed aside and deprived of all influence. Whether on account of her incapacity for business, or that the family held her responsible for their straitened circumstances, she received from them only sharp words and ill-humor. Margaret tells this in ambiguous words, without mentioning names. She takes extreme precaution not to reveal the guilty; but from the restrained emotion with which, twenty years after, she spoke in less reserved language, we can understand what a soul naturally so sensitive and impetuous as hers must have had to suffer.

" God permitted my mother," she says, " to be deprived of authority in her own house, and to be forced to yield it

[1] Mémoire, p. 291.

to others. Those in charge so lorded it over her that
both she and I were soon reduced to a state of captivity.
It is not my intention in what I am going to say to
blame those persons. I do not wish to think that they
did wrong in making me suffer. Far from me such a
thought, my God! I regard them rather as instruments
of whom God made use to accomplish His holy will.
We had no freedom in our own house, and we dared do
nothing without permission. It was a continual war.
Everything was under lock and key, so that I could not
even find my apparel when I wished to go to holy Mass.
I was even obliged to borrow clothes. I felt this slavery
keenly, I must acknowledge." The pain of such a position was still more increased by odious suspicions. "It
was at this time," says she, "that with all my strength
I sought my consolation in the Most Blessed Sacrament
of the Altar. But being in a country-house far from
church, I could not go there without the consent of
these same persons; and it so happened that the permission granted by one was often withheld by the other.
When my tears showed the pain I felt, they accused me
of having made an appointment with some one, saying
that I concealed it under the pretext of going to Mass
or Benediction. This was most unjust, for I would have
consented rather to see myself cut into a thousand
pieces than to entertain such thoughts." [1]

"Not knowing where to seek refuge," she adds, "I
hid myself in a retired corner of the garden, in the
stable, or in some other out-of-the-way place where I
could, unobserved, kneel and pour out my heart in tears
before God. This I always did through my good Mother,
the most Blessed Virgin, in whom I had placed all my
confidence. I remained there entire days without eating or drinking. Sometimes the poor villagers, pitying
my condition, gave me in the evening a little fruit or
milk. When I ventured to return to the house, it was

[1] Mémorie, p. 292.

with such fear and trembling as, it seems to me, a poor criminal endures when about to receive sentence of condemnation."[1]

She adds : "I should have esteemed myself much more happy begging from door to door the bread which frequently I dare not take from the table, than living in this way. The moment I entered the house, the batteries were opened more fiercely than ever. I was reproached with neglecting the house and the children of those dear benefactors of my soul.[2] I was not allowed to say one word. The night I passed as I had done the day, pouring out tears at the foot of my crucifix."

But this was not yet Margaret's greatest trial. She loved her mother tenderly ; consequently, she suffered fearfully at seeing her thus humbled in her own house. " The rudest cross I had to bear was my inability to alleviate my mother's trials. They were a thousand times harder for me than my own. I dared not even console her by a word, fearing to offend God by taking pleasure in talking over our troubles. But it was in my beloved mother's sickness that my affliction became extreme. She suffered much from being left to my care and little services. Necessary nourishment was withheld from her by our jailers, and I was forced to beg from the villagers eggs and other things suitable for the sick. This was a special torment to me, for I was naturally timid, and I was frequently received very rudely."[3]

It is useless to add that God never abandons His

---

[1] Mémoire, p. 293.

[2] No, not the children of the *married domestics*, as some historians ignorant of the process of her canonization have imagined. In that process we see that *those dear benefactors of her soul* " were the members of her own family." (Procès, p. 54.) We have named them above. The children here in question were the four little ones of Toussaint Delaroche—John, Margaret (to whom our saint was godmother), Antony, and Jane Gabrielle. The eldest was eight years old, and the youngest three.

[3] Mémoire, p. 293.

faithful servants in such sorrows. On one particular occasion, when her mother was ill of erysipelas in its worst form, a young village physician was called in. He bled her, but said on leaving that nothing short of a miracle could save her life. The holy child, not knowing what else to do, ran to the church. It was the feast of the Circumcision. Margaret implored God with tears to be Himself her poor mother's physician. We do not know exactly how the thing happened, for the saint's humble recital is full of reserve. But when she returned home, she found that the swelling of her mother's cheek had disappeared ; and, contrary to all human appearances, the wound healed in a few days.[1]

Behold in what hard trials Margaret's childhood passed ! She was now scarcely fifteen. Happily, suffering, humiliations, and contempt are no obstacles to sanctity ; they are, on the contrary, when accepted by the soul, the most active and powerful agents thereto. Persecuted, humbled, almost driven from her home, the pious child sought refuge in God. She prayed incessantly, and began at this tender age to practise most austere penances. Her brother Chrysostom asserts that from her earliest childhood she was not satisfied with long prayer in church. The deponent often found her praying on her knees[2] in retired corners of the house. She practised, he affirmed, almost from infancy, many austerities and macerations, as fasting, iron chains, disciplines, and cinctures. These last often penetrated the flesh. She slept on a plank, and passed the night in prayer. The servants of M. Alacoque declared that she sometimes forgot to go to bed, and that they often found her on her knees.

To sustain her in such trials, the Lord began to appear to her. She was not astonished, for she believed that others were favored in the same way. It was or-

[1] Mémoire, p. 295.
[2] Procès of 1715, Deposition of Chrysostom.

dinarily " under the form of the Crucified, or of the Ecce
Homo, or as carrying His cross." This sight roused her
soul to love so great, that the hardships she endured,
the slavery, contempt, beggary, and even the blows she
received, appeared to her light and sweet. "Sometimes," said she, "when they were about to strike me, I
was distressed that their raised hands were stayed, and
that they did not exercise upon me all their strength.
I felt constantly urged to render all sorts of good services to these persons, as to the true friends of my soul.
I had no greater pleasure than to do and say all the
good I could of them." [1]

Let no one imagine that Margaret was one of those
cold, apathetic natures that feel nothing. She was, on
the contrary, extremely tender and sensitive. She felt
keenly the slightest want of attention, and expanded
like a delicate flower under the least proof of affection.
Her innate pride rendered such a life insupportable.
She was gay, sprightly, intelligent, and fond of pleasure
to a degree that might at any moment have exposed her
to serious danger in the world. But she repeats on
every page of her Mémoire that it is not she that is acting thus, it is her Sovereign Lord, who was making
Himself master of her soul, and directing her in all
things.

It was, above all, to the Blessed Sacrament that she
turned for consolation and strength. As soon as a free
moment was hers, she ran, or rather she flew, to the
church ; and once inside the door, she could no longer
restrain her footsteps. Love impelled her to the foot
of the altar, and she could never get near enough to
the tabernacle. " I was wholly unable to recite vocal
prayers before the Blessed Sacrament," said she, " and
once in its presence I became so absorbed that I knew
no weariness. I could have passed days and nights
before it without eating or drinking. I do not know

[1] Mémoire, p. 295.

exactly how I employed those moments. I only know that, like a burning taper, I was consumed in its presence, rendering Jesus love for love. I could not remain in the lower part of the church, and, despite the confusion it might cause me, I had to draw as near as I could to the altar on which reposed the Blessed Sacrament. And yet I did not think myself happy even there. I envied those that could communicate frequently, and that were free to remain long in the Sacramental Presence. I tried to gain the friendship of such persons, that I might enjoy the privilege ot going with them to spend some moments with Jesus Christ in this mystery." [1]

Margaret did not always succeed in the accomplishment of the desire just expressed. As we have seen, "the consent of three persons was necessary, and what one granted the others refused." On such occasions the pious child ran to hide herself in some corner of the garden, to pray and weep before God. There was one spot specially dear to her. Some steps west of the house a steep declivity, clothed with a little thicket, led down to a very deep vale. It may have been in far-off times, when our globe was a mere molten mass, a passage of burning lava, or a torrent of water; for its remains might be a monument of either. It consisted of an immense block of granite of extraordinary dimensions, left there by the flow, unable to drag it farther. Our holy child loved this solitary spot, which was just on the boundary of her own garden, and there she often took refuge. Protected behind, and, as it were, veiled by the thicket at the side of the house, it had directly in view the apsis containing the main altar of the church, which was less than half a mile distant. From this block of granite, however, the ground rises so rapidly to the church that one might think the distance less; it seems to be only a few steps across the valley.

[1] Mémoire, p. 297.

At night the little lamp burning before the tabernacle could be seen from the windows of the Alacoque mansion. It was there that her Lord and Master dwelt, despoiled of glory, abandoned by creatures, a thousand times more neglected and humiliated than she could ever be. Such thoughts made her heart melt into love. Tears welled up and, leaning on the granite block, her eyes and heart riveted on the tabernacle, Margaret was lost for hours in contemplation.

CHAPTER III.

MARGARET'S VOCATION—SHE ENTERS THE VISITATION OF PARAY.

1662—1671.

" In charitate perpetua dilexi te."

"I have loved thee with an everlasting love."—*Jeremias* xxxi. 3.

" Posuit signum in faciem meam, ut nullum præter eum amatorem admittam."

" He has placed His seal upon my forehead, that I may admit no lover but Himself."—*Rom. Brev. Ant. of St. Agnes.*

THUS grew in the solitude of Lhautecour, beautiful and .pure, hidden from all eyes, even from those of her kinsmen, the holy child whom God had chosen for things so great. She herself was more ignorant than others of what was being done in her. She breathed only for God. Her only ambition was " to be consumed in His presence like a burning taper, and so return Him love for love."

From such a life to the cloister there is but one step ; and we might expect to see Margaret take it without one regret for a world of which she knew naught but its trials, and from which she could part without even a sigh. But had such been the case, her vocation would have been void of sacrifice, would have had neither in the eyes of God nor of man its true value.

It so happened that, as Margaret entered her seventeenth year, the circumstances of her surroundings entirely changed. Her eldest brothers, having arrived at the age of manhood, took charge of the business and restored their mother to the position and influence of which she had been deprived. On the other hand, Toussaint Delaroche, who had probably died, for we no longer find mention of him, had in his ten years'

rather arbitrary, though intelligent, administration re-
trieved the compromised affairs of the family. Freedom came with this change of fortune ; and that
gayety generally found where six or seven children are
just stepping from childhood into youth once more
shed its genial influence over the Alacoque home. In
the country the young marry at an early age, especially
the members of large families. Margaret was only
seventeen, and already several good offers had been
made her. Her eldest brother, now two-and-twenty
and the head of the family, needed a companion. "All
this," says our saint, "brought to our home much company whom it was necessary for me to meet." Inter-
course with society commenced, and more brilliantly,
perhaps, than her first historians suspect. When we
read the baptismal register of Margaret's brothers and
sisters, we see that almost all had for sponsors the most
noble lords and ladies of the neighboring castles.
Margaret, we remember, had been held over the font by
Mme. de Fautrières ; and although she was dead, we
cannot believe that the holy child ceased all communication with the castle of Corcheval. Her brother
Claude Philibert had for godmother Lady Couronne
d'Apchon, widow of John le Roux, Lord of Terreau.[1]
One of her sisters was carried to holy baptism by Lady
Gilberte Areloup, Baronne Després. It is the same with
all the others, whose god-parents belonged to the best
families of Charolais. Mme. Alacoque, desirous of
settling her children in life, began to bring them out a
little and to receive visitors at her own house. Mar-

---

[1] Couronne d'Apchon, widow of John le Roux, married for second
husband John Areloup, a gentleman squire of the king's chamber,
Baron of Saint-Péruse. By this marriage he became Lord of Terreau.
She had an only daughter, Gilberte Areloup Lady of Terreau.
who was married in 1640 to M. Claude de Thibaut de Noblet,
Chevalier, Baron Després, etc. Their son and heir, Pierre de Thibaut
de Noblet, was by the king created Marquis Després.

garet saw at once that she was much noticed and sought after. And what is singular and almost inexplicable is that this young girl who had been so strong in the midst of adversity, whom neither contempt nor humiliations could daunt, scarcely beheld the world smiling upon her, when she began to adorn herself to please it. She delighted in pleasure-parties, she shortened her prayers, she remained from confession, and her soul gradually sank from the height to which it had been elevated in early childhood. " I began to see the world and to dress to please it, and I tried to amuse myself as much as I could." [1]

Happily, God watched over this soul upon which He had designs so great. " But Thou, my God," she continues, " hadst other designs than those that I formed in my heart. Thou didst make known to me that it was hard to kick against the powerful goad of Thy love. My malice and infidelity made me use every effort and all my strength to resist its attraction and extinguish within me its movements. But in vain! In the midst of company and amusements, divine love pierced me with darts so inflamed that they seemed entirely to consume my heart. The pain stunned me, and yet it did not suffice to detach a heart so ungrateful as mine. I felt as if bound with cords, and so forcibly drawn that I was, at last, forced to follow Him who was calling me. He led me aside and severely reproved me. Alas! He seemed jealous of this miserable heart." [2]

Touched by such love, Margaret prostrated on the ground, begged pardon, and took a long and severe discipline. " In spite of all this," she adds, " I failed not to plunge again into vanity, and again I offered the same resistance."

One day during the carnival she masked to take part with several of her friends in a ball to which she had been invited. What tears she shed to expiate

[1] Mémoire, p. 299.   [2] Ibid.

"her great sin," as she called it! What fasts and macerations! And still, wonderful to say, Margaret had not yet conquered herself. Still bleeding from her self-imposed discipline, she began again to smile upon the world.

It was on her return from this ball that the Lord awaited her. "That evening," she says, "as I was taking off Satan's accursed livery, for thus I term my vain adornments, my Sovereign Master presented Himself before me all disfigured as He was during His flagellation. He reproached me, saying that it was my vanity which had reduced Him to such a state ; that I was losing infinitely precious time of which He would demand of me a rigorous account at the hour of death ; and that I had betrayed and persecuted Him after He had given me so many proofs of His love. This made so strong an impression upon me and wounded my heart so painfully that I wept bitter tears." [1]

Then, taking God's part against herself, jealous of seeing such love despised by so wretched a creature, feeling that there was no torment that she did not deserve and that she could not endure, Margaret un-covered her shoulders and disciplined them to blood. "To avenge in some manner on myself the injury I had done Him, I bound this miserable, criminal body with knotted cords, which I drew so tightly that I could hardly breathe or eat. I kept them on so long that they ate into my flesh. It was only by force and at the cost of cruel suffering that I could get them off again. It was the same with the little chains that I clasped around my arms. I could not remove them without tearing off with them pieces of flesh. I slept on planks, or strewed my bed with sharp sticks." But Margaret never spoke of these things. She so carefully hid her macerations that no one suspected them. Although in the flower of her age and the freshness of youth, they

[1] Mémoire, p. 300.

saw her, without apparent cause, "suddenly grow pale and thin."[1]

Let us remark that, on hearing the saints speaking thus bitterly of trifling faults, which they expiated so cruelly, we are sometimes tempted to think them more guilty than they are. But in our saint's case there was nothing in her first experience of the world and its pleasures to tarnish the immaculate purity of her heart. At twenty Margaret was innocent as a child. She abhorred the idea of marriage, and the thought of the slightest sin against holy purity forced tears from her eyes. Several witnesses in the process of her canonization solemnly affirmed that she ever preserved baptismal innocence. In default of such witnesses, it would suffice to open her Mémoire. One cannot read it without seeing at once the embodiment of Bossuet's beautiful illustration of the pure of heart. Let us, borrowing from him, say that, from the cradle to the grave, Margaret's heart resembled those beautiful streams one comes upon among the mountains of her native Burgundy. Hidden in deep caverns, overshadowed by the vast horizon, they offer to the traveller limpid waters whose crystalline purity is ruffled by no breath.

Protected by her innocence, Margaret would have triumphed sooner over the seductions of the world, had not the thought of her mother, whom she so tenderly loved and whom by her marriage she could extricate from many difficulties, shaken her purpose. "My relations," said she, "and especially my dear mother, urged me incessantly to marry. She wept as she told me that she saw no hope of release from her misery except in me; that she would find her consolation in being with me, as soon as I should be settled in the world. On the other hand, God's voice pursued me so vehemently that I had no peace. My vow was ever

[1] Mémoire, p. 301.

before my eyes with the thought that, if I violated it, I should be punished with frightful torments."

Truly, the battle was begun; and as the contest was between the two greatest and most powerful loves on earth, the love of God and the love of a mother, it was to be terrible. " O my God!" cried out Margaret, " Thou alone wast witness of the length of the fearful combat that I suffered interiorly. I should have yielded without the extraordinary assistance of Thy mercy."

She continues: " The devil, taking advantage of my love for my mother, incessantly represented to me the tears she shed; told me that if I became a religious I should cause her to die of grief; and that I should have to answer for it to God, since she was entirely dependent on my care. This thought was insupportable, for our mutual love was so tender that we could not live apart. At the same time, the desire to be a religious and to live a life of perfect purity pursued me without intermission. All this made me suffer a true martyrdom. I had no rest, I was constantly in tears; and having no one to whom I could disclose my grief, I knew not how to act. At last, my love for my mother began to gain the ascendency." [1]

Ah, how touching is this last word! The spectacle is the same as that which we admire a thousand times in the history of St. Chantal. It is ever in souls the most noble, the purest, that iies the source of the deepest tenderness; and never do the higher, the legitimate affections more freely expand, produce more beautiful flowers, more delicious fruits, than when forced in the hot-house of a heart warmed by the love of God.

But even Margaret's heart, so long turned to God, filial tenderness was about to mislead. She began to examine the terms of her vow. She had made it when only a very little child, wholly unconscious of what she was doing: was she, then, bound by it? Could she not

[1] Mémoire, p. 301.

readily obtain a dispensation? She would ask for it.
Then she examined the religious state. It was too high
for her; she could never reach its perfection. By em-
bracing it, she would lose the liberty of performing
penances and charities. By such reasoning she was
strongly tempted to renounce it altogether.

Three or four years, from 1663 to 1667, passed in these
terrible alternations between the world and God. At
the end of this period, as Margaret was entering her
twentieth year, she felt the desire of being a religious
rekindle within her. " My desire became so ardent,"
she said, " that I resolved to execute it at any cost."
She had constantly before her the beauty of the virtues,
particularly of humility, voluntary poverty, and chastity. She read the lives of the saints with delight ; but
she avoided those of the greatest servants of God, whose
heroism she felt unable to imitate. Opening the book,
she would say : " Let me look for a saint easy to imitate,
that I may do as she did." But hardly had she begun
to read before her tears flowed abundantly, on seeing
that the saint had not offended God as she herself had
done, or that she had spent long years in penance.[1]

Convinced that she could never love God as He deserves to be loved, Margaret resolved to devote herself
to the service of the poor. She so compassionated their
miseries that, had it been in her power, she would have
retained nothing for herself. " When I had any money,"
said she, " I gave it to some poor little ones, to induce
them to come and learn from me their prayers and
catechism ; and they flocked to me in such crowds that
in winter I knew not where to put them." For this
purpose, she made use of a large room still existing and
which formed part of the second building of her home.
It was reached by an exterior stairway. It is in the
middle of this chamber that Margaret's little cell is
found.

[1] Mémoire, p. 301.

Sometimes when her brother saw the crowd of poor children crossing the courtyard, he would say to his sister pleasantly, "Sister dear, are you going to be a school-mistress?" "Ah, brother!" she would reply, "who will instruct these poor little ones if I do not?"[1] Or again, her old aunt Catharine grumbled, and unfeelingly chased the children away. "They thought I would give to the poor all I could lay hands on; but that I would not dare to do, for fear of committing theft. I was obliged to coax and pet my mother, to obtain from her leave to give what I had. As she loved me dearly she readily granted the permission."[2]

Margaret was not satisfied with loving and instructing the poor little ones; she went to visit their families, especially when any of the members were ill. Delicate and sensitive, with a horror of everything unsightly, trembling in presence of a wound, never can we fully appreciate her efforts to overcome herself, or know what heroic acts she performed in this ministry. She spoke few words on the subject, but those few reveal prodigies of courage; and even under the reserve of a recital imposed by obedience, we discover miraculous cures. "I had extreme repugnance to look at wounds. I had to begin by dressing and even kissing them, in order to overcome myself. I was very ignorant as to how I should proceed in this duty; but my Divine Master so well supplied for my want of knowledge that, although the wounds might be very serious, they healed in a short time. I had, consequently, more confidence in His goodness than in my own remedies."[3]

In the midst of such occupations, her lively and ardent nature still inclined to pleasure. "I was naturally given to the love of pleasure and amusement; but I could not indulge my inclinations, although I frequently sought to do so. But the pitiful sight of the Lord, who

[1] Process of 1715, Chrysostom's Deposition.
[2] Mémoire, p. 302. [3] Ib., p. 303.

presented Himself to me covered with the blood of His flagellation, prevented my following out my intention; He reproached me in words that pierced me to the heart: 'Dost thou sigh for pleasure? *I* never tasted any. I gave Myself up to all sorts of bitterness for thy love and to gain thy heart,—and thou dost still wish to dispute it with Me!'" At such words, Margaret desisted. Although for several days after she was filled with confusion, she gradually resumed her search after vanities. "One day," she says, "when I was lost in astonishment that so many defects and infidelities were not sufficient to repel my Lord, He made me this reply : 'It is because I am desirous of making of thee a compound of My love and mercy.' " [1]

"On another occasion He said to me : 'I have chosen thee for My spouse, and thou didst promise fidelity when thou didst make to Me the vow of chastity. It was I who urged thee to make it before the world had any share in thy heart, for I wished to possess it pure and unsullied by any earthly affection.' "

Who would not believe that a heart like Margaret's, so pure, indeed so angelic, endowed with such generosity, would not enthusiastically respond to these tender and magnificent advances ? Nevertheless, even at this moment she hesitated ; and never, perhaps, in this terrible struggle of four years had she been more strongly tempted to yield. It was because serious events had changed the prospects of her family. Her two eldest brothers died one after the other in the prime of life. John, the oldest of all the children, he who on reaching his majority had taken charge of the business and restored to his cherished mother her position and influence, was the first taken. He died in 1663, at the age of three-and-twenty, leaving the entire charge of his affairs to his brother Claude Philibert. Two years after, September, 1665, the latter followed him to the tomb, at the same fatal age of twenty-three. There re-

[1] Mémoire. D. 204.

mained now only Margaret and her two brothers : Chrysostom, whom we have already met, and James, the
youngest of all, who was preparing for Holy Orders
Becoming thus sole proprietor of the estate of Lhautecoui
and head of the family, Chrysostom thought of marry-
ing. In 1667, at the early age of twenty-two, he married
Angelique Aumonier, of a good family of the Charolais.
It is thought that it was for this occasion the pictures
which decorate the house were painted. It is at least
singular that, at the period in which we see the tomb
of the two elder brothers opened and the wedding of
the third celebrated, we find among these allegorical
paintings two coffins surmounted by weeping cupids
with inverted torches, and opposite another representation of cupids lighting the hymeneal flame.

Chrysostom married, and Margaret's friends determined to make a last effort to induce her to do the
same. Her mother, with the remembrance of past sufferings, did not care to remain in a house ruled by a
daughter-in-law. With tears she implored Margaret to
come to some decision, and to take her to live with her.
At the same time the youngest son, James, who was preparing for Holy Orders, offered his sister half his patrimony as a dowry. Finally, Chrysostom, now head of
the family and Margaret's guardian, declared it time for
her to take a partner for life. The attack was so violent
that our saintly young girl was on the point of yielding.
" I could no longer withstand," she said, " the importunities of my relatives, nor the tears of a mother who
loved me tenderly, and who represented to me that at
twenty a girl ought to take a husband. The devil,
too, did his part. He whispered to me continually:
' Poor miserable creature, of what are you thinking in
wishing to become a religious ? You will make yourself
a laughing-stock to the world, for you will never per-
severe. What a disgrace to take off the religious habit
and leave the convent ! Where will you turn to hide

yourself after that?' I began, then, to share my
mother's sentiments with regard to remaining in the
world, though my horror of marriage was so great that
I could not think of it without bursting into tears." [1]

Margaret was in this state of hesitancy when God
came to her assistance. "One day," she relates, "after
holy Communion, He made me see that He is the most
beautiful, the richest, most powerful, most perfect, and
accomplished of all lovers. Being promised to Him,
whence came it, He asked, that I desired to break with
Him? 'Oh, remember,' said He, 'if thou dost thus con-
temn Me, I shall abandon thee forever; but if thou art
faithful to Me, I shall never leave thee. I will render
thee victorious over all thine enemies. I excuse thy
ignorance, because thou dost not yet know Me. But if
thou art faithful to Me, I shall teach thee to know Me,
and shall manifest Myself to thee.'" These words, in
which are combined authority, majesty, tenderness,
and the indignation that springs from love despised,
pierced Margaret's heart like an arrow. She shed
abundant tears, and felt new light dawn upon her soul.
She renewed her vow of chastity, resolved "rather to
die than violate it." On leaving the church, she announced her resolution to her family, imploring them
to dismiss every aspirant for her hand, however advan-
tageous the offer might be. [2]

Margaret's tone as she uttered these words conveyed
to her mother the conviction that her child meant what
she said; and so she no longer insisted upon her marry-
ing. "After this my mother shed no more tears in my
presence; but she wept before all with whom she spoke
on the subject. Those persons failed not to tell me that
if I left her I would be the cause of her death; that I
should have to answer to God; and that I could become
a religious as well after her death as before it. One
brother, in particular, who loved me much, did all in

[1] Mémoire, p. 305.   [2] Ibid.

his power to dissuade me from my design, and offered me his patrimony as a dowry. But to all such considerations my heart had become as insensible as a rock."

Margaret had, however, to remain nearly three years longer in the world. Her dowry was not forthcoming, the family being yet undecided. They acted slowly and sought pretexts for delay. Margaret waited patiently; but sure now of herself and of God, she lived in celestial peace.

Thinking the distractions of a pleasant city life would change her desires, she was sent to Macon, where her maternal uncle was royal notary. This uncle had a daughter who was very pious. She was on the point of entering the Ursuline convent of that city, and she made every effort to take her cousin with her. The uncle sided with his daughter, and was more insistent in the affair than was commendable. But to their importunity Margaret returned but one reply in which shone the elevation and purely divine disinterestedness of her vocation: "If I should enter your convent, it would be for love of you. I wish to go to a house where I shall have neither relatives nor acquaintances, that I may become a religious actuated by no other motive than the love of God." She was thus debating with her uncle and cousin, and almost ready to yield, for she could not explain to herself, and still less to others, her apparently groundless repugnance to entering a Community pious and fervent, and into which she would have been so joyously welcomed, when her brother Chrysostom arrived unexpectedly to conduct her home. Her mother was at the point of death. In fact, her good and excellent mother was dying of grief. They took advantage of her state, to force upon Margaret the thought of the responsibility she would incur by persisting in her project. "They made me understand," she tells us, "that my mother could not live without me, and that I should have to answer to God for her death. This was told me even by ecclesiastics. It caused me cruel sufferings, for I tenderly loved my mother. The devil made use of this ruse to make me believe that my mother's death would be the cause of my eternal damnation." [1]

Tortured in heart and conscience, Margaret cast herself at the foot of her crucifix and watered it with her tears. There she found peace. God came to her assistance. He consoled her mother, enlightened her brother, and gave her kinsfolk to understand that souls must follow whither God calls.

The more Margaret thought of the religious life, the more enraptured she became with it. It was there, she thought, that she would learn to pray as she had never yet known how; that she would obey and do penance to the full extent of her desires. There, too, she would communicate frequently; and this thought roused her soul to rapturous transports. " My greatest joy was to think I should communicate frequently; for the privilege was now granted me but rarely. I should have believed myself the happiest creature in the world, had I been able frequently to pass the entire night before the Blessed Sacrament. On the eve of my Communions, I felt my soul so abyssed in recollection that I could speak but with the greatest effort; I was wholly taken up with the sublimity of the action I was about to perform. After my Communions, I desired neither to eat nor drink, to see any one, nor to speak, so great were the peace and consolation I felt." [2]

Things were still in this state, when there arrived at Vérosvres, to preach the Jubilee proclaimed by Clement X. after his elevation to the Sovereign Pontificate, 1670, a religious of the Order of St. Francis. His name the old Mémoires do not tell. They inform us only that he was a man of eminent piety. To this child, who was to reveal to the world the pierced Heart of Jesus Christ,

[1] Mémoire, p. 307.   [2] Ib. p. 308.

God sent a disciple of him who on Mt. Alvernus had received in his hands and feet and heart the sacred stigmata of the wounds of Jesus Christ. "His charity was such," says she, "that he stayed at our house over-night to give us a chance to make our general confes-sion."[1] Margaret made hers with abundance of tears. Her least faults appeared to her crimes. The holy re-ligious, seeing her purity of soul, put her in the way of communicating every day, taught her to make prayer,—an instruction she hardly needed,—and promised her some instruments of penance; for, dreading vanity, she had not dared to speak to him of the mortification she already imposed upon herself. He did more. He went at once to find Chrysostom, and roused in him great scruples for putting obstacles in the way of such a voca-tion. Chrysostom loved his sister tenderly, but he feared still more to offend God. That same day he had a long conversation with Margaret, to find out whether or not she was really persevering in her design. Hav-ing received the energetic reply, "Yes, certainly, I would rather die than change my purpose," he at once took the necessary steps for her departure from home.

Shortly after, in the spring of 1671, Margaret, accom-panied by her brother, set out for Paray-le-Monial, where there was a convent of the Visitation, in which she had resolved to conceal herself for life.

Why the Visitation? She did not know. Never had she put her foot into a convent of this Order. She con-sidered the Poor Clares of Charolles too near to Véros-vres. As to the Ursulines of Macon, she was still in-fluenced by the motives that dictated her answer to her cousin: "If I should go into your Community, it would be for love of you. I wish to go where I shall have neither relations nor acquaintances, that I may become a religious through no other motive than the love of God." Once before when her brother insisted on her

[1] Mémoire, p. 309.

entering with the Ursulines, she replied: "No, that will never be. I wish to go to the Holy Maries, to a distant convent in which I have no acquaintances. I wish to be a religious only for God. I wish to leave the world entirely, to hide myself in some corner in which I can forget and be forever forgotten."[1]

This is all Margaret knew of the reasons that influenced her vocation. The rest was God's secret.

Several Visitation convents were proposed to her, Charolles, Macon, Autun, Dijon, and Paray. "As soon," said she, "as I heard mention of Paray, my heart bounded with joy, and I consented at once." She then set out with her brother for the term of her happiness, "dear Paray." On crossing the threshold, her soul was flooded with celestial sweetness, and a voice interiorly whispered: "Here it is that I wish thee to be." A short time before, seeing at Macon a picture of St. Francis de Sales, it seemed to her that the saint looked at her tenderly. It was something of the same kind that she now experienced. Turning quickly toward her brother, she said: "Be assured I shall never leave this house." Not so judged the good people of Paray who saw her enter. She was tastefully dressed, joy was beaming on her countenance, and she was making lively gesticulations. They smiled as they glanced at her, and said: "Look! has she the appearance of a religious?" "And indeed," she adds, "I then wore more vain ornaments than I had ever before done, and I gave expression to the great joy I felt at seeing myself all in all to my Sovereign Good."[2]

Margaret returned once more to Vérosvres, but only to take a last farewell. It was heart-rending. Her mother covered her with tears and caresses. Margaret at first bore this last assault without even growing pale. "Never did I feel my heart so joyous or so firm. I was, as it were, insensible to the affection and the sorrow of

[1] Mémoire, p. 310.　　　　[2] Ib., p. 311.

which I was the object and the cause. Even my mother's tears affected me not, and I shed not one myself on leaving her." But as God wished that none of the beauties of nature or of grace should be wanting to this great sacrifice, Margaret had hardly left her mother, when an immense wave of bitterness swept over her soul. "It seemed to me," she said, "that my soul was being torn from my body." When St. Teresa crossed for the last time the threshold of her father's house, she felt, to use her own expression, as if her bones were being snapped and her life was slipping away from her. Again, when St. Chantal tore herself from the embrace of her old father and the caresses of her little ones, she shed such torrents of tears that the lookers-on were astonished and scandalized. Margaret Mary had the same divine honor done her. On her way from Vérosvres to Paray, she tasted the agony of agonies.

Why, we ask, did she choose the Visitation, when so many other religious houses were open to her? Now we know. Margaret Mary went not to the Visitation like so many others, because this Institute, founded recently by two admirable saints, still exhaled its first perfume, a perfume so sweet to breathe in the cradle of religious houses. She went there by reason of a higher order. God, who has not raised a mountain, dug out a valley, directed the course of a river, without knowing for what people, for what souls He was laboring, in fashioning the Visitation thought of Margaret Mary. He made one for the other. He made the sweetness, simplicity, humility, the hidden life of the Visitation that Margaret Mary on the day of her entrance might expand as in her element: and there for twenty years He worked in the soul of our holy child. He made her sweet, humble, simple, pure, so that she might one day be the loveliest of Visitandine flowers, the sweetest of Visitandine fruits. Or rather He made one for the other—the grand Order for the humble virgin; the former to be the theatre, the latter the evangelist, the apostle of a great miracle, of which neither the one nor the other could have the shadow of a doubt. Long be-fore, in the far-away time, He had sent St. Francis de Sales and St. Chantal sublime presentiments of what was to take place. He had sown the living germs even in the foundation of the Visitation. He had given to it for its arms and armorial bearings a heart crowned with thorns and surmounted by a cross. These pious daughters, whom sixty years before He had formed in solitude to be one day the guard of honor of His adorable Heart, the people, though without knowing why, began to call " *The Daughters of the Heart.*"

But the humble virgin that was to cause those germs to flourish, throw light upon those early presentiments, and clothe with meaning that coat-of-arms, suspected nothing of her mission. In all these first years of her life, though the Divine Voice had already spoken to her, there was not one word of her extraordinary vocation; not one glimmer of light on her future destiny; not a reference to the wants of that Church to which, how-ever, she was sent as a liberating angel. She had ex-perienced but one attraction, and that had overruled every other. "Hide thyself, fly men, forget creatures. Seek a little corner, a solitude, a cloister, in which thou mayest forget all and in which, forgotten by all, thou mayest live for God alone"—such were the words spoken by the Divine Voice.

Behold the dispositions with which Margaret entered the Visitation, May 25, 1671. Three months after she was clothed with the habit, and eighteen months later she prostrated on the choir floor. The nuns covered her with a pall, from beneath which she rose up radi-ant; for between her and man there was raised an im passable barrier—the tomb was sealed!

CHAPTER IV.

THE CONVENT OF PARAY.

1671.

"Surge, illuminare, Jerusalem, quia venit lumen tuum, et gloria Domini super te orta est."

"Arise, be enlightened, *O Paray*, for thy light is come, and the glory of the Lord is risen upon thee."—*Isaias* lx. 1.

"When the time had come, the sanctuary doors opened, and the King of Love entered the dear convent of Paray, introducing therein His well-beloved."—*Année Sainte*, vol. i. p. 746.

WHAT kind of convent was this toward which God directed our saint, and which was to be the theatre of such marvels? What souls was she to meet therein? What virtues and what traditions? What the faith and fervor of their religious life?[1]

This was the time in which the Visitation Order, for thirty years bereaved of its foundress, the great-souled Mother de Chantal, 1641, drew from the recent feasts of the canonization of St. Francis de Sales fresh vitality, and continued to cover the world with its pious solitudes. Every year saw them opened to souls weary of the world and thirsting for divine love. In 1642, Ville-

---

[1] It is customary at the Visitation for each monastery to send out every three years a *Circular* addressed to the whole Institute. In this *Circular* is first related whatever of importance has transpired in the community, and then is given a sketch of the lives of the Sisters that have died during those three years. Hence we see the importance of such documents. It is the complete history of a convent, the general history of the community, and the individual history of each Sister. We have, consequently, most carefully examined all the *Circulars* of Paray belonging to the epoch with which we are now occupied. It is from these documents we draw this chapter, and shall turn to them for light on the obscure questions of many following.

franche, Verceil in Italy, Montbrison, Agen, Avignon, the second of Rouen; in 1643, Salins, Montélimart, Limoges; in 1644, Issoudun, Castellane, Vienne, and Tulle; in 1645, Saint-Marcellin and Soleure; in 1646, La Flèche, Avallon, and Dole; in 1647, Toulouse, Chartres, and Saumur; in 1648, Loudun, Bourbon-Lancy, the second of Grenoble ; in 1649, Compiègne and Clermont ; in 1650, Abbeville and Mons, in Hainaut ; in 1651, Chaillot, Seissel, Aurillac, and Larochefoucauld ; in 1652, the second of Marseilles and the second of Aix ; in 1653, Saint-Amour and Langres ; in 1654, Varsovie, in Poland ; in 1657, Arone in Italy ; in 1659, Auxerre, Alençon, and Brioude ; in 1660, Thiers and the third of Paris ; in 1663, Bourg, Saint-Andéol, and Monaco ; in 1664, Nîmes ; in 1666, Saint-Remo ; in 1667, Brussels and Munich ; in 1669, Modena and the second of Nice ; finally, in 1671, Rome. An inexhaustible current of life flowed from the tomb that had just closed over St. Chantal. And although her first daughters, they who had listened to her energetic words, had gone to rejoin her in the sojourn of light after which they had so ardently sighed, they left behind souls whom they themselves had formed, inheritors of their virtues, some of whom had even caught a glimpse of the venerable countenance of their holy foundress.

Among all these pious solitudes, that of Paray, in Burgundy, was recommendable for its antiquity and fervor.

The little town of Paray is situated in a charming valley, encircled with mountains and crossed by fresh running water. The most beautiful vines in the world lend it their shade, and it rests at the foot of an old basilica built by St. Hugh, in the twelfth century, to test the plan to be used for the colossal church of Cluny. Born of the breath of the monks, and for that reason called Paray-le-Monial; reared under the paternal government of the abbots, of whom, in Burgundy as well as

on the borders of the Rhine, they say, " One lives at
ease under the crosier," it has preserved even to our
own day a purity of morals, a nobleness and distinction
of manners, a loyalty of friendship, and a fervor of piety, that the misfortunes of the times could not diminish.   Protestantism, it is true, appeared there for a moment ; but it was, as in other parts of Burgundy, only a
surprise visit, from which it quickly recovered, and soon
regained its former fruitfulness.   To repair the breaches
made by its inroads, Paray made haste to build a convent in which the Ursulines might rear her children ; a
hospital for the care of her sick ; a house for the Jesuit
Fathers to teach again Jesus Christ ; and, finally, a convent of the Visitation to embalm all around with the
perfume of piety.   Some years later, the little town,
whose population did not then exceed four or five thousand, witnessed one of those outbursts of faith and
charity that would have done honor to the largest me-
tropolis ; namely, the rejoicings occasioned by the arrival of the Sisters of the Visitation, September 4, 1626.
In 1642, their convent was entirely rebuilt in a beautiful plain to the east and, as it were, pillowed on the
back of the old basilica.   It may still be seen in all
its primitive simplicity, for it has not changed.   Four
large buildings form a square, which incloses a court.
A cloister extends around them, its vast colonnade opening on a court, in whose centre plays the traditional and
symbolical fountain.   On the walls of irreproachable
whiteness, and in the arch formed by the rising roof,
may still be read sentences which St. Francis de Sales
recommended to be written everywhere, that no eye
might be raised without meeting a thought for the mind
and food for the soul.   The community-room, chapel,
sacristy, and refectory open on the cloister, from the four
corners of which lead stairs to the cells on the story
above.   That of Margaret Mary is still in existence,
though now converted into a chapel.   But we have seen

it in its primitive state, narrow, chalk-white, with no other furniture than a bed, a table, and a chair; no other ornament than a wooden crucifix, and a paper picture of the Sacred Heart. All the other cells are like it, simple, poor, neat. The large gardens dotted with statues and chapels surround the whole convent with verdure, silence, and peace. The sojourn of the saint here undoubtedly exhaled around it a perfume that otherwise it would not have had ; and has made it, as it were, a reliquary filled with precious mementos of the Lord. One cannot take a step without inhaling peace, fervor, forgetfulness of creatures, and the presence of God.

On Margaret's arrival, in 1671, the convent was governed by the venerable Mother Hieronyme Hersant, just then finishing her sixth year of superiority. She belonged to the Visitation of Paris, rue Saint-Antoine, where she had for mistress of novices the great and holy Mother Lhuillier. Whilst young, she had been able to open her heart and soul to the venerable Mother de Chantal, and for twenty years she had for director St. Vincent de Paul.[1] In such a school she had become a saint, and had, moreover, learned that science of government and that art of directing minds which, joined to the most solid virtue, had already secured to Paray five years of fervor and progress in the spiritual life. True, she was at the time, having almost finished her six years of superiority, 1666–1672, about to leave the Sisters of Paray and return to Paris. But from her hands the government was to pass into those of Mother de Saumaise, a soul neither less tender nor less strong, who was to come from Dijon. After having governed that convent for six years, 1672–1678, she was to give place to Mother Greyfié from Annecy, 1678–1684. In this Visitation of Paray, where we are to see virtue so sublime, vocations so extraordinary, love of Rule so

[1] Année Sainte, vol. i. p. 745.

great, courage so masculine, humility overruled the
other virtues to such a degree that it would not allow
the religious to feel that they were able to govern themselves. Their fervor impelled them to seek at Annecy,
Paris, and Dijon, Superiors the most capable of keep-
ing them united and of advancing them in the true
spirit of the Visitation. Rising higher, let us say, God,
who was bringing to this cloister so rare a marvel, and
through her perfecting the Visitation, completing the
work of St. Francis de Sales and St. Chantal, wished to
call there to direct Margaret Mary the most eminent
Superioresses from the three convents in which were
still existing the oldest traditions and remembrances of
the holy founders.

The mistress of novices into whose hands Margaret
was to be placed on her arrival was a venerable religious who had passed four-and-forty years of conventual
life, and whose vocation dated back even to the foundation of the Visitation of Paray. Her father, M. de
Thouvant, was one of the two founders of the convent,
and she was the first of the young girls of Paray to take
the veil. Contemporary with the eight religious whom
Mother de Blonay had sent from Lyons to make the
foundation,—and " who were so extraordinarily favored
by God; whose obedience was proof against all difficulties; whose gift of prayer was sublime; and, finally,
whose perfume of virtue was so powerful that the people
clipped their clothing to obtain some shreds as relics," [1]
—Sister de Thouvant had not yet finished her novitiate
when St. de Chantal arrived at the convent. The saint
looked at the novice, who was only sixteen years old,
and, knowing by prophetic light what she would one
day be, laid her hand on her head with a blessing. She
earnestly recommended that they would take great care
of her and moderate her fervor, " and, in particular,

[1] Unedited Foundations of the Convent of Paray (MSS. in 4to,
belonging to the Visitation of Paray), p. 308.

allow her to make only half an hour's prayer until she was eighteen, for fear too great application might weaken her health; adding that she foresaw that her virtues and good judgment would render her eminently serviceable to the Community." [1]

The saint's prophecy was fully realized. After having governed the convent of Paray twelve years as Superioress, 1645–1651 and 1657–1663; after having, as mistress of novices, formed the greater part of the Community; endowed with the gift of sublime prayer, tender devotion to the Lord, and a deep knowledge of souls, she was going to finish her successful career by forming Margaret Mary to the religious life.

Under the administration of the venerable *Mother* Hieronyme Hersant, and the enlightened direction of the pious Sister de Thouvant, the convent of Paray recruited rapidly. A crowd of young girls, overcoming the most painful opposition, were seen hastening to bury themselves in the cloister, at the cost of the greatest sacrifices. They belonged to the best families of Burgundy: Catherine-Antoinette de Lévis-Châteaumorand for example, who had been detained in the world by the tenderness of her mother. After the death of the latter, she scattered so generously the treasures of her large fortune on her native province, that when the people learned her design of entering religion there was a general outcry. It was resolved to oppose her departure, and even to arrest her *en route ;* [2]—Marie-Hyacinthe Courtin, as "remarkable for beauty as for virtue, and who was followed by her suitors even into our parlors;" [3]—Marie-Thérèse Basset, belonging to one of the

[1] Unedited Foundations of Paray, p. 310.

[2] Abridgment of the life and virtues of our dear Sister de Lévis-Châteaumorand (without date).

[3] Circular of Paray, March 23, 1725. Abridgment of the virtues of twelve of our dear Sisters who died in the convent of Paray from September 9, 1719.

richest families of Roanne, who saw two aspirants to her hand decide their claim by a duel, in which the loved one was slain by his jealous rival. Wounded to the heart by this blow, she sought forgetfulness and consolation in the love of Him who cannot be taken away; [1] —Madeleine de Vichy-Chamron, of the two illustrious houses of Chamron and d'Amanzé, who entered the Visitation only after having refused the abbatial crosier offered her by Mgr. de Villars, Archbishop of Vienne; [2] —Séraphique de la Martinière, who, forced to remain in the world by the devotedness of her parents, fell so ill that she soon resembled a skeleton. Allowed at last to fulfil her desire, "the ardor of her fever yielded to that of divine love, which conducted her to the celestial Spouse." [3] We are about to see group around Margaret Mary so many who, had they deigned to give it their heart, might have hoped everything from the world; in fine, the ladies Damas, Coligny, d'Amanzé, Varenne de Glétin, d'Athose, des Escures, who might at least, since they desired to be religious, have borne the crosier of an abbess, or worn the pectoral cross of a canoness, but who relinquished all, attracted by the humility, poverty, and fervor of the humble retreat that St. Francis de Sales and St. Chantal had just opened "to the great of heart and the weak of health." There were seen even high-born ladies who thought it not sufficient if, in becoming religious, they did not descend to the rank of domestic Sisters : Frances-Angélique de la Mettrie, for example, or Claude-Françoise Chappui, granddaughter of M. de Marselison, of a very rich family of Charolais. "All the importunity of her rela-

---

[1] Circular of December 17, 1717. Abridgment of the virtues of our most honored Sister Marie-Thérèse Basset.

[2] Circular of February 20, 1738. Abridgment of the life and vir tues of our very honored Sister Madeleine-Victoire de Vichy de Chamron.

[3] Circular ot March 23, 1725. Abridgment of the twelve, etc.

tives could not dissuade the latter from taking at **Paray** the white veil of the domestic Sisters, nor constrain her at the close of her life to become a choir Sister. She declared that her wish was to die in the white veil." [1]

Just because these young girls belonged to great families, and possessed a great heart, the trials of the novitiate were excessively severe. Fifty years later their remembrance made them tremble. " As they were not sparing of trials then," says the Sister who relates the entrance into religion of Rosalie Verchère, " she displayed all the generosity of her soul." " Her great piety caused her to be joyfully received to the novitiate," is written of Françoise-Marguerite d'Athose. " She endured the trials, which at that time were very great, with a fervor that merited for her the reception of our holy habit." [2] " Her intrepid courage," it is said of Marie-Catherine du Chailloux, " consumed, so to say, the rigor of those early days, and she plunged with all the ardor of holy love into the ocean of severe trials then in force." [3] " One can say of Catherine Heuillard that she carried to the grave the fervor of her novitiate, having never had any other reproaches addressed her than that she did too much and labored above her strength." [4] Like words one meets on every page of the manuscripts that record the foundation of the Visitation at Paray.

How could this character of austerity, of holy and generous abandonment to the rigor of holy love, fail the novitiate, since the professed Sisters, one and all, were possessed of it? We have already seen something of it; but it would be necessary to relate the life of each member, in particular, to give a true picture of this fervent and generous Community. Marie-Suzanne Piédenuz was a prodigy of austerity. " Wholly penetrated

---

[1] Circular of April 18, 1713.
[2] Circular of March 23, 1725.
[3] Circular of October 1, 1743.
[4] Circular of December 17, 1717.

with the majesty and sanctity of God, she would have wished to abyss herself in His presence even to the centre of the earth. She appeared before Him as a criminal crushed under the weight of His justice. Her bloody disciplines diminished nothing of the ardor of her love. Loving her Divine Saviour with all the powers of her soul, yet feeling that she could not love Him as much as she desired, she looked upon herself as a reprobate, and this painful state lasted till her death." [1] Catherine-Augustine Marest had yet a stronger attraction for penance. " This admirable daughter, although not to be imitated in her mortifications, drank wine rarely, hardly ever approached the fire, the ardor of divine love serving her at all seasons. She was clothed in winter as in summer, not thinking herself worthy even to wear that which could no longer be used by others." [2] " God had prevented Marie-Hyacinthe Courtin with His holy fear and so lively a horror of sin that, though shunning even its shadow, she dreaded to approach the sacraments. Endless time was necessary for her to prepare for confession, in which, however, she failed not to be short and clear, in spite of the great scruples by which she was devoured on the score of the Office. This, joined to her great abstinence and mortification, reduced her to a slow decline." [3] Marie-Charlotte Benoit was still more penitential. " Her strong and generous soul made her aim at perfection in the most vigorous manner. She did nothing by halves. She sacrificed herself and carried her severity so far that her conduct on this point is more admirable than imitable. She treated her body so harshly during her lifetime that, like St. Bernard, fearful of having shortened her days, she was constrained at the hour of death to ask its pardon. This state of continual death makes

[1] Circular of March 15, 1703.
[2] Circular of April 18, 1713.
[3] Circular of March 23, 1725.

us regard her as another St. Jerome."[1] They compared
Rosalie de Farges to another Elias, whose ardor and
penance she possessed. We shall see her pass her entire
life on Calvary in the midst of austerities that make one
tremble.[2]

To this austerity, this mortification, which left their
traces on the countenance of the Sisters of Paray, was
joined a love for Rule carried, perhaps, to so high a degree in no other convent. Sister Jeanne-Aimée lay at the
point of death. The Superioress found her absorbed in
God, her hands clasping the book of Constitutions. To
the questions addressed to her, she answered: "Ah!
Mother, the Lord has made known to me that I can
enter heaven only by these three doors: the observance
of our holy Rules, the love of our neighbor, and humility."[3] " Marie-Joseph Bouthier, dying at the age of
twenty-one, and pained at leaving life so young, exclaimed: 'Alas! I have only begun to live, and behold,
I must die.' To reconcile herself to the sacrifice, she
kissed the book of Constitutions and found therein
strength to submit to the holy will of God."[4] Marie-
Hyacinthe Courtin always had her Rules in her hand.
By them she regulated all her actions, not wishing " to
do anything more or less," which words she had taken
as her device.[5] The zeal with which Sister Catherine-
Augustine Marest was animated, not to say inflamed, for
the holy Rule, would not suffer a failure in the least
point of it; but God made her understand, at last, that
it would be more meritorious to moderate her rigor.
"Attached to her Rule alone, she understood nothing
of the mysteries of direction, as she herself said smiling.
Her Rule, her Superioress, her ordinary confessor, suf-

[1] Circular of December 17, 1717.
[2] Circular of May 14, 1743.
[3] Circular of December 17, 1717.
[4] Circular of March 23, 1725.
[5] Circular of December 17, 1717.

ficed for her." [1] They said as much of Sister Séraphique
de la Martinière, whose chief attraction was love of the
hidden life and exact observance of Rule. " All that was
high and sublime was suspected by her." [2] And in another place we read of Sister de Damas de Barnay: " What
was singular and admirable was not for her."

Let us carefully note all these traits: that exact observance of Rule; that care of regulating their actions
by the motto, " Neither more nor less;" that fear of
everything high and sublime, everything singular and
admirable, that sweet smile when speaking of those
mysteries of direction, etc. In them we touch upon
one of the most striking characteristics of the convent
of Paray, the true cause of the passing opposition that
Margaret was going to meet there, and which has been
till now so little understood and so unfairly estimated.

Let us add that these ardent souls, so generous, so
strongly attached to their Rules, were incredibly humble
and obedient. " Sister Anne-Alexis was like a ball of
wax in the hands of God and of those that held to her
His place. It was this that made them put her into all
the offices high and low, by which she was neither
elated nor cast down, but always frank and cordial, and
of exemplary regularity." [3] When they informed Sister
de Vichy-Chamron, who had broken her abbatial crosier
to enter the Visitation, that they thought of making her
directress, tears filled her eyes, she trembled and
swooned. [4] It was the same with Mother de Lévis-
Châteaumorand when there was question of making her
Superioress. Obliged to submit, she left at her death a
written request that, contrary to custom, they would
write nothing about her, but leave her memory in
eternal oblivion. [5] The Sisters did not obey this order.

[1] Circular of December 17, 1717.   [2] Ibid.

[3] Abridgment of the Life and Virtues of Sister Anne-Alexis de
Maréschalle (a small quarto of 10 pages).

[4] Circular of February 20, 1738.   [5] Abridgment of Life.

Would to God they had not obeyed a similar recom
mendation left by Sister Marie-Madeleine des Escures,
at first Margaret's most intimate friend, whose affection,
a little too lively, was in those first days the trial of her
novitiate; later, her most zealous adversary, because,
though fervent, but less enlightened than our saint, it
seemed to her that the latter strayed from the Rule
and the spirit of the Visitation, above which she herself
prized nothing and finally, when she saw her error,
the most humble, most zealous of the adorers of the
Sacred Heart and of the disciples of Margaret Mary.
It is also to be regretted that the Sisters conformed so
exactly to the written requests left by Sisters Angélique
de Damas de Barnay, Jeanne-Françoise Chalon, de
Coligny, and a number of others. Their love having
led them to quit all and bury themselves in the cloister,
it now led them to desire to be forgotten even by the
cloister.

It is needless to say that love for God crowned these
numerous virtues and inflamed all souls. It was love a
little timid, we must admit, though strong and austere
after the fashion of the seventeenth century, in which
generosity was unlimited, but in which tenderness
should have predominated. The great devotion of
Marie-Anne Cordier was to the immensity of God, and
she incessantly buried herself in this abyss as a nothing
that He is about to destroy.[1] That of Séraphique de la
Martinière was for the infinite majesty of God. This
idea she had constantly before her eyes; therefore she
always worked on her knees.[2] Marie-Émerentianne
Rosselin was almost always buried in the contemplation
of God's justice, which thought tinged her life with
fear.[3] It was the same with Marie-Catherine du Chailloux, whose days were passed in terror of His judg-

[1] Circular of April 18, 1713.
[2] Circular of March 23, 1725.
[3] Ibid.

ments. All that she heard in sermons, all that she read on the end of man, predestination, or fidelity to grace, impressed her so forcibly that she was ready to die of fright. We would be unable to rehearse all the penances she performed to obtain the peace of the children of God, which she at last possessed after having purchased it so dearly." [1]

But these grand views, which have so deteriorated in our days, and which then filled souls with so lively respect for God, do not hinder love. Sister Séraphique de la Martinière, who, as we have said, always labored on her knees, appeared inflamed with that fire of divine love which Jesus Christ came to enkindle upon earth. The assaults of divine love often reduced her to death, and she complained tenderly to her God, saying: " I can bear no more! Have regard to my weakness, O Lord, or I shall expire under the violence of Thy love!" [2] That other Sister, Marie-Anne Cordier, who always felt herself annihilated before the immensity of God, had at the same time for Him a love so lively, so, strong, so ardent, that, according to her own expression, she would die of sorrow at not being able to die of love. [3] " O Mother!" said Sister Émerentianne Rosselin, " I long passionately to die in order to see my God;" and her eyes, whilst saying these words, shone with so vivid a light that in them could be read the truth of what she affirmed. [4] Sister Marie-Suzanne Piédenuz made every day one hundred acts of the love of God; [5] and eyes filled with tears on beholding Sister Catherine Séraphique Bouillet, a venerable old Sister, on her knees, her hands joined, asking the little novices what

[1] Circular of October 1, 1743.
[2] Circular of March 23, 1725.
[3] Ibid.
[4] Ibid.
[5] Année Sainte, vol. v. p. 353.

she must do to love God. "For I languish with love of Him," said she, "and I cannot be satisfied." [1]

The two great devotions of the convent were, as we see, the Cross and the Holy Eucharist—the tomb of sacrifice and the tomb of Love Eternal. The religious went to the first to entertain and there excite that thirst for immolation, for penance, for austerity and humiliation, which devoured them. There is not one of those lives in which we do not discover that the second source of their piety was the Lord in the Holy Sacrament. According to the old Mémoires: "They ran thither as if famished."

We begin now to discover the true features of Paray. In founding his grand work of the Visitation, the saintly Bishop of Geneva had, we remember, two lofty, prevailing ideas. They were tutelary angels far in advance of their time, and which for that reason met a thousand difficulties that stranded the one and kept the other in constant jeopardy. The first idea of St. Francis de Sales was to found religious for the service of the poor. The world cried out against it, and constrained the holy prelate to erect the grates of the cloister. Baffled in this, the saint thought of that multitude of souls who, from want of robust health, could not enter Carmel or the Poor Clares, and drew up a kind of life in which recollection, sweetness, the spirit of mortification, and amiable charity were to supply for corporal austerities, which the want alluded to rendered impossible. But here that vast tide of compunction which swept through the seventeenth century began to swell and carry on its breast crowds to the Visitation. Paray was of this number. Behold those cloister-grates, more austere than St. Francis de Sales demanded ; those frequent disciplines, those continual fasts! See that multitude of Sisters forced to ask pardon of their body for having treated it so badly!

[1] Circular of May 4, 1704.

See them trembling before God with holy fear, over-
powered by the feeling of His immensity, His awful
greatness! In a word, look at that love, generous but
not sufficiently tender, and you have a picture of Paray
in 1671. It was more austere than St. Francis de Sales
wished, but it was not less fervent than he could have
possibly desired.

Were the generous-souled inmates of this convent
sad? Listen to a remark repeated a thousand times
and with perfect truth: "The more severe the Rule, the
gayer the religious." In the lives of the Sisters who
then composed the Community of Paray, one reads with
surprise words most pleasing. There is hardly one of
those religious of whom they do not say that she was
a good friend;[1] one of the best friends that could be
found;[2] a soul sincere and frank in her friendship;[3] a
royal heart;[4] a noble and liberal heart;[5] a heart the most
sensible to affection and most grateful for the least
service.[6] Their records sing on every note of the scale
of the amiability, gayety, sweetness, eagerness to give
pleasure, lively and spiritual repartee, beautiful talents of
all kinds.[7] Marie-Thérèse Basset, daughter of the mayor
of Roanne, understood business so well as to surprise
the lawyers of her day. "She has been most useful to
us," say the Mémoires, "in the care of our papers; and
her distinct and beautiful penmanship has been of
marvellous assistance. On entering the cloister she
brought with her a library so well furnished that it was
for us a valuable present.[8] Sister Marie-Catherine du

---

[1] Circular of March 23, 1725.

[2] Ibid.

[3] Circular of November 1, 1715.

[4] Circular of March 8, 1701.

[5] Circular of December 17, 1717.

[6] Circular of July 7, 1743.

[7] See the above-mentioned Circulars, along with others already
quoted or from which we are going to quote.

[8] Circular of December 17, 1717: see her detailed Life.

Chailloux wielded a not less able pen. It was she who wrote the *Annales* of the convent of Paray, "a work that immortalized her among us."[1] Sister Anne-Alexis de Maréschalle wrote charming verses. "She possessed a joyousness of heart that was reflected in her countenance and entered into her conversation, always gay and holily joyous. She also wrote very beautiful couplets to animate herself to fervor ever new."[2] Sister Marie-Suzanne Piédenuz did better still, for she composed a great number of poems and canticles. She transposed into verse the Psalter of the Blessed Virgin, consisting of one hundred and fifty Psalms, composed by St. Bonaventure.[3] Madeleine-Victoire de Vichy-Chamron also cultivated poetry. The time passed in her cell was so agreeable that, far from being wearisome, she always found it too short. She composed spiritual canticles full of energy and fervor. Some of the poems then written in the convent of Paray have been preserved. They are not inferior to those cited by M. Cousin composed at the same epoch by Mlle. de Bourbon, Mlle. de Rambouillet, Mlle. de Bouteville and Mlle. de Brienne at the château of Chantilly.[4] Margaret Mary is about to join this choir of voices sweet and pure, and our dear little country-girl will warble melodiously as they.

> "A chased and panting fawn,
> I seek the flowing stream.
> The hunter's flying dart
> Has pierced my inmost heart."

Let us now bring an artiste to the front. Marie-Anne Cordier covered the convent with her pictures. Seizing the brush herself, she painted the chapel of the Blessed Virgin, the ceiling azure sown with golden stars, which produced a lovely effect. Again, she in-

---

[1] Circular of July 7, 1743.
[2] Circular of March 9, 1733.
[3] Année Sainte, vol. i. p. 353.
[4] Cousin, La Jeunesse de Mme. de Longueville, p. 217

spired painters and sculptors with her own ideas, with which workmen even the most expert were charmed. She had the altar-piece made, she herself furnishing the idea to a very skilful sculptor. She had made, also, some figures in copper representing the mysteries of the Passion. They were placed in a corridor leading to the infirmary, at the end of which was a Calvary. She had, in fine, painted all around the Blessed Virgin's chapel the mysteries of her life.[1] The chapel of the Sacred Heart, however, she had not the happiness of thus embellishing. Whether she was suffering at the time or other reasons intervened we do not know, but that honor was reserved for Marie-Nicole de la Faige des Claines. Born of a great family, the recipient of a brilliant education, she had, perhaps, a more exquisite talent. She, also, it was who painted the first picture representing the Sacred Heart surrounded by angels.[2] Another Sister, Françoise-Eléonore de Vichy-Chamron, succeeded so well in small crayons "that some of her work, after exciting the admiration of Mgr. Cardinal de Bouillon, was sent by him not only to his noble relatives in Paris, but one also to the Holy Father, Pope Clement XI. His Eminence assures us that it was honored with a place in the breviary of His Holiness, who praised its delicacy very much."[3]

Whilst some of the nuns charmed thus the leisure hours of their cloistered life, warming their heart by devout poetic effusions and beautiful paintings, others plied the needle. Through a spirit of devotion for the ornamentation of the holy altar; or through a penitential spirit of labor; or again, after the pestilence, through the necessity of supplying their own wants, they busied themselves in similar occupations, in all which, however, they showed themselves most expert, and per-

[1] Circular of April 18, 1713.
[2] Année Sainte, vol. ix. p. 727.
[3] Vie et Œuvres, vol. i. p. 482.

formed wonders. Françoise-Marguerite d'Athose, we are told, "was one of the most skilful in weaving laces of gold and silver, which we made at that time for a merchant of Lyons."[1] When Sister Madeleine de Vichy-Chamron took the veil, she was attired in a magnificent dress of cherry-colored moire with under-skirt of silver moire, which she afterward devoted to the altar. With the assistance of her dear Sisters, she embroidered it beautifully in gold and silver. Their skilful fingers succeeded so well that their work was long used as our most beautiful ornaments.[2] Sister de Vichy-Chamron had as friend and rival in this sort of work Catherine-Augustine Marest, who employed her time and extraordinary talent in making laces of *point à la reine* to trim albs and surplices. She was also remarkably skilful in making gold and silver laces to be sold in Lyons, and the result of her labor was so suc-cessful as to furnish the necessary funds to erect in the church the chapel of St. Francis de Sales.[3] They praise the exquisite tapestry of Sister Marie-Catherine du Chailloux, wrought in her early religious days; for later, through humility, she asked and obtained per-mission to make a vow to employ her time in shoe-making. With the same hand that had arranged the *Annales* of the convent, she for forty years made the shoes of its inmates.[4] It was the same sentiment of humility that induced Madeleine de Vichy-Chamron to abandon her embroidery in gold and silver for the cloth-factory that the Sisters of Paray had established in their house to defray the expenses of their convent, desolated by the pestilence. She passed many years there making

[1] Circular of March 23, 1725.

[2] Circular of January 20, 1738. Those beautiful ornaments have not perished. Splendidly restored, they were used at the feast of the Beatification.

[3] Circular of December 17, 1717.

[4] Circular of July 7, 1743.

cinctures with a little loom or frame, and spinning the woof of the stuff with which the frames were covered.

When Mme. de Maulvrier expressed astonishment at seeing a girl of her birth in so low an employment, she received the beautiful reply that, low as it was, it was far too honorable for her.[1] She had in this work as teacher and mistress Sister Anne-Alexis de Maréschalle, who had been the first to learn the art from a cloth-weaver and his wife, very poor, plain people, " under whom she suffered much in acquiring her knowledge of spinning and weaving." But nothing could daunt her. She had the establishment of this cloth-factory at heart, and she afterward devoted seventeen years to it.[2] Another brave soul devoted to this humble and laborious work was Catherine-Augustine Marest, a skilled point-lace maker. She remained long years in the factory, turning her great wheel with recollection that edified the beholders, and strength that no fatigue could overcome, looking upon herself the while as the dolt of the house. Thus did Mother Greyfié smilingly call her. Not that Sister Catherine was wanting in spirit. She possessed the gift of repartee, the most lively and the most spiritual, along with judgment the very best. It was in allusion to the labors with which she overburdened herself that she received the characteristic epithet.[3]

To possess a picture true and complete of the convent of Paray, we must add that from the first days was established in it a boarding-school to which the great families of the Charolais, of the Maconnais, of the Autunesse hastened to send their daughters, too happy at being able to confide them to women like Mother de Lévis-Châteaumorand, Sister Marie-Catherine du Chailloux, Sister de Vichy-Chamron, Sister d'Athose, Sister

[1] Circular of February 20, 1738.
[2] Circular of March 23, 1725.
[3] Ibid.

de Damas, Sister de Coligny, and so many others, so pious, so distinguished in gifts of mind and heart, who in abandoning the world had not parted with their charms nor dispossessed themselves of their talents. We shall mention only one of these little boarders, Marie-Madeleine de Chaugy, whom St. Chantal found there on her last visit, whom she took with her to Annecy, and whom later on we know as so great a religious and so brilliant a writer.

Such was the convent of Paray. It was one of the most fervent of the Order, one of the most generous. They called it " dear Paray," and " the Tabor of Superioresses," on account of the sweet union and perfect obedience of the Sisters. God visibly blessed this house, though none knew as yet His mysterious designs upon it. Finally, when all was ready, May 25, 1671, the doors of the sanctuary opened, and the King of Love entered " dear Paray" to introduce therein His well-beloved.[1]

Margaret was then twenty-three years old; and, although no correct likeness has been left us of her, we may picture her to ourselves from what we know of her appearance by hearsay. She was tall, a little above the ordinary height, and her constitution delicate. Her expressive face was lighted up by soft, clear eyes, and her manners were gay and graceful,[2] her whole air agreeable and vivacious.[3] Add to this great intelligence, a judgment solid, keen, and penetrating, a noble soul and a great heart,[4] and we have the portrait of Margaret Mary on her entrance at Paray. Her features

---

[1] Abridgment of the life and virtues of our very virtuous Mothei Margaret-Hieronyme Hersant, Superioress of the convent of Paray. (Année Sainte, vol. i. p. 742.)

[2] Visit made at the parlor to Margaret Mary by Père Leau, S.J. (Vie de la Bienheureuse, by Père Daniel, p. 352.)

[3] Deposition of Mother Greyfié.

[4] Vie de la Bienheureuse, par P. Croiset.

bore the impress of the most lively piety, but she had not yet " that incomparable recollection,[1] that meek and humble exterior,[2] that air of lowliness even to the centre of her nothingness"[3] by which later on she was distinguished. The Sisters extended to her that tender and maternal welcome that all young girls, after tearing themselves from the embraces of their families, received upon their arrival at the convent. They surrounded her with kindness and affection; but none suspected the treasure with which God had just enriched their humble convent.

[1] Deposition of Sister Anne-Alexis de Maréschalle.
[2] Visit made to the parlor by the Rev. Fathers Villette and Croiset.
[3] Circular of March 23, 1725.

CHAPTER V.

MARGARET MARY'S NOVITIATE—GOD PREPARES HER FOR THE GREAT MISSION ABOUT TO BE ENTRUSTED TO HER—HER PROFESSION.

May 25, 1671–November 6, 1672.

"Ecce venio ad te quem amavi, quem quæsivi, quem semper optavi."

"Behold, I come to thee whom I have loved, whom I have sought, whom I have always desired."—*Rom. Brev., Ant. of St. Agnes.*

THE first word addressed to Margaret by the venerable Mother Thouvant, the day after the entrance of the former at Paray, will ever remain celebrated. Margaret, inflamed with the desire of giving herself entirely to God, went to ask her mistress by what means she should do so, imploring her especially to teach her the secret of making prayer. Mother Thouvant replied: "Go place yourself before God like canvas before a painter"—words brief but full, in which Margaret discovered the whole secret of prayer.[1] To kneel at the Lord's feet, to contemplate Him, to allow His holy image to be impressed upon us; and for that end to present Him a soul simple, recollected, pure like those beautiful silver plates on which, thanks to the discoveries of modern science, only the perfect image can be

---

[1] The expression *une toile d'attente*, which may be translated "prepared canvas," was current in the convent of Paray as one of its most ancient traditions. In 1628 one of its religious foundresses fell ill. During her fearful torments she was heard to cry out: "O sweet hand of my Spouse, sketch ! sketch !" The Superioress asked her what she meant by those words. "Ah, Mother," she answered, "I mean I am before God as canvas under the hand of a painter. I am supplicating Him to delineate in me the perfect image of my crucified Jesus." (Année Sainte, vol. x. p. 313.)

depicted,—behold the true method of prayer. Margaret went to prostrate herself at the Lord's feet, and to fulfil the word of her instructress. "As soon as I knelt before Him," she said, "my Sovereign Master made known to me that my soul was the canvas on which He desired to paint the features of His suffering life; of that life which He passed until its consummation in love, silence, and sacrifice. But perfectly to produce these features, He had first to purify it from every stain, from every affection to earthly things, from love of self and of creatures, to whom I was still greatly inclined." [1]

From this moment Margaret felt enkindled within her so ardent a desire for suffering that rest was no longer hers. One thought possessed her soul, and that was how should she crucify herself for a God who had allowed Himself to be crucified for love of her. To no purpose had she guarded inviolably the white robe of baptism; to no purpose had she at the age of three made a vow of virginity, and renewed it at six; to no purpose at twenty-three had she placed between herself and the world the impenetrable cloister-grate: all this was too little for the flame now kindled within her. Her life, though so pure, filled her with horror. She burned to wash in her tears and bathe in her own blood, that by so doing she might purge from her veins the last vestige of sin. O tears of Margaret Mary! blood-stained scourges, avenging whips, insatiable thirst for humiliation and penance; holy industry to purify and adorn her soul for the coming of the Spouse! How shall I describe you? St. Francis de Sales himself was necessary to interpose limits to the young postulant's ardor. One day he had smilingly said to his daughters gathered around him that if, in order to assume austerities contrary to their Rules, they ever forgot the spirit of moderation and sweetness in which he desired them to live, he would return and make so much noise

[1] Mémoire, p. 313.

in their dormitories as to make them readily understand
that they were acting against his will. Margaret knew
something of this. "My blessed Father," said she,
"reproved me so sternly for going beyond the limits of
obedience that I have never since had the courage to
repeat the offence." "Ah, what, my daughter," said he
to me, "do you think to please God by trespassing the
bounds of obedience? Obedience, and not the practice
of austerities, sustains this congregation."[1]

But if St. Francis de Sales could interfere to moderate
this thirst for immolation and penance which awoke in
Margaret's heart stronger than ever on the day she
crossed the threshold of the convent door, he had only to
bless and encourage another desire that appeared at the
same time: that of casting herself headlong, as she said,
into obedience, humility, self-contempt, and the attaining, as perfectly as she could, the perfection of his holy
Institute. To be a religious only by halves horrified her.
And, indeed, it is scarcely worth one's while to leave
the world for so little! The daughters of St. Francis de
Sales were styled at that time "*The Holy Maries*," and
Margaret resolved to be, in the full sense of the word,
a *holy Mary*. We shall soon see whether or not she succeeded.

Three months passed in those first efforts, at the end
of which the nuns gave her the holy habit, on the feast
of St. Louis, August 25, 1671. No details of this ceremony have been preserved. Her sister-novices tell us,
however, in their deposition that her countenance
breathed but modesty and humility, and that a joyous
light played on every feature.[2] This was but a feeble
indication of what was passing in the depths of her heart;
for on this same day the Lord showed Himself to her as
the true Lover of her soul, as the One whom she had
chosen above all others, as the One that would indemnify

---

[1] Mémoire, p. 314.
[2] Process of 1715, Deposition of Sister Contois.

her for all that she had left for Him. " My Divine Master," she said, " let me see that this was the time of our betrothal, and, like the most ardent of lovers, He made me taste what was sweetest in the sweetness of His love." " Indeed," she adds, " His favors were so excessive that they frequently transported my soul, and rendered me incapable of acting. This caused me so deep confusion that I dared not show my face." [1] Torrents of tears flowed at times from her eyes, and again her countenance sparkled like a star. She was, for the most part, so absorbed that she seemed to be no longer on earth. This state was so noticeable that the Sisters, astonished, began to say to themselves: " What is this little novice about ? What is going on within her ?"

What was passing in Margaret's soul none knew at that time. It was only long after that obedience, more powerful than humility, wrested from her the secret of the wonders with which she was honored in those first days.[2] She had, indeed, hardly taken the habit when she received from God an extraordinary grace, one very rare in the lives of the saints. The Lord began to appear to her, not from time to time and from afar, as we read in the life of St. Catharine of Siena and of St. Teresa, but in a constant and ever-present manner.[3] " I saw Him," she said, " I felt Him near me, and I understood Him much better than if I had seen and heard Him with my corporal senses. Had it been by the latter, I should have been able to distract my attention, to turn away from it; but not having any part in it, I could not prevent this kind of communication."

[1] Mémoire, p. 314.

[2] Mémoire of Mother Greyfié on the life and virtues of our pious Sister Margaret Mary. This Mémoire, of thirty pages, is very precious. We shall frequently quote from it.

[3] It would seem, at first sight, that this admirable privilege was not conferred on Margaret Mary till after her profession. She does not, in fact, mention it until this time. But in two other places she says expressly that she enjoyed it even before that event.

"He honored me," she adds, "with His conversation sometimes as a friend, sometimes as an ardently loving spouse, or as a tender father full of love for his only child, and in many other ways." [1]

There were in this rare and marvellous privilege, in this Divine Presence, less seen than felt, though continual and penetrating. two diverse aspects, like two poles, that the Lord showed her in turn. Margaret Mary, not knowing how to define them, called one the sanctity of justice, the other the sanctity of love. The first, the sanctity of justice, made her tremble at the sight of His infinite Majesty. He impressed on her words cannot say what sentiment of annihilation, which made her long to hide in the depths of her own nothingness. She dared remain only on her knees before this awful Majesty. A number of witnesses deposed at the process of canonization that when alone, working, reading, or writing, she always knelt on the ground as if overwhelmed with respect before the invisible presence of an invisible Being. "She was so united to God," said Sister Marie-Nicole de la Faige, "that, whether working, writing, or reading, she was always on her knees with such recollection as one might expect to see in church." The deponent adds that several times she beheld her for three or four consecutive hours in the same position, on her knees, immovable, absorbed in God; and she was often found bathed in tears.[2] "I was often witness of the fact," said Sister Marie Chevalier de Montrouan, an Ursuline and an old pupil of the Visitation of Paray, "that Sister Margaret Mary always worked on her knees. Her recollection was such that curiosity often impelled me to gaze at her a long time, and I used to invite my little companions to come look at her. This they did, though unperceived by her,

[1] Mémoire, p. 319.

[2] Process of 1715, Deposition of Sister Marie-Nicole de la Faige des Claines.

so absorbed was she in God."[1] "This union with God," says another witness, "was such that one might say she preserved it even in sleep."[2]

But working on her knees through respect for the infinite Majesty that everywhere accompanied her, was in Margaret the least of the effects of the sanctity of justice. She would have wished to annihilate herself before that Presence; and she would have desired that every fibre of her being might be destroyed, since she saw not one that was pure. Not being able to effect this, she tried, at least, to immolate and sacrifice herself. "If we had not snatched the scourge from her hands," says Mother Greyfié, "her blood would have never ceased to flow."[3]

Behold what the sight of that which she called "the sanctity of justice" produced in her! If the Lord then depicted under her view "the sanctity of love," it was as if He enkindled a star before her a thousand times more brilliant. The sight of justice and of the Divine Majesty may be supported; but not that of infinite love. To be loved on earth, to be loved by a being noble, elevated, distinguished ; to be faithfully loved, loved devotedly,—oh, what enchantment! But to be loved by God—and loved even to folly! Margaret's heart dissolved at the thought, and, like St. Philip Neri and St. Francis Xavier, she cried out to God: "Withhold, O my God, these torrents that ingulf me, or enlarge my capacity to receive them!"[4]

But the benign Saviour was not satisfied with accompanying the young novice at every step, darting on her at every turn rays of His love and justice. He appeared to her from time to time visibly. He spoke to her, encouraged her in her difficulties, consoled her in her sacrifices, and reproved her for her faults. One day when

[1] Process of 1715, Deposition of Sister Marie-Nicole de la Faige des Claines.
[2] Ibid.　　　　　　　　　　　　[3] Mother Greyfié's Mémoire.
[4] Mémoire of Mother Greyfié, p. 317

she was yielding to some little negligence, " Learn," said He to her, " that I am a holy Master, who teaches sanctity. I am pure and cannot suffer the least stain." This was said in so stern a tone that there was no sorrow, no suffering she would not have preferred.[1] Another day when she seated herself to say her Rosary, He appeared and darted upon her a glance in which was mingled so much love and anger that, twenty years after, she trembled with fear and happiness at its remembrance. Again, she tells us: " Once I yielded to an emotion of vanity in speaking of myself. O God, how many tears this fault caused me!—for when next alone He reproved me with: ' What art thou, O dust and ashes, and in what dost thou glory, since thou hast of thyself naught but nothingness? That thou mayest never lose sight of what thou art, I shall place before thy eyes a picture of thyself.' And then He allowed me to see what I am. The sight filled me with surprise and created in me such horror of self, that if He had not sustained me, I should have swooned with grief. It was by suffering such as this that He punished the least emotion of self-complacency. This forced me to say to Him sometimes: ' Alas, O my God, either let me die, or hide from me this picture! I cannot behold it and live. The sight inspired me with hatred and vengeance against myself; whilst, on the other hand, obedience did not permit me to perform the rigorous penances that they suggested. I cannot express all that I suffered." [2]

If, however, the Lord was severe toward faults against the virtue of religion, faults against respect before the Blessed Sacrament, for defects of uprightness, of purity of intention, of humility, nothing could equal His inflexible severity when there was question of faults against obedience, apart from which the greatest virtues become crimes; the most costly sacrifice, fruits of cor-

[1] Mémoire of Mother Greyfié, p. 323.   [2] Mémoire, p. 330.

ruption deserving only His wrath. "You deceive yourself," said He to her, "in thinking to please Me by such actions and mortifications. I am much more pleased to see a soul take some little alleviation through obedience than to overwhelm herself with austerities and fasts by her own will."[1] "All this the Lord said to me so frequently, so distinctly, in terms so precise, under figures so touching, that I determined," said she, "to die rather than trespass, however little, the limits of obedience."[2]

Tender and good to this soul as toward all others, though operating in her a little more, since she was destined for a grand and perilous mission, the Lord formed her Himself. He aided her to ascend rapidly the first degrees of perfection, and fitted her gradually to receive in humility and entire self-forgetfulness His divine communications. "Nothing was difficult to me," she writes, "because at this time Jesus steeped the severity of my sufferings in the sweetness of His love. I frequently besought Him to withdraw that sweetness from me, that I might taste the bitterness of His anguish, the pangs of His death. But He bade me submit to His conduct, and said that I should see later how wise and able a director He is who knows how to guide souls when, forgetful of self, they abandon themselves to Him."[3]

Whilst things were thus going on in the soul of Margaret Mary, the Sisters, who saw only the exterior, began to experience astonishment and alarm. In vain did the humble novice try to hide the graces with which she was inundated. They could not be concealed What most astonished the Sisters was, not only the long hours that she passed on her knees in the choir or in her cell, her face radiant, her eyes full of tears, but the state of constant abstraction from which it was necessary to arouse her. Her work fell from her hands,

[1] Mémoire p. 324. [2] Ibid. [3] Ibid., p. 325.

and she forgot everything. The poor child's soul was in heaven, and she knew but imperfectly how to conduct herself on earth.

Her Superiors were still more disquieted than the Sisters. From the very first, Mother Thouvant, the mistress of novices, thought it her duty to inform Margaret that her manner of acting was not in accordance with the spirit of the Visitation, and that if she did not change she could not be admitted to profession.[1]

The words threw Margaret into great desolation of soul, and she did her best to change her manner of life. But how accomplish it? "This spirit," she said, " had already acquired such ascendency over mine that I could no longer control it, any more than my other powers which I felt absorbed in it."[2]

What the venerable Mother Thouvant desired, and very justly too, of one so young and inexperienced was the exterior renunciation of extraordinary lights, and the practice of prayer according to the simple way in which the other novices were instructed. Margaret did not hesitate to obey, but her efforts were fruitless. "I made," she said, "every effort to follow the method of prayer taught me, along with other practices; but my mind retained nothing of all those teachings. The beautiful points of prayer vanished, and I could neither learn nor retain anything but what my Divine Master taught me. This made me suffer greatly, for His operations in me were frustrated as much as possible, and I had to resist Him as much as I was able."[3] It was like Jacob's wrestling with the angel. Margaret Mary came forth bruised and wounded, though having gained more and more the heart of her mistress by her admirable obedience.

To assist her in her efforts, and to aid her to overcome, if possible, her state of absorption, which was what the Community most remarked, Margaret Mary

---

[1] Mémoire, p. 314.   [2] Ibid., p. 20.   [3] Ibid., p. 320.

was given as aid to Sister Catherine-Augustine Marest, the infirmarian, who had instructions to keep her constantly employed, and not to allow her a moment's rest. This Sister Marest was one marvellously well chosen for her work. She was "incomparable in strength of body and mind;" greatly given to the active life, very little to the contemplative; caring little for the mysteries of direction, as she pleasantly said; knowing only her Rule, nothing more, nothing less; but nobly observing that Rule even to heroism. To all this she joined a love of God, not tender nor contemplative, but warm and ardent. She was a true Martha with whom was now associated a true Mary. And it turned out just as we read in the Gospel. Martha complained of Mary, who, transported, in spite of herself, with excessive joy, constantly relapsed from the activity imposed upon her into the sweet sleep of contemplation.[1] If permitted to enter the choir to hear the subject of meditation read, scarcely was it over before Margaret Mary was instructed to go sweep the corridors, clean the cells, weed the garden, etc. Overburdened with work, and longing for that prayer which she had not been allowed to make, she went to her mistress to beg time to resume it. But the latter reprimanded her sharply. She told her that it was strange she knew not how to unite prayer and labor, and sent her to other occupations more numerous and more overwhelming.

But these Sisters did well. The Lord, who was enriching Margaret Mary's soul, reigned supreme Master in it and, in spite of every obstacle, inebriated it with delight. Pacing the corridors, broom in hand, whilst the Sisters were sweetly kneeling at the foot of the holy altar, Margaret Mary had ever before her eyes the invisible Object of her love. She contemplated Him, she listened to Him, she lived under the charm of the per

[1] Circular of December 17, 1717. Année Sainte, vol. ii. p. 242.

petual vision granted her by her Celestial Spouse. Work·
ing, she sang:

> " The more they contradict my love,
>   The more that love inflames.
> By day, by night, they torture me,
>   But cannot break my chains.
> My Lover's love's of such a kind,
>   The more I suffer pain,
> The closer does He my poor heart
>   Unto His own enchain." [1]

The anniversary of her admission to the habit was now
approaching, August 25, 1672, and yet she was not called
to her holy profession. The embarrassment of the
Community increased every day. The Sisters admired
her virtues; her unbounded humility; her obedience;
her love of Rule, so much the more striking as it seemed
to lead her in the most extraordinary ways; and her
charity, which placed her at the service of all. She was
not very skilful in ordinary domestic ways, but she was
so good, so eager, that whilst thanking her for services
badly rendered, the recipient could not fail to be
touched by her goodness of heart. Mother Hersant did
not hesitate to say that Margaret Mary was called to
extraordinary sanctity;[2] and from two or three circumstances it could be seen that she was capable of the
most heroic sacrifices. Once, for example, she struggled
against a natural repugnance till she fainted. Again,
being tenderly attached to Sister Marie-Madeleine des
Escures, one of the companions of her novitiate, she was
warned interiorly that this sweet union saddened the
jealous love of her Divine Master; and she resolved to
disengage her heart from it. For this three months of
battle were necessary, so affectionate was she by nature.
But in this point, as in all others, she triumphed; for
neither repugnances nor sympathies were capable of
daunting her courage. Nevertheless, although it is

[1] Mémoire, p. 315.   [2] Process, p. 71.

customary at the Visitation for the profession to take place one year and one day after the date of reception, August 25, 1672, rolled by without Margaret Mary's having had the happiness of pronouncing her holy vows. "I have learned from many old Sisters," says one of the witnesses, " that her profession was deferred only on account of her extraordinary ways; for, as to the rest, they esteemed her a saint." [1] "I have heard from the Superioress and mistress of novices, who conferred together about the Blessed One," says Sister Jeanne-Marie Contois, "that she would one day be a saint. But she was so extraordinary that perhaps she was not intended to live out her life at the Visitation." [2] "Margaret Mary," says a third witness, "was an example of fervor. All had an excellent opinion of her, though all did not approve her extraordinary ways." [3] "The Blessed One," says a fourth witness, "was astonishingly fervent during her novitiate. But her extraordinary ways made us fear." [4] All the Sisters spoke in like manner. They reveal to us the very just precautions taken by the monastery in which suddenly appeared one of the rarest phenomena of sanctity: an humble girl whose life was already in heaven, who was everywhere accompanied by the visible presence of God; who in the midst of her Sisters was wholly absorbed, her eyes suffused with tears; her countenance now sparkling like a star, or cast down as if in utter annihilation; admirably obedient, and yet incapable of obedience; avaricious of extraordinary penances, and so eager for suffering that her Superiors knew neither how to moderate nor how to satisfy her. Assuredly, if any convent would have hesitated, for the chances of error are great in things so delicate, how much more the Visitation, to which St. Francis de Sales so much recommended humility, simplicity, love of the hidden life, and

---

[1] Process, p. 70.
[2] Ibid., p. 68.
[3] Ibid., p. 72.
[4] Ibid., p. 73.

in which he had supplicated the Sisters to conform simply and purely to the Rule with no innovations! One day, after his holy Mass, he knelt with St. Chantal at the foot of the altar, and both supplicated God never to send to the Visitation any extraordinary grace. Thus the idea gradually took possession of the Order that the Visitation was not called to brilliant gifts; that it was to live hidden and obscure, like an humble little violet, and leave to others exceptional favors and great missions. Such thoughts as these gave rise to their delay in allowing Margaret Mary to pronounce her vows; but, on the other hand, when they fixed their eyes upon her, why were they not reassured? Had there ever been a vocation more supernatural, more disinterested? Who but God had led Margaret to the Visitation, of which she knew nothing? Who enabled her to overcome every obstacle? If God willed to make this gift to the Visitation, why should the Visitation refuse it? The Spirit breatheth where it will. Love is the master. And already what signs that the Spirit breathing on Margaret was truly the Spirit of God, and that she was conducted by His divine love!

Finally they decided, and after three months' reflection she entered her great retreat, October 27, 1672, to prepare for her holy vows. What pen could portray Margaret's silence, recollection, profound union with the Lord during this blessed time? From the second day, abstraction became such that, in order to moderate a little the intensity of the love that consumed her,[1] the Superioress sent her into the field to mind an ass and its foal which had been purchased for the use of a sick Sister. Orders were given the holy novice to see that the animals did not enter the kitchen-garden by which the field was surrounded, and that the enclosure was protected. Margaret, in consequence, passed the day in running now after the ass, now after the foal, both

[1] Contemp., p. 37, note.

strongly tempted by the garden-herbs. The fervent novice would unquestionably have much preferred being
on her knees at the foot of the holy altar; but she was
where God wished her to be, and what more could she
desire? "If," said she simply, "Saul found the kingdom of Israel when seeking his father's asses, why
should I not obtain the kingdom of heaven while running after these animals?" She did, indeed, find it; for
it was in this place, in the midst of these humble occupations, that, kneeling in a little cluster of hazel-nut
trees which have survived the wreck of time [1] and which
are still pointed out to the pilgrim, that she received
one of the greatest favors of her life. She has, however,
given it to us in terms too brief and, above all, too obscure. "I was so contented in this occupation," she
said, " and my Sovereign kept me such faithful company,
that the running did not disturb me. It was whilst
thus employed that I received favors greater than I had
ever before experienced. It was then that He made
known to me particulars of His holy Passion and death
never before communicated to me. But to write them
would be interminable. Their number makes me sup-
press all. I shall only say that it was this communication that filled me with such love for the cross that I
cannot live one moment without suffering. But this
suffering must be in silence, without relief, consolation,
or compassion. I long to die with the Sovereign of my
soul, overwhelmed by crosses of all kinds, by oppro-
brium, forgetfulness, humiliation, and contempt.[2]

The end of this retreat corresponded to its com-
mencement. Never did greater delights inebriate a
soul. Margaret Mary knew all the sweetness of love,
the most tender, most ardent, most divinely consoling.

[1] This cluster still exists. On the enormous roots that support it are
nourished the strong green branches. Their leaves are distributed to
pilgrims.

[2] Mémoire, p. 322.

All was, however, mingled with the assurance of future crosses that would equal in bitterness the sweetness she had just tasted from the divine caresses.

At last, November 6, 1672, in the present chapel of the convent of Paray, at the grate still in existence, Margaret Mary pronounced her holy vows. The details left us of this ceremony are as meagre as those of her taking the habit. But better than these, we know perfectly the sentiments that filled her heart, and the graces with which she was inundated. The Lord appeared to her and said: "Up to this moment I have been only thy Fiancé. I shall henceforth be thy Spouse." He promised never to leave her, but to treat her as His spouse, which promise He began at once to fulfil "in a manner," she says, "that I feel incapable of expressing, and of which I shall only say that He spoke to me and treated me as a spouse of Tabor."[1] Margaret, touched to the depths of her soul, in a transport of love wrote with her blood a total consecration of herself to the Lord. This act concludes in words that recall the sublime cry of St. Teresa or of St. Catharine of Siena:

> " All in God, and nothing in self!
> All to God, and nothing to self!
> All for God, and nothing for self!"

She subscribed herself: " His unworthy spouse, Sister Margaret Mary, dead to the world."[2]

---

[1] Mémoire, p. 318.

[2] " We must here express a deep regret. That sacred relic of the soul and the blood of Saint Margaret Mary is probably lost forever. It was in the possession of the worthy Mother Baudron, Superioress of the hospital of Paray, at the beginning of the Revolution. She knew well its value, and refused to part with it even for one instant. She consented to lend it only on the entreaty of an aged confessor of the faith, M. l'Abbé Jean Gaudin, curé of Vaudebarrier, arch-priest of Charolles. He asked for it in the same spirit that led St. Hugh when dying to have exposed at his bedside the relics of St. Marcel, pope and martyr. M. Gaudin died in the odor of sanctity, but what has be-

We must recall those words of hers just read above. that we may comprehend the true beauty of the voca- tion given her by God. In the day of her youth the Lord had said to her : " I shall be to thee the most beau- tiful, the richest, most powerful, most perfect of all lov- ers." [1] On the day of her entrance to the novitiate, He added: "This is the day of our betrothal." [2] Now there is only one step more. "Until this time I have been thy Fiancé; from this day I wish to be thy Spouse." This is the whole religious life; for in the cloister as in the world, "It is not good for man to live alone." God, who has made us for an infinite love, has placed in us its hid- den sources. At six years it begins to spring or gush deeply and tenderly. We go out of ourselves to find some soul in sympathy with our own. Noble emotion, given by God and worthy of Him, whence are born family ties with all its joys! But in the multitude of souls devoured by the want of human sympathy, who are they that look above the earth? Human hearts are not deep enough for them, human love not sufficiently strong nor beautiful. They have scarcely seen the world, and yet they despise it. They have not yet tasted the cup of love, and still they put it far from them. Not that they are destitute of sensibility and ten- derness; on the contrary, no heart is so insatiable as theirs; but not for created things they yearn—beaming and radiant they fly to offer their heart to Jesus Christ. Twenty times I have had this sight under my eyes. I have seen girls, young and charming, tearing themselves from the embraces of father and mother, abandoning at twenty the hopes and illusions of life; and it was from the greatness of their emotion at parting, the keen ten- derness of their adieux, that I discovered the beauty of

come of the sacred blood whose presence enabled him to die so well ?" (*Histoire Populaire de la Bienheureuse,* par M. l'Abbé Cucherat, al moner of the hospital of Paray, p. 84.)

[1] Mémoire, p. 305.   [2] Ibid., p. 314.

their heart and the power of the attraction that drew them. Three or four months pass, and behold, they reappear at the choir-grate for the sweet ceremony of the taking of the habit. Look at them! No tears dim their eyes. Arrayed as young brides, ornamented with jewels and diamonds that they accept for one instant for the pleasure of casting them off publicly and trampling them under foot, their brow bespeaks serenity so pious and so divine that I have never seen its like in an earthly union. They know to whom they give themselves! And when, after twelve months of a second and definite trial, they reappear at the *grille* for the last time, to pronounce the irrevocable vows; when their voices are raised in the silence of the holy assembly to say: "*O ye heavens, hear what I say, and let the earth listen to the words of my mouth! It is to Thee, my Jesus, that my heart speaketh!*"—it is not only joy, it is enthusiasm that makes their heart beat, and that betrays in the tremulous tones of their voice the divine passion that consumes them.

But who, then, is this Being, dead on a gibbet more than eighteen hundred years, and who still excites such enthusiasm? Who is this invisible Lover hidden from all eyes, who every day snatches from our side and from our very heart beings the dearest, the purest, the most charming, the most suited to enchant and console our life? Who is He? It is He who said to Margaret at the age of twenty: "I shall be to thee the most tender of lovers;" who said to her on the day of taking the habit: "This is the day of our betrothal;" who at her profession added: "Till now I have been thy Fiancé; henceforth I wish to be thy Spouse." He, in fine, who made such promises is alone able to accomplish them. Whilst human loves perish one by one; whilst flowery wreaths fade on the brow of the young bride; whilst all other love deceives, because, alas! it promises more than it can give, and thus an inevitable melancholy tinges every earthly union,—Jesus Christ, on the contrary, throws around souls consecrated to Him a charm that is incessantly renewed. Young, intrepid, and valiant hearts that have left all for Him, that can no more detach themselves from Him, He unites to Himself by sorrow as well as by joy; and, as He is a crucified Spouse, whether He inebriates with consolations or overwhelms with sufferings, He rejoices them all the same.

CHAPTER VI.

FINAL EXTERIOR PREPARATIONS. LAST FINISHING
STROKE WITHIN.

November 6, 1672—December 27, 1673.

"Ego dormio, et cor meum vigilat."
" I sleep, but my heart watcheth."—*Cant.* v. 2.
" Satiabor cum apparuerit."
" I shall be satisfied when Thy glory shall appear."—*Psalm* xvi. 15

THE year following the profession of Sister Mar_
garet Mary resembled the first days of spring-
time when, after a long and silent preparation,
nature suddenly bursts forth perfumed and blossomed
under the influence of a genial dew. Thus it was in the
soul of our saintly professed. From the day of her solemn vows, so rapid was her increase in virtue that the
whole community was astonished and touched. The
rapidity of this progress was understood later, for only
some months then separated us from the grand revelations of the Sacred Heart. But before that moment it was
easy for observant minds to see with what delicacy God
was preparing all things, that when He should speak
His voice might be heard. The day after the Ascension,
1672, four or five months before Margaret Mary's profession, the venerable Mother Hersant, having completed
her six years of government, was recalled to Paris. She
had not definitively decided Margaret's vocation, though
she had given her the habit and declared that she would
some day attain extraordinary sanctity. She was replaced by Mother Marie-Françoise de Saumaise, whom
God had chosen to be the first confidant of His intimate

communications to our saint. Born at Dijon, in 1620, she was at this time fifty-two years old. Descended from an old parliamentary family, she had inherited their distinguished manners and solid judgment. The latter was remarked even in her early childhood by the venerable Mother de Chantal, who predicted that she would some day be one of the best Superioresses of the Order. Though never having exercised that charge, she arrived at Paray marvellously well prepared to fulfil it. She was possessed of good judgment and great decision of character. With a just mind, firm and clear, she was full of ardor, tempered, however, by exceeding kindness and the rarest modesty. To these qualities she added a perfect knowledge of the Visitandine Rules, and one not less profound of God's workings in souls. To acquire the first science she had been in a grand school, that of the venerable Mother Brulard, Superioress of Dijon. She belonged to the old parliamentary family of Brulards, in which honor and justice, talent and business qualifications were hereditary with virtue.[1] And, as to the second science, she had acquired it at a still higher school, one altogether incomparable—that of Mother Anne-Séraphine Boulier, Superioress of Dijon, who has left on prayer and the love of God pages truly sublime, which disavow not her claims to being countrywoman of Bossuet.[2] Thus prepared by that tender and delicate hand which does

---

[1] Annales du Monastère de la Visitation de Dijon, published by M. l'abbé Colet, Vicar-General of Dijon (present Bishop of Luçon), Dijon, 1854, chap. xvii. and following. Mother Brulard's grandmother was that Mme. Brulard, wife of the first President of the Parliament of Bourgogne, who was the intimate friend of Mme. de Chantal, and one of the dearest spiritual daughters of St. Francis de Sales.

[2] Vie de la Vénérable Mère Anne-Séraphine Boulier, died Superioress of the Visitation of Dijon, Sept. 1, 1683. Mgr. Colet has given this Life in the continuation of the *Annales*, p. 271. He has also given those pages of profound mysticism known under the name of " Avis de la Vénérable Mère Anne-Séraphine Boulier," Annales, p. 393.

all with sweetness and strength, Mother de Saumaise
had hardly crossed the threshold of the convent of
Paray when her eyes were fixed on this humble and fervent novice, then in the eighteenth month of her novitiate, and whose extraordinary ways made her the subject of so much inquietude. Mother de Saumaise was
not slow to recognize in Margaret Mary the characteristics of the Spirit of God, and it was she who decided
her admission to the holy profession of vows. She first
took a precaution which most significantly reveals her
prudence and faith. Margaret, distressed at the hesita-
tion of the community, breathed out her sorrow at the
feet of her Divine Master, and said to Him: " Ah, Lord,
Thou wilt, then, be the cause of my being sent away!"
The Lord reassured her, and charged her to say to her
Superioress not to fear. Mother de Saumaise, animated
with holy confidence, replied: "Very well; ask the Lord
as an evidence of His promise to render you useful to
the community by the practice of all our Rules. The
Lord answered that she would be useful to the community in a way they should see later on. And laying down
Himself the great law that preserves from all illusion,
He promised to adjust His favors to the spirit of the
Rules and the judgment of Superiors, to whom He
wished her to be submissive in all things.[1] We are now
to see Mother Saumaise directing our saint in the midst
of her perplexities and trials; recognizing the truth of
her revelations; and later, when she shall have left
Paray, propagating everywhere devotion to the Sacred
Heart, of which she was the first confidant, the first to
acknowledge its divine origin.

But great and providential as it was to be raised into
regions so high by the support sent her by God in
Mother de Saumaise, this support could not suffice. It
is not to virgins even the purest, the most enlightened,
that God has given the gift of discerning His ways and

[1] Mémoire, p. 317.

supernatural missions in His Church. This gift belongs
to those to whom Jesus Christ has said: " Go teach all
nations." [1] Priests teach under the direction of bishops;
bishops, subject to that of the Pope; and the Pope
teaches under the infallible guidance of the Spirit of
God. Explain the Scriptures, scrutinize public prophecies and private revelations, and let all baptized souls
render you, in the limits of the holy hierarchy, the
obedience due to Jesus Christ. Such is the divine constitution of the Church. Consequently, after having
placed near the humble Margaret a virgin enlightened
by God, to console, sustain, and guide, to serve her as
a mother and confidant, it was further necessary to ap-
point a priest, to say to her at the destined hour the
word that calms doubts and unerringly points out the
way.

Such a priest God chose from the Society of Jesus.
He desired by this to recompense that valiant Society
for services rendered the Church in the midst of the
great conflict of the sixteenth century, when it had by
its illustrious founder, his first and heroic disciples, and
its grand theologians, so powerfully contributed to the
arrest of heresy and the vindication of the faith. Perhaps by this most delicate attention God willed to
thank the Society for the position it assumed in the
seventeenth century in the terrible struggle begun by
incipient Jansenism against the Church. Without weak-
ening the respect due to the infinite majesty of God,
the Jesuits ceased not to exalt His goodness, His tenderness for sinners, His infinite love. Even if it were
true, in view of that haughty rigorism which cast souls
into despair, that some of the members of this illustrious
Society, by one of those reactions that cannot be con-
trolled, should have leaned a little too much toward the
opposite side and rendered the road to heaven a little
too easy, it must at least be admitted that they did 't

[1] St. Matt. xxviii. 19.

not to their own profit. Whilst preaching moral sweetness, they rigorously preserved among themselves moral severity; and neither the proximity of courts, the favor of the great, nor the wealth flowing in upon them from the gratitude of the people, was ever able to tarnish the purity of morals or the amiable austerity and generous fervor of the Society. Let us add that as the price of so many services, to recompense them for having reared the youth of all Europe, for having civilized Paraguay, evangelized Japan, shed their blood on thousands of inhospitable regions, enriched civilization by a multitude of curious discoveries, and, what is much better, embalmed the world with the perfume of every virtue, the Society of Jesus was to be persecuted and disgraced, its most venerable members cast into prison or sent into exile. It was only just, therefore, that God should give it under circumstances so critical not only support and consolation, but above all, a public sign of His love. For reasons such as these, the priest charged to recognize and proclaim to the world the truth of the revelations of the Sacred Heart was taken from the Society of Jesus.

He was called Claude de la Colombière, and even then his name was not without glory. His appearance in the pulpit was remarkable. One felt on beholding him that, though fitted to shine in the world, he was one of those refined natures, a being innocent and pure, whom nothing human or vulgar could ever captivate. His distinguished manners, his charming conversation, his mind lively and polished by nature, his address and grace under every circumstance, added to the correctness of his judgment, were surpassed only by his austerity and virtue. Born in 1641, he was at this time thirty-two years old ; and, though still so young, had just been called by his Superiors to pronounce his last vows. To those demanded of religious by the Church he added a fourth sufficient to frighten the most fervent.

We have the twenty-two articles written by his own hand ; and we know not if there ever was any one who vowed to attain perfection so eminent.[1] At the close of his great retreat, he was appointed Superior, with residence at Paray. He arrived there at the time in which the third of the three grand revelations of the Sacred Heart took place, that which was to be the last in the cycle of those solemn entertainments.

Whilst God was thus preparing the support of which Margaret was soon to have need, He was also putting the finishing stroke to her own soul. Her novitiate was passed in joy and consolation so great that, in her inability to sustain them, she cried out: "O my God, diminish Thy favors or increase my power to receive them !" Delights continuing to inundate her soul after her profession, she began to be astonished and disquieted. She had espoused a crucified God, annihilated, humiliated, buffeted, and she wished none other. She complained to the Lord, saying : "Ah ! my God, Thou wilt never, then, permit me to suffer !" Then was witnessed the beginning of a singular contest between her and her Spouse. He desired to overwhelm her with loving caresses and consolations. She desired only sorrow, contempt, and humiliation, and that so ardently that the Lord is forced to yield. He withdrew, but slowly, little by little, like a conquered general skilfully retreating. Once, when He loaded her with the delights of Tabor, which, on account of the want of conformity to her wounded and crucified spouse on Calvary, were more painful to her than death, He said to her interiorly: "Let Me do it ! Everything in its own time. Now,

[1] Sermons of P. Claude de la Colombière, third edition, 1689. This preface, slightly oratorical, and containing few precise details, is, however, all that we have of Father de la Colombière. How much it is to be regretted that nearly two hundred years have rolled around without the written Life of this great servant of God!

My love wishes to amuse itself with thee as it pleases. But thou wilt lose nothing by it." [1]

On another occasion, urged by Her importunity, He said to her : " Have a little patience ; later I shall make thee experience what thou must suffer for My love." [2]

O adorable goodness of the Lord ! He could not resolve to begin the crucifixion of His spouse. One day she conjured Him never to make anything known about her, unless to humble her before creatures and destroy their esteem for her. ' For alas ! my God," she said, " I feel my weakness, and I fear to betray Thee." " Fear nothing," was the reply. " I shall be thy Protector." " What ! Lord, wilt Thou, then, always let me live without suffering ?" she cried. Then Jesus showed her a cross covered with flowers. " Behold !" He said, " the bed of my chaste spouses on which I shall make thee consummate the delights of My love. One by one these flowers will fade, and naught will remain but the thorns they now hide from thy weakness. But thou wilt feel their points so keenly that all the strength of My love will be needed by thee to enable thee to accomplish thy martyrdom." [3]

One involuntarily pauses before this vivid and startling picture of life. A bed of thorns covered for a few moments with flowers. The flowers fade, the dream vanishes, the illusion disappears, and nothing remains but points so sharp, so piercing, so penetrating, that God alone can nerve to the endurance of their pain But whilst we weep and groan, Margaret Mary trembled with joy. Jesus' words rejoiced her, for she had feared never to have sufferings enough to satisfy the burning thirst for them that gave her no rest by night or by day. [4]

The Lord generously multiplied His promises, and assured her that the hour was not far distant in which

[1] Contemp., p. 39.   [2] Ib., p. 44.
[3] Mémoire, p. 322.   [4] Contemp., p. 45.

He would satiate her with suffering and humiliation. Nothing could satisfy the desire that tormented her. " It seemed to me," she wrote, " that I should never be at rest until I found myself unknown to all, and abyssed in humiliations and suffering ; until I should be lost in eternal oblivion, in which, if remembered at all, it would only be to be the more deeply despised. If, in truth, my Sisters knew the desire I have of being humbled and despised, I doubt not that charity would induce them to gratify me on this point." [1]

" I experience," she again said, " so strong a desire to suffer that I cannot find any sweeter rest than to feel myself inundated with pain, my mind the prey to all kinds of dereliction, and my whole being drowned in humiliations, contempt, and contradictions." [2] " Suffering alone can render life endurable to me," this is the cry that will henceforth be heard in all her letters. Its form of expression may, indeed, vary ; but in substance it will ever be the same.

Her actions corresponded to her words. The plainest and coarsest food that could be found in the convent appeared to her too delicate for a sinner like herself ; so she seasoned it with ashes to render it more unpalatable. She deprived herself of every kind of beverage ; and at one time she took the resolution not to drink anything from Thursday until Saturday of every week. Reproved by her Superiors, and obliged by them to slake her thirst, she resorted to a thousand inventions to do so only with water tepid and unpleasant to the taste. At night she put planks in her bed, and even strewed it with fragments of broken potsherds. " Had she been permitted," wrote her Superioress, Mother de Saumaise, " she would have martyrized her body with vigils, disciplines, and other mortifications, although

[1] Languet, Vie de la Vénérable Sœur, p. 115.
[2] Mémoire, p. 336.

during six whole years I saw her in the enjoyment of health for only five months."[1]

What shall we add? That with which the dainty of the century have reproached the illustrious author of the "Life of St. Elizabeth," that with which they have reproached us in the "History of St. Chantal," it must be permitted us to relate here. And yet we warn fastidious souls that we have suppressed the half. Margaret Mary's sole happiness was to kiss the wounds of the sick, and press her lips to the most disgusting ulcers. Once, in particular, when nursing a Sister dying with cancer of the stomach, and who could not retain anything upon it, she wished to clear away her vomit. She did it with her lips and tongue, saying to Jesus Christ: "If I had a thousand bodies, a thousand loves, and a thousand lives, I should wish to sacrifice them all, in order to be Thy slave." "And," she added, "I found so much delight in this action that I longed for daily occasions to teach me to overcome myself in the same manner, and to have God alone for witness."[2]

Every day exhibited similar scenes, similar desires after humiliation and contempt, a thousand little stratagems to procure herself suffering, and extraordinary aspirations after the most frightful self-immolation. There were, according to her own expression, three tyrants inclosed within her heart, which gave her neither rest nor truce, which were never satisfied, and which incessantly urged her on to fresh exertions. The first was love of contempt; the second, love of suffering; the third, the sweetest, the most powerful, the most insatiable, the least easily satisfied, was the love of Jesus Christ. "Jesus Christ! Jesus Christ!" she cried in tones that expressed more than a lengthy sermon. "The longer I live, the more clearly I see that a life without the love of Jesus Christ is the misery of mis-

[1] Languet, Vie de la Vénérable Sœur, p. 108.
[2] Mémoire, p. 337.

eries. If to go to Jesus Christ I had to walk barefoot on a pathway of flames, it would seem to me nothing. After having received Jesus Christ, I remain as it were annihilated, but filled with joy so entrancing that sometimes for seven minutes my whole interior is hushed in profound silence, listening to the voice of Him whom I love." [1]

"I know not whether I deceive myself," she again wrote, "for one grows not weary of hearing the accents of this Divine Voice, so strong, so heroic, so elevated above our weakness and human impotence. It seems to me that my pleasure would be to love my amiable Saviour with a love as ardent as that of the seraphim. But I should not be grieved even were it in hell that I loved Him. The thought that there could be a place in the universe in which, for all eternity, an infinite number of souls, redeemed with the Precious Blood of Jesus Christ, would never love this amiable Redeemer, afflicts me deeply. I would wish, my Divine Saviour, if it were Thy will, to suffer all the torments of hell, provided I could love Thee as much as all souls, doomed ever to suffer and never to love, would have been able to love Thee in heaven." [2]

The more one advances, the more this love of God consumes. Margaret's frail and delicate constitution could not resist such emotions. Thin and pale, the glowing ardor of her mind was visible through her transparent skin; she realized more perfectly the threnody of her novitiate:

> "A chased and panting fawn,
> I seek the flowing stream.
> The hunter's flying dart
> Has pierced my inmost heart."

Such was Margaret Mary in her twenty-fifth year, and such are all the saints. For us, for the greater part

[1] Contemp., p. 46.
[2] Languet, Vie de la Vénérable Sœur, p. 95.

of men, God is known and saluted from afar and but
with difficulty. To some of us He is a friend; for
very few, an intimate friend. But there are others for
whom He is more than a friend, more than a father,
more than a spouse. Their love for Him amounts to
passion, yea, even to folly. This is a mystery the world
does not understand; it laughs and scoffs : but what
matters it ?

Astonishing as it may be at all times to the witnesses
of this stupendous life to see that ever-increasing desire
after sufferings, that hungering after humiliations and
contempt, that thirsting after the love of God,—there is
something that will still more amaze ; namely, that
state of entire absorption in God to which we have already alluded, and which will now strike the beholder
with astonishment and admiration. In recreation, in
the refectory, in the choir, Margaret's companions
were constantly obliged to rouse her. She no longer
lived on earth. Were she needed for anything, they
never thought of seeking her in her cell. They ran to
the chapel, for she now never left it.[1] There she passed
entire hours, kneeling motionless, her hands joined, her
eyes closed. She saw nothing, heard nothing ; she did
not even feel the Sisters tapping her on the shoulder.
But at the sound of the word "obedience," she arose
quickly, and did whatever they requested.

Let us listen to the witnesses of these extraordinary
scenes, and for an instant gaze upon the greatest contemplative that has appeared in the Church since St.
Teresa:

" I attest," said Sister Marguerite d'Athose, " to having seen the venerable deceased pass *almost the entire day,*
particularly Sundays and feasts, before the Blessed
Sacrament, *on her knees, immovable,* in recollection so
profound that the whole community was surprised that

---

[1] Process of 1715, Deposition of Sister Rosselin.

she could remain so long in the same position, though her constitution was not the strongest." [1]

"Having lived long years with the venerable Sister, I affirm," says Sister Claude-Rosalie de Farges, "that she was always the first at morning prayer. So rapt was her attention before the Blessed Sacrament that on feasts she never stirred almost the whole day, but remained before it in an attitude of respect and abasement that inspired the beholder with devotion." The deponent affirmed, also, that she had seen her *from seven o'clock, Holy Thursday evening, till four o'clock the next morning* on her knees, *immovable,* her hands joined on her breast; and that the Sisters who succeeded her (the deponent) beheld her in the same position until the Office. This gave cause to the deponent to say to Margaret: "My dear Sister, how can you remain kneeling so long?" To which Margaret answered: "At such times I do not even know that I have a body." [2]

Another deposition is still more explicit and curious, that of Sister Elizabeth de la Garde, Superioress of the convent of Paray. She entered the convent almost at the same time as the venerable Sister, and had been her companion of the novitiate. "I certify," she said, "that the venerable Sister was always most faithful to pass all her free time before the Blessed Sacrament, her hands joined in profound adoration. No movement on her part ever betrayed a wandering of mind. On feast-days, *from the time she rose until dinner,* and *from the end of the recreation till Vespers,* there she was in prayer. But on Holy Thursday, for several consecutive years, she passed from *seven in the evening until the next morning* kneeling in the same place, neither coughing nor moving." This led the deponent to notice Margaret Mary whilst she herself was in the choir, and commission

[1] Process of 1715, Deposition of Sister Marguerite d'Athose, p. 67.
[2] Process of 1715, p. 69.

others to do the same when she went to rest, that she might know whether Margaret preserved the same atti-tude. The Sisters thus commissioned assured Mother Elizabeth that Sister Margaret Mary knelt in the same posture all night.[1]

What was then done by Mother de la Garde's orders was ever after continued during Margaret Mary's life. "One Holy Thursday night," says one of the witnesses, "we went from time to time to look at Margaret Mary through a half-open door of the choir. There she was kneeling, immovable, her hands joined on her breast, her countenance radiant. *This lasted twelve hours without the slightest motion on her part.*"[2] "I have often watched her," says Sister Marie Rosalie de Lyonne, "and I once saw her myself kneeling *from seven o'clock in the evening till midnight,* and others observed the same *from midnight until the next morning at seven o'clock.* During all this time Margaret remained immovable on her knees, her hands joined." "Next day," continues the deponent, "having asked her how she could remain so long in the same posture, and of what she was thinking all that time, she replied : 'I am then so occupied with the Lord's Passion that I do not know that I have a body. I feel nothing.'"[3]

It was not only the Sisters succeeding one another in adoration before the Blessed Sacrament who watched her through the half-open choir door, but the little boarders asked leave to rise during the night that they too might see "their saintly mistress praying to God so fervently."[4] The Faithful, also, on days of Exposi-tion flocked to peer through the choir grate and to point her out with the finger, saying: "See the saint!" But their notice had not the power to distract her.[5]

The Sisters of the Community carried their pious cu-

---

[1] Process, p. 72.   [2] Ib., p. 64.
[3] Ib., p. 66.   [4] Ib., p. 81.
[5] Ib., p. 102.

riosity still further. They approached her, they spoke to her, they tapped her on the shoulder, but without obtaining a word of reply. "I attest," said Sister Jeanne-Françoise Chalon, "that I several times saw the servant of God in His holy presence before the Most Blessed Sacrament of the Altar. I spoke to her without being able to draw a word of response from her. She was immovable as a marble statue, she was wholly rapt in God."[1] "I have heard my brother, the chaplain and confessor of the convent, say," deposed M. Claude Michou, an advocate of the parliament, "that when on her knees before the altar, Saint Margaret Mary appeared *ecstatic.*"[2]

This word *ecstasy* will perhaps cause some to smile. But allow me to ask: Is there any love without contemplation, any ardent passion without ecstasy? What is the life of a mother during the first months of her child's life? Is it other than a rapturous transport before the crib? And what takes place around a death-bed on which still rest the remains of a cherished being? The living regard the dead, they contemplate the remains, they forget themselves. Are they seated or on their knees during this contemplation? How long has it lasted? Who can say? The more they love, the less they know.

This is what Saint Margaret Mary did during those long nights. Twelve consecutive hours on her knees, her hands joined on her breast, her eyes closed, without coughing or moving, like a marble statue, like an ecstatica! She loved, and in loving she forgot herself!

Only one thing could recall her to earth, and that was the word *obedience.* At that word she became conscious, bowed sweetly to the altar, and rose to go whither obedience called. "I affirm," says Sister Françoise-Rosalie Verchère, "that I have seen her for entire hours in prayer, and so rapt that I have

---

[1] Process of 1715, p. 106.   [2] Ib., p. 87.

approached without being able to distract her. But at
the least sign of obedience she left all to respond to it.'
Said witness confessed to having told her once as if
coming from the Superioress, though in fact it was of
witness' own suggesting and merely to see whether
Margaret Mary would leave her prayer or not, to go
warm herself. On the instant she set off to obey.[1] "I
remember," says Mother Elizabeth de la Garde, "that
once, wishing to make a trial of the obedience of the
servant of God, I sent a Sister to whisper in her ear:
'Sister, Mother says go and warm yourself.' It was
Holy Thursday night, and very cold, and she had asked
permission to remain. But immediately Margaret Mary
made her genuflection, withdrew, and went to the fire
for a quarter of an hour. On coming back, she resumed
her place in the choir till Prime of the next day, just
seven hours."[2]

Extraordinary as was Margaret Mary's immobility
during twelve consecutive hours notwithstanding the
cold of the night, it was not the most astonishing feature in her wonderful life. At times, whilst thus kneeling in the choir, she suddenly fainted, and had to be
borne out trembling and radiant, her countenance on
fire, her eyes suffused with tears. To the questions put to
her she could answer nothing, nor was she able to support herself. Once they found her thus extended in the
choir, torrents of tears flowing softly and uninterrupt-
edly from her eyes.[3] On another occasion she said:
"I neither felt nor knew where I was. When they came
to take me away, seeing that I could not answer nor
support myself without great difficulty, they led me
to our Mother. I was quite out of myself; I trembled
and seemed to be consumed by fever. They thought I
would die."[4]

It was repeated scenes like this that astonished and

---

[1] Process of 1715, p. 52.   [2] Ib., p. 72.
[3] Mémoire, p. 327.   [4] Ib.. p 328

alarmed the Sisters, inspired some with tender pity and respect, others with admiration and enthusiasm, and caused all to say: "What can it be? What passes between God and this soul during those long hours? Is it an illusion? or is it God acting in her? If so, for what end?"

We now know the answer to all these questions. Obedience unsealed the lips of the humble virgin, and the Church has authenticated her words. Guided by this authority, let us penetrate without fear of deception into the secret of her raptures, and contemplate their beauty.

But first we must collect them. We must do like the pilgrim on approaching Jerusalem. He hears his guide suddenly cry out: " El Cods! La Sainte!" Deeply moved, he pauses, kneels, and adores before presuming to rest his eyes on that city in which appeared the Word made flesh, on that hill upon which expired Infinite Love!

CHAPTER VII.

THE AURORA OF THE DEVOTION TO THE SACRED HEART.

"Quasi aurora consurgens."
" As the morning rising."—*Cant.* vi. 9.
" Omnia in mensura, et numero, et pondere disposuisti."
'' Lord, Thou hast ordered all things in measure, and number, and weight."—*Wisdom* xi. 21.

GOD had taken three-and-twenty years to prepare the heart of **Saint** Margaret Mary for the prodigious marvel whose secret He was about to confide to her; but He was going to employ still more time in preparing the world to understand that wonder and to accept it. All beautiful things here below have an aurora that precedes and announces them, that turns toward them all eyes and hearts. The devotion whose history we are going to relate had its rosy dawn, and the time has come to portray it.

Can we imagine the Church existing seventeen hundred years without a thought of the Adorable Heart of her Divine Spouse? Can we fancy her innumerable virgins, so inflamed with love for Jesus, never craving the happiness of St. John, the happiness of reposing on the breast of the Divine Master? Did none of her Doctors ever contemplate that pierced side whence flowed he wonderful mixture of blood and water? If it be true that our forefathers believed as we that the heart is the seat of love; if all nations have guarded with respect and carried in triumph the hearts of their deceased heroes, how admit that those far-off Christian ages, so filled with enthusiasm for the person of the Saviour, cast no glance, breathed no prayer toward His Sacred Heart, the most beautiful, most noble, most tender, the purest and greatest of all hearts?

Far up through past centuries, off in the catacombs of Rome or Lyons, in those remote ages whose writings are rare, whose chiselled marble and frescoed walls form the annals of their Christian generations, we behold the devout gaze fixed upon the pierced side of the Saviour, on the stream of love flowing from it, and the Heart that forms its source. When, at Lyons, the young deacon Sanctus appeared before his executioners and astonished them by the firmness of his heroic courage, the historian of his martyrdom asked how he could endure fire and sword and other most atrocious torments. Sanctus had but one answer: "It was," said he, "because the holy deacon was sprinkled and strengthened by the source of living water gushing from the Heart of Christ."[1] There was recently discovered in the cemetery of the *Via Strata*, at Autun, a Greek inscription placed in the second century on the tomb of a Christian. With the confession of the Divinity of Christ, with the names of Saviour, Jesus, Redeemer, we find in it special mention of the Adorable Heart, toward which, even as early as the second century, souls turned for the gifts of faith and hope and love.[2] From those far-off ages, of which we have so few memorials, we pass to those of the Doctors, the brightening aurora of the Church, and find Tertullian contemplating the pierced side of the Saviour and reading therein the title of our vocation and election to salvation.[3] It was St. Cyprian who passed before the singular mixture of blood and

---

[1] Eusèbe, Lettre des Martyrs de Lyon.

[2] Card. Pitra, Spicil. Solesm., tom. i. p. 554.

[3] Tertull. De Baptismo, cap. xvi., et De Anima, c. xliii. "Somnus Adæ mors erat Christi dormituri in mortem, ut de injuria perinde lateris ejus, vera mater viventium figuraretur Ecclesia."

water flowing from the wounded breast of the Christ, and from it saw the Church springing forth in radiant beauty.[1] It was St. Ambrose who immortalized this divine wound through which the Saviour's graces have flowed upon and embalmed the world, like those odoriferous plants that emit their perfume only when wounded.[2] It was, above all, St. Augustine who, by the tenderness and heavenly elevation of his soul, was so capable of understanding the mysteries of the Heart of Jesus. "Oh!" he cried, "of what a perfect word the Evangelist made use when he said: '*One of the soldiers opened His side with his lance.*' He does not say, '*His side was struck;*' he says, '*His side was opened;*' that is to say, the door of life was opened to allow the sacraments and all other graces to flow upon the world."[3] Under a thousand forms the saint develops the sublime doctrine that from the wounded side of Jesus Christ the Church was born and the sacraments came forth. From it beams light upon souls, and from it issues love. The Heart of Jesus, he tells us, ought to be the special asylum, the refuge of all in need of consolation, strength, or pardon. "Consider, O man," he says, speaking in the person of the Lord, "how much I have suffered for you. My head was crowned with thorns, My feet and hands pierced, My blood shed. I have opened My side to you and given you to drink the precious blood that flows from it! What more can you desire?" "Approach, then," continues the holy Doctor, "this fountain of living water, of which He will give us the water of salvation without money and without price. He invites us to come and draw: 'If any man thirsts let him come to Me.'[4]

---

[1] Cyprian, De mont. Sinæ et Sion. "Percussus de lancea, sanguis ex aqua mixtus profluebat, unde sibi Ecclesiam sanctam fabricavit in qua legem passionis suæ consecrabat, dicente ipso: *Qui sitit, veniat et bibat.*"

[2] Ambros. Serm. III. in Psalm xxviii. et cxviii.

[3] Aug. Tract. cxx. in Joan.

[4] St. John, vii. 37.

Behold the purest of fountains gushing up in the midst
of paradise and watering the whole earth." [1]   In these
words of St. Augustine, we hear St. John Chrysostom,
St. Basil, St. Gregory of Nazianzen, St. Ephrem, St.
Cyril, and other Fathers of the fourth century. [2]

Deeply impressed with this doctrine, artists of the first
centuries impressively depicted it to the eye, when they
represented Jesus on the cross.   His side presents a
gaping wound, from which gushes an impetuous torrent of blood ; and at the foot of the cross stands the
Church collecting the precious blood in a chalice. [3]
Sometimes, to give the Blessed Virgin the first place
near the dying Saviour, they depict the Church in a
kneeling or half-sitting posture, and holding the chalice
in the direction of the open side.   Most frequently,
however, she is standing nimbus-crowned, her standard
in her hand.   Farther back in the picture are seen the
Blessed Virgin and St. John standing and in tears,
though the Church weeps not.   In her eagerness to
catch the precious stream, whence she draws her existence, she holds up her chalice as high as possible so as
not to lose one drop. [4]   No description can convey to
him who has not studied these old paintings the enthu--
siasm with which the Church contemplates the wound
of the Heart from which she came forth as Eve from
the open side of Adam. [5]   Thus it was that for centuries

[1] Aug. De Symbolo ad catechum., vi., in Psalm l.

[2] If some scholar well versed in Greek and in Latin patristic lore
would make a collection from age to age of all that the Fathers have
said upon the Sacred Heart, he would be of eminent use to the Church
in our day.

[3] See, in particular (Melanges d'archéologie, par le P. Chas. Cahier),
an ivory crucifix sculptured after the model belonging to M. Carraud.
The blood flows in a stream upon a large cloth.

[4] See, among others, the crucifix of Cividale del Frinli (Gori, The-
saur. Diptych., tom. iii. p. 321.

[5] Crucifix of Bamberg (Biblioth. of Munich).   It belonged to the
Emperor St. Henry   Nothing is more admirable than the ardor with

the first and fondest regards of all Christians were fixed on the wounded side of their Saviour.

But let us leave these far-off times and enter the epoch of the great Doctors of the Middle Ages. What progress! They contemplate not only the pierced side, for, passing through it, they catch a glimpse of the Heart of burning love, and to it offer their adoration. " Thy Heart has been wounded," exclaims St. Bernard, " that the visible wound may reveal to us the invisible one of love. For who would allow his heart to be wounded if love had not already attracted it? But also who would not seek, who would not love, a heart thus wounded?"[1]

Elsewhere he explains this text: " My dove in the clefts of the rock, in the hollow places of the wall;" and shows that the clefts of the rock are the wounds of Jesus Christ, above all that of the side through which may be seen His Heart. " Oh!" he cries out, " how good and how sweet to dwell in this Heart! Precious treasure, rare pearl that Thy Heart, O good Jesus, found in ploughing up the field of Thy body! Who could reject this pearl beyond price? Ah, I should rather give all to purchase it! And there, in this temple, in this Holy of holies, in that sacred ark, I shall live, I shall praise, I shall adore! O Jesus! draw me into Thy Sacred Heart; and that I may dwell there, wash me from my iniquities, purify me from every stain. O most beautiful of the children of men, Thy Sacred Heart has been opened only that we may be able to dwell in it in safety and in peace."[2]

These and similar words constantly escaped the lips of St. Bernard. He filled the solitude of Citeaux and Clairvaux with them. It suffices to open the works of St. William, of St. Guerric and his principal disciples, to

which the Church rose up to catch the divine blood, which not only flowed but poured out in streams.

[1] St. Bernard, Tract. de Passione, cap. iii.

[2] Ib.

be convinced of this. But he did not proclaim it in public. Did he find the world still too barbarous, too gross, to grasp this doctrine so delicate, so high? Or rather, had the hour not yet come for that star to rise on the world? This is more probable. The period of which we speak was but the dawn of devotion to the Sacred Heart, whose sweet, strong light was to penetrate only some few chosen souls.

We must not omit from the rank of those chosen ones a man whom the imagination cannot contemplate without being inflamed with devotion to the Heart of Jesus. Look at that pale, emaciated, ecstatic figure on the rocks of Mt. Alvernia. On his forehead we read meekness, humility, tenderness, and peace. In his eyes burn a pure and brilliant flame which reveals his ardent love of God. The wounds of the Saviour's feet and hands are reproduced on his flesh, and he bears in his side the impress of the stroke of the lance that opened the side of Jesus! Oh, who can depict his emotion when, on the summit of Alvernia, from the heart of the serapu that appeared to him darted those rays of fire and love to pierce his own heart! Francis has written nothing. We have no word of his revealing the extent of his devotion to the Heart of Jesus. But all around him, among his most cherished disciples, there is a trace of light more brilliant than that which surrounded St. Bernard. We shall quote St. Bonaventure. What light and what tenderness! "Oh!" he cries out, "had I been the lance that pierced the Heart of Jesus, thinkest thou that once having entered I should ever, ever have come forth? No! no! I should have remained therein. I should never have been able, I should never have desired, to leave that abode. I should have said: ' This is my rest forever and ever. Here will I dwell, for I have chosen it.'"

And, again: "O my soul! thy most sweet Saviour desires to take thee for spouse, to tell thee the secrets of

His Heart; and delayest thou to flee to Him ? In the excess of His love He longed for the lance that opened His side, that He might prove to thee that He had given thee His Heart. Oh, didst thou know how sweet this Heart is ! Enter therein, and when thou shalt be in that most sweet Heart of Jesus, do thou close after thee the doors of His wounds, so that it may be impossible for thee ever to go forth. Thy heart will then be so inflamed with love that it will seem to thee that thou wouldst gladly escape from thy body to dwell in the wounds of Jesus Christ." " O most holy, most amiable, most sweet wounds of Jesus Christ ! One day I entered therein, I penetrated even to the most secret recesses of love. There inclosed on all sides, I knew not how to retrace my steps. Behold why I remain therein and rest forever. There I am all ardor, all love. There I enjoy without stint abundance of all riches ! O man, take my word ! If thou dost try to enter the Heart of the most sweet Saviour by the opening of His wounds, not only thy soul but thy body shall taste a sweetness most admirable." [1] What more could one wish ? The seraphic soul of Margaret Mary holds for us, concerning the honor of the Heart of Jesus, neither accents more tender nor teachings more explicit.

With whatever discretion these holy Doctors environed themselves, and although, in general, they confined their teaching to the cloister, it was difficult for them to prevent some sparks from bursting forth. We begin, besides, at this epoch to see even those bound to the world cultivating the habit of retiring from it and themselves, and making their dwelling in the pierced side of their Lord. Blessed Elzear, Comte d'Arian, in Provence, having, says St. Francis de Sales, been long absent from his devout and chaste Delphina, she sent a messenger to him to inquire expressly for his health. Behold the reply she received: " I am very well, my dear

[1] Bonav. Stimulus amoris, pars I. cap. i. et vii.

wife; but if you wish to see me, seek me in the wound of the side of our sweet Jesus: for it is there that I dwell, and there you will find me. Elsewhere you will seek me in vain." This was a Christian chevalier indeed.[1] Whilst this sweet aurora darted its beams on the silent solitudes of Clairvaux and Citeaux, on the fervent monasteries of St. Francis of Assisi, and on some chosen souls in the midst of the world, it beamed brightly, also, in the erudite schools of St. Dominic. Listen to St. Thomas, the Angel of the Schools, who, seeking for marks of predestination, found them in the assiduous contemplation of the pierced Heart of Jesus.[2] Hear Blessed Henry Suso, called the Ecstatic Doctor on account of the sublimity of his contemplation: " O Jesus! remember the cruel lance that wounded Thy side and pierced Thy Heart! That Heart, wounded and opened for us, is become to us, O Jesus, a fountain of living water!" [3] Listen to John Tauler, surnamed the Sublime Theologian, who, meditating on the Passion of the Saviour and contemplating the wound of His Heart, exclaims: "What more could He do? He has opened His own Heart for us to enter. He has given us this Sacred Heart cruelly wounded as our dwelling-place, so that, being purified therein and having acquired perfect conformity with it, we may be worthy of being received with Him in heaven." [4] In fine, all the theologians of the Order of St. Dominic. even to Blessed Louis of Grenada, "the Bossuet of Spain," as he was called, who opened an admirable chapter of his Memorial with this cry: "I adore Thee, O most sweet, most amiable, most merciful Heart, wounded for love of me." [5]

[1] Introduction to the Devout Life, part II. chap. xii.
[2] S. Thom. in cap. xix. Joan.
[3] Life of Blessed Henry Suso, ch. vii. See at the end of his life his " Contemplations on the Passion of Jesus Christ."
[4] Tauler, Exercises on the Life and Passion of Jesus Christ, ch. ix. Jesus Pierced with a Lance.
[5] Louis of Grenada, Memorial, ch. vi.

Thus did the aurora brighten with succeeding centuries. It was not only the pierced side that was contemplated, it was the Heart, and in the Heart was adored the immense love of a God for man; nevertheless, neither St. Francis of Assisi, nor St. Dominic, nor St. Bonaventure, nor Henry Suso, nor Tauler thought of spreading throughout the world devotion to the Sacred Heart. They delighted their own soul with it, they embalmed their cloisters with it; and, although millions of Christians crowded on their track as they traversed the country preaching peace, reconciling cities, appeasing passions, causing faith, humility, and the love of God to flourish everywhere, never one word from their lips called the people to honor that adorable Heart, the Source of purity and devotedness, of love and peace. The aurora, undoubtedly, increased; but the hour destined by God for the star to rise was not yet come.

This progress and, at the same time, this prudence are read in the beautiful works of the painters and sculptors of that epoch. Contemporaries of St. Bernard, St. Dominic, St. Francis of Assisi, and St. Bonaventure, and the greater part of the disciples of these saints, not one of them ever dreamed of representing the Heart of Jesus or the rays proceeding from the Saviour's breast, though some significant facts made known the new direction of their piety. The first was a subject treated by them with singular complacency; namely, the ecstatic slumber of St. John on the Saviour's breast. They returned to it constantly; they clothed it with a delicacy of sentiment, a depth of expression, a sort of jealous enthusiasm which is really a revelation, and which we again find in the magnificent sequences dedicated at this epoch to the Beloved Disciple.[1] Moreover, when they

[1] See in particular the Four Sequences of Adam of St. Victor, the greatest lyric poet of the Middle Ages, if St. Thomas had not on two or three occasions shown himself as capable in this branch as in all others.

represented the crucifix, it was no longer in the gross manner of preceding ages: that open side, that torrent of blood, that chalice held with so much eagerness. It was something more intimate, more tender. The wound, which had hitherto been represented on the right side of the Saviour, now gradually passed to the left;[1] and there it was that all eyes concentrated, and all lips began to rest. There are numbers of touching and ingenuous examples, in which is seen the contemplative genius of the Middle Ages. I shall only cite that of the descent, or rather the taking down from the cross, represented on the shrine of the great relics at Aix-la-Chapelle. One of the arms, the right one, is detached, and Mary supports it weeping; Nicodemus draws the nail from the left hand; Joseph of Arimathea, supporting the sacred body, embraces the wound of the Heart. Sometimes, even, but rarely, as at the portal of the cathedral of Mayence, artists have ventured to represent Christ sitting, opening His tunic and showing His Heart. At the right and on the left are seen a man and a woman, the woman at the side of the Heart, both prostrate, adoring the open side, upon which their tender gaze is riveted. Nowhere, I repeat, is the Heart itself represented, nowhere are seen rays.[2] It is always shown to us **like the first** gleam of dawn, heralding the advent of the **sun.**

But to behold the sweet aurora developing in brilliancy we must cast our gaze on the virgins whom the sacred solitudes of the Middle Ages hid from all eyes. Who but a woman can comprehend the mysteries of the heart? Who will rise so far as to have a presenti-

[1] See in the museum of Cluny a Christ of the twelfth century; the hands extended, and a large wound in the left side. See also an incrusted enamel of the thirteenth century, the chalice on the left side.

[2] I have, however, seen at Cologne a pall of the thirteenth century, upon which is embroidered in red silk a heart pierced with a lance. But this is the only example of the kind of which I know; and I am not sufficiently assured of its authenticity to adduce it as a proof.

ment of the mysteries of the Heart of Jesus, if it be not
a virgin? The lights, the Fathers of the early ages, the
Doctors of the Middle Ages, pale before the intuition
of virgins hidden in the silence of cloisters. It is in
them not only a light, an adoration, a devotion, it is
more still. In these tender intimacies of Jesus with His
spouses, the heart is all. They forget, I do not say, only
His grandeur, His majesty, but even the wounds of His
feet and hands; they see only His Heart. And when
Jesus appeared to them, He also showed them only His
Heart. One day, for example, when St. Gertrude said,
" My Lord Jesus Christ, I supplicate Thee, by Thy
Heart transpierced by a lance, to pierce the heart of
Gertrude with darts of Thy love," the Lord appeared,
and showing her His open side, said, " Look at my
Heart. I wish it to be thy temple." At these words
Gertrude felt herself drawn in a marvellous manner
into the Heart of Jesus, where " to say what she tasted,
what she saw, what she heard, belongs not, as she tells
us, to any tongue neither human nor angelic."[1] On
another occasion, though making efforts to pray with
attention, she was besieged by those distractions which
the saints knew as well as we, but which they bewailed
more than we. The Lord, to console her, presented her
His Heart, saying: " Behold my Heart, the delight of
the Holy Trinity! I give it to Thee that it may supply
for what is wanting to Thee." From that moment Gertrude prayed only through that Divine Heart. By it
she offered to God her adoration and thanksgiving, the
insufficiency of which she now no longer felt. In it she
rested, and her whole life was only one long and sweet
sigh of love toward that Heart wounded by love still
more than by the lance that had entered it. From that
abode she wished never to come forth. [2]

St. Mechtilde, who astonished the thirteenth century

[1] Revelations of St. Gertrude, bk. III. ch. xvi.

[2] Ib. ch. xv.

by the splendor of her illuminations, was honored by no less favors. One night when she could not sleep on account of a violent pain in her head, Jesus Christ let her see the wound of His Heart, and invited her to enter and repose in it. From that day she felt touched by so lively devotion toward the Divine Heart of Jesus Christ, and received from it such graces, that she was accustomed to say: "If I should write all the favors that I have received from the most amiable Heart of Jesus, it would make a larger book than my breviary."[1]

St. Lutgard received still more tender favors, perhaps. One day, whilst yet a young girl, she was entertaining a suitor, when suddenly Jesus Christ appeared to her, opened His sacred breast, and showed her His Heart. "Look," said He to her, "this is what thou oughtest to love. Forsake the attractions of human love, and thou shalt find in my Heart ineffable delights." Some time after, in recompense for her immediate renunciation of human happiness, the Lord again appeared to her, fastened to the cross and radiant with love. As she was contemplating Him in ravished delight, He detached one of His arms and drew her to His adorable breast. There He made her, swooning with rapture celestial, press her lips to the wound of His Heart.[2]

To these illustrious virgins of the thirteenth century must be added another saint. She is still more celebrated, for she bore on her flesh the secret impress of the Saviour's wounds; and less hidden, since she was invested with the mission to lead the Pope from Avignon to Rome, and thus become the Joan d'Arc to the Papacy. She it was that excited in the Middle Ages deep and universal enthusiasm. This was St. Catharine of Siena. One day when meditating on this verse, "Create in me a new heart," she beheld her Divine Spouse approach and touch her left side with His hand.

[1] Vie de Sainte Mechtilde, liv. II. ch. xxii.
[2] Boll. Act. SS. Junii, tom. iii. p. 239.

She immediately experienced such a shock of pain and love in it as to cause her to swoon with happiness. Amazed and dumfounded, for it seemed to her that her Spouse had taken her heart from her breast, she saw Him reappear with a luminous heart in His hand. At this sight, the virgin sank trembling and fainting. The Divine Spouse approaching, these tender words reached her ear: "My daughter, I have thy heart and I give thee Mine, that thou mayest forever live in Me." From that day Catharine had not only a wound in her left side, which crowds came to contemplate respectfully after her death, but in her heart so active a fire that, in comparison with it, all material fire seemed cold. Along with that fire, she felt an elevation of soul, a purity, a generosity, and such transports of love as commanded the admiration of the fourteenth century.

After such a favor it might seem that, if any one ought to propagate devotion to the Sacred Heart, it should have been St. Catharine. One day the Lord even spoke to her in terms as precise as those He used in speaking to Margaret Mary; for when Catharine asked Him why His side had been pierced, He answered: "It was to reveal to men the secret of My Heart, and make them understand that My love is far greater than the exterior manifestations I have given ot it. My sufferings have had an end, but My love has none." But neither the light of such a revelation, nor the favor with which the Sovereign Pontiff surrounded her, nor the popular enthusiasm with which her slightest words were received, could transform Catharine into an apostle of the Sacred Heart. She did not even dream of such a mission.

Similar things must be said of St. Magdalene di Pazzi. The Lord one day appeared to her and showed her His Heart, from which moment she was so filled with divine love that, to moderate the fire which consumed her, she was obliged to open her habit, or to pour forth burning words in strains of highest praise and joy.[1] St. Catherine of Genoa, also, being in prayer, suddenly received so violent a wound that the fire enkindled in her heart rapt her into ecstasy. She appeared like one demented, as she sought relief from the fire of her wound. One day, astonished and frightened at this phenomenon, and feeling she would certainly die, she asked the Lord the cause of the wound that was consuming her heart. Then she saw herself tenderly drawn to the breast of Jesus Christ crucified; His Sacred Heart all inflamed with love was shown her; and she learned that from that source came the flames that devoured her.[2]

In this history of the Heart of Jesus we must not forget St. Margaret of Cortona, who, seeing once, the pierced side of Jesus Christ open like a cavern of love, hastily laid her hand on her own heart, to prevent its leaping out of her breast.[3]

Nor must we pass you over, sweet St. Rose of Lima, little flower of the Indies, who constantly saw the Heart of Jesus burning like a fiery sun over your head; and who one day, when one of its rays fell on your heart, felt the sweet languor of happiness and love.[4] Nor you, Blessed Angela of Foligno, Clare of Montefalco, Margaret of Hungary, Beatrix of Citeaux, Hosanna of Manteau, Frances of Rome, Jane of Valois, rivals of St Catharine of Siena and of St. Gertrude, who having once seen the Heart of Jesus, no longer knew how to languish on earth. At this we are no more astonished than at perceiving in all of you the same phenomenon, namely, the Heart of Jesus inflaming yours. Of infinite love must be said what is often remarked of human

---

[1] Boll. Act. SS. Maii, tom. vi. p. 232.
[2] Vie de Sainte Catherine de Gènes, ch. ii., vii.
[3] Boll. Act. SS. Februar., tom. v. p. 330.
[4] Boll. Act. SS. August., tom. v. 927.

love: "Love has but one word; and though constantly uttering it, it never repeats itself." [1] But what does astonish me, O holy lovers of Jesus, is your silence. Why, though so inflamed with love for this Sacred Heart, have you revealed its beauty to none? We seek among you apostles and evangelists of the Heart of Jesus, but we find only contemplatives, on fire, 'tis true, but silent. Your silence we should be unable to explain; for from the abundance of the heart the mouth speaks, had not one of you taught us the mysterious reason.

Once St. Gertrude asked the beloved disciple St. John why he, who first had the happiness of reposing on the Saviour's breast, had taught us none of the secrets of the Adorable Heart. St. John answered that God had reserved to Himself to make them known in a time of great coldness, and that He held back these wonders to rekindle the flames of charity at a time in which it would have grown cold and almost extinct. [2]

This is the explanation of that aurora, at once so luminous and so secret. The Heart of Jesus has never ceased to be contemplated, adored, loved; never was it not preached. Its devotion is transmitted from soul to soul, from solitude to solitude. The more sensitive the souls and the more lonely the retreat, the more intimate and ardent, the sweeter is the devotion. But to illustrate with souls even the most devoted to the Heart of Jesus throws on it no ray of light. It comes not forth from shadow. Several times the devotion seemed on the point of bursting forth. But it did not, though the dawn went on increasing; the light became more distinct, the devotion more tender. The seventeenth

---

[1] Lacordaire, Vie de Saint Dominique, ch. vi.: Institution du saint Rosaire.

[2] Revelations of Saint Gertrude, bk. iii. ch. xvii.

century found all ready to hail it; but a single voice was needed to call it forth.

Almighty God, indeed, would be able to satisfy Himself with a single voice. But as the devotion preceded by so long preparation was to spread throughout the Church and preside for ages over the renewal of fervor and piety, He resolved to confide this holy deposit to a religious Order, a band of virgins scattered over the face of the earth, who, inflamed by that burning Heart, would radiate its beams beyond the grates of their cloistered homes.

As yet, as far as we know, no one has studied the history of the Visitation from this point of view. No one has shown that it was established for the Sacred Heart; and we ourselves who have written its origin, why may we not now confess that we did not then know to what a degree the broad lines and least details of that Institute relate to the Heart of Jesus? We shall now fill up this void. After having seen devotion to the Sacred Heart arise and spread throughout the whole Church, we shall go back to gaze upon it as it increases in beauty and brilliancy in the bosom of the Visitation.

CHAPTER VIII.

THE VISITATION ESTABLISHED TO BE THE SANC-TUARY OF THE SACRED HEART.

"Inspice, et fac secundum exemplar quod tibi monstratum est."

"Look and make it according to the pattern that was shown thee."— *Exodus* xxv.

"Arcam de lignis setim compingue, et deaurabis eam auro mundis-simo intus et foris; faciesque propitiatorium de auro mundissimo; duosque cherubim expandentes alas, versis vultibus in propitiatorium."

"Thou shalt construct an ark of setim wood, covered with the purest gold within and without; the propitiatory make also of the purest gold; and there shall be two cherubim, spreading their wings, and their eyes fixed on the propitiatory."—*Ibid.*

I DO not know," said St. Francis de Sales in his own gracious style, "why they call me the founder, for I have not done what I wished; in fact, I have done just what I did not wish."[1]

The Visitation, such as it came from the hands of St. Francis de Sales in 1615, is indeed something very differ-ent from what he had at first projected. Every step in the organization of his work was marked by some ob-stacle invincible and unforeseen, which forced him to modify his plans, and sweetly impelled him to form his religious in a mould quite contrary to his original design.

He desired to make of them Marthas, and he made Maries. He wished to throw them out into the active life, and he led them into the contemplative. He wished to send them into cities and villages, to seek out the suffering—and behold, he hid them from all eyes behind impenetrable bars! This Visitation, which

[1] Esprit de Saint François de Sales, Migne, tom. ii. p. 78.

was to resemble a hive whose bees were to carry the honey of charity to all wounds of soul and body, was suddenly closed. It enveloped itself in silence. No longer an active hive, it became a sweet, recollected sanctuary, altogether interior; something like that which God demanded of Moses when He said to him: " Thou shalt construct, according to the model that I shall show thee, an ark of setim wood, covered with the purest gold within and without ; with cherubim, their wings spread and their eyes fixed on the propitiatory." This is what St. Francis de Sales hardly thought to do, and this is what the Visitation became—a silent ark lined with gold, the abode of prayerful cherubim.

But dare we say that in erecting the Visitation St. Francis de Sales did not suspect what it was one day to become ? Is it certain that from this period he did not organize it with the idea of the Sacred Heart in view, and according to the model that had been mysteriously shown him ?

On June 10, 1611, he wrote to his holy co-operatrix : " Good-morning, my dear Mother ! God gave me last night the thought that our house of the Visitation is by His grace noble and important enough to possess its coat-of-arms, its escutcheon, its motto, and its legend. I think, then, dear Mother, if you agree, that we shall take for our coat-of-arms a heart pierced with two arrows, encircled by a crown of thorns, and surmounted by a cross graven with the sacred names of Jesus and Mary. My daughter, when next we meet I shall tell you *a thousand little thoughts that have occurred to me on this matter;* for, in truth, our little congregation is the work of Jesus and Mary. The Saviour when dying generated us *by the opening of His Sacred Heart."*

Thus wrote St. Francis on June 10, 1611. Now, do we know what this 10th of June was ? It was this year, 1611, the first Friday after the octave of the Blessed Sacrament ; that is, the very day chosen from all eternity to be consecrated to the Sacred Heart ; the day of which the Lord said sixty years after to Margaret Mary : " I desire that the Friday after the octave of the Blessed Sacrament shall be a solemn feast throughout the Church in honor of My Divine Heart." It was on this selfsame day that St. Francis de Sales, ravished in ecstasy, gave to his rising Institute for device and standard a heart crowned with thorns !

This certainly affords matter for reflection.

But what were these " thousand little thoughts" that St. Francis had had on that ecstatic night, and that made him wish so eagerly for morning, that he might communicate them to his holy co-operatrix ? In writing the history of St. Chantal I asked myself this question. I was then ignorant ; but now I know. A closer study of the manuscripts of the Order has given me a deeper insight into the most secret thoughts of the holy bishop at the moment in which, his eye resting on the model, he designed the plan of the Visitation. " This is the model," he said to himself, " the Heart of Jesus !" And when, his work finished, he lay in the silence of death, St. Chantal, fearing that he had not been understood, collected a thousand little secret, confidential papers, received from him, and completed the revelation.

Let us dive into these details so marvellous and yet so little known.

A century before opening his adorable breast and declaring to Margaret Mary that He wished to make the daughters of the Visitation the depositaries of His Heart, the Lord cast a look of love on him who was to be the founder of the Institute, formed his heart on the model of His own, and rendered it the meekest and humblest of all hearts. " I do not know," says a certain author, " whether there has ever been a saint that practised more excellently the lesson of the Saviour : ' Learn of Me that I am meek and humble of heart.' " [1]

[1] See the " Heart of St. Francis de Sales:" One-and thirty Considerations, published by the Visitation of Annecy, p. 35.

Some years after, God also prepared for foundress the saint who, formed by St. Francis de Sales, became, as she was pleased to call herself, " the child of the Heart of Jesus," [1] and who was to practise in a high degree, in the natural and supernatural greatness of her strength, the virtues of meekness and humility. "It was revealed to a soul eminently favored by God," relates Mother de Chaugy, " that, when Jesus pronounced this high lesson : ' Learn of Me that I am meek and humble of heart,' [1] He cast a look of love and predilection on our holy Mother de Chantal." [2]

But it is especially during the years that the two saints worked together to form the Visitation, that it is sweet to study by what mysterious ways they were led to dispose all things in order that this Institute, " founded on the golden basis of meekness and humility," [3] might become the sanctuary of the Sacred Heart.

At the moment of Mme. de Chantal's departure for Annecy to begin the foundation of the Institute, St. Francis de Sales wrote her a line to animate her courage : " My advice, my daughter, is, that henceforth we live no more in ourselves, but that in heart, intention, and confidence *we lodge forever in the pierced side of the Saviour.*"

Again, on the eve of her entrance : " My daughter, I must tell you that I have never seen so clearly how much you are my daughter as now. But I say it as I see it in the Heart of our Saviour.[4]   O my daughter, how I desire that your life be hidden with Jesus Christ in God !

---

[1] " God, who has taken her, and made her the child of His Heart, will have care of her." (Letter of Mother de Bréchard, Migne, p. 1007.)

[2] See the " Heart of St. Jane de Chantal:" One-and-thirty Consid erations, published by the Visitation of Annecy, p. 67.

[3] Esprit de Saint François de Sales, Migne, tom. ii. p. 399.

[4] Lettre, April 24, 1610.

I am going to make a little prayer for this, in which I shall implore the royal heart of the Saviour for ours." [1]

And to his daughters gathered around him in those first sweet moments of the little "Gallery House" he says : "The other day, considering in prayer the open side of our Saviour, and gazing upon *His Heart*, I seemed to see all our hearts around His, doing Him homage as the Sovereign King of hearts."

Thus, in the far-off time, we behold the image under which St. Francis loved to represent to himself his little congregation, his daughters lodged in the Heart of Jesus, or their hearts surrounding and rendering homage to the Heart of Jesus. Some days later, when their first home was disputed with the Sisters, St. Chantal and her daughters remembered the true dwelling assigned to them by their holy founder. "Who could have told you," wrote the holy bishop, "that our good Sisters of the Visitation have met with opposition to their locating and building ? O my dear father, the Lord is the refuge of their souls; so are they not too happy ? And as our good Mother (Mother de Chantal), although languishing, yet vigorous, said to me yesterday : 'If the Sisters of the Visitation are very humble and faithful to God, they shall have the Heart of Jesus for a dwelling and sojourn in this world.' " [2]

But let us continue. This little incident, though very insignificant, becomes more definite and strikingly clear. As the Heart of Jesus was to be the abode of the daughters of the Visitation, St. Francis de Sales exhausted all his eloquence, all his piety, in showing them its beauty. "O my daughter," he wrote to one of them, "if you look at this Heart, so meek, so sweet, so condescending, so loving toward miserable creatures, provided only they recognize their misery ; so gracious toward the unfortunate, so good to penitents ! Ah ! who would

[1] Lettre, June 5, 1610.
[2] Lettre à un ecclésiastique, September, 1617.

not love this royal Heart so paternally maternal toward us?"[1] To another religious he wrote: "O my daughter, put it—your dear heart—in the *pierced side of the Saviour*, and unite it to the *King of hearts*, who is as on His royal throne to receive the homage and obedience of all hearts, and who holds the door open that all may approach for an audience."[2] And to the venerable Mother de Chantal, on the feast of St. Catharine of Siena: "O God! my well-beloved daughter, apropos of our heart, may it happen to us as to this saint: may the Saviour take our heart and put His own in its place! But should we not rather render ours all His, absolutely His? Yes, let Him do it, this sweet Jesus! I conjure Him by His own and by the love that He incloses in it, which is the love of loves! But if He will not do it, (oh, but He will!) at least let Him not prevent us from going to take His!" And the amiable saint adds: "And if He were to open our breast to place therein His own Heart, would we not let Him do it?"[3]

Thus it is not enough for St. Francis de Sales to lodge his humble little Visitation in the Heart of Jesus. It is this Sacred Heart that he now wishes to lodge in his humble little Visitation. "And He [Jesus] cannot," he says, "prevent our taking it from Him for that purpose."

Farther on his words are still more clear, more precise: "My very dear daughter, are we not children, adorers, and servants of the loving and paternal Heart of our Saviour? Is it not on this foundation that we have built our hopes? He is our Master, our King, our Father, our all. Let us but think of serving Him well, and He will think of rewarding us well."[4] And again, in almost the same terms: "Do you not wish to be

[1] Lettre, February 18, 1618.
[2] 143d Letter, no date.
[3] Lettre, April 29, 1622.
[4] Lettres, liv. iv. Letter 96, without date.

daughters, adorers, and servants of the loving Heart of
this Divine Saviour? Is it not on this burning furnace
of dilection that you have cast all your hopes?"[1] "Unite
your heart by holy submission to the Heart of Jesus,
which, grafted on the Divinity, will be the root of the
tree of which you will form the branches."[2] And finally
this word which threw light on all else, and which baptized the Visitation by its true name : "The religious of
the Visitation who shall be so happy as to observe their
Rules well may truly bear the name of Evangelical
Daughters, established in these latter times to be the
imitators of the Heart of Jesus in meekness and humility, the basis and foundation of their Order. It will
give them the privilege and incomparable grace of bearing the title of Daughters of the Sacred Heart of Jesus."[3]

Daughters of the Sacred Heart of Jesus! This is the
name that St. Francis de Sales gave to his religious sixty
years before the revelation made to Margaret Mary. He
established them to be "the adorers of the Sacred
Heart," "the imitators of the Sacred Heart," "the
servants of the Sacred Heart." The Heart of Jesus will
be "their sojourn," "the root of the tree of which they
will be the branches," "the foundation of their hopes
and the cause of their being." "They were to take
from Jesus His Heart," and "to open their breast to
lodge Him therein," as in a sanctuary.

This is what the holy Bishop saw; and, carried out of
himself by such thoughts, he felt that something great
was being prepared. "Believe me, my dear Mother,
God wishes I know not what great things from us."[4]
And to Mother Favre: "His all-powerful hand will make

---

[1] "Abridgment of the Interior Spirit of the Religious of the Visitation," explained by St. Francis de Sales, collected by Mgr. de Maupas,
ch. vi. (Rouen, 1644): De l'abandon à la Providence, p. 34.

[2] Ib., ch. ix. p. 53.

[3] "Sentiments of St. Francis de Sales on the Sacred Heart," p. 194.

[4] Lettre, February, 1615.

of this little Institute more than men can imagine." [1]
Whilst contemplating these things, and beholding his
little Visitation "coming forth from the pierced side of
Jesus Christ," and called to the honor of being "the
sanctuary of His Adorable Heart;" like an eminent architect, who skilfully causes the general lines and the least
details to converge to the determined end, he organized
his whole Institute with a view to its marvellous mission.

The Visitation was, then, to become a contemplative
Order, and as such its whole plan is changed! But
then "it is in the Heart of Jesus that it is to make this
continual contemplation." [2] St. Francis studied the
kind of prayer proper for the Visitation, the prayer of
simple attention, of simple remission and repose in God.
He wished this look to be fixed on the Sacred Heart;
and this repose, a sweet sleep "on that same well-
loved Heart." [3] Hear how he exalts this kind of prayer:
"O my daughters, it is much better *to sleep on the sacred
breast of the Saviour* than to watch elsewhere, wherever
else it may be." He made each of his daughters take
the following resolution: "I shall every day give a certain time to this sacred sleep, so that my soul in imitation of the beloved disciple may *sleep in all security on the
amiable breast,* nay, *in the loving Heart* of the loving
Saviour." [4]

"Our blessed Father," said St. Chantal, "who understood excellently well all sorts of prayer, has always
approved of this [the prayer of simple regard]. He
said that, whilst others ate diverse viands at the Lord's
table, we ought to rest our soul and all our affections
on *His loving breast.*" [5]

---

[1] Lettre, October, 1617.

[2] "Interior Spirit of the Religious of the Visitation," by Mgr. de
Maupas, p. 19.

[3] "Treatise of the Love of God," Migne, p. 664.

[4] XXIII. Entertainment of St. Francis de Sales: "De la crucifixion
de Notre-Seigneur Jésus-Christ.'

[5] Answer of St. Chantal on Article XXIV.

Not, of course, that in this contemplation you should forget the neighbor. Oh, this dear neighbor! You must always think of him. But St. Francis de Sales wishes that his daughters see him no more except in the Heart of Jesus and as if through His sacred breast. "There," said he, "who would not love him? who would not bear with his defects? Yes, he is there, this dear neighbor, in the breast of the Saviour. He is there, so loved and so amiable that the Lover dies of love of him." [1]

All the Rules of the Visitation proceed from the same thought, and conduct to the same end. "I assure you, my beloved daughters," says the saint, "you will captivate the Heart of Jesus if you are faithful to the practice of your Rules." [2]

"O God!" he cries elsewhere, "how necessary it is that our poor heart should live no more but under obedience to the Heart of Jesus! And since this Sacred Heart has no more affectionate law than meekness, humility, and charity, we must perforce hold firmly to these dear virtues." [3] He repeats on every key that all the Rules converge to two points, humility and meekness, and that he has expressly chosen these two virtues because they are those of the Heart of Jesus. St. Chantal speaks in the same way: "Inculcate to all your daughters," she writes to a Superioress, "the practice of these words of the Lord: ' Learn of Me that I am meek and humble of heart' They are the substance, the life of our holy vocation." [4]

It was after organizing thus the interior of the sanc-tuary, "after giving it for golden foundation, humility and meekness," because these are the virtues of the Heart of Jesus, that St. Francis de Sales, as if wishing

[1] XII. Entertainment: " De la cordialité."
[2] " History of the Gallery." See also, in the "Little Customs," the Entertainment with Sister Claude Simplicienne.
[3] " Life of the Venerable Mother Clément," published in 1685, p. 264.
[4] Letter to Sister de Blonay, Migne, tom. ii. p. 1069.

to tear away the last veil and initiate the world itself into the grand thought that ruled him finally realized the project of which he had spoken to his saintly co-operatrix, June 10, 1611. He gave to his Institute as coat-of-arms the Heart of Jesus crowned with thorns. The religious wear it engraven on their pectoral cross. It blazons at the head of all their writings, private or public. It is used as a seal for their letters. They have it sculptured on the exterior doors of their convents.[1] He acted like a skilful architect who, after having constructed a palace, puts on the main door the escutcheon of the noble lord who is to reside therein.

All this, assuredly, is very striking, when we reflect that every one of these facts is over sixty years prior to the revelations of Margaret Mary. But what follows is perhaps still more astonishing.

St. Francis de Sales was hardly dead when his saintly and faithful co-operatrix, in a spirit of filial piety, collected all the little papers, the most secret, most confidential that she had received from her holy Father, and directed them to the Order to be an eternal memorial of him. "My very dear Sisters," said the venerable foundress in the letter that forwarded them, "we cordially address to you this writing, because it is taken from the works of our blessed Father. I am particularly pleased to send you several little collections that we have found written by his dear and saintly hand. They are his own thoughts, his own words; and in them you will easily recognize his spirit. We have tried to abridge them, and arrange the whole into meditations."

---

[1] "The seal of all the monasteries shall be engraved with a heart, in the middle of which there shall be the most holy name of Jesus and of Mary together, surrounded by a crown of thorns, and transpierced by two arrows, with a little cross, the lower end of which shall be in the cavity of the heart, and the head within the crown. There shall be no other form of seal in the house. The letters shall all be sealed with it." ("Custom Book" of the Religious of the Visitation, compiled by St. Chantal, p. 78.)

There are two series, called in the Order respectively
"the Great" and "the Little" Meditations. In the first
collection,[1] signed by St. Chantal and bearing date of
July, 1637, there are some remarkable things; for example, the eighteenth meditation: "By what means the
Religious Soul ravishes the Heart of her Beloved."
But it is the second collection, particularly, that is
astonishing from this stand-point.[2] There is one meditation on the subject that now occupies us, so clear, so
explicit, in which the saint calls his daughters to meditate on the *honor that God has done them in confiding to
them His Heart.* This meditation is in terms so precise
that we at first believed it written at a later date. It
appeared to us impossible that such a page could have
been extracted by St. Chantal from the papers of St.
Francis de Sales, unless both were prophets. We
yielded only when we had in our hands a copy published undoubtedly during the life of St. Chantal and
more than sixty years before the apparition of the Lord
to Margaret Mary.[3]

[1] Live ✚ Jesus. "Meditations for the Annual Retreats," taken from
several collections by the hand of our holy Father. This collection is
prefaced by a letter of St. Chantal, and dated thus: "From this first
monastery of the Visitation of Holy Mary of Annecy, August 15, 1637,
begun under the triumphant protection of the Mother of God." One
vol. in white parchment. On the first page a silver heart in rays, in the
centre of the heart Christ's monogram, I. H. S., and below three nails.
This volume contains thirty-three meditations.

[2] Live ✚ Jesus. "Spiritual Exercises for a Ten Days' Solitude, according to the spirit of St. Francis de Sales, taken for the greater part
from his writings." One vol., republished on white parchment, without
date or publisher's name. It comprises only ten meditations, one for
each day, but they are most beautiful.

[3] What created the difficulty for us is that the second collection is not
dated; it does not even give the name of the publisher. But we could
not doubt the compilation was St. Chantal's. The traditions of the
Order, the preface, the Directory on page 16, the introduction of the
different parts, a multitude of counsels, of directions, which could come
only from the foundress,—all, even the style, the orthography, and

This is the meditation that St. Chantal herself copied from several little collections found written by the holy hand of our blessed Father, and which she recommended to her daughters. Again I ask, is this a prophecy? Is it mere chance? It is entitled " Eighth Meditation: Of the Love that Jesus Christ Bears us."

After having made her dear daughters consider the *i*ove that Jesus Christ bore them, first, in the mystery of the Incarnation; second, in that of the Eucharist; third, in that of the Dolorous Passion, she comes to a fourth consideration, altogether unique when we reflect upon the date at which she wrote:

" CONSIDERATION IV.

" Consider that the sweet Saviour not only showed His love for us, as well as for all other Christians, by the work of our redemption; but that He obliges us especially, as daughters of the Visitation, by the gift and favor that He has made to our Order and to each of us in particular of His Heart, or rather of the virtues it contains, since He has founded our most lovely Institute on these two precepts: Learn of Me that I am meek and humble of heart. This is the portion of His treasures that has fallen to us. Having given to other

that beautiful cover of white parchment, gave us the date of the compilation and the certainty that it was St. Chantal's. But what we there read was so important that we wished to have the material proof of it. At Rouen first, then at Nantes, Boulogne, Dijon, wherever we went we asked to see the oldest copies of the " Meditations for Retreats." We found them bearing like the others no date, but an approbation of the Doctors of the Sorbonne which was dated. Here it is: " We the undersigned, Doctors of Theology of the Sacred Faculty of Paris, approve, praise, and highly esteem this book of meditations for retreats, etc., after the corrections and abridgments made by us, by which we hope that the Lord will be blessed. Given this day, Feast of St. John Evangelist, Dec. 27, 1643." Now, St. Chantal died in 1641, and the corrections referred to a previous edition that we had had until then in our possession. The proof could not be more complete.

Orders, to one eminent prayer, to another solitude, to another austerity, He bequeathed to us what, undoubtedly, He esteemed more dear, since His precious Heart is its depository. Ah, could we but have this satisfaction, could we learn and practise well the lesson that this loving Saviour gives us, we should then be honored in bearing the title of '*Daughters of the Heart of Jesus.*'"

Mother de Chantal then concludes with this cry of gratitude and thanksgiving:

"It is very sweet, O my soul, that this gracious Jesus has chosen us to make us the daughters of His Heart. Why, O my Saviour, hast Thou not so favored others in Thy Church? What have we done for Thy Goodness *to have from all eternity destined for us this treasure in these last ages of the world?*"

In founding every religious Order, God ordinarily opens to it a source of love for the interior aliment of its divine life and the means of its apostolate. To one, the cross and the rigors of penance; to another, the desert and the invisible perfumes of contemplation; and to a third, the love of souls and apostolic ardor. The Visitation was to have its special portion, namely, the sacred deposit of the Heart of Jesus. But who will not be astonished, recognizing with what clearness, what increasing precision St. Francis de Sales and St. Chantal had, sixty years before, the intuitive perception of it? It was at first only a sign, a word, a vague lineament: "The Heart of Jesus will be the refuge, the sojourn of the daughters of the Visitation." The idea becomes more distinct, better defined: "It is on the Sacred Heart that the Visitation is founded." "The Sacred Heart is the root that bears the Visitation." Is this enough? No: the idea seems now to be endued with life; it is warmed, it takes color as in a picture: "The religious of the Visitation shall be the adorers of the Sacred Heart." Again: "They shall be the servants of the Sacred Heart. Their spirit shall be the imitation of the Sacred Heart; their arms, a heart crowned with thorns; their title, 'Daughters of the Heart of Jesus.' And to accomplish all this, their gift, the privilege laid up for them from all eternity, and which shall be theirs in the latter times, in preference to all other religious Orders, will be the Heart of Jesus." Behold the words of St. Francis de Sales echoed by St. Chantal. Then both died, and half a century passed before the humble yet illustrious virgin appeared who was to give sense and meaning to their words, who was to cast around their divine presentiments the halo of prophecy.

We may, however, well believe that this half-century did not roll round without the Visitation's turning its eyes and its heart to the Heart of Jesus. St. Francis de Sales had spoken too loudly, and his words were too tenderly meditated by his daughters, for his pious inspirations to be forgotten. Indeed, when one enters the convents during those sixty years that separate us from the first revelations made to Margaret Mary, we perceive everywhere, not indeed public devotion, but in a multitude of the religious eminent for piety, a devotion deep, tender, and heart-felt, neither public nor propagated, but which God preserved by extraordinary graces.

Let us quote some facts. At Annecy, for example, Sister Anne-Marie Rosset went one day to the novitiate oratory to kiss, according to her custom in passing, the feet of a large crucifix still preserved there. " It seemed to me," she said when relating the fact to the venerable Mother de Chantal, " that my Jesus stooped toward me, and that my lips, which were on the wound of His foot, were suddenly removed to that of His side. My heart was so forcibly drawn into my Lord's that I cannot express what I experienced, nor what passed within me during its passage into the Sacred Heart of Jesus."

This was in 1614, hardly four years after the foundation.[1] A little later, in 1618, in the same convent of Annecy, our old manuscripts show us Mother de la Roche teaching the young novices to read in the Heart of Jesus dying;[2] Mother de Bréchard incessantly studying this Heart all luminous, in which, she said, the most simple very quickly became the most learned;[3] Mother Bally, of whom it was said that between the Heart of Jesus and her own there was room for nothing;[4] and, in fine, so many others whom the Annecy Annals show us holily enamored of the Heart of Jesus, at a time the most remote from the establishment of its devotion.

At Melun, in 1636, the venerable Mother Clément, being in prayer, was vouchsafed a privilege like to that with which God honored St. Catharine of Siena. " It seemed to me," she wrote, " that God took my heart out of my breast, and put His own in its place; so that, as it appeared to me, I had no other heart than that of Jesus." Ravished thus into ecstasy, she saw her blessed Father St. Francis de Sales making his sojourn in the Sacred Heart of Jesus, and there receiving the inspiration to erect an Order which would have only one end, that of honoring the Divine Heart of Jesus. In another ecstasy she saw the Blessed Virgin Mary drawing from the pierced side of Jesus Christ and pouring over her dear Visitation all the graces of which it had need to fulfil its mission.[5]

At Turin, in 1635, an humble domestic Sister, Jeanne-Bénigne Gojos, received still more wonderful favors. She spent her life in adoring and invoking the Heart of Jesus in these words: " O Heart of Jesus, pardon the

---

[1] Life of Mother Anne-Marie Rosset, by Mother de Chaugy.
[2] Annals of the Visitation of Annecy.
[3] Ib. Life of Mother de Bréchard, by Mother de Chaugy.
[4] Life of Mother Bally.
[5] Life of the Venerable Mother Anne-Marguerite Clément, etc. Paris, 1686, p. 109.

whole world and punish only Jeanne-Bénigne! Make her bear all the chastisements due to the guilty world." Rapt frequently into ecstasy, united in an ineffable manner to the Heart of Jesus, sharing its sadness, and inflamed with the desire of making it known and loved, she foresaw in divine light the virgin of Paray, and announced the great mission with which she would one day be charged.[1] At the same time, 1635, at Lyons, Mother M. Geneviève de Pradel devoted herself in quality of victim to the Heart of Jesus, "for which she had all her life the most tender devotion," and from which she drew strength that frequently raised her to heroism.[2] Shortly before, at Paris, 1627, Mme. de Boutelier left the world where God had given her a great name, a handsome fortune, children elevated to the highest honors of Church and State, and a number of charming grandchildren. She left all for the sole reason that she was too happy, and that on account of her great happiness she trembled for her eternal salvation. She came to the Visitation, and there found herself still more happy. But why did she not tremble there? " Ah!" said she, " it is that now I see myself entirely hidden in the Heart of Jesus, and in it there is no room for fear."

At Chartres, 1661, Sister Marie-Guillemette Dunas made her ordinary residence in the wound of Jesus' side. The Lord had taught her that there she would be near His Heart, and that there she might await in peace His judgment at the hour of death. The same year, in the second convent of Lyons, they make mention of a religious, Mother de Rioux, who lived only for the Sacred Heart. She left some writings which we have read, and which are embalmed with the most tender and ardent devotion for the Heart of Jesus.[3]

[1] " The Charm of Divine Love; or, Life of the Devout Sister Jeanne-Bénigne Gojos," p. 353.

[2] Annals of the Visitation of Lyons.

[3] Archives of the Second Monastery of Lyons, MSS. of Mother de Rioux.

At Périgueux, in 1664, the feast of the Conception, a pious and fervent religious, Marie-Pacifique Collet, being in prayer, asked for purity of heart. " All at once," said she, " God did me a favor of which it makes me tremble to think. It seemed to me that our Saviour told me to approach His Divine Heart, the source of all purity. At the same instant, He appeared to me, if I do not deceive myself, and made me repose on His Sacred Heart." [1] Shortly after, at Amiens, Mother Anne-Séraphine Cornet felt an attraction to consecrate herself to the Heart of Jesus. The manuscript annals of the house have carefully noted that this was " before knowing anything of the favors that the saintly Sister Margaret Mary received from the Lord;" and they enter into details that show Sister Anne-Séraphine to be one of the most generous lovers of the Heart of Jesus. [2] We read the same of Mother Marie-Séraphine de Gaillard, who passed from the Order of Cîteaux to the Visitation, from the school of St. Bernard to that of St. Francis de Sales, and who has left us some meditations redolent with the most ardent devotion to the Heart of Jesus. [3]

How many names we could add to these! In almost all the Visitation convents we find religious of high sanctity favored with the most striking lights on the Sacred Heart. But what is most astonishing is that nowhere do we perceive the least temptation to propagate the devotion. The worship is entirely private and personal. We discover no exterior manifestation. Not a single religious thinks of communicating it even to the Sisters of her own convent; and, for still stronger reasons, not one dreams of spreading it beyond the grate. Here, as in the Middle Ages, the Heart of Jesus has its adorers and lovers, but no evangelists or apostles.

[1] Life of Sister Marie-Pacifique Collet.
[2] Annals of the Visitation of Amiens.
[3] Annals of the Visitation of Aix.

In the list of the convents in which we have seen the devotion to the Heart of Jesus flourishing in the seventeenth century, it may be surprising that we have not cited Paray. But neither in its Annals, which we have read carefully, nor in the lives of the religious, nor in the archives, so rich and so well kept, is there one word, one line relative to the Heart of Jesus. And what is still more remarkable, Margaret Mary is not less than her Sisters a stranger to this devotion. Read her Mémoire, study her first steps in the religious life, and we find not the slightest allusion to it. She herself declares that her eyes were never turned to the sacred side until the day on which God, drawing aside the veil, presented to her His Adorable Heart with the injunction to make it known and adored by the whole world.

This day is come. After having for six hundred years embalmed the solitudes of the Church, it is time for this mighty devotion to go forth, to quicken faith and inflame hearts. The world had grown cold. Faith, like love, had diminished. Minds were darkened, hearts saddened. On the other hand, souls sensitive as those that in the Middle Ages chose to shut themselves up in cloisters are now multiplied in the world. The perfume has escaped from its vase. Its odor is everywhere: in the bosom of Christian families, and in recollected hearts truly capable of understanding all that is most exquisite in the mysteries of Christianity.

O Jesus! Jesus! The Church and the world claim Thy Heart. Some detached sparks from this burning flame will not suffice us. The furnace itself is what we want. The virgin is ready, likewise the sanctuary. Holy angels who guard our soul, lead to the altar the faithful virgin, and by her, through her purified hands, send forth over the face of the earth the fire that warms, renews, and vivifies!

CHAPTER IX.

THE REVELATIONS OF THE SACRED HEART.

1673–1675.

" Si scires donum Dei."

"If thou didst know the gift of God!"—*St. John* iv. 10.

" Eo usque procedens ut ipsius recumberet pectore Salvatoris."

" She mounted up and reposed on the breast of the Saviour Himself."
—*Leonine Sacramentary, Pref. of the Mass of St. John.*

" Beatus qui supra pectus Domini recubuit! Fluenta Evangelii de ipso sacro Dominici pectoris fonte potavit."

" Blessed is he who has leaned on the breast of the Lord! He drew from the sacred fountain of the Saviour's Heart the living waters of the Gospel."—*Rom. Brev., Feast of St. John.*

WE must recall what has been said in the fifth chapter of this Life. What most astonished the Sisters of Paray on examining the life of Margaret Mary is the length and ecstatic character of her prayer. On certain days, for example, when the Blessed Sacrament was exposed, she never left the choir. Feeble in health, and sometimes even rising from sickness, she remained entire hours motionless on her knees, without support, her hands joined, her eyes lowered. To her devotions of the day she began, toward the end of 1673, to add prayers during the night. We have seen that, particularly during the night between Holy Thursday and Friday, she remained twelve consecutive hours on her knees, so absorbed that she heard nothing of what passed around her. The Sisters, not knowing how to describe such a state, compared her to a statue of marble, and called her an " ecstatic." Frequently she came from prayer flushed and trembling, unable to stand, and ready to faint.

Three or four times, even, it was necessary to carry her swooning under the assaults of a love too strong for mortal to bear.

It was under such circumstances, and during such ecstatic prayers, that, unsuspected by the Community, took place the grand revelations of the Sacred Heart. We say *revelations;* for there were three of them, three and distinct, with several months intervening between them. The first was on December 27, 1673, when Margaret Mary was twenty-six years of age and had been professed only a little over a year. The second was in the following year, 1674. Of the precise day we are ignorant. The Blessed Sacrament was exposed in the chapel; and, from the customs of the time, we may conjecture that it was during the octave of Corpus Christi. The third took place June 16, 1675, on a day of the same octave. There was, then, between these apparitions a very considerable interval—some months between the first and the second, and one year at least between the second and the third. This was not too much. Margaret had time to recover from the state of emotion consequent upon each of these apparitions; for her agitation and weakness were such that, once in particular, it was thought she would die.

When we consider these three apparitions in their entirety from another point of view, we are struck by their order, their gradation, their increasing beauty. It is like a drama in three acts, in which God raised little by little the mind of His servant to the full understanding of the mission that He was so unexpectedly about to confide to her.

For the rest, we have an irrefragable witness of the apparitions—Margaret Mary herself. Obliged by her Superiors to put the recital of these marvels into writing, she did it watering the paper with her tears; and when it was returned to her she threw it in the fire. Only a single one of those copy-books remains; and there is in it a tone of humility so sincere, a frankness so true, forgetfulness of self so great, and traces of emotion so deep, that, even were the Church not convinced of the truth of the apparitions, it would be impossible to doubt them after listening to Margaret Mary's accents whilst relating them.

"It is for Thy love alone, O my God," she began, " that I submit to write this in obedience, and I ask Thy pardon for the resistance I have made. But as no one except Thyself can know the extent of the repugnance that I feel, so it is only Thou that canst give me the strength to overcome it." Then she added these admirable words: " I receive this order as coming from Thee; and by its fulfilment I wish *to punish the excessive joy and precaution that I have taken to follow the great inclination that I have always had to bury myself in eternal oblivion of creatures.* O my Sovereign Good, may I write nothing but for Thy greater glory and my still greater confusion!" [1]

She then took her pen and began her recital. But soon she stopped dumfounded, speechless, confused, utterly unable to overcome her repugnance. " O my Lord and my God, who alone knowest the pain that I suffer in fulfilling this obedience and the violence that I must do myself to overcome the repugnance and confusion that I feel in writing all this, grant me grace to die rather than put down anything but what springs from Thy Spirit of truth, and which will give Thee glory and me confusion. In mercy, O my Sovereign Good, let it never be seen by any one excepting by him whom Thou wishest to examine it, *so that this writing may not prevent my remaining buried in eternal contempt and forgetfulness of creatures.* O my God, give this consolation to Thy poor miserable slave." [2]

A little farther on, having resumed her recital, and again crushed by the work, we read: "I proceed through

[1] Mémoire, p. 289.   [2] Ib. p. 344.

obedience, O my God, without any other design than that of satisfying Thee by the martyrdom which I suffer in penning these lines, every word of which seems to me a sacrifice. But mayest Thou be glorified by it eternally!"

The same plaintive tone is heard throughout her Mémoire; the same contest is witnessed between humility and obedience. At one instant humility lays down the pen; at the next obedience makes her take it up. It was thus that was finished, in an incomparable glory of sanctity, the recital of the three revelations relative to the Heart of Jesus. We shall now make them known in Margaret Mary's own words. The Church has studied the triple recital with the severity she always brings to this kind of examination, and has solemnly declared their authenticity.

FIRST REVELATION.
December 27, 1673.

The first of the three revelations took place, no one can doubt, on the feast of St. John the Evangelist, December 27, 1673. It was the same day on which, three hundred and fifty-three years before, St. Gertrude had learned in a vision that if the well-beloved disciple had said nothing of the sacred pulsations of the Sacred Heart, it was because God reserved to Himself to speak of them at a time in which the world would begin to grow cold. The day could not have been better chosen for this revelation. We have the account of it written by Margaret Mary. She gives us the whole scene to the life.

"Once," said she, "being before the Blessed Sacrament and having a little more leisure than usual, I felt wholly filled with this Divine Presence, and so powerfully moved by it that I forgot myself and the place in which I was. I abandoned myself to this Divine Spirit, and yielded my heart to the power of His love. He made me rest for a long time on His divine breast, where He discovered to me the wonders of His love and the inexplicable secrets of His Sacred Heart, which *He had hitherto kept hidden from me. Now He opened it to me for the first time,* but in a way so real, so sensible, that it left me no room to doubt, though I am always in dread of deceiving myself." [1]

We see it was " the first time " that the Lord showed His Heart to Margaret; until then " He had always kept it hidden." And such is the character of this apparition, and the impression that she receives from it, that the humble virgin, ordinarily so timid, so distrustful of self, " could conceive no doubt of it."

Jesus had then spoken; and " This," adds Margaret, " as it seems to me, is what passed: The Lord said to me, ' My Divine Heart is so passionately in love with men that it can no longer contain within itself the flames of its ardent charity. It must pour them out by thy means, and manifest itself to them to enrich them with its precious treasures, which contain all the graces of which they have need to be saved from perdition.' He added: ' I have chosen thee as an abyss of unworthiness and ignorance to accomplish so great a design, so that all may be done by Me.' "

Thus, according to the conditions of this first revelation, the new devotion was going to be the grand effort of the Heart of Jesus, " passionately in love with men," and wishing at any cost to draw them from the abyss of perdition. Until then ordinary means had sufficed. But in the sad state in which the world was, Jesus could no longer " contain the flames of this burning charity in His Heart," which wished to save all men. His pierced side opened, and His Heart longed to come forth. It had as yet only shown itself in cloisters and to chosen souls, and in showing it to them had made them faint from love. But now it wished to show itself to the

[1] Mémoire, p. 325.

multitude, and try whether, in revealing the hidden secrets of love, it might succeed in melting the ice that was being heaped up in the midst of Christian people. Such was the sense of the first apparition.

Jesus said nothing else to Margaret Mary, excepting that, for the accomplishment of His design, He made use of her; not in spite of her weakness and ignorance, but rather on account of them, that all should be done by Himself. But when? how? in what manner? The Lord did not say, and Margaret Mary had neither the thought nor the strength to ask Him.

Since, however, there was question of a public ministry, the Lord desired to leave her a living and unquestionable proof of the truth of what had just passed.

Before disappearing, He asked if she desired to give Him her heart. But let her speak for herself:

" He demanded my heart, and I supplicated Him to take it. He did so, and put it into His own Adorable Heart, in which He allowed me to see it as a little atom being consumed in that fiery furnace. Then, drawing it out like a burning flame in the form of a heart, He put it into the place whence He had taken it, saying: ' Behold, My beloved, a precious proof of My love. I inclose in thy heart a little spark of the most ardent flame of My love, to serve thee as a heart and to consume thee till thy last moment.' He added: ' Until now thou hast taken only the name of My slave; henceforth thou shalt be called the well-beloved disciple of My Sacred Heart.' " [1]

One can easily imagine what effect might be produced by such a favor in a creature already wholly inflamed with divine love. "After so great a grace," said she, " one that lasted so long and during which I knew not whether I was in heaven or on earth, I remained several days wholly inflamed, wholly inebriated. I was so out of myself that it was only by doing violence to myself [1]

[1] Mémoire, p. 326.

could utter a word. I was obliged to make so great an effort to eat and recreate that my strength was exhausted in my endeavor to endure my suffering." [1]

Again was she led to Mother Saumaise, but she could scarcely pronounce one word. " I experienced," she said, " so great a plenitude of God that I was not able to express myself to my Superioress as I wished." As to her Sisters, she experienced only one temptation; namely, to throw herself at their feet and confess to them her sins. " It would have been a great consolation to me," she says, " to have made my general confession aloud in the refectory, that my Sisters might see the depth of my corruption; for then they would attribute to me none of the graces I received." [2]

Besides this sentiment of profound humility, the first fruit of the luminous apparition, a sentiment that must necessarily be conceived by one that has rested on the breast of the Saviour (for astonishment, admiration, and love create humility), Margaret preserved a memento, or rather an ineffaceable mark, of divine love. She did not bear it visibly on her breast, like St. Francis of Assisi or St. Catharine of Siena, but all her life she retained an invisible wound in her side. " The pain of this wound," she said, " is so precious to me, causes me transports so lively, that it burns me alive, it consumes me." [3] This divine memorial did not grow faint with time, for the Lord renewed it every first Friday of the month, and again showed her His Heart. " The Sacred Heart," she said, " is shown me as a sun brilliant with sparkling light, whose burning rays fall direct on my heart. I then feel myself inflamed with such a fire that it seems about to reduce me to ashes." [4]

Such was the first act of this triple revelation of the Sacred Heart. One sees as yet only the principle and, as it were, the inspiration of this new devotion; but in what touching beauty ! A God forgotten by men, and

[1] Mémoire, p. 326.   [2] Ib.   [3] Ib. p. 327.   [4] Ib.

unable to resign Himself to such forgetfulness; despised by man, and wishing to punish him; hearkening to His anger, endeavoring to silence the voice of His love, and yet not succeeding; unable to contain within Himself the flames of His ardent charity, and yet not able to chastise His ungrateful creatures, He resolved to vanquish them by force of tenderness, and for this end daily inventing new and most divine contrivances of love! After the splendors and benefits of creation came the annihilations of the crib. The crib is followed by the sorrows of the Cross; the Cross, by the Holy Eucharist! Is there anything left? Yes; for we now behold the supreme effort of the Sacred Heart! It is always the same law. Every new evidence of coldness on the part of man causes God to descend a degree in order to touch the heart from which He cannot succeed in detaching Himself.

The day following this lively and ineffaceable apparition, in which Margaret Mary had learned two things,— the first, that God could not contain in His Heart the secrets of His love; the second, that He would make use of her to reveal them to the world,—the life of our saint resumed its accustomed course. Very nearly six months were granted her to recover from the profound impression just received,—and she had much need of them. Six months of peace, recollection, silence, brilliant progress in humility and the love of God! And now, at the moment she least expected, comes the second revelation! More penetrating, more luminous than the first, it made a still deeper impression on her soul. She fell ill from the violent emotion it caused; so ill that all thought she must die.

SECOND REVELATION.

1674.

This second revelation is the only one of which we know not the exact date. It certainly took place in

1674, before the arrival at Paray of Father de la Colombière, who came in the autumn of this year. As the
Blessed Sacrament was exposed, it could not be, according to the custom of the times, other than the feast of
the Visitation, or during the octave of Corpus Christi.
On the other hand, it seems to follow from Margaret's
account that it was on Friday, and the first Friday of
the month. We think, therefore, that it was in the beginning of June, and the Friday in the octave of Corpus Christi.

Let us hear the Sister's recital: " Once when the
Blessed Sacrament was exposed, my soul being absorbed in extraordinary recollection, Jesus Christ, my
sweet Master, presented Himself to me. He was brilliant with glory; His five wounds shone like five suns.
Flames darted forth from all parts of His sacred humanity, but especially from His adorable breast, which
resembled a furnace, and which, opening, displayed to
me His loving and amiable Heart, the living source of
these flames." [1]

In recounting the first apparition, Margaret Mary had
not described the adorable person of the Lord, because,
probably, it had not the same glorious character as this
one. It was a less royal, perhaps a more intimate, communication. " He made me," she says in speaking of
the first, " rest a long time on His breast," which it
might seem would agree not well with the splendors,
the flames that enveloped Jesus in the second apparition. However, this difference in form corresponds to
the difference of spirit in which they were made. Till
that hour Jesus was the Friend, the Father, making a
tender effort to save His children. Now He is the outraged Spouse, the unacknowledged King about to demand reparation. Whilst Margaret, trembling with
emotion, was contemplating Him, " He unfolded to me,"
she says, " the inexplicable wonders of His pure love,

[1] Mémoire, p. 327.

and to what an excess He had carried it for the love of men, from whom He had received only ingratitude. 'This is,' He said, 'much more painful to Me than all I suffered in My Passion. If men rendered Me some return of love, I should esteem little all I have done for them, and should wish, if such could be, to suffer it over again; but they meet My eager love with coldness and rebuffs. Do you, at least,' said He in conclusion, 'console and rejoice Me, by supplying as much as you can for their ingratitude.'"[1]

After having shown in the first revelation the true principle of the new devotion, namely, a love whose flames He could no longer confine in His Heart, Jesus now revealed its character. This devotion would be an *amende honorable* and an expiation for all the crimes of the world, a consolation for His forsaken Heart. He appealed to some chosen souls to come and supply at the foot of the altars for those that do not love Him; and, by their love and adoration, to render the homage He no longer receives from the multitude grown cold and indifferent. "Do thou, at least," and in speaking thus the Lord addressed Himself to all pious souls, "give Me the consolation of beholding thee supplying for their ingratitude, as far as thou canst."

Margaret excused herself on the plea of incapacity. "Fear not," said Jesus; "behold, here is wherewith to furnish all that is wanting to thee." "And at that moment," continued Margaret, "the Divine Heart being opened, there shot forth a flame so ardent that I thought I should be consumed by it." Admirable symbol of what this new devotion was going to become in the Church, of that universal re-warming of hearts of which we shall try later to trace the consoling picture!

Thoroughly penetrated with this burning flame, and unable longer to endure the fire, Margaret implored our Saviour to have pity on her weakness. "Fear nothing,"

[1] Mémoire, p. 327.

said He to her; "I shall be thy strength. Listen only to what I desire of thee to prepare thee for the accomplishment of My designs." Then the Lord asked two things of her: the first, to communicate every first Friday of each month to make Him the *amende honorable;* the second, to rise between eleven o'clock and midnight on the night between Thursday and Friday of every week, and to prostrate for an hour with her face to the ground, in expiation of the sins of men, and to console His Heart for that general desertion, to which the weakness of the apostles in the Garden of Olives had been only a slight prelude.

"During all this time," says Margaret Mary, "I was unconscious, I knew not where I was. Some of the Sisters came to take me away, and, seeing that I could neither reply nor support myself on my feet, they led me to our Mother, who found me quite out of myself, trembling and as if on fire." When Margaret Mary told her what had just taken place, whether she believed or not, or whether she feigned not to believe it, Mother de Saumaise humbled her as deeply as she could—"which gave me extreme pleasure, caused me inconceivable joy," says Margaret Mary; "for I felt myself such a criminal, I was filled with such confusion, that, however rigorous might be the treatment bestowed upon me, it would still have seemed to me too lenient." [1]

"The fire that devoured me," continues Margaret Mary in a style that grows eloquent with the subject, "brought on continual fever; but I rejoiced too much in suffering to complain of it. I never spoke of it but when my strength was completely gone. Never have I felt so much consolation. My whole body was racked by extreme pain, and this relieved a little the parching thirst I felt to suffer. This devouring fire could neither be fed nor satisfied but with the wood of the cross; namely, with contempt of all kinds, humiliations, and

[1] Mémoire, p. 328.

pains. Never was my bodily suffering equal to what I experienced from not suffering enough. The Sisters thought I would surely die."

Dr. Billiet, the attendant physician, declared that Saint Margaret Mary had sixty consecutive fevers that resisted every remedy employed to moderate their ardor. Mother de Saumaise, very much perplexed, at last resorted to the following expedient. She approached the bed of the apparently dying Sister, and commanded her in the name of obedience to ask her restoration of God, adding that she would recognize it as a sign of the supernatural character of all that had taken place in her regard. She would then, she said, permit her to make the Communion of the first Friday of every month, and the hour's prayer during the night between Thursday and Friday. Margaret experienced strong repugnance to asking a termination of her sufferings, fearing, she said, "to be heard." But at the word *obedience*, she no longer hesitated. Scarcely had she uttered a short prayer before her fever fell, her pulse beat less rapidly, and the astonished physician pronounced her cured. There was, however, little need for the doctor to make this assertion, for the saint arose; and from that day the Sisters remarked a total change in her health. Mother de Saumaise did not resist the voice of God. She granted Margaret Mary the permission to communicate the first Friday of the month, and for the future to rise on the night between Thursday and Friday.

Meanwhile Mother de Saumaise became more and more embarrassed. This cure, which looked like a miracle and which perhaps was one, caused her to reflect most seriously on the propriety of acknowledging the incontestable sanctity of Sister Margaret. But, on the other hand, Margaret was very young, hardly six-and-twenty, and counted but two years of religious life. The visions that she related were, moreover, very extraordinary. Was not some illusion to be feared? Finally, Mother de Saumaise resolved to consult others; and breaking silence for the first time, she conferred on the subject with some religious whose names we do not know—"learned people," say our old Mémoires. But whether Margaret, so timid and so humble, was herself not understood, or whether the advisers of Mother de Saumaise entertained certain prejudices on the score of supernatural manifestations, a thing not unfrequent even among priests and pious religious, her conferences led to the conclusion that in Margaret Mary's case there was much imagination, a little natural temperament, and perhaps even some illusion of the evil spirit, so skilfully disguised that the good Sister could not perceive it.

The perplexity of Margaret's judges was thus increased instead of diminished. Condemned by her Superiors and confessors, the poor Sister knew not which way to turn. "I made," said she, "every effort to resist my interior attractions, believing that I was assuredly in error. But I could not succeed. I no longer doubted that I was abandoned, since I was told that it was not the Spirit of God that governed me; and yet it was impossible for me to resist the Spirit that moved me."[1] One day, when drooping under the weight of this continued anxiety, and pouring out her plaintive wail at the feet of her Lord, she seemed to hear a voice saying to her: "Have patience, and await My servant." She knew not what the words meant, but they poured a little balm into her soul, and she felt that God would come to her assistance in His own good time.[2]

Things were in this state when Mother de Saumaise announced to her Community one day that a pious conference would be given them by a religious of the Society of Jesus who had just arrived at Paray, and who had the reputation of speaking eloquently of the things of God.

[1] Contemp., p. 81. [2] Mémoire, p. 345.

His name was Father de la Colombière. We are astonished that a man who, in spite of his youth, was already
so celebrated, and who from his entrance into the
Society had given promise of attaining high renown,
should be sent to so small a place as Paray. We read
in the sequel the divine purpose of this sending. Father
de la Colombière came in time for the greatest perplexities (for it was very likely the morrow of the second
revelation, so badly understood by "the learned people"
of Paray, and the eve of the third and last, the most
important of all). He was going, in few words, to evoke
light in the midst of darkness.

Sister Margaret Mary went with the other Sisters to
the conference, Father de la Colombière's name not
having made upon her the slightest impression. But
he had hardly opened his lips when she distinctly heard
these words: "Behold him whom I send to thee."
Accustomed to await God's moments without antici-
pating them, scarcely had she rested her eyes on the
Father when she remitted to God, who had sent him,
the care of making her known to him.

The Ember days came. Father de la Colombière
having been deputed to hear the confessions of the
Community, Margaret Mary remarked that, although
he had never seen her, yet he spoke as if he knew what
was passing in her soul. He detained her a long time,
and even offered to see her again the next day, in order
to receive a thorough manifestation of her interior state.
These advances could not come more opportunely.
But Margaret did not wish to open her heart to him;
and as to the second proposition, she replied humbly
and timidly that she would do what obedience ordered
her.

Very probably it was the venerable Mother de Saumaise who had spoken to Father de la Colombière of
Margaret's state, that she might be able to add the opinion and advice of a pious and eloquent man to those

that she already had: though perhaps it was God Him‚
self who had thus enlightened His servant, that He might
extend to His faithful spouse the direction of which she
had so great need. Be this as it may, a few days later
the Father returned and asked for Sister Margaret
Mary. "Although I knew," said she, "that it was the
will of God for me to speak to him, yet I felt extreme
repugnance to answering his summons." Her repugnance, however, lasted but a moment. Gained by the
piety and sweetness of the holy religious, and interiorly
excited by grace, Margaret Mary confided to him the
secrets of her heart. The interview was long, and Sister
Margaret Mary came forth from it enlightened and consoled. "He assured me," she said, "that there was
nothing to be feared in the guidance of this Spirit, inasmuch as it did not withdraw me from obedience; that I
ought to follow its movements, and abandon my whole
being to it, to be sacrificed and immolated according to
its good pleasure. He admired the great goodness of
our God in not withdrawing His favors in the face of so
much resistance, taught me to esteem the gifts of God,
and to receive with respect and humility the frequent
communications and familiar entertainments with which
He favored me. The Father added that my thanksgiving for so great goodness ought to be continual.
When I had told him that my soul was pursued so
closely by the Sovereign Goodness without regard to
time or place, that I could not pray vocally without
doing myself violence so great that I sometimes remained with my mouth open unable to pronounce a
word, and that this happened particularly whilst saying
the Rosary, he told me to make such efforts no more,
and to confine myself to my vocal prayers of obligation.
When I told him something of the special caresses and
loving union of soul I received from my Well-beloved,
and which I cannot describe here, he replied that I had

great reason to humble myself, and to admire with him the wonderful mercy of God in my regard." [1]

We have quoted this entire page, because in very brief form it contains true light. There is something elevated, sensible, sweet, and pious in it. It is, besides, the great word of Father de la Colombière. He did, undoubtedly, utter many others. He preached long, he made known God's truth in France and England. But, notwithstanding all this, he was most probably created, led from afar, divinely prepared by a chain of hidden marvels expressly to speak this word. That done, he retires, his mission finished. He had played his part. Assuredly there is none either more glorious or more useful; for in enlightening one such soul he has enlightened millions. He contributed largely to the good of the Church by giving her bark tossed by a frightful tempest the stroke of the oar that was to enable her to clear rugged obstacles. But Father de la Colombière did not retire and leave his work unfinished. We shall see him again at the decisive moment of the third revelation, when he will once more sustain and enlighten the Sister. He will study seriously this last and highest manifestation of God's will, after which he will be the first to prostrate with our saint and consecrate himself to the Sacred Heart.

THIRD AND LAST REVELATION.

June 16, 1675.

It was on June 16, 1675, that the last of the grand revelations relative to the Sacred Heart took place. It was to close the cycle of those solemn disclosures. Until then the humble virgin had received from the Lord only personal favors, very like those with which other holy souls had already been favored. He had only demanded of her some individual practices of devotion. Now, how-

[1] Mémoire. p. 346.

ever, the hour was come for Him to invest her with her grand, public mission.

During the octave of the feast of the Blessed Sacrament, June 16, 1675, Margaret Mary was on her knees before the choir-grate, her eyes fixed on the tabernacle. She had just received "some of the unmeasured graces of His love." We have no particulars of these graces. Suddenly the Lord appeared on the altar and discovered to her His Heart.

"Behold," said He to her, "this Heart which has so loved men that it has spared nothing, even to exhausting and consuming itself, in order to testify its love. In return, I receive from the greater part only ingratitude, by their irreverence and sacrilege, and by the coldness and contempt they have for Me in this sacrament of love. And what is most painful to Me," added the Saviour, in a tone that went to the Sister's heart, "is that they are hearts consecrated to Me." Then He commanded her to have established in the Church a particular feast to honor His Sacred Heart. "It is for this reason I ask thee that the first Friday after the octave of the Blessed Sacrament be appropriated to a special feast, to honor My Heart by communicating on that day, and making reparation for the indignity that it has received. And I promise that My Heart shall dilate to pour out abundantly the influences of its love on all that will render it this honor or procure its being rendered."[1]

This was the last revelation, and the most celebrated of all. Justly the most celebrated, for all that regards the Divine Heart of Jesus is contained in it. Its principle is no other than the overflowing love of God, love making a grand effort to overcome evil; its end, to become a public devotion, having been so long a private one; and, lastly, its effects, a new effusion of divine love

[1] Mémoire, p. 355.

on the Church, and more particularly on the pious souls that become its apostles and propagators.

But whether the Lord, to leave her the full use of her natural faculties at a moment so serious, had concealed a little the splendor of His divine presence, or whether Margaret Mary, reassured by Father de la Colombière, had banished all fear and abandoned her soul entirely to the happiness of contemplating her Divine Master, we do not know. But at the close of this third revelation no trace of the violent emotion that had followed the first two was perceived. The humble virgin is recollected, attentive, happy. Although astonished at such a mission, (for who was she to establish a feast in the Church, she who could not succeed in convincing her Superiors?) but one word escaped her: " Lord, how can I ?" To which the Lord answered by telling her to address herself to that servant of God who had been sent to her " expressly for the accomplishment of this design." [1]

Margaret Mary did, indeed, recur to Father de la Colombière, and confide to him this third revelation. The venerable priest asked for a written account of it, that he might be able to study it at leisure. We shall see later on with what religious respect he preserved the document. He examined the revelation attentively before God, and, enlightened from on high, declared to Margaret that she could rely on it, for without doubt it came from Heaven. Thus reassured, Margaret Mary no longer hesitated. She knelt before the Divine Heart of Jesus, solemnly consecrated herself to it, and thus rendered it the first and one of the purest acts of homage that it was ever to receive on earth or in heaven. Father de la Colombière, wishing to unite with her, also consecrated himself to the Heart of Jesus. It was Friday, June 21st, the day after the octave of the Blessed Sacrament; the day that had been designated by the Lord to

[1] Mémoire, p. 355.

be forever the feast-day of His Adorable Heart. Thus He received, in the person of a holy priest and of an humble virgin, the first-fruits of those acts of adoration soon to be rendered Him by all mankind.

Thus ended this glorious drama, at the same time three and one, of the revelations of the Sacred Heart. Thus was successively developed, in profound and mysterious order, that incomparable vision vouchsafed to one of the most humble of virgins. And that which in silence and ecstasy she had three times consecutively beheld in that chapel, through that grate, on that altar, the Church also was going to see. She examined this testimony, this recital, forced by obedience from the saint's touching modesty; she declared them true and authentic; and, following the example of the humble virgin, she prostrated before the Sacred Heart.

What the Lord asked has been done. The faithful flock from all quarters on the first Friday of every month to kneel before the Sacred Heart of Jesus, and to make reparation for the incomprehensible ingratitude of creatures whom He has passionately loved. In every region, also, are found Christians—wives, mothers, young girls, priests and virgins consecrated to God—who rise in the night between Thursday and Friday, who come to watch with Him, to weep with Him, and sometimes even to impress on their flesh the sacred marks of His Passion. Everywhere, in fine, throughout the Catholic Church, the Friday following the octave of the Blessed Sacrament is a solemnity consecrated to the contemplation of the tenderness, the devotedness of the best of all hearts.

But let us continue our recital. As yet only one part of our Saviour's will on this august subject is known to us. We shall see others appear, and we shall behold their realization. Time is undoubtedly necessary. It is necessary also to the sun on a hazy autumn day for it to pierce the fog that obscures the horizon; but though slow to appear, its sweet light is none the less loved or desired. So it is, likewise, with the Adorable Heart of Jesus in our own sad times. It is but two centuries since it appeared on the horizon. Let us not complain. Already the greater part of the clouds are dissipated. The hour is approaching in which it will illumine the heavens and rejuvenate the earth.

CHAPTER X.

ALMIGHTY GOD PREPARES THE CONVENT OF PARAY
TO BECOME THE SANCTUARY OF THE SACRED
HEART.

1675 - 1678.

" Sanctificamini; cras enim faciet Dominus inter vos mirabilia."
" Be ye sanctified, for to-morrow the Lord will do wonders among
you."—*Josue* iii. 5.

BEHOLD Margaret Mary invested with a mission
the most formidable! She who shut herself up
in a cloister as in a tomb, to flee forever from
the eyes of men; who so carefully hid herself therein,
was now commissioned to address the whole world, to
turn all eyes toward the Divine Heart of Jesus, hitherto
known only to some chosen souls. She was even to
petition the Sovereign Pontiff for a new feast to be inscribed on the cycle of the Christian year.

To accomplish such a mission, what support had
God prepared for her? There was at Meaux a bishop
who had reached the pinnacle of glory. He was Margaret's countryman. Had he learned from her the
mysteries of the Heart of Jesus, he would have taught
them to the world with such brilliancy of genius, with
common-sense so good, that he would in advance have
overthrown the stupid objections of the eighteenth
century. At Cambray, not far from Meaux, was another bishop who, though lacking the genius of Bossuet,
had, by the tenderness of his soul, the purity of his
heart, the noble elevation of his affections, admirably
inculcated this doctrine of love so suited to charm
a heart like his own. Again, there was at Paris an old

man who, like St. John, died exhausted by the ardor of
his charity. He knew nothing better in his green old
age than to repeat the words of the Prophet of Patmos:
" My little children, love one another." This was St.
Vincent of Paul, a worthy apostle of the Sacred Heart.
In exhaling this charming devotion with his last sigh,
he rendered it forever venerable. St. Vincent had had
in his school two young priests, M. Olier and Father de
Condren, to whom God had confided the great mission
of reanimating the hearts of the clergy and rekindling
charity in the breasts of those who were to be the
apostles and missionaries of the devotion. It would
seem that, if they themselves had added this light to
their sublime ideas on the priesthood, they would have
found in it strength invincible, and it would have added
another charm to their grand life-work.

But by one of those inscrutable designs of Divine
Providence, met at every step in the history of the
Church, in which we see God making it a delight to
triumph in weakness, not one of those illustrious stars
rose upon the horizon of Margaret Mary's humble
sphere. The only man, one not illustrious, though
pious and eloquent, who appeared for one instant at
Paray, departed almost as soon as he came, as if God
had sent him only to calm Margaret Mary's anxiety
and then abandon her to her own weakness.

Shortly after the sublime revelation of which we have
spoken, Father de la Colombière received orders to go
to England as almoner to the Duchess of York, Marie
de Modena, a Catholic princess espoused to the heir
presumptive of the crown of England. The holy priest
set out in haste; not, however, before he wrote a word
to Margaret, recommending her to abandon herself to
God and to the practice of holy humility. In answer
he received a prophetic line, in which she stimulated
him to courage in the midst of difficulties, meekness
toward his future enemies, and humility in success

Such were the words of their adieux. The saint now found herself alone in the face of her perilous mission. For a moment she was alarmed and troubled; but, calming her fears, she retired into the depths of her soul, and heard a voice saying to her: " Will not God suffice for thee ? " [1]

It might seem that an hour more badly chosen could not be found in which to take from Margaret Mary the enlightened guide so lately given. The time was approaching in which, called to proclaim to the world the ineffable mysteries of the Heart of Jesus, she was to learn them herself by bitter experience. The Heart of Jesus, crowned with thorns and pierced with a lance, was about to impress upon her its own living image. We recall with what delight God inundated her soul during her novitiate and on the day of her profession; delights tempered, however, with the assurance of a future cross that, without special help from God, she would be unable to support. Far from shrinking from it, Margaret had never ceased to plead for it. It came at last. She was by it to be made worthy of Him who had promised it, of Him from whom she had so earnestly petitioned it.

Physical sufferings were the first intimation of its presence. The little health she had, vanished. She could but languish in her misery; and some strange attendant circumstances threw around her state of suffering an air of mystery. One morning, when drawing water from the well in the middle of the yard, the bucket, after being filled, slipped from her hands and fell with velocity proportioned to its weight. At the same time, the long iron handle that served to raise it swung violently round and round, and struck Margaret on the head. She fell to the ground, several of her teeth knocked out, her gums cut and bleeding. Her sisters ran to raise her, bruised and livid, covered with

[1] Mémoire, p. 356.

blood, but smiling through it all. The terrible pain
consequent upon this accident threw light upon a vision
she had had a short time before. The Sacred Host had
appeared to her resplendent as the sun, and in the
centre of that glory was Our Lord holding a crown of
thorns in His hand. He laid the crown on Margaret's
head with the words: " My daughter, receive this crown
as a sign of that which shall soon be given thee to
render thee conformed to Me." And, in truth, from
that day Margaret's forehead was encircled with a band
of fire. She could rest her head not even on her pillow.
But she made no complaint. Courageously and joyously she endured this conformity with her thorn-
crowned Spouse. " I confess," she said, " that I am
more grateful to my Sovereign Master for this precious
crown than if He had presented me the diamonds of
the greatest monarchs of the world; and this so much
the more, as no one can take it from me. Of necessity,
it often affords me long hours of wakefulness in which
to converse with the only Object of my love; for, like
my good Master, who could not rest His adorable head
on the bed of the cross, I am unable to rest mine on
my pillow."

Margaret, at the same time, felt greatly increase that
mysterious thirst from which she had already suffered,
and which nothing could assuage. It was caused either
by the fire that consumed and dried up her blood, or by
God's desire to give her this new resemblance to her
crucified Lord. Obedience alone could prevail on her
to take some relief. " Reflecting," says Mother de
Lévis-Châteaumorand, " that Jesus' last suffering on the
cross was a burning thirst, Margaret resolved to abstain
from drinking anything from Thursday till Saturday of
every week. At another time, she passed fifty days
without taking any liquid; and when, by orders of
Superiors, she was obliged to refresh herself a little,

water, tepid and most disagreeable, was, she said, much too good for her." [1]

Let us not forget, in this enumeration of Margaret's sufferings, that invisible wound received at the first of the three grand revelations. Our Lord having darted to the heart of His servant " a little spark of the most active flames of His Heart," she felt a mysterious pain in her side, which increased on the first Friday of every month. " This wound," Margaret tells us, " whose pain is so precious to me, causes me suffering so intense that it consumes me, burns me alive." [2]

But this was not all. After giving her His crown of thorns, after having communicated to her something of the thirst He endured in His agony, and some portion also of the sacred wound of His side, Jesus put the finishing stroke to His work by appearing to her with a cross in His hand. He said: " Receive, my daughter, the cross I give thee. Plant it in thy heart. It will cause thee to experience the most cruel torments, mysterious and continued." From that day Margaret became, in fact, a compound of suffering that made her an object of pity, a living image of the Heart of Jesus, wounded, bleeding, and crowned with thorns. " In truth," said a holy bishop, " neither her feet, hands, nor side have received the visible marks of her Saviour's wounds, and never was she favored with those miraculous stigmata that glorified St. Francis of Assisi and many other saints. But her conformity with the Divine Master, though more hidden, was not less real." [3] She endured a band of fire around her head; a thirst that nothing could assuage; a pain in the side from the stroke of a lance; and a cross so heavy, so crushing in its weight, that sometimes, in spite of her energy and

[1] Process of 1715, Deposition of Mother de Lévis-Châteaumorand.

[2] Mémoire, p. 326.

[3] Pastoral of Mgr. de Marguerie, Bishop of Autun, for the Beatification of Saint Margaret Mary, p. 19. Autun, 1865.

her avidity for suffering, she was tempted to lay it down. But at such moments the Lord interposed by stretching Himself upon it. One day, for instance, that she was ill and wished to relieve herself by changing her position from one side to the other, He appeared to her and, in ineffable accents, said: "When I was carrying My cross, I did not change it from side to side."

God thus accomplished in His servant what He had promised when, at the beginning of her novitiate, she placed herself at His feet like a piece of canvas and He had engaged to delineate in her the features of His suffering life. "Like Veronica's veil," continues the holy bishop just quoted, "Margaret Mary received the impress of Jesus' features bruised and humbled."[1] This was necessary; for there is no perfection, even human, no intellectual pre-eminence, no moral grandeur, and, with still greater reason, no sanctity, apart from suffering. But above all was it necessary for Margaret Mary on account of the mission confided to her. How would she be able to understand the Heart of Jesus, that furnace of immolation and sacrifice by love; how would she be able to speak of it to the world, had she not begun to make of her own heart a furnace of love and, consequently, of immolation and sorrow?

Although God assisted her by multiplied trials, by sacrifices and tribulations that, far from ceasing, were ever on the increase, it was wholly insufficient to satisfy her desire to love, to suffer, and to die. "From her ardent love for Jesus Christ," says Mother de Lévis-Châteaumorand, "proceeded that other for contempt and sufferings, which she called her daily bread. And although God acted liberally toward her on this point, she was never satisfied, but always hungering. She was never sufficiently humbled, never sufficiently crushed. A day without this food was to her a day of

[1] Pastoral of Mgr. de Marguerie, p. 16.

special suffering. Had not obedience stayed her, she would have fallen into excesses." [1]

"Margaret's love for pain and suffering," say her contemporaries, " was insatiable. With St. Teresa, she desired to suffer or to die. She declared that she would willingly live till the day of judgment, provided she might always have something to suffer for God; but that to live a single day without suffering would be intolerable to her." [2] Again, she said that she was " devoured by two insatiable fevers: one for holy Communion, in which she received the God of her heart and the Heart of her God; the other for suffering, contempt, and humiliation." [3]

Whilst these things were going on in the soul of Saint Margaret Mary, others were being prepared for her in the interior of the convent, and they were to furnish ample food for that hunger after immolation which tormented her. To her Sisters her life became more and more of an enigma. They understood nothing. Instead of dissipating, the clouds that overshadowed their mind grew heavier; and Margaret found around her only doubts, suspicion, contradictions. Let us note well what, in 1675, our humble Margaret was to her Sisters, the religious of Paray. God had just conferred on her an admirable mission, and an inestimable honor, in making her the confidant of the anguish and sufferings of His Sacred Heart; but the Sisters knew nothing of it. Not one word from Father de la Colombière, Mother de Saumaise, nor, for still greater reason, from Margaret herself, betrayed the secret. The Sisters knew of her only what they saw; that is, hours of prayer prolonged beyond those of the Community; rising in the night, permitted, undoubtedly, by the Superioress, but extraordinary in the Visitation; customs that seemed singular, as that of working on her knees, or others that

---

[1] Process of 1715, Deposition of Mother de Lévis-Châteaumorand.
[2] Contemp., p. 141.   [3] Ib.

astonished without giving light, as the fainting or swooning that took place in the choir, and necessitated her being carried out by the Sisters; and, in fine, what appeared yet more serious, frequent conferences with the Superioress, with Father de la Colombière, and with extraordinary confessors. Though not desiring such interviews, Margaret Mary was obliged to hold them. All this was to the Sisters inexplicable, and very natu, rally brought to their lips such remarks as these: "Why does our dear Sister do nothing like any one else? Why ambition such singularities?"

To all this must be added the strange absorption of which we have spoken, which increased every day and rendered Margaret Mary more and more incapable of special duties. Her Superioress had tried her skill as infirmarian, but without marked success, although her goodness, zeal, and devotedness were there displayed to all, and her charity found vent in such acts of heroism that our readers could not endure the relation of them. She had been tried in the kitchen, but that proved even a greater failure, for the dishes fell from her hands. The admirable humility with which she repaired her awkwardness did not prevent such accidents from being very prejudicial to the order and regularity that ought to reign in a Community. She was next placed in the boarding-school. There she was loved by the little girls, who, venerating her as a saint, even clipped off pieces of her habit. But her preoccupation of mind prevented necessary vigilance. Poor dear Sister! In 1675, even more than in 1672, she lived not on earth; and so they were forced to let her live in heaven! Join to this her strange maladies, with their sudden cures and as sudden relapses, incomprehensible to the physicians and still more so to the Sisters, and then let us ask, should not one be astonished? Why not say: But may not the imagination play an active part in all this? Is not she of whom we speak laboring under an ill-regulated temperament? Is she not perhaps the victim of illusion? Vainly was Margaret Mary thus interrogated. Her answers, vague and unsatisfactory, afforded no light to the members of the Community. Some said that Sister Margaret Mary was under delusion. They even accused her of having won over Mother de Saumaise and Father de la Colombière, and of imparting to them a share in her delusions. Some went even farther, and asked if she were not possessed by the devil; whilst others sprinkled holy water when they passed her. One advantage of this diversity of judgment, which God permitted as formerly the incredulity of St. Thomas, was to place in clearer light the divine origin of the revelations on the Sacred Heart. But it had, too, its disadvantages, for it was the occasion of faults, little murmurs, and words contrary to charity. Among some of the Sisters it gave rise, also, to obstinate blindness touching the ways of God, and to the forming of parties, a circumstance well calculated to render the convent of Paray wholly unworthy to become the sanctuary of the Sacred Heart. All this led to a singular result, until now very badly understood, and which has been strangely exaggerated by Mgr. Languet, Margaret Mary's first biographer. He had received the recital from some aged religious who, unable to forgive themselves the part they had taken in the affair, magnified the injury they had done their saintly Sister. It is now our duty to re-establish the truth and explain its grand signification.

When about to give His Law to the people on Mount Sinai, God ordered them to purify themselves, because "To-morrow," He said to them through Moses, "the Lord will do wonders among you." Again, before beginning His ministry at Jerusalem, the Lord, wishing to inaugurate it by the purification of the Temple, drove from it all those that dishonored its sanctity. Thus at the moment of confiding to Paray the treasure of the

Sacred Heart, Almighty God resolved to demand of it a solemn expiation of all the faults that had been there committed, especially in regard to His servant. Behold how this was done:

On the 21st of November of every year, the feast of the Presentation of the Blessed Virgin in the Temple, the religious of the Visitation renew their vows at holy Mass, having prepared for that solemn act by a little retreat and some penitential exercises. On November 20, 1677, when the Sisters went at eight o'clock in the evening to take their collation in the refectory—for they fast on that day—they were much astonished to see Saint Margaret enter, or rather drag herself in, fall on her knees in the middle of the floor, and there, violently agitated, her eyes full of tears, make unavailing efforts to speak. She was out of herself, she trembled in every limb, and uttered from time to time the words: "My God, my God, have pity on me!" After vainly trying to force some words from her, the Sisters conducted her to the Superioress, Mother de Saumaise, who was at the time ill in the infirmary. Margaret Mary, still in a transport of sorrow, and perfectly overwhelmed with grief, appeared before her. She was questioned as to what was the matter with her; but she could say nothing, until the Superioress, who knew that obedience alone could unseal her lips, ordered her to speak. Then came the startling announcement that God was displeased with the Community; that He had determined to punish it, unless Margaret herself consented to be a victim in its stead and endure the chastisements He had prepared for it. She told them that, frightened at the sight of such humiliations and sufferings, she had long resisted; that since the day on which He had said to her, " Thou must become a victim of immolation to My Heart, to avert the chastisements in store," and on which she had hesitated through fear, God had not ceased to pursue her; that again, in the

morning, God's anger was shown her in a terrible manner, and He had said to her: "It is hard for thee to
kick against the goad of My justice." In the same
spirit He added: "Since thou dost make so much resistance to humiliations, I shall give them to thee double;
and instead of a secret immolation, I demand of thee a
public sacrifice accompanied by the most humiliating
circumstances." It was for this that Margaret Mary
had dragged herself to the refectory to make aloud on
the spot the sacrifice that God had demanded of her for
the sins of the Community; but the words had died on
her lips. She had fainted in terror and confusion under
the eye of the irritated God who was pursuing her.
All this was told to the Superioress with sighs and sobs,
with a voice and demeanor that excited pity.

Mother de Saumaise, who knew the sublime traditions
of the Sacred Heart, who doubted not their truth, and
who was daily expecting God to make them known to
the Community, was not astonished that He wished
it to be purified, that it might deserve to be the first
sanctuary of that Adorable Heart. She sent at once
for the Sister Assistant, and told her to say to the Sisters
that God was angry with them, and that to appease
Him every one must go to her cell and take a discipline
in expiation of the sins of the Community.

If, in imposing this penance, the Superioress had been
able to give the reason for it, namely, the necessity of
purifying the place in which God was going to illustrate the wonders of His love, there would have escaped
from the Sisters a cry of answering love. But Mother
de Saumaise, not feeling herself obliged to speak more
at large, kept silence, and thus subjected the whole
Community to a severe trial. That apparition of Margaret Mary in the refectory, her tears, her choking sobs,
her cries, "Have pity, have pity, my God!" followed by
the long conference with the Superioress, in which she
announced that God was dissatisfied, that the Com-

munity was not sufficiently holy, that it should be purified by penance,—all this to-day, when the saintly
Sister appears before us with an aureola on her brow,
this command on the part of God to purify the future
sanctuary of the Sacred Heart is beautiful and full of
signification; but at the time of which we speak it was
far from being so. Margaret Mary was young, scarcely
eight-and-twenty, only yesterday professed, giving lessons to her Sisters, to the venerable Mother by whom
she had so recently been received! Such conduct, to
say the least of it, was certainly singular. However,
such were the piety and fervor of this Community, of
which Mother Greyfié said, " This dear Paray is the
Tabor of Superiors, on account of the obedience that
therein reigns,"[1] that the Sisters retired in silence to their
cells, and performed without murmur the painful expiation imposed upon them, the reason of which they
did not even ask. Some only, called by duty to the infirmary, or a few whose dissatisfaction brought them to
Mother de Saumaise, found Margaret Mary there trembling and still overcome by her feelings. They approached and questioned her, but her silence only increased their chagrin. As the hour of retiring had
sounded, and the saintly Sister was unable to go to her
cell, they carried, or rather they dragged, her thither,
plying her meanwhile with questions in which there
may have been some small dash of irony. As they
knew nothing of the mysterious sufferings of their holy
companion, some of them proposed that a physician
should be called in, whilst others retorted that to have
recourse to holy water would be all-sufficient. How
many took part in this scene? Five at most; and were
we to raise the veil, we might almost tell their names.
They were Sisters by no means relaxed and tepid, as
has been asserted, but souls pious and even fervent.
Their only fault was a little too narrow an attachment

[1] Mémoire of Mother Greyfié.

to the letter of the law. Dreading innovations of any kind, they interpreted the word of St. Francis de Sales in a servile manner, and thought that instead of thus disturbing the quiet and good order of the convent, their Sister would do far better simply to follow what is prescribed.

For a proof of what we say, as also of their own piety, we have only to see them at a later period kneeling before Mgr. Languet, and humbly accusing themselves of their share in the scene of that memorable night. This they did with a trifle of holy exaggeration, thus misleading him as an historian. The next morning, also, distressed at having broken the " great silence," and, in their excitement, of having allowed some words contrary to charity to escape them, they asked to go to confession before holy Mass. On their return from holy Communion, Margaret Mary heard the Lord saying to her: " My daughter, the peace is concluded, and the sanctity of My justice is satisfied." The temple had been purified.

This sublime act, the signification of which can escape no one, and which was none other than the divine purification of the convent of Paray before the day on which Jesus would make of it the first sanctuary of His Divine Heart, was the last act of the drama in which we shall see appear the venerable Mother de Saumaise. Her six years of government were drawing to a close, and shortly after, she left Paray to return to Dijon. She had deserved well of God and the Church by her intelligence and meekness, her firmness and prudence; for, after hesitating an instant in view of Margaret's extraordinary ways, she recognized her true call to the Visitation, and admitted her to holy profession. She afterward directed her with a rare mingling of meekness and strength; and when the sublime revelations began, sought counsel, that she might not err in things so difficult. She had listened humbly to Father de la Colombière and, reassured by him, had continued to keep Margaret in humility and peace. Convinced, finally, that God was preparing a great light for His Church, instead of turning the part she had taken in it to her own glory, she silently withdrew, discreetly carrying the secret in her own heart, and humbly leaving to others the honor of assisting at these wonders and of laboring at the promulgation of that august mystery. From her we have a magnificent testimony on our saintly Sister, in which she particularly praises her humility, her obedience, her mortification, her avidity for contempt, and that impatience for the cross which increased with trials. " During the six years that I knew our Sister Margaret Mary," she wrote, " I can affirm that she never for one instant relaxed the resolution taken at her profession to make God reign in her before all, above all, and in all, and never to grant any pleasure to mind or body. This fidelity attracted upon her from the Divine Goodness some special graces, which brought with them a very great desire for the cross, humiliations and sufferings. We may truly say without exaggeration that no one was more ambitious of honors and pleasures than she was of contempt and humiliations which, in spite of her highly sensitive nature, formed her only joy." [1]

Nothing can be added to these words.

[1] Contemp., p. 114.

CHAPTER XI.

MOTHER GREYFIÉ SUBMITS MARGARET'S EXTRAORDI
NARY WAYS TO A NEW EXAMINATION—HER SEVER
ITY AND HER FEARLESSNESS—FATHER DE LA CO
LOMBIÈRE RETURNS TO PARAY—HIS DEATH.

1678–1684.

" Probate spiritus, si ex Deo sint."
" Try the spirits if they be of God."—*I. St. John* iv. 1.

JUNE 17, 1678, Mother Péronne-Rosalie Greyfié, a
religious of Annecy, arrived at Paray, having
been elected Superioress in place of Mother de
Saumaise.

The first of the three Superioresses deputed by God
to examine the extraordinary ways of Margaret Mary,
Mother Hersant, was from Paris. The second, she who
had admitted her to profession and who was the confidant of the revelations of the Sacred Heart, Mother de
Saumaise, was from Dijon, the natal place of St. Chantal.
Now we have Annecy, " the holy source," coming in its
turn to take up this grand and solemn examination, and
going, if we may so express ourselves, to close it.

Coming to Paray after the period of the grandest
revelations and before the public manifestation of Margaret's apostolate, Mother Greyfié seems to have been
delegated for no other end than, by the severity and
courage of her examination, to throw splendor upon
Margaret's virtue and the supernatural character of her
mission. It must be granted that no Superioress was
more fitted than she to fuifil the task intrusted to her.
Blessed in her earliest childhood by the venerable
Mother de Chantal, admitted to the " little habit" and
boarding-school by Mother de Blonay, received to her

profession oy Mother de Chaugy, Péronne-Rosalie
Greyfié had been reared from her earliest years in
the purest atmosphere of the Visitation. The stories
told of her during her childhood, and later in her novitiate, record actions full of generosity and strength of
character that show the grandeur of her soul. " She is
a distinguished subject," wrote the Superioress of Annecy, Marie-Aimée de Rabutin, on sending her to Paray,
" who perfectly possesses the spirit of meekness and
strength proper for governing. Upright and sincere,
she is a perfectly humble soul, and very exact to the
observance. Indeed, my dear Sisters, only my great
love for Paray induces me to send it this Mother with
whom, I am persuaded, you will be perfectly satisfied." [1]
Superioress at Thonon, Paray, Lémur, Rouen, and Annecy successively, she died at the age of seventy-nine
years, after sixty-two years of profession. She was one
of those great Superioresses of the Visitation during its
second period. But there is a difference in souls.
Sweetness predominated in Mother de Saumaise. In
her one loved that breadth and frankness of mind,
unmixed with weakness, that led her to all that is good.

Mother Greyfié was, on the contrary, characterized by
rigorism and austerity. "She had," say the old Mémoires, "an extreme distrust for the guidance of extraordinary souls." [2] "Her wonderful attachment to the
Rule made of her a living rule." [3] With such a character and such inclinations, one might expect Mother
Greyfié to neglect no precaution to assure herself of the
nature of Sister Margaret Mary's extraordinary ways.
Perhaps it was for this that the convent of Annecy,
which knew of the trouble at Paray, had suggested her
election to the Sisters. Let us, to rise above thoughts

---

[1] Abridgment of the Life and Virtues of our very honored Mother
Péronne-Rosalie Greyfié, who died Superioress of this First Monastery
of Annecy, February 26, 1717. Small octavo of 19 pages. Annecy, 1718.
[2] Life and Works, vol. i. p. 448.   [3] Abrégé, etc.

so low, say that it was certainly for this purpose God had brought her to Paray, that there might no longer be room for doubt of Sister Margaret Mary's sublime mission. The precautions taken by Mother Greyfié were of such a nature, her severity so great, that she afterward experienced remorse for it; nor could she end her life without publicly expressing regret "for having yielded too much to Margaret's desire to be humbled and mortified." [1]

At the time of Mother Greyfié's coming to the convent of Paray, the community, "very good," she says, "and full of virtue and piety," [2] was decidedly divided on the subject of Margaret Mary. The great act that we have related in the preceding chapter, always inexplicable, had left a deep impression. No one could doubt Margaret's virtue, though her conduct astonished. Discussion went on, not with regard to the revelations of the Sacred Heart, absolutely unknown to the Community, and of which the Sister had not yet said one word, but on her long prayers, her faintings in the choir, her unusual practices, her strange maladies. Religious the most grave, the most fervent, and at their head Marie-Madeleine des Escures, "whom they always regarded as a saint," [3] inclined to believe that Margaret was in error.

No doubt Mother Greyfié had from the beginning demanded entire and filial confidence. She learned in this way, and perhaps also from Mother de Saumaise, of the three revelations of the Sacred Heart. What impression had this recital made upon her mind? Did she believe it? Did she doubt it? It is difficult to say, although everything seemed to indicate that, at first, she was not perfectly convinced.

[1] Mémoire of Mother Greyfié.   [2] Ibid.

[3] Abridgment of the Life and Virtues of our very honored Sister Marie-Elizabeth de la Salle, died in this Convent of Paray, February 10, 1735. Small octavo of 13 pages.

However that may be, her resolution very quickly followed. It was this: to make no account of what she had heard, and to subject Margaret in all things to the common life of the Community. She herself tells us with what rigor she executed her resolve: "When I entered the service of your house," she wrote later to the Sisters of Paray, "although your Community was very good, full of virtue and piety, I nevertheless found sentiments very much divided with respect to this true spouse of the crucified Saviour. Therefore, to keep each Sister in peace and tranquillity, I made up my mind rarely to pay any attention to the extraordinary things that she said took place in her. I never introduced her to any one, neither within nor without the convent. If it happened that she did something which displeased, though by my order or with my consent, I suffered that others should disapprove it, and I even blamed her myself if she were present." [1]

With an imperfect soul such conduct might have been dangerous, leading perhaps to revolt. But with Margaret Mary, whatever efforts Mother Greyfié made, she could not succeed in humbling her as much as she desired to humble herself. Mother Greyfié continues: "It was always Sister Margaret Mary who was called to account for whatever went wrong; it was she who did all the mischief, all the evil, or who was the cause of God's permitting it in others. Thus she ceased not to ask to do penance, to satisfy Divine Justice. Had she been allowed, she would have martyrized her body with fasts, vigils, bloody disciplines, and other macerations."

This first means not succeeding, Mother Greyfié tried another. She not only affected to make no account of Margaret, whom she ever sacrificed to the murmurs of the Community, even when the saintly Sister had acted by her orders; but to calm minds, she began to withdraw from Margaret the permissions that had been

[1] Mémoire of Mother Greyfié.

accorded her. She had been allowed to make the Holy
Hour; that is to say, every week on the night between
Thursday and Friday, at the end of Matins, she remained in the choir until eleven o'clock, prostrate on
the floor, her arms in the form of a cross. It was there
the Lord made her ineffably participate in the sorrows
of His agony. At first, Mother Greyfié made her
change her posture, requiring her to kneel with her
hands joined; and soon she spoke of suppressing this
exercise altogether. So long as there was question of
merely changing her posture, the humble Margaret said
not a word. But when the Holy Hour was suppressed,
though she obeyed (for nothing could shake her obedience), two or three times on coming from prayer she ran
frightened to the Superioress to say that the Lord appeared irritated, and that she was afraid some terrible
punishment would reveal His anger. Mother Greyfié
paid no attention to her, but persisted in the order she
had given. While things were going on in this way,
there died suddenly, and under circumstances that
astonished Mother Greyfié, one of the youngest and
most amiable Sisters of the Community, one on whom
were founded the greatest hopes. Mother Greyfié
thought she saw in this stroke the divine anger threatening her, and she hastened to restore Margaret's permission for the Holy Hour. It is she herself who tells
this humbly and simply. But obliged thus to yield in
this one point, she held firmly to the rest of her orders;
and our poor Sister Margaret Mary, drawn by a force
more powerful than herself and having already taken
her upward flight, was obliged humbly to subject herself to the pace of the other Sisters.

Soon Mother Greyfié went farther. She affected to
pay no more attention to her maladies than to her attractions and to the permissions that had been accorded her. She obliged her, though in a raging fever and weighed down by illness, to follow every

exercise of the Community. It might have drawn tears to all eyes to see this perfectly obedient soul dragging herself to the choir and there remaining on her knees, her hands joined and motionless, with the exception of the slight movements the fever forced from her. One of these occasions will be forever memorable. Margaret was in bed in the infirmary. Mother Greyfié went to see her, and told her to rise and follow the exercises of the annual retreat. "Go," said she to her, "I remit you into the hands of God. Let Him direct you, govern you, and cure you according to His will." Margaret Mary was, at first, a little surprised to find herself put into retreat, notwithstanding her raging fever; but the joy of being, as the Mother had said "placed in the hands of God" overruled every other consideration. She rose at once from her bed, and began her retreat. God, who loves generous souls, appeared to her as soon as she had retired to her little cell. She was lying on the floor, benumbed with cold. He raised her up with a thousand caresses, saying: "Lo! thou art now committed entirely to Me and My care; consequently, I wish to restore thee in perfect health to her who remitted thee into My hands." In effect, after eight days passed in ineffable delights, Margaret Mary came out of retreat physically renewed, and so strong that Mother Greyfié was in admiration.

One might be tempted to accuse Mother Greyfié of cruelty, but she was far from deserving such a reproach. She wished to see clearly, for she felt the weight of her responsibility in matters so grave. By nature little given to extraordinary things; "knowing," as St. Chantal says, "that women are sometimes very imaginative;" fearing to be deceived and drawing the convent and the whole Institute into error, she knew not what precautions to take to assure herself of the truth of the sublime revelations of the Sacred Heart. And supposing that she did exceed in measure, which, however, we do not believe, who will dare blame her?

Resolved to rise above her doubts, she wished to have at any cost some authentic act to prove that it was God who was conducting Sister Margaret Mary. Consequently, full of that holy audacity to be found in the lives of the saints, she had the hardihood to demand a miracle that would have numberless witnesses and the greatest publicity.

" One day," says Mother Greyfié, " when the fervent Sister was recovering from a serious illness and had not yet left her bed, I know not whether it was on a Saturday or the eve of a feast, I went to see her. She asked my permission to rise next morning for holy Mass. I hesitated a little at her request, and she perfectly understood that I did not consider her strong enough to grant it. Whereupon, responding to my thought, she said to me, sweetly and graciously: ' My good Mother, if you wish it, the Lord will also wish it and give me the strength.' ' Then,' I replied, ' I shall tell the Sister Infirmarian to give you some nourishment in the morning and let you rise about Office time, so as to bring you to holy Mass.' " [1]

The infirmarian was Sister Catherine-Augustine Marest. Now, on the evening of that same day, Margaret Mary, feeling better, thought she could not only hear Mass the next day, but also receive holy Communion, of which she had been so long deprived. She spoke of it to the Sister Infirmarian, and implored her to go and ask the Superioress' permission to remain fasting, that she might communicate. Sister Marest promised, but soon forgot the commission. Next morning she made Margaret rise very early and still fasting. All at once she remembered that she had not asked permission for Margaret to remain fasting, so she left the infirmary to seek the Superioress and ask the desired leave. " God

[1] Mémoire of Mother Greyfié.

permitted," says Mother Greyfié, "that, as she left by one door, I should enter the infirmary by the other. Hardly had I seen the poor invalid up and learned from her that she was fasting with the intention of being able to communicate, than, without inquiring into the fact, I gave her a sharp reprimand, exaggerated her fault and called it the effect of her own will, want of obedience, submission, and simplicity. In conclusion, I told her to go to Mass and communicate. But since her own will had given her sufficient strength and courage for that, I wished in my turn to command. I then prescribed that she should carry her bed-clothes to her cell and her napkin to the refectory, and that she should go to the Office at the sound of the bell, and follow all the Community exercises for five consecutive months, without once returning to the infirmary. Margaret Mary received my correction on her knees, her hands joined, her countenance sweet and tranquil. After listening to the end, she humbly asked pardon and penance for her fault, and at once set about fulfilling to the letter all that I had commanded." [1]

There were at this time in the infirmary two Sisters, Françoise-Marguerite d'Athose and Catherine-Augustine Marest, the latter having returned in time to witness the scene. Both testified at the process of canonization to the impression received from Margaret's humility. They saw her humbly fall on her knees before her Superioress, ask her pardon for a fault that she had not committed, and, without reply or excuse, go simply where obedience sent her.

It was, perhaps, lightly and under some excitement that Mother Greyfié had told Margaret to carry the clothes from her bed and not again to set foot in the infirmary for five months. But when the saint had gone, reflecting that, humanly speaking, obedience to her orders was impossible, the venerable Superioress

[1] Mémoire of Mother Greyfié.

felt inspired that this was the occasion for which she had so long been seeking, the miracle that would banish every remaining doubt. Retiring to her cell, she wrote the following note, which she laid under Margaret's eyes, as she was already kneeling in the choir to hear holy Mass.

"Live ✠ Jesus!

"I, the undersigned, by virtue of the authority God has given me in quality of Superioress of Sister Margaret Mary, command her, by virtue of holy obedience, to ask health of the Lord with so much fervor and importunity that she may prevail on His goodness to grant it, in order not to be always a burden to holy religion and to be able assiduously to practise all the exercises of the Community, and this until the Presentation of Our Lady of this year, 1780, on which day we shall deliberate upon what we shall do for the future.

"Sister Péronne-Rosalie Greyfié, Superioress."

Mother Greyfié did not mince matters. More than once we have had proofs that on great occasions God loves such bold tests of faith. The miracle asked by Margaret Mary was instantaneous and brilliant; or rather there were two of them. First, the sudden and extraordinary cure, followed by perfect health; then, at the end of five months, the feast of the Presentation, a relapse so sudden, so lamentable, into so unusual a state, that God's intervention was evident. The entire Community witnessed these two prodigies. A number of Sisters testified to them at the process of canonization; and all declared that they knew not which to admire more, the swiftness of the cure or the precision of the relapse.

Let us listen to Margaret Mary recounting the circumstances of the first miracle: "At the elevation of holy Mass, I felt sensibly relieved of all my infirmities. It was as if a robe of suffering had been taken off me;

and I found myself with the health and strengtn of a very robust person that had never been sick."

Listen now to contemporaries, who testified to ьhe second. " We all admired so manifest a miracle, especially as at the same hour upon which the five months expired, she fell suddenly as ill as she had been before." [2]

Several religious testified at the time to these two miracles. " The venerable Sister," says Sister Françoise Chalon, " was suddenly cured the day on which the Superioress asked it. She went to the choir with the other Sisters, all of whom were much astonished by the sudden change in her state. All went well for five months, at the end of which she relapsed into her former infirmities." The said deponent added that the venerable Sister had made her read the note which the Superioress had given her, and in which she exacted her cure as an evidence of the divine origin of what took place in her. [3] " I attest," says Sister Rosalie de Lyonne, " that I saw our venerable Sister at the time of her greatest illness, when she received from the Superi oress the note ordering her to ask of God her cure as a sign that all that took place in her came from Him. Margaret Mary accepted the alternative, and submitted. That same day she was cured, and, to our great astonishment, began to follow all the exercises of the Community. She continued in perfect health for five months, needing no remedy; but at the end of that time she relapsed into all her infirmities. I saw and read the note. I am an eye-witness of both the cure and the relapse." The venerable Sister said to her in confidence, as she tells us, that if the Superioress had asked five years instead of five months she would undoubtedly have obtained them from her amiable Saviour. [4]

---

[1] Mémoire, p. 363.

[2] Contemp., p. 150.   [3] Process of 1715, p. 57.

[4] Process of 1715, Deposition of Sister de Lyonne.

Besides other witnesses, Sister Catherine Marest and Mother Elizabeth de la Garde spoke of the miracles and stated the facts in identical terms, to the surprise and admiration of the Sisters.

While things were taking this turn at Paray, Father de la Colombière was obliged to leave England. He returned to France crushed, almost dying. Had any one been tempted to envy Father de la Colombière's position as almoner to the Duchess of York and confessor to the heir-presumptive to the crown, he might now estimate in his person the small value of worldly honors. After passing four years in the Duchess of York's palace, where he lived as a religious and in such detachment that he did not even visit the great capital of England, and at the same time as an apostle, preaching incessantly and with the greatest success, Father de la Colombière, along with some English Catholics, was suddenly involved in a grave accusation of plotting against the safety of the state. The accusation was apparently political, intended, they said, to protect the threatened life of the king; in reality, however, its object was to dishonor the Duke of York, his heir-presumptive, because he was a Catholic, and thus prevent his ascending the throne. In revolutionary times, when people are excited, a word suffices to enkindle a fire. The idea of this pretended plot hatched by the Catholics against the life of the king of England was received by the people of England with a credulity at which their greatest historians now blush. Father de la Colombière was conspicuous by his high position, his apostolic zeal and great talents. He was, therefore, one of the first arrested even in the palace of the Duchess of York, and cast into prison. There, resigned to death, he languished a whole month by order of his judges. At the end of this time he was made to assist at the execution of four English Jesuits, his confrères and friends, who were put to death under his eyes.

Then, as his enemies dare not touch his person, by reason of his being a Frenchman, they condemned him to perpetual banishment from England. A vessel landed him on the shores of France. The dampness of his prison, the racking emotion of a sensitive soul like his at the sight of the sufferings of his friends, the sorrow of leaving a great church desolated for so long a period, brought on hemorrhages of the lungs, which in some months conducted him to the grave.

Hardly had he set foot on the soil of France when he wrote to his Superior in terms that portray the most touching humility. He begged forgiveness for returning to France almost incapable of work, a burden to the Society, and he asked for orders. "It is very painful to me," he wrote, "to return to the province in a condition in which apparently I shall not be able to work much this year."[1] Lyons having been assigned him as his place of residence, he passed rapidly through Paris, and proceeded through Burgundy, stopping at Dijon to see Mother de Saumaise. He had always had an uncommon esteem for this soul, so generous, so good, and he wanted to converse with her about Sister Margaret Mary, and learn in detail the end of those marvels of which they had together been the first confidants. It is bitterly to be regretted that the conversation of those two great souls has not been preserved. We know not whether Mother de Saumaise carefully guarded the secret, or whether the Sisters to whom she related it had no thought of committing it to writing. We only know that during the visit he made at the parlor to all the Community, Mother de Saumaise having been called out for a moment, he took advantage of her absence to congratulate the Sisters on having such a Mother, adding humbly that he would esteem himself happy to be under such direction.

From Dijon Father de la Colombière went direct to

[1] Letter of January 16, 1679.

Paray, conducted to Mother Greyfié by the same Hand that had hitherto led him, in order to throw on the extraordinary ways of Sister Margaret Mary some last light. At Paray they hardly recognized him. He was no longer the young religious, at once so humble and so brilliant, who was so communicative, and who spoke with so much warmth. He could scarcely breathe. They felt that he " had," as Holy Scripture says, " come out of great tribulation." [1] But his peace of soul, the fire that lit up his emaciated countenance, his recollection and lively faith, particularly at the altar, told more plainly than words that this tribulation had been good for him, and that he had finished " the washing of his robe in the blood of the Lamb." The whole town, and the Visitation in particular, welcomed him with that veneration which the first Christians had for those confessors whom the sword had spared in spite of themselves. According to the expression of one of the Fathers of the Church: "He had not failed to be a martyr, if martyrdom had not failed him." [2]

Paray seemed to restore him a little strength. Some days after his arrival, he wrote to Mother de Saumaise: " I was ill on arriving at Paray; but in two days I was re-established. I worked straight on for a week from morning till night, without feeling any inconvenience. I cannot tell you how many subjects of consolation God has given me; I found matters in an admirable condition. *It seems to me that everything has taken an increase since my departure.* . . . You can easily believe that in eight days I have not had time for long interviews with those who wished to speak to me; and yet it has pleased the infinite mercy of God to shed so many blessings on the few words I have said that all have been, as it were, renewed in fervor." [3]

[1] Apoc. vii. 14.

[2] See the Approbation of Father de la Colombière's Sermons, December 21, 1681.

[3] Letter written at Lyons, March 23

He saw Mother Greyfié several times, and had long interviews with her, but with Sister Margaret Mary only once. This accorded with the course he always followed in conversing with the latter. He saw her rarely, then but for a short time; and they hardly ever wrote. If Margaret had a word to say to him, she put it on a scrap of paper and confided it to Mother Greyfié, who either sent it, or did not send it, to London. The reply came under cover to the Superioress, or rather in her letter. A heavenly detachment existed in those rare and hasty communications. One sees nothing human in them. This unique visit was, besides, full of consolation. "I have only been able to see Sister Margaret Mary once; but I have had much consolation in the visit. I always find her extremely humble and submissive, with a great love of the cross and of contempt. Behold the marks of the spirit that guides her, and which never deceives any one." [1]

What Father de la Colombière wrote then to Mother de Saumaise he had said in the same tone to Mother Greyfié, with whom he had conversed a long time. He declared to her very decidedly that, as for himself, he did not hesitate to believe that "what passed in this dear Sister came from God." He gave her the true reason for it: "There is in her no appearance of illusion; it would be found that the devil, in wishing to deceive her, deceives himself: humility, simplicity, exact obedience, and mortification are not the fruits of the spirit of darkness." [2] "By this advice," said Mother Greyfié, "I have been strongly reassured; for in whatever way I have taken Sister Margaret Mary, I always found her in the faithful practice of these virtues and the exact observance of our holy duties." [3]

During those eight or ten days passed at Paray, Father de la Colombiére remarked, as he wrote to Mother

---

[1] Letter written at Lyons, March 23.
[2] Contemp., p. 130. [3] Mémoire of Mother Greyfié.

de la Saumaise, *that all was very much increased during his absence.* It was the truth. Mother Greyfié's severity had made resplendent both Margaret's virtue and the divinity of her sublime revelations. Her boldness in demanding a miracle had begun to crown our humble Margaret with the aureola of the saints. Besides, it is the privilege of true love that the more it is persecuted the more it becomes inflamed, like fire, which the air fans and excites. This is what she sang in her novitiate days:

> " The more they contradict my love,
> The more that love inflames!"

Checked in her most earnest aspirations, deprived of those exercises that would satisfy her love by allowing it expression, Margaret felt her passion for God and the Sacred Heart increase. We have purposely said " her passion," for the word *love*, so sublime, so deep, so excessive when there is question of the majority of men, expresses in a very cold manner the flame enkindled in her heart. To sigh after contempt and humiliations, to plunge into sufferings, was for her an ordinary thing. She renewed her donation of self, making it more fully than ever before, and by it delivering to the Heart of Jesus her entire being in the present and in the future. It was in these sentiments that she received the inspiration to make a kind of last will and testament, in which she abandoned to the Lord, to use as best pleased Him and make over to whom He wished, not only her prayers and sufferings, her present merits, but even the prayers and holy sacrifices that would be offered for her after her death; thus despoiling herself of all merit in favor of Him whom alone she loved. This testament conceived and prepared, she had the courage to ask Mother Greyfié to witness; for, as she said, she came on the part of the Lord.

Mother Greyfié, by nature little given to such acts, felt the importance of this one, and, encouraged by

Father de la Colombière, enlightened by the miracle of the Sister's cure and by other incidents in which she had experienced her power with God, did not hesitate. She herself wrote out the donation, and signed this humble formula: "Sister Péronne-Rosalie Greyfié, at present Superioress, and for whom Sister Margaret Mary daily asks conversion with the grace of final penitence."

This done, Sister Margaret Mary implored Mother Greyfié to allow her, in turn, to sign, but with her blood. The Mother having assented, Sister Margaret Mary went to her cell, bared her breast, and, imitating her illustrious and saintly foundress, cut with a knife the name of Jesus above her heart. From the blood that flowed from the wound she signed the act in these words: "Sister Margaret Mary, Disciple of the Divine Heart of the Adorable Jesus."

The world may see in this but foolishness and excess. True; but it corresponds to other excesses more inexplicable still: here, the scourges of penance; there, the blows of flagellation; here, the name of Jesus written in bloody characters on the breast; there, the feet and hands of the Saviour pierced, His Heart opened. Two follies instead of one, and those of man obliged to yield the palm to those of God! But if worldlings sometimes commit similar acts of foolishness for the love of creatures, who are here to-day and away to-morrow, and who at the very time they captivate our heart possess only a shadow of perishable beauty,—why do they fail to comprehend such actions in regard to Him who is infinite beauty, and whose only fault lies in this, that He hides Himself under a veil?

If He would raise it for a moment, the sight would at once disturb our reason, and we should all experience those extravagances of love, now the happy privilege of only a few choice souls.

The Lord expressed His pleasure at the total gift that

Margaret had made of herself: "My Divine Master," she wrote, "testified to me great satisfaction at this act. He told me that since His love had stripped me of everything, He did not wish that I should have any other riches than those of His Sacred Heart. 'I constitute thee,' said He to me, 'the heiress of My Heart and of all its treasures. I promise thee that assistance shall never be wanting to thee till power is wanting to Me. Thou shalt be forever its well-beloved disciple.'"[1] He had a word also for Mother Greyfié: "He promised to grant her the same grace formerly bestowed upon St. Clare of Montefalco; to clothe her actions in the infinite merits of His own; and on account of the love she had manifested for His Sacred Heart, to enable her to merit the same crown."[2] "This gave me great consolation," Margaret Mary adds, "for I loved her much, because she nourished my soul generously with the delicious bread of mortification and humiliation."

However, in the midst of the peace and joy that this great act had procured her, the generous and fervent Margaret Mary experienced one regret, namely, that the letters of the holy name of Jesus, which she had engraven on her heart and which she wished to be as lasting as her love, began, after some time, to grow faint, and to disappear. Resting on the permission that she had received, she tried once or twice to renew them by opening the lines with a knife; but not succeeding according to her liking, she determined to apply fire. This she did, but so incautiously that she soon had reason to fear having exceeded the limits of obedience. Trembling and humbled, she went to acknowledge her fault. Mother Greyfié, true to her custom, apparently paid little attention to what Margaret said, but ordered her in a few dry words to go to the infirmary and show her wound to Sister Augustine Marest, who would dress it. Margaret had not foreseen this increase of

[1] Mémoire, p. 349.   [2] Ibid.

humiliation. Must she, then, disclose to a simple Sister the effects of love's holy ardor? And to what a Sister! For Sister Augustine Marest's rough, strong nature held such things in very low estimation.

Timid and blushing, Margaret Mary went to complain to the Lord: " O my unique Love, wilt Thou suffer that another should see the injury I have done myself for love of Thee? Art Thou not sufficiently powerful to heal me, Thou the Sovereign Remedy of all my evils?" Touched by her affliction, her good Master promised that she should be cured the next day. This indeed was the case; for next day, instead of bleeding wounds, there remained only large scars. Meanwhile, Sister Madeleine des Escures was sent to Margaret by Mother Greyfié, who was less indifferent than she seemed. Preoccupied with the thought of what Margaret had told her, she deputed this Sister to examine and report to her the gravity of the statement. Sister des Escures accordingly asked to see Margaret's wounded breast. The latter, knowing herself to be cured, thought herself dispensed from obeying, thanked the Sister graciously for her proffered services, but refused to show it. It was not thus, however, that Mother Greyfié understood the matter. Informed of Margaret's refusal, she went to her, reproved her sharply for disobedience, deprived her of holy Communion for that day,—" which was for me," says Margaret, "the severest of all penances,"—and commanded her to show her wounds to the Sister.[1] Sister Marie-Madeleine des Escures found them healed, though the glorious scars were visible. The deep wounds had disappeared, but the large, dry crusts forming the holy name of Jesus were still there. The characters were of unusual size and such as are impressed on very large books.[2]

But Mother Greyfié's displeasure at obedience of this

[1] Contemp., p. 140.
[2] Process of 1715, Deposition of Sister de Farges.

kind was nothing compared with that shown Margaret by the Lord. He appeared to her with an angry air, reproached her for her fault, and for five days kept her at His feet, without permitting her to raise her eyes for one instant to His Sacred Heart. " I saw myself banished," she said, "under His feet, where for nearly five days I did nothing but bewail my disobedience, and ask pardon by continual penances." [1] She goes on: " In punishment of this fault, Jesus told me that the impression of His holy name on my heart should never appear exteriorly." And, in truth, after Margaret's death Sister des Escures, who had beheld the deep wounds, had the holy curiosity to examine whether they still existed; but there was no trace of them. " You were well inspired," wrote Mother Greyfié, who was then at Annecy, " to examine whether the impression of the holy name of Jesus which Margaret had engraven on her heart remained. And that you assure me there is no trace recognizable is to me a confirmation of the truth of the favors vouchsafed her. For I know that, in punishment of a certain fault, the Lord told her that this sacred name should not appear exteriorly." [2]

Father de la Colombière's health was not re-established. He grew weaker every day. The lung trouble contracted in the London prisons were little by little conducting him to the grave. His Superiors sent him to Paray, thinking that the mild, pure air of that little valley would be favorable to him; but, in reality, he came to die. His last sigh was to be a last approbation of the sublime revelations of the Sacred Heart; and, like a faithful witness sleeping at the feet of his Master, his bones were to rest near the altar whereon Jesus Christ had appeared. He arrived at Paray in the beginning of August, 1681, and there his last six months were passed. His life now was not much more than a breath; but that breath was more and more inflamed

[1] Mémoire, p. 362.   [2] Contemp., p. 143.

with the pure love of God. He occupied himself with the establishment of a hospital for the poor. His efforts were successful, and his work still exists. He scattered around him, though in vague terms and with extreme reserve, all the pious practices that the Lord had demanded of His servant: the Holy Hour, Communion on the first Friday of the month, and, above all, the observance of the Friday after the octave of Corpus Christi. " He had learned," he said, "from a very holy soul that there were special graces for those who would be faithful to these practices." He came from time to time to say Mass at the Visitation, on that altar of whose extraordinary sanctity he was almost the only one that knew, and in secret to press his lips on that stone upon which the feet of the Lord had rested. More rarely still, and very discreetly, he visited Margaret Mary in the parlor, to reanimate the fervor of his soul and carry away with him a greater love of God.

It was thus his life came to a close. His death was somewhat singular. The physicians, seeing that, far from improving, he grew weaker every day, advised him to return to his brother's home in Dauphiny. His Superiors consenting, his departure was fixed for January 29, 1682. But to spare the invalid the emotion of adieux to his numerous penitents, they agreed to keep secret the day appointed for his departure. Only one pious girl whom he guided and who was a friend of Sister Margaret Mary, Mlle. de Bisefrand, begged an exemption in favor of the latter. Having obtained it, she went to the convent to inform the saint of the Father's projected departure on January 29th. Sister Margaret Mary reflected for an instant and then, after a moment's silence, commissioned Mlle. de Bisefrand to go to Father de la Colombière and say to him from her that, if he could postpone his departure without in the least violating the orders of his Superiors, he should not set out. Either fearing that her commission would

not be properly delivered, or not wishing to confide her
secret to any one, "she wrote a little note to the Father
and confided its delivery to Mlle. de Bisefrand. Now,
this little note delayed the Father's plans, and he died
some days after."

Shortly after its receipt his fever increased, and on
February 15, 1682, at 7 o'clock, he died as the saints die
—holily in the Lord.

As soon as she heard of his death, Sister Margaret
Mary tried in every way to have the note she had sent
Father de la Colombière returned to her. She sent
Mlle. de Bisefrand for it. "But the Father Superior of
the Jesuits," said the latter in her deposition, "refused
to return it. He made me read it. The contents were:
'He has told me that He wishes the sacrifice of your
life in this country.'"[1] Another witness, Sister de
Lyonne, confirms this fact, and adds some details.
She testified that she knew through Rev. Father Bour-
guignet, then Superior of the Jesuits, that the venerable Sister, having learned that Father de la Colombière's
brother had come to take him to his native air, warned
him by a note not to undertake this journey, that he
had something of more consequence to do soon, and
that it was at Paray that God wished the sacrifice of his
life.[2] Other attempts were again made by Sister Margaret Mary to have returned to her this note that betrayed
her sanctity; but the Superior cut them short by declaring that he would rather give all the archives of the
house than return that note.[3]

God, who had revealed to Margaret Mary the death
of His servant, deigned also to reveal his glory. When
Mlle. de Bisefrand went, February 16th, five o'clock in
the morning, to announce Father de la Colombière's
death, which had taken place the evening before, she

---

[1] Process of 1715, Deposition of Mlle. de Bisefrand.
[2] Process of 1715, Deposition of Marie-Rosalie de Lyonne.
[3] Contemp., p. 155.

could utter but one word. " Pray and get prayers everywhere for him." "But at one o'clock the same day,"
continues the latter in her deposition, " I received from
said Sister a note to this effect: 'Cease to grieve. Invoke him; fear nothing. He is more powerful to assist
you than ever.'"[1] And to Mother Greyfié, who was
astonished that Sister Margaret Mary had not asked
to impose upon herself some extraordinary penances,
her usual custom on the death of her acquaintances:
" Mother," said she, " he has no need of them. He is in
a state to pray for us, being, through the goodness and
mercy of the Sacred Heart of our Saviour Jesus Christ,
well fixed in heaven. Merely to satisfy for some negligence in the exercise of divine love, his soul was de-
barred the sight of God from the time it left the body
until the moment it was laid in the tomb."[2]

This was not the only revelation that Margaret Mary
had of the supernal happiness of her holy director.
Some time after she had a celebrated vision, in which
God showed her, at one and the same time, the glory
of Father de la Colombière and the double and distinctive mission confided to the Visitation and the Society
of Jesus relative to the Sacred Heart. This page is of
the first importance in the history we are writing.

" He was, it seemed to me," wrote Margaret Mary, " in
a place very high and spacious, admirable for its beauty.
In the centre of it was a throne of flames upon which
was the loving Heart of Jesus, its wound shedding
forth rays so fiery and luminous that the whole place
was lighted and heated by them. The most Blessed
Virgin was on one side, and our holy Father St.
Francis de Sales on the other, with Father de la Colombière. The daughters of the Visitation, each holding a
heart in her hand, were there also, their guardian
angels at their side.

[1] Process of 1715, Deposition of Mlle. de Bisefrand.
[2] Contemp., p. 155.

"The Blessed Virgin spoke: 'Come, my beloved daughters,' she said, 'approach, for I wish to make you *the depositaries of this precious treasure.*'

" And showing them the Divine Heart, she said: ' Behold this precious treasure. It is especially manifested to you on account of the tender love my Son has for your Institute, which He regards and loves as His dear Benjamin. For this reason, *He exacts more from it than from all others.* It must* not only enrich itself with this inexhaustible treasure, but endeavor with all its power to distribute abundantly this precious money and try to enrich the whole world with it.' "

Thus, according to the wording of this revelation, God created the Visitation to guard the *precious deposit* of the Sacred Heart, to be a fervent, recollected sanctuary, in which they shall contemplate incessantly the Heart of Jesus, in which every soul may enrich herself from its inexhaustible treasury. This is the first end of the Institute. But this is not all. If the Visitation does not do this, it will fail in its mission. The knowledge and love of the Sacred Heart, which it contemplates in the sweetness of prayer, it must propagate beyond its grates, that its light may shine everywhere. *It must, to the full extent of its power, distribute it, give it abundantly to the world.* It is not a favor that God confers upon it, it is an order that He gives it. *It must;* that is to say, God restores to it, under a new form, its first vocation. It again becomes a Visitation. But, instead of carrying food and clothing to the poor, *it must* carry to souls: to virgins hidden in solitude; to apostles exhausting their strength in the labor of preaching; to priests and bishops who grow gray with the sad thought ever before them of the multitude of sinners that are lost;—the Visitation must, we say, carry to them the light, the consolation, the sublime strength that flows abundantly from the Sacred Heart. Behold why God has instituted the Visitation! Behold the mission He gives it! For the rest, silence, forgetfulness, the hidden life; and for the Sacred Heart, an incessant promulgation, an apostolic flame.

Such is the first part of this vision. The second is not less memorable.

" Then turning toward Father de la Colombière, the Mother of mercy addressed him: ' And thou, faithful servant of my Divine Son, thou hast a great part in this precious treasure; for if it is given to the daughters of the Visitation to make it known and loved, and to distribute it to others, it is reserved to the Fathers of thy Society to make the value and utility of it understood, so that they may profit by gratefully receiving a benefit so immense. In proportion as they shall console the Heart of Jesus, that Divine Heart, fruitful source of graces and benedictions, will pour itself out so abundantly on the functions of their ministry that they will produce fruits above their hopes and labors; and the same for the perfection and salvation of each one of them in particular.' "

Thus, whilst the Visitation shall guard the deposit of the Sacred Heart and distribute it through its grates to enrich the world, the Fathers of the Society of Jesus will be its teachers, its preachers, its doctors, to prepare the way for it. Catechists, preachers, apologists, apostles, and, if need be, martyrs of the Sacred Heart—this is to be their part. Let not other religious Orders envy them their privilege; for each has had its own. When, in the Middle Ages, God inspired an humble religious to exalt, more than preceding ages had done, devotion to the Blessed Sacrament, He called to serve and aid Him, as mouth-piece, as speaking-trumpet, the Order of St. Dominic. After having established it the Order of the Holy Rosary, He made of it the Order of the Holy Eucharist; and far on to the threshold of eternity the vaults of our cathedrals will re-echo the Dominican hymns, *Lauda Sion* and *Tantum Ergo*. In like manner, when God desired that Christians should wear on their breast, as a buckler, the name and habit of the Blessed Virgin, He chose the Order of Carmel, and commis- sioned it to propagate in the world and distribute every- where the holy Scapular. He had previously confided to the children of St. Francis the devotion to the Cross and to the Five Wounds of Our Saviour. It was necessary for each Order, in its laborious mission, to have its arms, its banner, its means of action, and its burning flame. However, that which belongs to some is not so exclusively theirs that it cannot belong to all; for of the love of Jesus, still more than of a mother's love, can we say with the poet:

" Each has his own share, and all possess it entire."

Let us not be jealous of one another. In the grand army of Jesus Christ, let us hold aloft our standard, and desire only the happiness of making more con- quests.

Father de la Colombière's death took place February 15, 1682. It was the same year in which was held at Paris the famous assembly of the French clergy con- voked by Louis XIV. to consider the dangers menacing Christendom. All were there united: power, genius, eloquence, experience, popularity. And to what did such efforts amount? Their declaration in four ar- ticles, whose least words have been so studied, so care- fully weighed, so skilfully connected—to what purpose have they served? Only to increase, instead of avert- ing, the danger. Whilst that assembly was being held, an humble virgin in the solitude of an obscure convent, directed by a poor religious, saw the true evil that desolated the Church and society, and prepared herself to show the world the only remedy for it.

Meanwhile Mother Greyfié's six years of Superiority were nearing their term. She was to leave the convent of Paray for that of Lémur in Auxerre, where she had been elected Superioress. The Community of Paray must think of replacing her. For the last eighteen years the Sisters of Paray had sought a Superioress beyond their own home. Paris had sent them Mother Hersant; Dijon, Mother de Saumaise; and to Annecy they were indebted for Mother Greyfié. This time they thought of seeking a good Superioress among themselves. Their unanimous choice fell on a Sister who had edified the Community of Paray for four-and-thirty years. The only reproach that could be made to Mother Marie-Christine Melin, whom they elected, was that she was too kind—not a bad thing after the rather severe reign of Mother Greyfié. But she was pious and, moreover, dearly loved by our saint, whom for a long time she had understood and almost divined, and with whom she shared all the new devotions. Her first act was to nominate Margaret Mary Assistant; and shortly after, " as the incomparable sweetness of Mother Marie-Christine diffused a delicious peace in the sacred desert of holy religion," [1] and novices came flocking in, she confided to her the care of forming them to virtue. It was there, in that little novitiate, in the midst of six or seven young novices, pure as angels and all inflamed with love of God, that was to escape from the heart of Margaret the secret of love hidden therein for nine years.

[1] Manuscript Annals of the Convent of Paray.

CHAPTER XII.

THE SAINTLY SISTER AMONG HER NOVICES—THE SECRET OF THE SUBLIME REVELATIONS ESCAPES HER IN SPITE OF HERSELF—FIRST PUBLIC ADORATION OF THE SACRED HEART.

1684–1685.

" Adjuro vos, filiæ Jerusalem, si inveneritis dilectum meum, ut nuntietis ei quia amore langueo."

"I adjure you, O daughters of Jerusalem, if you find my beloved, that you tell him that I languish with love."—*Cant.* v. 8.

" Adducentur regi virgines post eam. Afferentur in lætitia et exultatione; adducentur in templum regis."

"After her shall virgins be brought to the king. They shall be brought with gladness and rejoicing: they shall be brought into the temple of the king."—*Psalm* xliv. 15, 16.

IN appointing Sister Margaret Mary mistress of novices, Mother Melin had yielded less to her own attraction than to the requests made her by all around. The sanctity of the humble Margaret Mary was becoming known. Some young professed, about to leave the novitiate, expressed their willingness to remain if she were given to them for mistress; and some older religious solicited on the same condition the favor of returning. Even one or two novices who had had the happiness of conversing with her profited by the kindness of Mother Melin humbly to express their desire. They were nearing the hour in which Margaret's sanctity was to pierce the last clouds.[1]

Let us see who composed the novitiate when Margaret Mary assumed its direction.

The eldest of the novices, Claude-Marguerite Billiet

---

[1] Process of 1715, Deposition of Sister de Farges.

oi Paray, was the daughter of a physician, "the most famous of the province,"[1] he who, at all hours, was by the pillow of the saintly invalid, and who assisted at her deathbed. Full of pleasantry and good-humor in the world, Claude-Marguerite became in the cloister "a purely interior soul," "a daughter of prayer and silence, whose union with God and ardor for holy Communion cannot be described." She was so on fire with the divine flames of the Eucharist that she would have overwhelmed herself with austerities for God's sake, had she been permitted. Her hunger after them was insatiable, and the sweetest pleasure one could afford her was to grant them to her; they were the most delicious refreshment. Bound in friendship with Margaret Mary, enthusiastic over her virtues, she joyfully put herself under her direction, and began to run with ardor in the odor of her perfumes. She was one of the first to comprehend and relish devotion to the Sacred Heart, one of the first to plunge into the love of the Adorable Heart, and she was not slow in being consumed by its flames.[2]

The second novice was Françoise-Rosalie Verchère. She, too, was the daughter of a physician, and one of thirteen brothers and sisters, all of whom, with the exception of two, consecrated themselves to God. Called to the religious life, but not knowing into what Order, Françoise, more than usually agitated, was walking one day in a very pleasant garden belonging to one of her relatives. She entered a summer-house and, to dispel her weariness, opened a book that was lying on the table. Happily, it was the life of our venerable Mother de Chantal, and Françoise opened at the page that records how the Celestial Lover had engraven His name on St. de Chantal's heart. At that selfsame moment He impressed Himself so strongly on that of

[1] Circular of March 23, 1725.

[2] Abridgment of the Life and Virtues of Sister Claude-Marguerite Billiet.

this young lover that, feeling violently attracted by His divine fire, she resolved to become a daughter of the Visitation.[1] Mother Greyfié joyfully received her, and did not spare her trials to test her courage. Seeing her valiant and intrepid under them, she resolved to lead her to the summit of perfection. We may say that there was scarcely any height which Françoise did not ascend. Her chief attraction was the practice of the almost uninterrupted presence of God, whence sprang angelic modesty and recollection. Her exterior alone inspired devotion. They compared her to St. Catherine of Genoa. Margaret Mary loved her tenderly, and predicted one day that it would be in her arms that she would die. This prediction was realized, as we shall see, in a wonderful manner and contrary to all expectation. "As if the fire and ardor of the dying saint were poured into the heart of our dear Sister Françoise-Rosalie Verchère, having no longer the support of this incomparable and virtuous friend, she gave herself up entirely to the power of divine love, and on November 5, 1690, at the age of five-and-twenty, made a vow to do all that she knew to be most perfect. Very far from being embarrassed by her chains, she found them all her life infinitely amiable. Nothing cost her; and as God loves generous souls, He poured so many consolations into her heart that, in the midst of crosses and austerities the recital of which makes one tremble, she swam as if in a stream of peace."[2]

Sister Verchère had a sister younger than herself, also a novice, Péronne-Marguerite Verchère, whose biography we have not been able to find. She was very fervent, lively, and intelligent. At first she disputed a little with God the full possession of her heart. It was she who, speaking of Margaret Mary, said one day

[1] Circular of March 23, 1725.

[2] Ibid. Abridgment of the Life and Virtues of Sister Françoise-Rosalie Verchère.

to her sister: " Let us take care, else she'll make us more pious than we wish to be."

Françoise-Rosalie Verchère had a companion, born like herself at Marcigny, and led by her example to the Visitation. She was called Péronne-Rosalie de Farges. Friends in the world, yet more so in the cloister; novices together, and both disciples tenderly loved by Blessed Margaret Mary, they held her when dying, their arms entwined about her. They guarded her memory; they collected and preserved her letters; they wrote her life. They are deserving of our eternal gratitude, especially Péronne-Rosalie de Farges, who prevented Margaret Mary from throwing into the fire her invaluable Mémoire, as she had done all her other writings. Péronne's act thus preserved to the Church the crowning monuments of Margaret's sanctity, and the only one, perhaps, that gives us to know a little the greatness of her soul.

At the age of seven Péronne-Rosalie de Farges made a vow of chastity. Shortly after, under the direction of Father de la Colombière, who prepared her for it, she made her first Communion, " like an angel." She entered the Visitation at sixteen, in spite of the opposition of her family, one of the best and richest of the country. From her entrance she was confided to Margaret Mary, whom she closely imitated in the greatness of her courage and heroic virtue. Like her she had engraved on her heart the holy name of Jesus, to testify to God the vehemence of her love. She plunged so deeply into that holy love, she exercised on herself such cruelties, and practised such charity toward her neighbor,—for "to that noble end she turned her too fiery temperament,"— that she made continual progress in perfection. Though so closely imitating the actions of her holy mistress, she still preserved her own individuality. "For a long time she was regarded by her companions as a St. Jerome, who granted nothing to nature, neither to her-

self nor to others. In this she differed from our saintly Sister Margaret Mary, whose demeanor was gentle
and humble, as if seeking the centre of her own nothingness; who never censured any one; and who insensibly
gained hearts by the honey of her words."

We cannot recount the numerous victories Péronne
gained over her sprightly and ardent temper, having
taken for device, "To conquer or to die." She saw
nothing but duty, and like a heroine she tried to fulfil
it. The sword was ever in her hand to conquer her
passions, which would have been very turbulent had
she not repressed them. She came out so victorious
from the struggle that, at the close of her life, "she
passed in the town for a second Margaret Mary," and
when she died "the people ran to her funeral to see the
saint." [1]

To the four novices to whom we have now introduced
our readers we must add three others not unworthy of
a place in society so holy and so amiable: Marie-Françoise Bocaud de la Clayette, who died young, leaving us
few reminiscences; Marie-Christine Bouthier de Semur
en Brionnais, whose religious life was inaugurated by
a miracle. Having suffered during her novitiate from
weakness so great that she appeared to be pining away,
she received from Margaret on her profession day the
command to ask God for her cure. Pale and debili-
tated, Marie-Christine prostrated under the pall, and
rose from beneath it full of strength and vigor, her
countenance glowing with the hue of health. Marie-
Nicole de la Faige des Claines was the seventh, and she
left in the Community a memory both sweet and lasting. She was Margaret Mary's child of predilection,—
her "little St. Louis of Gonzaga," as she called her.
"Beautiful and graceful; looked upon in her family as a

---

[1] Circular of March 23, 1725. Abridgment of the Life and Virtues
of our dear Sister Péronne-Rosalie de Farges. See, also, Année
Sainte, vol. v. p. 282.

little prodigy; flattered by her parents, whose house she ruled at the age of ten; idolized by her grandmother, —great was the astonishment when, at the age of fourteen, she asked to enter the Visitation, and with such persistence that the permission had to be granted." At fifteen she took the holy habit, and began her noviceship under the direction of Margaret Mary. Such were her fervor and angelic modesty that our saint, so strict and so enlightened, allowed her to pronounce her vows at the age of sixteen, and she herself placed the sacred veil on her head. Shortly after, though so young, she made a vow to do what was most perfect. Full of talent, of grace, of sweetness, skilled in every sort of employment, she did everything with ravishing tranquillity. Her innocence and candor were remarkable. She was so like an angel that her companions used to say laughingly that God had lent her a body. This was, perhaps, the foundation of the predilection Margaret always had for her. Most delicate privilege, which recalls that of the beloved disciple, and forms the most beautiful eulogium of this dear novice. At the moment of death Margaret Mary sent for her, "wishing to have this little angel at her pillow."[1]

In the midst of these young novices, we must rank apart a religious older than they. Though professed in 1680, and having already filled some important charges in the house, she so earnestly solicited permission to return to the novitiate, that good Mother Melin knew not how to refuse her. This was Sister Anne-Alexis de Maréschalle, a singularly grand soul. She had been born in Calvinism, of one of the oldest and noblest families. Dissatisfied with the course of things, its members, through a spirit of opposition and the hope of reform, threw themselves into heresy. When her father, who wished to return to the true faith, which he left only through complaisance to his wife, was dead;

Circular of April 17, 1746. Année Sainte, vol. ix. p. 727.

and when the latter, who had violently opposed her weak husband's conversion, had, through the persuasive voice of Father de la Colombière, abjured heresy; in order to induce her daughter Anne-Alexis to follow her example, she took her secretly to the Visitation under pretext of placing her there as a pupil. The child, perceiving her mother's design, burst into a fury. She poured out torrents of abuse, and laying her head on the trunk of a tree, cried out with all her strength: "Cut off my head. I would rather die than be made a papist and remain with these wolves and demons of religious." The Sisters thought for a time that they would be obliged to send the child back to her mother. She scoffed at everything. When in church, she turned her back to the Blessed Sacrament; when in the garden, she climbed the highest trees, and throwing a rope on the walls, tried to scale them. Such she was then: ardent, energetic, passionate; such she was on the day of her conversion and abjuration. True stroke of Heaven! It was not enough for her to be a religious; she flung herself headlong and fearlessly into what was highest and holiest in religion or most appalling in virtue. Mother Greyfié did not spare her trials, "giving her even extraordinary ones, but they cost Sister Anne-Alexis nothing at all." Never was she more joyous than when most overwhelmed by them. Were we to detail the austerities that she imposed upon herself, their number would be almost infinite. She never laid aside her iron cincture, not even when watching by the sick, helping in the washing, or performing other labors yet more painful. She sang the entire Office with this instrument of penance around her waist; she even slept with it, "so natural to her were corporal macerations." With all this, she exhibited the greatest contentment. A certain joyousness shone in her countenance, and glided into her conversation, which was always gay and holily recreative. She composed couplets and very beautiful canticles to animate herself to new fervor. She was the best friend in the world, and the most obedient of daughters to her Superioress; for she was like a ball of wax in the hands of God and of those who held His place. It was she whom "they could put into all employments great and small, without either elevating or lowering her." She had been a religious seven years when she asked to return to the novitiate, where she was the astonishment and spur of the young Sisters.

Such was the novitiate of Paray at the time that Margaret Mary assumed its direction, such were the souls confided to her care. They were worthy of having a saint for mistress; and she, inflamed with the love of God, and desirous of enkindling it in all breasts, could not wish for material better prepared. Indeed, hardly had she entered upon her charge when, to use the expression of the old Mémoires, she "enkindled the fire of divine love in all those hearts so well disposed."[1] She animated them by her words, whilst her example led them to emulate her. Sometimes she simply explained to them the Rule or the observances, but in such a tone, with unction so penetrating, that every difficulty seemed at once to disappear. "Although," said Sister de Farges, "we had learned all these observances from three mistresses who had preceded her, our venerable Sister explained them to us with a clearness and unction altogether heavenly. Her words seemed to flow from the Heart of Jesus, and they delightfully facilitated virtue."[2] "Sometimes she spoke to them of the love of God. But," says Sister Verchère, "He whom she had on her lips was nothing compared to Him whom she had in her heart. Hers was a passionate love for God. At every instant she gave utterance to such cries as: 'Oh, if you knew how sweet it is to love God! Oh, what is there that we cannot cheerfully suffer for the love of our neighbor!' She returned so frequently to this point

[1] Circular of March 23, 1725.   [2] Ib.

that we compared her to the beloved disciple, St. John the Evangelist. The ardor of her charity inflamed her with the purest zeal, and she often said that she would willingly suffer every torment to save one soul."[1] Again, it was on humility or self-forgetfulness that she entertained her novices. But "her sweet and lowly exterior, abased even to the centre of her nothingness," spoke more eloquently than any discourse. "It was a pleasure," says Sister des Claines, "to see her reproved by her Superioress. It would be impossible to receive a correction with truer humility. The tears that she shed over her least faults impressed the beholder with the idea that she was dead to self-love and absolutely given up to the love of God."[2]

Ordinarily she spoke to them of the Sacred Heart. She so timid, and who, "through natural reserve, never mentioned a word about it to the Community, nor to her friends, of whom she counted a large number, nor even to the Superioress or ordinary confessor,"[3] gave free vent to her heart in the midst of this amiable and pious band. Without saying anything of the revelations with which she had been honored, but upon which she maintained inviolable silence, she spoke to them of the Adorable Heart of Jesus, of its beauty, of the treasures it contains, of the graces with which it will inundate those that study, adore, and love it. She could say all that without betraying herself. In speaking thus, she was imitating her Father, St. Francis de Sales: and who has spoken better of the Heart of Jesus than he? She was imitating, likewise, her Mother St. de Chantal: and who has more piously contemplated and comprehended the beauty of Jesus' Heart than she and the first Mothers of the Visitation? In speaking thus, Margaret Mary went not beyond the purest spirit, the most venerable traditions of her Order.

[1] Année Sainte, vol. ix. p. 215.
[2] Circular of April 17, 1746.   [3] Ib.

God seemed, besides, to multiply at this time His revelations to her. She understood more and more clearly the Adorable Heart of Jesus, and it imparted to her words that warmth, that light, that fire which rises without effort to the lips of an emotional and enthusiastic person. They recall the character of the sublimest revelations of the Sacred Heart,—the Lord appearing to her in glory on the altar, His breast open, and His Heart palpitating with love. Later, as if God had wished to concentrate her regards on the Heart itself, it began to appear to her alone, on a throne, and amid dazzling light. "Once," said she, "the divine Heart was represented to me on a throne of fire and flames, transparent as crystal, more brilliant than the sun, and radiating beams on all sides. The wound it received on the cross was visible. Around the Sacred Heart was a crown of thorns, and above it a cross."

"The Lord," she adds, "assured me that He takes particular pleasure in being honored under the figure of His Heart of flesh. He wished a picture of it to be publicly exposed, that it might touch the insensible hearts of men; and He promised me that He would pour out abundantly on all that honored it the treasures of grace with which it is filled. Wherever this image shall be exposed, it will bring down all sorts of benedictions." [1]

At another time Margaret Mary had a still clearer revelation. To excite her to ask with more importunity for the adoration of men, God made her contemplate the adorations of the angels. "One day, when we were all working together picking hemp, I retired into a little corner, to be nearer the Blessed Sacrament. There my God lavished upon me the greatest graces. Whilst doing my work, I suddenly became perfectly recollected, interiorly and exteriorly. The Adorable Heart of my Jesus, more brilliant than a sun, was present to me. It

[1] Contemp., p. 87.

was in the midst of the flames of His pure love, and surrounded by seraphim, who sang in ravishing harmony:

> " ' Love triumphs, love enjoys;
> The love of the Sacred Heart gladdens! '

" The blessed spirits invited me to join with them in praising the amiable Heart, but I dared not do it. Then they told me that they had come to unite with me in rendering it a continual homage of love, adoration, and praise, and at the same time they wrote this association in the Sacred Heart, in letters of gold and ineffaceable characters of love. This favor lasted two or three hours. All my life I have felt its effects, as well by the assistance I received from it as by the sweetness that it infused into my being and which its remembrance always produces in me. I remained abyssed in confusion. Henceforth in praying to the angels, I could no longer mention them but as my associates." [1]

Such visions were frequently vouchsafed Margaret Mary. " Every first Friday of the month," she says, " the Sacred Heart of Jesus was represented to me as a brilliant light, whose rays fell on my heart and inflamed it with a fire so ardent that it seemed as if about to be reduced to ashes." [2]

This, then, is what Jesus showed to Margaret Mary in her luminous ecstasies,—a Heart: a Heart palpitating with love! She sees only that! In heaven and on earth—adorable spectacle!—all is contained in a Heart! Some religions have been made for the adoration of wisdom; others—oh error!—for the adoration of happiness, even pleasure; and others, more degrading still, have been made for the worship of human strength. They all deceive themselves. Love only is adorable!

Even sanctity, before which the Jews prostrated in the midst of the thunderbolts of Sinai, before which the cherubim veiled themselves with their wings, has not

[1] Contemp., p. 75.   [2] Ib.

the highest claim to man's adoration. Love wields the sceptre.

It is love that has decreed that Christianity shall be the eternal religion of humanity. "If I say to a man, 'I esteem you,' can I say to him anything else?" cried out a great orator one day. "Yes; for I can say to him, 'I venerate you.' And if I say to a man, 'I venerate you,' can I say to him any more? Have I in this word exhausted my vocabulary? No; I have still one thing to say to him—one only, the highest of all. I can say to him, 'I love you!' Ten thousand words may precede it, but none other of any language can follow it. When one has said it once to a man, there is nothing left but ever and ever to repeat to him that selfsame word."[1] In like manner, after power has been deified, wisdom also may be divinized; but after that comes love, and there ends the scale: we have nothing left but to adore it forever.

What is the love that Christianity has been made to adore? We may have remarked what our saint said when the Heart of Jesus was shown to her on a throne of fire and flames: "The wound that it had received was visible, and there was a crown of thorns around the Divine Heart." This vision frequently presented itself to her, and this character of immolation and of sacrifice was impressed upon her under a thousand forms. "Once," said she, "this loving Heart was shown me transpierced and torn with blows."[2] Another time it appeared to her "pierced with light, like a fathomless abyss, opened by an immeasurable arrow."[3] "Generally the thorns of the crown surrounded the Heart so closely and pressed it so violently that it was wounded in every part, and the blood flowed in streams."[4] This was the meaning of the divine words of the *Imitation : Et sine dolore non vivitur in amore!* "Without sorrow there is no living in love."[5]

[1] Contemp., p. 54.   [2] Ib.   [3] Ib.   [4] Ib.
[5] Imitation of Christ, bk. III. ch. v

Admirable thing! There are in the heart two poles:
one by which we enjoy, and one by which we suffer.
Of these two poles, one is meant to last forever. We
shall carry it with us into eternity, for it is that by
which we enjoy. But who would believe it? Here below, on this sad earth, it must scarcely ever be brought
into action. It is full of peril to the soul. It is neither
great nor productive of great things. If one aspires to
glory, to genius, withdraw this pole from the heart,—
this divine pole, this celestial pole, by which we enjoy. Its hour is not yet come. It can achieve nothing
here below but low and vulgar things. The laurel
crown has ever rested on wounded foreheads, and the
aureola of sanctity has never encircled any but crucified
hearts. How beautiful, then, were these visions in
which Margaret perceived, not only a Heart, but a
Heart wounded, a Heart bruised, a Heart crowned and
bleeding! She knew not how to detach herself from
it. Her soul was never satiated with this vivifying
sight, and her longest hours were employed in contemplating that wounded Heart, and trying to understand
the ravishing mystery it proclaimed of immolation and
of sacrifice.

This was not, however, the only form under which
the Sacred Heart was shown to Margaret Mary. There
were others, also very beautiful, which incessantly reappeared: "a burning furnace;"[1] "a furnace of love;"[2] "a
lover attracting souls;" "an abyss into which the soul
must plunge in order to be regenerated."[3] Sometimes
Margaret Mary saw cold souls, frozen souls approach
that furnace; and when about to warm themselves,
they suddenly and foolishly took flight and lost themselves in darkness. She saw others come to the Heart
of Jesus, cold, stunted, and deformed. On approaching
it they were enlightened and inflamed, and they ended
by losing themselves in it like sparks in a furnace. One

[1] Contemp., p. 90.   [2] Ib., p. 193.   [3] Ib., p. 49

day the Heart of Jesus appeared to her under this form of a burning furnace, into which two other hearts hastened to plunge. At the same moment she heard a voice saying to her: " Thus does My pure love unite these three hearts forever!" She knew that it was the heart of her holy director and her own that thus abyssed themselves in the Heart of Jesus.[1]

These visions passed at every moment before her eyes, raising her above the earth, making her a prophetess, and revealing to her the secrets of souls and the laws of a superior world. As in nature there is for the visible universe a centre of gravity around which revolve all the celestial bodies, now impelled toward it, now held back from it, thus governed by a double force that everywhere establishes harmony; so is there a centre of gravity in the moral universe, spotless and immovable amidst the tumult of the world : and that is the Heart of Jesus. There is only this difference between it and the attractive forces that govern the stars; the latter, though borne to their centre by attraction, are happily restrained by centrifugal force; but souls must break loose from this second force, this egoism, this personality, that they may allow themselves to be carried to the Heart of Jesus and therein abyssed, for there will be no order, no happiness, until all are lost in it.

This is what the saintly Sister saw. Can we marvel that she passed entire nights in contemplation, and that, when left on her knees at the foot of the tabernacle at seven o'clock in the evening, she was found next morning in the same position, immovable and ecstatic ? But can any one imagine what must then have been her words, the light of her countenance, the ardor, the passion of her sentiments, and the inflamed eloquence that flowed from her lips ? However, discreet, and mistress of herself, having learned from the Holy Book that one should not divulge " the secret of the king," Margaret

[1] Contemp., p. 90.

Mary said nothing of her sublime revelations. If forced to speak, she did so vaguely and obscurely. One day, when Sister de la Farges, in the simplicity that belongs to the true Visitandine, asked her what she was doing on her knees perfectly immovable for so many long hours before the Blessed Sacrament, Margaret Mary merely replied that she was wholly occupied with the sorrows of Jesus in His Passion. But the young novice insisting, received the reply: "Whether I have or have not a body at that time, I should find it hard to say." On another occasion, walking with Sister Claude-Marguerite Billiet, and passing near the little cluster of hazel-trees: "There," said she to her, "behold a spot redolent of graces for me! It is here that God made known to me the happiness of suffering, by the knowledge He has given me of His Passion." And to Sister Verchère, who had fallen suddenly ill in consequence of the significant prohibition to Margaret Mary to make the Holy Hour, she revealed for her consolation the secret of her prayer on the night between Thursday and Friday, and of her Communion of the first Friday of the month.[1] There was undoubtedly nothing in all this that could betray the secret of the grand revelations of the Sacred Heart. But as time went on it became more evident to all that God favored Sister Margaret Mary with singular graces. At this period of the divine manifestations, although nothing definite was known, it was clear that a word, a single word, the least imprudent word, would suffice to reveal all, to throw light upon the obscure presentiments brooding in all souls. This was just what happened, and behold in what way:

There had been two consecutive providential lights: one weak, but which aroused attention; the other absolutely brilliant, and which banished all doubts.

Sister Péronne-Rosalie de Farges, who was going

[1] Année Sainte, vol. ix. p. 216.

into retreat, went to ask her mistress on what she should make her prayer during it. Margaret Mary gave her a book to help her. "In this book," says Sister de Farges, "she had by mistake left a note written by her own hand, and in very nearly these terms: ' *The Lord made me understand this evening at prayer that He desires to be known, loved, and adored by men; that for this end He will communicate many graces to them when they shall have consecrated themselves to love and devotion toward His Sacred Heart.*' "[1] We may well believe that Sister de Farges failed not to show this note to her dear companions of the novitiate, and that by it Margaret Mary's reputation for sanctity increased. Her novices now began to suspect that it was not in books that she had learned what she said of the Adorable Heart of Jesus.

Shortly after, an absolutely unforeseen event raised the veil. We must recall the fact that Father de la Colombière was now dead two years, February 15, 1682. Among his papers had been found notes written during a retreat. These notes were so redolent of sanctity; they furnished so beautiful an idea of his great soul; they might, besides, be so useful to the pious in general, that the Jesuits resolved to publish them. The work appeared at Lyons, under this title: "Spiritual Retreat of Rev. Father Claude de la Colombière:" and, naturally enough, one of the first copies was sent to the Visitation of Paray. The good Mother Melin, before reading it herself, had it read aloud in the refectory, wishing thus to gratify more quickly the pious desires of all the Sisters. The little volume, which had excited veritable enthusiasm in the Community, was almost finished when the reader stumbled unexpectedly upon a certain passage; and, strange to say, Sister de Farges was reader that day. After saying that, should it please God to restore him to health, he resolved to promote with all his strength devotion to the Blessed Sacrament,

[1] Process of 1715, Deposition of Sister de Farges.

Father de la Colombière added these words, which the Sister read with ever-increasing devotion:

"I have recognized that God wishes me to serve Him by furthering the accomplishment of His desires concerning a devotion He has suggested to *a person to whom He has communicated Himself very intimately, and to serve whom He has graciously pleased to make use of my weakness.* I have already taught it to many in England. I have written of it in France, and implored one of my friends to endeavor to make it appreciated. It will be very useful to them, and the great number of chosen souls in that Community makes me think that its practice in that holy house will be very agreeable to God. Why, my God, cannot I everywhere publish what Thou dost expect from Thy servants and friends?

"God, then, having revealed Himself to a person who, from the great graces that He has given her, we have reason to believe, according to His Heart, she explained them to me, and I obliged her to put in writing all that she told me. I have much desired to write it myself in the journal of my retreats, because the good God wishes, in the execution of this design, to make use of my poor services.

"'Being before the Blessed Sacrament during one of its octaves,' said that holy soul, 'I received from my God some most sublime graces of His love. I was filled with the desire of making Him some return, and of rendering Him love for love; but He said to me: *Thou canst never do anything greater for Me than what I have already so many times asked thee.* And exposing to me His Divine Heart, *See this Heart,* said He, *which has loved men so much that it has spared nothing, even to exhausting and consuming itself, in order to testify to them its love. In return I receive from the greater part only ingratitude, by reason of the contempt, irreverence, sacrilege, and coldness that they show Me in this sacrament of love. But what I feel yet more is that there are some hearts consecrated to Me that treat Me thus. It is for this reason that I ask thee that the first Friday after the octave of Corpus Christi be set apart as a special feast to honor My Heart, by making an act of reparation, and by communicating on that day to repair the indignities it sustained during the time of exposition on the altars. I promise thee that My Heart will expand to pour out abundantly the influence of its divine love upon all that will render it this honor.'*"

We have said that Sister Péronne-Rosalie de Farges was the reader. At the first word she divined all, and cast a furtive glance at Margaret Mary, who sat facing her in the refectory. "When," said she in her deposition, "I came to what concerned the revelation of the Sacred Heart, I looked at the venerable Sister. She was sitting with her eyes lowered and looking profoundly annihilated."[1] The Community felt the same emotion. "Not only deponent," continued Sister de Farges, "but the Community understood then that it was the said servant of God who had made these predictions."[2]

The young alone recoil not in the presence of what would deter or awe others. On leaving the refectory, Sister de Farges unhesitatingly approached the saint with: "Aha! my dear Sister, haven't you heard your manifestation in the reading to-day[3] to your heart's content?" What could Margaret Mary do before so direct a question? Deny it? Impossible! Acknowledge it? Her humility forbade such a course. "Saint-like she bowed her head, and replied that she had great cause to love her abjection."[4]

From that moment the novices entertained no more doubt on the subject. To them Margaret Mary was a saint honored by most secret communication with the

---

[1] Process of 1715, Deposition of Sister de Farges.
[2] Ib.   [3] Ib.
[4] We are astonished that like facts have not yet been found in any life of Margaret Mary.

Lord. They divided among themselves little scraps of her clothing, and when Sister Anne-Alexis de Maréschalle cut her hair, they eagerly strove for the relics. It is also probable that from this day Sister Margaret Mary maintained a little less reserve in her communications with her young novices. She regarded the revelation made by Father de la Colombière as providential, and the Friday after the octave of Corpus Christi "she ventured to hang on the novitiate altar a little pen-and-ink picture of the Sacred Heart." [1]

The feast of the saintly mistress, July 20, 1685, was now approaching, and the novices resolved to celebrate it with pious solemnity, in accord with the sentiments they entertained for her. Margaret Mary, noticing this preparation, asked them smilingly if they desired to make her very happy. Reading the answer in the glowing countenances of her dear novices, she begged that all the testimonies of affection they were preparing for her should be offered to the Divine Heart of Jesus. The novices understood, and in an instant changed their plans. Under a stairway that led to the tower or belfry, was an apartment large enough to accommodate a little altar, and very capable of being transformed into an oratory. Sister des Claines seized her brush, and covered the walls, the ceilings, the rafters, the planks with flowers and stars and fiery hearts that may still be seen.[2] They erected an altar, ornamented it with roses, and placed in its centre the little picture of the Sacred

---

[1] The original is at the Visitation of Turin. We read at the bottom: "This picture is the first ever venerated under the title of the Sacred Heart of Jesus, in the novitiate of the Visitation convent of Paray." The Heart is surrounded by a crown of thorns and surmounted by a cross. Not knowing how to express the love that consumed it, the opening with a lance is represented, and in the centre is written "*Charitas.*" Around the crown we read "Jesus, Mary, Joseph, Joachim, Anne." We do not know whether this picture is by the hand of Margaret Mary herself or by that of one of her novices.

[2] Année Sainte, vol. ix. p. 730.

Heart from the novitiate. With Mother Melin's consent they had noiselessly employed part of the night in this work. In the morning, however, they were less fortunate ; for having advanced their duties, in the refectory, in their eager joy, they forgot themselves a little, and thus attracted the attention of some of the dear Sisters. Informed by them of what was taking place, Mother Melin went to seek the novices. But they soon gave her reasons so good for what she had heard that she went away satisfied, and the little troop finished their humble preparations in peace.

At nine o'clock, Prime being over, Margaret Mary went to the novitiate, whence, without saying a word, she was led to the little oratory. Surprised and delighted, she thanked her dear novices for the joy they gave her. Radiant, and with the ardor of a seraph, she addressed to them some glowing words; and then, prostrating before the picture, her example followed by the novices, she publicly consecrated herself to the Sacred Heart. Each of the novices did the same, repeating in turn the words of the formula Margaret Mary had used. After this she invited them to retire awhile with her into solitude, there to write the sentiments with which they had just been penetrated, promising them to add a word below their act of consecration. The whole morning was thus piously and joyously passed.

After the noon-obedience Margaret Mary again reunited her novices around the little altar. She was even more radiant than in the morning, the happiness of her holy soul beaming in her countenance. She congratulated her novices, and blessed God. In her transports of love, she would have wished the rest of the Community to come to offer their homage to the Heart of her good Master.[1]

Hearing her speak thus, the amiable and impetuous Sister Verchère hurried off to the Sisters, who were walk-

[1] Contemp., p. 206.

ing in the garden, related to them what was taking place in the novitiate, and begged them to come offer their homage to the Heart of Jesus. But she was rather ungraciously received. "As they were daughters of strict observance," wrote their contemporaries, "to whom this just proposition was made, they sent her back more quickly than she had come, telling her that it was not the province of little novices to introduce novelties,[1] and quoted a point of the Rule by which such things are absolutely prohibited."[2] Sister Verchère said, also, in her deposition: "The most exact were decidedly the most opposed, because they feared novelty."[3]

Of this number was Sister Catherine-Augustine Marest, renowned for the ardor of her penance, frequently carried to heroism; Sister Marie-Séraphique de la Martinière, always recollected as an angel, and so tenderly united to God that our old Mémoires say she died of love ; finally, and especially, Sister Marie-Madeleine des Escures, whom the contemporary manuscripts call "the saintly Mother Marie-Madeleine."[4] It was she who was most persistent in her refusal, "although she was the intimate friend of their incomparable mistress."[5]

[1] Contemp., p. 208.

[2] Constitutions of the Visitation, Constitution XVIII. "Now, as human minds are apt to take a secret complacency in their own conceits, even under a pretext of devotion or of an increase of piety ; and as it nevertheless happens at times that a multiplicity of offices hinders due attention, alacrity, and reverence, the Community shall not be allowed, under any pretext whatever, to charge itself with any other Office, or ordinary prayers, but those that are assigned in these Constitutions and in the Directory. For thus it will be better qualified and better able to say and sing the Office with that gravity and respect now observed in it."

[3] Process of 1715.

[4] Contemp., p. 208.

[5] "Abridgment of the Life and Virtues of our dear Sister Marie-Elizabeth de la Salle." She was placed under the direction of our very honored Sister Marie-Madeleine des Escures, one of the best friends of our saintly Sister Alacoque, who always regarded her as a true saint.

"Go say to your mistress," she replied to Sister Verchère, "that the best devotion is the practice of our Rules and Constitutions ; and that that is what she ought to teach you and the others to practise well."

Little Sister Verchère did not expect this reception ; she was, consequently, much astonished and embarrassed. However, not to sadden her mistress on such a day, she merely said, on returning, that the Sisters could not come.

"Say, rather," quickly responded Margaret, "that they will not come. But the Sacred Heart will force them to render it homage." And alluding to Sister Marie-Madeleine, she continued : "There are some now opposed to it, but the time will come when they will be the first to forward the devotion." This, indeed, happened in the most unexpected manner before the end of the year.

Margaret Mary was in reality right in calling the whole Community to render homage to the Heart of Jesus, because she had received that commission from God. In refusing to go, Mother Marie-Madeleine had done no wrong ; for Margaret Mary's mission was not yet vouched for by any one,—not by the Pope, the definitive and sovereign judge of devotions in the Church; nor by the diocesan bishop, the judge in the first instance, nor even by Margaret Mary's Superiors. Mother Marie-Madeleine waited, then, faithful guardian of the Rules, holding to them, and doing well to hold to them, since she was not yet authorized to stray from them ; although, assuredly, if she had looked into them a little more carefully, and if she had had a broader and more liberal mind, she would have understood that this devotion came forth from the very bowels of Christianity; or, without going so far, she would have found it born of the books of even St. Francis de Sales and St. Chantal. But though very holy, Mother Marie-Madeleine rose not so high. In this house she represented the positive side, the practical and literal interpretation : and in that is contained all that is absolutely necessary to a Community. It is, moreover, the most secure, provided its members acknowledge that God can make exceptions, and know how to submit to them when the trial shall be made. This will happen at the time fixed, and will crown saintly Mother Madeleine with an aureola most pure. After having resisted so long as the will of God was not manifested to her by the voice of her Superiors, she was the first to submit after they had spoken. We shall see her prostrating before the Sacred Heart, bringing after her the entire Community, and making a public consecration, which will at the same time be an act of contrition and reparation.

The rest of the day was passed in the novitiate in peace and recollection almost heavenly. That evening Margaret Mary again assembled her novices. She appeared to them as if transfigured. The manuscript here repeats an expression already used twice before, and which better than any other conveys the general impression : "She looked like a seraph." It is probable that with prophetic gaze she saw far ahead of her own age. In this little novitiate adoration she beheld similar acts multiplied in the future ; she saw them become universal and perpetual, rewarming the Church, saving France, and bringing to God new and greater accidental glory.

Good Mother Melin had sanctioned this feast; but seeing how it was received in the Community, she now believed it her duty prudently to efface it. She was a peace-loving soul, unequalled in sweetness, her great condescension gaining for her the title of a true daughter of St. Francis de Sales, a title acquired by the imitation of the great saint's virtues.[1] That evening, therefore, the novices having retired, she went to find Margaret

[1] Contemp., p. 210.

Mary ; and, though permitting her to adore and teach the Heart of Jesus in the novitiate, yet, in order to calm minds, she forbade her to do anything that could attract the attention of the Community.

Margaret Mary obeyed : first, because she always obeyed; and secondly, because, having cast a look on the Adorable Heart of her good Master, she thought she heard a voice that said to her : " Fear nothing, My daughter. I shall reign in spite of My enemies and those that wish to oppose Me." [1] Of enemies He had none in the convent, since " it was the most exemplary ; " though there were some that, " fearing novelty, made opposition." We shall not be slow, however, to meet them in the world ; and the way in which the Heart of Jesus will triumph over them, and " reign in spite of them," will furnish the greatest proof that the finger of God is here.

[1] Contemp., p. 211.

CHAPTER XIII.

THE APOSTOLATE OF THE SACRED HEART BEGUN— WITH WHAT MODESTY AND ZEAL MARGARET MARY BEGINS TO SPREAD DEVOTION TO THE SACRED HEART.

1686–1689.

"Ite, angeli veloces, ad gentem convulsam et dilaceratam; ad populum terribilem, post quem non est alius; ad gentem expectantem et conculcatam, cujus diripuerunt flumina terram ejus."

"Go, ye swift angels, to a nation rent and torn in pieces: to a terrible people, after which there is no other : to a nation expecting and trodden under foot, whose land the rivers have spoiled."—*Isaias* xviii. 2.

"Trahe me, post te curremus in odorem unguentorum tuorum."

"*O Heart of Jesus*, draw me! We will run after Thee to the odor of thy ointments."—*Cant.* i. 3.

IN asking Sister Margaret Mary to desist for the present from any effort to spread the new devotion in the Community, Mother Melin had not forbidden her to labor at making it known outside the grate. The hour was come. Margaret Mary was more and more consumed with love of the Adorable Heart. This divine fire, having been restrained so long, must now be allowed to burn unchecked. With the Lord, Margaret Mary might have said: "I am come to bring fire on the earth."

At the beginning of this year, 1686, she wrote: "It seems to me that I can breathe only to increase devotion to the Heart of Jesus. He sometimes enkindles in my heart so great a desire to make it reign in all other hearts that there is nothing I would not wish to do and suffer for this end. Even the pains of hell, without sin, would be sweet to me."[1] "I am no longer able to occupy myself with any other thought than that of the Sacred Heart of my Jesus. I should die content could I procure it any honor, even should my efforts bring me as recompense only eternal pain. Provided I love Jesus and that He reigns, it is enough for me. Contradiction often made me almost resolve to cease speaking of His Heart; but I was so severely reproved for my vain fears, and afterwards so strengthened and encouraged, that I have determined, whatever it may cost me, to pursue my purpose to the end. But if obedience should not permit me, I shall stop; for to it I defer all my views and sentiments."[2] "Life is to me so heavy a cross that I can find no consolation in it, excepting that of seeing the Heart of my Saviour reign. For this there is nothing that I would not wish to suffer."[3]

The first two of the foregoing extracts are from a letter addressed to Mother Greyfié, who, after leaving Paray in 1684, had been nominated Superioress of the Visitation of Semur-en-Auxois. The third is taken from a letter to Mother de Saumaise, who was then Superioress at Dijon. Mother de Saumaise had passed three years at Moulins, where she prepared Mother de Soudeilles to understand and relish the mystery of devotion to the Heart of Jesus. These were the three religious chosen to begin the work of the apostolate. Hidden in her humility, not wishing to appear in anything, having a "horror of letters and the parlor," Saint Margaret Mary will be their inspiratrix. They, more advanced in years; more at liberty, since they are at the head of Communities; and more fearless, since it was not to them that the revelations had been made;—they, to use the expression of Mother de Saumaise, will be the speaking-trumpets, the precursors, the heralds of the Sacred Heart. The first thing that Saint Margaret

[1] Letters of Blessed Margaret Mary. Letter XXXV.
[2] Letter XXXV.   [3] Letter LXXX.

Mary desired was a picture that would attract the gaze and prepare the heart. No devotion can become popular without this condition, and all great love has need of it. Hardly were the first Christians inclosed in the catacombs, before they wished to provide for themselves this gratification. They tried to paint on the walls of their obscure abodes the features of the Saviour, of His Virgin-Mother, and of the apostles. Unskilful as were their brushes, coarse and imperfect as may be their sketches, they are even at the present day, even after Fra Angelico and Raphael, not without some charm for those that contemplate them. They are wanting in art, but not in heart. Similar things will take place at Paray, whose inmates were at first satisfied with " a simple pen-and-ink drawing on paper," but who now long for something better. The difficulty was, however, very great. There was question not only of representing but of idealizing a heart, and, by some magical stroke of the brush, to show forth in it both divinity and love. Van Eyck has skilfully depicted in the face of a lamb all the majesty of a God. But there was no Van Eyck at Paray. Alas! no Van Eyck has since arisen, neither at Paray nor elsewhere. After two whole centuries of trial and methodizing, we are still awaiting the master-hand that shall make the canvas breathe the immaterial beauty of the passion that consumed Margaret Mary, the Adorable Heart of Jesus Christ. Meantime, as in the catacombs, Paray is trying some strokes of her timid brush.

One month after the novitiate fête, Margaret Mary wrote to Mother de Saumaise, to beg her to come to her assistance. " There has been here," said she to her, " a young man from Paris, a relative of one of our Sister-novices. The latter having spoken to him of it, he generously offered to procure for us a picture as beautiful as we can desire. All that we have to do is to find

the model."[1] This was the difficulty. To encourage
Mother de Saumaise to overcome it, and to seek at
Dijon, the old capital of Burgundy and the focus of
letters and art, a painter capable of a task so difficult,
Margaret Mary spoke to her of a vision she had just
had. In it Our Lord had told her that souls devout to
His Sacred Heart should never perish; and that, as it
is the source of all benedictions, He would pour them
out abundantly upon every place in which the image
of this amiable Heart should be exposed for love and
adoration; that He would by this means reunite divided
families; that He would protect souls in necessity; and
that He would give a special grace of salvation and
sanctification to the first who would have this holy picture made.[2]

On another occasion she wrote with even more importunity: "I should be very much pleased to know
whether you can do something that the Sacred Heart
of our good Master has destined and reserved for you.
. . . It is that, as you have been the first to whom He
is well pleased that I disclose His ardent desire of being
known, loved, and adored by His creatures, He wishes
you to be the one that will have a plate made of the
picture of the Sacred Heart; so that all that wish to
render Him special homage may have those pictures in
their houses, and smaller ones to carry on their person.
It seems to me that it would be a great happiness for
you to be able to procure Him this honor, for which you
will be more abundantly recompensed than for anything that you have hitherto done in your whole life."[3]

In similar terms, and with yet more ardor of soul,
Margaret Mary wrote of it to Mother Greyfié: "If you
knew, my good Mother, how much I feel urged to love
the Sacred Heart of our Lord Jesus Christ! It seems
to me that life was only given me for this! . . . He has
favored me with a visit that has been extremely advan-

[1] Letter XXXVI.   [2] Letter XXXII.   [3] Letter XXXVI.

tageous to me, owing to the good impressions it has left in my heart. He has repeated that the pleasure He takes in being loved, known, and honored by His creatures is so great that, if I do not mistake, He has promised me that they who shall have been devout to His Heart shall never perish; and that, as He is the source of all benedictions, He will pour them out abundantly upon every spot in which shall be exposed and honored the image of His divine Heart." Margaret Mary, having specified those benedictions almost in the same terms as in her letter to Mother de Saumaise, adds: " He has given me to know that His Sacred Heart is the Holy of holies, the sanctuary of love; that He wishes to be known in our day as the Mediator between God and man, for He is all-powerful to restore us peace, by turning from us the chastisements our sins deserve, and to obtain mercy for us." [1]

Mother Greyfié had just finished reading Père de la Colombière's *Retreat*. That reading on the one side, this letter on the other, the perfect knowledge that she had of the sublime revelation of the Sacred Heart and of the Sister's sanctity, convinced her that the hour for a solemn act was come. Having, probably, at her command a painter of some merit, she caused a picture of the Adorable Heart of Jesus to be executed in oil, and hung it above the altar of a little oratory. There, at the head of the Community, she knelt and solemnly consecrated herself to the Heart of her Divine Master. No one could have repaired more simply her former hesitancy, nor given to the whole Order, of which she was one of the most eminent Superioresses, a more brilliant example. Moreover, wishing to give Margaret Mary a present that would go straight to her heart, she had a copy of the picture made, added to it a dozen little pen-and-ink drawings of the Sacred Heart, and sent them to her for a Christmas gift.

[1] Letter XXXIII.

The saintly Sister could not contain her joy. She wrote at once to Mother Greyfié and thanked her heartily: "I cannot tell you the consolation that you have given me both by sending me the representation of the amiable Heart and by wishing to help us honor it with all your Community. You have caused me transports of joy a thousand times greater than if you had put me in possession of all the treasures of the world."[1] A little later she says: "I shall now die content, since the Sacred Heart of my Saviour begins to be known and I remain unknown. I remind you of your promise to me, namely, to do all you can to prevent any mention of me after my death, except to ask prayers for the most needy and wicked religious of the Institute. . . ." She concludes with: "He wishes that I should say to you that your Community has so won His friendship, by being the first to render adoration to His Heart, that it has become the object of His complacency. When praying for it, He does not wish that I should name it other than *the well-beloved Community of His Heart.*"

Whilst thus, in terms of admirable humility, pouring out her gratitude to Mother Greyfié, Margaret Mary lost no time in distributing the little pictures to those who would most profit by them. She sent one to the Jesuit Fathers of Paray, two to Mother de Soudeilles and to Sister de la Barge at Moulins, and one to Mother de Saumaise at Dijon. The last mentioned was accompanied by an imploring request to have a copper-plate engraving of it made, for the little pen designs could not be distributed in sufficiently large numbers. "If," said she, "we had a plate, we could scatter them far and wide."

Mother de Soudeilles, having received the two pictures of the divine Heart, kept the smaller one to wear always on her heart; and the larger she exposed for the veneration of the Sisters in the room in which

[1] Letter XXXIV.

their sainted foundress had died. From that day the oratory was more than ever frequented; and on the first Friday of every month the whole Community used to assemble there to make on their knees the Act of Reparation.

Deeper, perhaps, than even the joyous impression made upon Margaret Mary herself on learning of the solemn consecration of Semur to the Sacred Heart was that produced on the Community of Paray, and on Sister Madeleine des Escures in particular. The convent of Paray was, so to say, divided at that time into two large parties: the party of the aged, the rigid observers of the Rule, fervent guardians of the customs, having at their head Sister Marie-Madeleine; and the younger members, formed by Margaret Mary, over whom reigned her holy influence and into whom she had instilled some of her own devotedness to the Heart of Jesus. Between these two parties the prudence of good Mother Melin maintained peace. Mother Greyfié, so rigid and so firm in her goodness, had once belonged to the first-mentioned party; consequently, when what she had just done became known, a profound sensation was created, and no one felt it more sensibly than Sister Marie-Madeleine. In her heart she had always been tenderly united to Margaret Mary, whom she both loved and venerated; but her reason inclined toward Mother Greyfié. She knew her as a rigorous observer of the least point of the Rule; she knew her as no innovatrix, and as one that acted only after most serious reflection. She had lived six years under her administration, and she regarded her as one of the pillars of observance, one of the firmest columns of the Institute. If, then, Mother Greyfié had prostrated before the Sacred Heart, and solemnly inaugurated the new devotion, why should she still hesitate? Who could doubt after such an example? Surely there was nothing contrary either to the letter of the Rule or to the spirit

of the Visitation, much less to the doctrines of holy
Church. Sister Madeleine spoke of it to Mother Melin,
who had long been a secret adherent of the sacred cause,
and in union with her she quickly and quietly prepared
for a public act of reparation.

For this they chose the Friday after the octave of
Corpus Christi, the day fixed by the eternal decrees to
be in the Church the great day of adoration of the
Heart of Jesus. That morning, on entering the choir,
the Sisters perceived in the middle of it something like
a little repository. They drew near, and looked at it.
On a little altar covered with tapestry was exposed, in
the midst of flowers and blessed tapers, a picture of the
Sacred Heart, the same that Mother Greyfié had sent
to Margaret Mary. A card, signed by Sister Madeleine,
was fastened to the altar. It bore on it an invitation to
the Sisters to kneel and consecrate themselves to the
Adorable Heart of the Lord. No longer did they
hesitate. The old without exception, led by Sister
Madeleine, the young conducted by Margaret Mary, in
whose enthusiasm they shared, prostrated like two
choirs of angels. The latter offered to their Lord
joyous adoration; the former, prayers mingled with
regrets,—all uniting to form the purest incense most
agreeable to God. If the young had glorified Him by
their eagerness, the others had hardly done less by their
prudence. Saint Margaret Mary and Sister Madeleine
embraced, and henceforth there throbbed in that convent
but one heart to praise God and to adore the divine
Heart of Jesus. In the fervor of their enthusiasm, all
agreed upon the erection of a chapel in which to expose
a beautiful, large picture of the Sacred Heart.

Whilst awaiting the realization of this project, and
the better to repair what she termed her fault, Sister
Marie-Madeleine asked to be allowed the care of the
little oratory consecrated by the novitiate to the Heart
of Jesus. " I tell you that we have a second picture of

the Sacred Heart, and it is our dear Sister de Farges who painted it. It is, as I have desired, for the little chapel that was first erected to the honor of the divine Heart. Our dear Sister des Escures has charge of it, and it is a little bijou, so beautifully does she adorn it." [1]

Margaret Mary did not, however, lose sight of her first project. A picture in oil was all very well, though capable of being used only in one place. Some on vellum done with the pen were, consequently, executed everywhere,—at Paray, Dijon, Semur, and Moulins. But notwithstanding this activity, the demand for these pictures was constant. A copper-plate became absolutely necessary to produce them in considerable numbers and enable them to be distributed among the faithful. Margaret wrote about it to Mother de Saumaise, who was busily occupied at the time in having a large picture painted, and insisted that that was not what the Lord demanded of her. " It was to be," said Margaret, " a picture struck from a stamp, or a plate, so that every one could freely purchase according to his devotion." [2]

Meanwhile a Jesuit Father from Lyons proposed having a copper-plate made. He urged the matter, and showed great zeal for its prosecution. But when, at last, he received the commission to attend to it, he failed to take any further steps. He was, in truth, always travelling, always on missions. He promised everything, but accomplished nothing. At last, when sent to Aix, he proposed taking the picture with him and having it executed there. But this offer was not feasible. After a thousand difficulties, Margaret Mary succeeded in getting the model out of his hands. She sent it next to Mother de Saumaise, earnestly conjuring her to undertake the work. " Behold, my dear Mother," she wrote, " the drawing that the good Father has returned to us, though not without real dissatisfaction *a*'

[1] Letter LXXX.   [2] Letter XXXIX.

not being able to accomplish the work. But God does all for the best. He wills the picture to be better done; for the model, of which the Father sent us the copy, is neither pretty nor to my taste. You will oblige me infinitely by changing it." [1]

Mother de Saumaise had with her at Dijon a young Sister, Jeanne-Madeleine Joly, who was distinguished by her most tender devotion to the Sacred Heart. To her she communicated the contents of this letter, and expressed the wish that she would try to draw another that would better correspond to Margaret Mary's ideal. The Sister undertook the task with simplicity, and fully succeeded. "I cannot express," the saintly Sister wrote immediately, "my sweet transports of joy on receiving your model. It is just what I desired. The consolation I experience from the ardor you evince for the Sacred Heart is beyond my power to express. Go on with your work, my dear Sister, for I hope this divine Heart will reign in spite of all opposition. As for myself, I can but suffer and be silent." [2] The model which corresponded so well to Margaret Mary's wishes was not, however, executed at Dijon. After many unsuccessful preliminaries, it was sent to Paris, where, by the help of the first convent, the copper-plate so long desired was finally engraven.

The first step had now been taken for the royal glorification of the Heart of Jesus, and the diffusion of its devotion. Besides the pictures in oil, which began to multiply, the miniatures on vellum, the little pastels the pen drawings that circulated from convent to convent and were already distributed on the missions, there was now, after innumerable difficulties, a plate from which could be struck as many copies as were needed for distribution throughout the world.

Useful, however, as was the picture in making known and propagating the devotion to the Sacred Heart, it

---

[1] Letter LX.   [2] Letter LXI.

was in itself far from being sufficient. A book explain-
ing the picture now became necessary; a book to inter-
pret the devotion, and offer to the faithful suitable
prayers, litanies, and acts of adoration and reparation.
Had Margaret Mary been commissioned to do so, she
could have composed on this subject so many meditations, so many rapturous effusions, aspirations, and
prayers, that to choose from them would have been an
embarrassing task. But who would have dared suggest
such a thing to her ? That would have been to plunge
her "even to the centre of her nothingness." Sister
Jeanne-Madeleine Joly, the successful *artiste* of the
Sacred Heart, conceived the idea of writing a little
book of a few pages only, to explain the picture. She
notified Saint Margaret Mary of her intention, and
received in return most hearty congratulations with an
urgent request to hasten the work.[1] Submitted to Mgr.
de Langres and approved by his Vicar-General, the
tiny manual was printed before the end of the year, and
copies despatched at once to every convent of the
Order.[2] It accompanied the picture and rendered it
intelligible.

At Moulins, Mother de Soudeilles had conceived the
same idea as Sister Joly. She, too, composed a little
work on devotion to the Heart of Jesus. But, less discreet than Sister Joly, she inserted some prayers and
acts of consecration composed by Margaret Mary, thus
raising a corner of the veil under which the latter had
so carefully concealed herself. "We send you," wrote
Margaret Mary to Mother de Saumaise, "the little book
that Mother de Soudeilles has had published. After its
appearance, some persons of consideration (but who
they are I do not know) made her a present of the Litanies of the Sacred Heart, the Act of Reparation, and the
rest; and that has given me what I deserve, namely,
frightful confusion. As you read it, you will clearly

[1] Letter XLVII.   [2] Letter LXVI.

understand what I would say. I need not explain further. I have in some manner reason to accuse you; but the will of God be done!"[1]

Soon a Little Office of the Sacred Heart appeared, composed by a saintly religious, upon whom Margaret pronounced an extraordinary eulogium. He is so concealed under the cloak of humility that it was with difficulty that we were able to discover his name. The details of his life remain to us a secret. All we know is that he belonged to the Society of Jesus, and was called Father Gette. "You ask me the name of the saintly religious who, in the thought that the divine Heart required it of him, has composed a Little Office of the Sacred Heart. Excuse me at present from telling you. I can say only that he will be a second Père de la Colombière."[2] The Office was published, and shortly after put into French verse. "Adieu, my dear Mother! I think it will not be disagreeable to you for me to present to you a copy in verse of the Office of the Sacred Heart. It is considered very beautiful."[3]

The success of these little works, joined to the picture of the Sacred Heart, was considerable. The demand for them everywhere increased. Every one wished to have them. "We pray your charity to let us know whether they still publish those little Sacred Heart books; and if you do us the favor of sending us some, we shall remain infinitely obliged to you. You cannot conceive how eagerly they are asked for."[4] And again: "There is such a demand here for those little books that we can never have sufficient to satisfy the devotion of every one."[5] And elsewhere: "They have put the price of this book at seven sous. The first edition having been exhausted in a wondrously short time, behold already a second; and I do not believe it will stop there."[6]

The above could be said not only of Paray, Dijon,

[1] Letter LVIII.
[2] Letter LXXXIII.
[3] Letter LXXXVII.
[4] Letter LXXXVIII.
[5] Letter XCI.
[6] Letter CII.

Semur, Moulins, the places in which the devotion took birth; but at Lyons, Marseilles, Paris, everywhere, the same eagerness was manifested. "I must tell you something to the glory of the divine Heart, which will lead you to bless it anew. I gave a person from Lyons one of the little books of Dijon. She sent it to a young Father, who, having read it, showed it to his scholars at Lyons. They liked it so much that they made numbers of copies of the litanies and prayers, which they now recite with great devotion. These children, moreover, having shown them to others, the devotion took flights so grand that, as the manuscript copies failed to meet the demand, they resolved to have the book printed, and eagerly offered to defray the expense dependent upon it. A young workman urged the point with so much earnestness that it was found necessary to yield to his importunities. One of the most prominent publishers [1] of Lyons was applied to for the purpose; and, touched by the love of the divine Heart, he took the resolution to do it at his own expense. This gave rise to a pious struggle between the young workman and himself. The latter having gained his point, he demanded the book on the Sacred Heart, and took it to one of his friends to make some additions to it. A saintly religious undertook the task.[2] They have had a new edition printed, which is very beautiful and well bound. The demand for it has been so great that they have had a second edition of it since June 19th. This is only August 21st, and they are bringing out the third edition." [3]

The little book begins to be known out of France. "I assure you, my unique Mother, that it is a consolation for all that love it to see the devotion extending everywhere. The most honored Mother of our first convent of Lyons has sent it to Poland—I mean the little book for which they asked, and which they are going to translate into Italian."

[1] Horace Molin. [2] Père Croiset.
[3] Letter CV. [4] Letter CXIII.

Margaret Mary again writes, October 22d, 1689: "What consolation to hear of the happy progress of this sweet devotion! They write us from Lyons that the ardor and eagerness with which souls take to it are truly miraculous. They mention three or four cities in which the book is going to be published. Marseilles is one of them, and they have taken a thousand for that place alone. Of the twenty-seven religious houses in that city, there is not one that has not taken up this devotion so ardently that some are already *raising altars, others erecting chapels for it.*"[1] The devotion grew of itself. After the picture, the altar; after the altar, the chapel. They arose everywhere. This was a species of homage that was still wanting to the Adorable Heart of Jesus; one superior to all others, because more brilliant, more popular, and more lasting.

The first of all these chapels, that which had been enthusiastically agreed upon the day on which the entire Community of the convent of Paray prostrated before the Heart of Jesus, was finished September 7th, 1689, and dedicated with extraordinary solemnity. "The curés of the city and neighboring parishes, accompanied by immense crowds, assembled at the parish church, and then came in procession to our inclosure. The ceremony began at one o'clock, and lasted two hours."[2] On the altar was exposed the picture of the Sacred Heart that Mother de Saumaise had had enlarged from Mother Greyfié's miniature, and of which Margaret Mary had said: "I could not refrain from looking at it, for it is so beautiful."[3]

During the two hours that the pious ceremony lasted, our humble and happy Margaret knelt in the chapel, so ravished and abyssed in God that, among the many who so greatly desired to speak to her, not one dared do so. Numbers that had never before seen her regarded her with curiosity. They surrounded her on all sides.

[1] Letter CVIII.   [2] Contemp., p. 282.   [3] Letter LXXVIII.

Some even watched to see whether she would change her position; *but she knelt immovable as a statue.*[1]

What was passing at that moment in the interior of this holy lover of Jesus? That is a secret she never betrayed. But on beholding the triumph of the Sacred Heart, her soul must have cried out with the aged Simeon: " Now I shall die content, since the Heart of my Saviour begins to be known and adored."

The only regret we can have is that this chapel is built in the middle of the garden, in a place inaccessible to the people, instead of being located on the street. But piety was not to be checked by any obstacle. The people made the tour of the garden; and peasants were seen kneeling outside, leaning against the walls, their gaze turned toward that first temple in which was publicly adored the Heart of Jesus.[2] Then began the triumphal march of this great and tender devotion to Infinite Love! We can trace its progress in each of Margaret Mary's letters. Hidden and obscure at first, concealed, so to say, in the shadow of the cloister, we behold it clearing the grates, overcoming all barriers, and appearing in full daylight. The chapel of Paray was soon followed by a second, that of Bois-Sainte-Marie, built by Margaret's own brother. Then came that of Dijon, and a little later those of Moulins and Semur. Each Visitation house was soon to have its own. The devotion was begun. " I am most consoled to be able to tell you that great devotion is here entertained to the divine Heart of Jesus. Some persons who made novenas with lighted tapers have received what they asked."[3] " I have heard that a congregation is about to be erected under the title of the Sacred Heart of Jesus. I do not know whether it is at Paris or not, but I do know that there is another entirely dedicated to its honor."[4]

[1] Contemp., p. 282.
[3] Ib.
[2] Letter CXIV.
[4] Letter CI.

The last and highest act of homage, however, still remained to be rendered. Hitherto the devotion had been individual and private. To crown the honor thus far rendered the Sacred Heart, public worship must be joined to private, the Holy Sacrifice must be solemnly offered in honor of the Adorable Heart. Again it was to little Sister Jeanne-Marie Joly that this initiative glory belonged. Grown courageous in her love, she dared even to compose a Mass in honor of the Heart of Jesus. This she did in French, for she knew no other language. Then she begged good M. Charolaise, confessor to the Community, to put it into Latin, after which it was sent to Bishop de Langres, with importunate entreaties that he would be pleased to authorize its public celebration in the convent. The kind and saintly prelate joyfully accorded the favor asked.

So far so good. But even this could satisfy neither Sister Joly nor Mother de Saumaise nor the Community of Dijon. The bishop's approbation, they declared, must be followed by that of the Pope. A copy of the Mass was sent to the Superioress of the Visitation at Rome, with the request that it might be shown to Cardinal Ciborio, and by him to the Sovereign Pontiff. They implored His Holiness, very humbly indeed, but very importunately, to be pleased to accord his authorization to the public celebration throughout the whole Church of the feast of the Sacred Heart.

This was a bold stroke on the part of humble religious. What the prayers of our saint were during the negotiations, none can say; but in her letters is discerned a species of impatience not at all usual to her.[1] "It seems to me that I shall die content if you obtain the authorization of the Mass in honor of the Adorable Heart of Jesus."[2]

Rome's answer was long in coming. Rome is never in a hurry. Rome is patient, because she is wise. Rome

[1] Letter LXXXIII.   [2] Letter XCIII.

is slow, because she is eternal. But when the answer did come, it pierced the heart of Margaret Mary as with a sword of sorrow.[1] Rome replied that the time had not yet come for an approbation that would extend to the universal Church.

But on the kind representations of Cardinal Ciborio, the Mother Superioress of the Visitation at Rome added that there was no reason for discouragement; that it was necessary, first, to have the devotion publicly established in the diocese with permission of the Ordinary; and, when it should have been in existence for some time, it would be more easy to obtain Rome's decision in its favor.

Directed by counsel so wise, and sustained by Margaret Mary, who most confidently affirmed that, in spite of contradiction, the Heart of Jesus would triumph, Mother de Saumaise, or rather Mother Desbarres, now Superioress at Dijon, addressed herself to Bishop de Langres, and supplicated him to be pleased to permit the public celebration of the feast of the Sacred Heart, not only in the convent of Dijon, but in the whole diocese. The authorization having been granted, preparations were begun at the convent for the solemn honoring of the Heart of Jesus. However, as the public ceremony could not take place until after Easter, to satisfy the impatience of the Sisters a little private feast was organized. A picture of the Sacred Heart was placed in the sanctuary of the religious, and M. Bouhier, the Superior of the Visitation, celebrated the Mass, February 4, 1689, on the first Friday of the month, in presence of the Community alone. This Mass was the first ever said in the Catholic Church in honor of the Heart of Jesus. We leave you to imagine the delight of Mother de Saumaise, Sister Joly, Mother Desbarres, and of all those chosen souls who, urged on by love so pure for the Heart of their Beloved, to reach the result just at-

[1] Letter LXXXVII.

tained, had done so much, had struggled so hard. It was a heavenly day like unto that on which the first adoration of the Sacred Heart took place in the little oratory of Paray. From that time the picture of the Sacred Heart was exposed every first Friday in the sanctuary of the religious, who passed almost the entire day kneeling before the Heart of their Divine Master. Nothing could drive them from it.

The public fête took place after Easter. The Ducal Chapter of the Holy Chapel went in procession to the church of the Visitation, and there with musical accompaniment sang the Mass of which we have spoken.[1] The Blessed Sacrament was exposed all day in the midst of an unusual concourse, and shortly after a Confraternity for the Perpetual Adoration of the Sacred Heart was established. The whole city wished to belong to it ; and in a few days were recorded " six large volumes of names, among them some of the most illustrious of the province." The first hour of adoration was made by a venerable canon of the Holy Chapel, M. Benigne Joly, a man of extraordinary sanctity, the St. Vincent de Paul of Burgundy, the founder and promoter of all the great works of Dijon, whom the people had surnamed *the Father of the Poor*, and to whom the Church has decreed the title of *Venerable*. Public devotion to the Sacred Heart had been solemnly inaugurated.

Thus, little by little, remaining hidden as far as she possibly could, without noise, without issuing from her obscurity, did Margaret Mary begin to enlist adorers for the Heart of her well-beloved Spouse. Public devotion succeeded private. Already, even without effort on the part of the humble Margaret, excepting that made by her desires and prayers, the new devotion had been knocking at the doors of the Vatican, and had awakened the attention of the Sovereign Pontiff. It was

[1] Annals of the Visitation, by M. l'Abbé Colet (now Bishop of Luçon), p. 146.

easy to foresee, whatever might be the prudence of the Church in things so delicate, that a little sooner or later devotion to the Heart of Jesus would be enthroned on every altar of Christendom.

The facts thus far rehearsed were accomplished toward the middle of 1689. And now Saint Margaret Mary had only a few months more to live. We might think her mission ended; but most unexpectedly her sinking to rest was lighted up by new celestial beams. On the brink of the tomb, she received a new revelation, as brilliant as any of her youth. In it God showed her His great designs upon France, as well as another unexpected and admirable phase of the devotion to the Heart of Jesus.

CHAPTER XIV.

THE LAST GRAND REVELATION—THE KING AND FRANCE.

1689.

" Vive le Christ, qui aime les Franks!"

" Long live Christ, who loves the Franks! "—*Prologue of the Salic Law.*

" Non fecit taliter omni nationi."

" He hath not done in like manner to every nation."—*Ps.* cxlvii. 20.

THE revelation of the Sacred Heart is, beyond doubt, after that of the Incarnation and the Holy Eucharist, the most important of the revelations that have enlightened the Church. It is the most resplendent ray of light since Pentecost. Margaret Mary went so far as to declare that the Heart of Jesus would be in the Church as a " New Mediator;"[1] that is to say, as we can reach the Father only through the Divine Son become incarnate for us: in like manner we can henceforth reach the Son only by addressing ourselves to the infinite love of His Heart. This was Almighty God's first design. He had for end, as we have seen, to dissipate the darkness, to melt the ice that had accumulated, and to revive in the Church the fire of immolation and sacrifice.

But besides this first design, He had another relative to France, and in which we shall again discover that love of God for the Franks which for fifteen hundred years, notwithstanding our infidelities, has never abandoned us, and which is in a measure increased in proportion even to our ingratitude. We might have been able to suspect something of this second design, seeing first

[1] Letter XLIII.

that France was the chosen of all nations for the theatre of the manifestations of Infinite Love; and that it was to a French virgin, to a French religious Order, that God showed the high honor of being the confidants, the apostles, and the first adorers of His divine Heart. If we remark the nature of our wounds during the seventeenth and the eighteenth centuries, we shall not fail to see how sweetly, how delicately, how efficaciously this sublime devotion was adapted to their cure. Lastly, one might have been able to arrive at this conclusion, had he observed that it corresponds not less perfectly to the noble and sublime side of the French nature. Hence, one might have been able to foresee that, sooner or later, France would succumb to the charm of such a doctrine; and that, when all Christendom would have been subjected to the adoration of a Heart wounded by love, there would be between the French heart and that devotion so great an affinity that it would enthusiastically vow itself to its propagation; and that, once regenerated in its flames, it would regenerate the world. The distance, however, between the epoch of which we speak and that which was to realize the perfect beauty of God's designs over France was very, very great.

There are some saints, even contemplatives, who acquaint themselves with the affairs of their times, and who take part in them with the double glory of divine and human light. Witness a St. Teresa, whose admirable correspondence with Philip II. deserves to be better known, and which shows that great saint in an aspect altogether new. But our saintly Sister appears not in such a character. Born in an obscure village, hardly had she buried herself in an unknown cloister, in the midst of an unimportant town, than she is no more of this earth. She cares not for the politics of nations; she alludes not in her letters to what was then agitating her contemporaries. If Jansenism, in denying or depreciating Infinite Love, began to straiten and dry up the heart of man; if rationalism, the involuntary son of Descartes, in isolating mind from the other faculties, and particularly in separating the soul from the heart, continues and aggravates its detestable work; if sensism finishes by corrupting the heart; if ancient morals decay; if Louis XIV. passed from the guilty love of Mlle. de la Vallière to the shameful rule of Mme. de Montespan, leading the dance that merrily whirled the French Empire to its ruin; if the heart, attacked by so many enemies at the same time, was on the point of perishing, —would it not, at least, be elevated, purified, restored to health by contact with a pure heart? We repeat, it was not thus that things presented themselves to the eyes of Margaret Mary. She saw only her Well-beloved. She knew only that men do not love Him; that they forget Him and betray Him; that for the benefits He lavishes upon them He reaps only outrage. About their various degrees of sinfulness, about the difference between their offences of to-day and those offered Him in past ages, she cared little. And, in truth, that was of little consequence.

Once, however, she received a divine illumination on the disorders of the king and the court. The Superioress said to her one day: "Go and take the king's place before the Blessed Sacrament." Margaret Mary obeyed. All the time that she remained there, she, angelic purity itself, was assailed by thoughts and imaginations that filled her with horror. This experience was several times renewed. Her Superioress was obliged, at last, to withdraw her from a ministry in which she experienced torments to her so strange and new.

On another occasion she remarked, in one of her letters, that she perceived " *a strange spirit of pride* " prowling around the Visitation,—a strange spirit of pride, which wished to substitute itself for that of humility and simplicity, the " foundation of the whole edifice." [1]

---

[1] Letter XLIII.

That "spirit of pride" was Jansenism. But the saint did not know its name. She had seen it, not in the light of history, but in that of God. She had beheld it in ecstasy.

These are the only allusions in Margaret's writings that refer to contemporary events. Nothing, then, had prepared her for the grand revelation now about to be made to her. Her companions, her friends, her old and valued Superiors, were even less prepared for it than she. The first revelation related to the Church, and it gave rise to tempests. Those regarding France seem to have remained either unknown or ignored, for contemporaries make no mention of it. Mgr. Languet himself did not even suspect their existence: and how could he, since they have been known scarcely ten years? Like those pages whose invisible characters appear only when approached to fire, the flame of revolutions was necessary to draw from the obscurity of their archives the writings that record those revelations, and to direct attention to them after they had appeared. And who knows whether or not we possess all the monuments of that national revelation, as glorious to France as the conversion of Clovis or the mission of Joan of Arc?

Behold, at least, what we do possess of it, namely, three letters addressed in 1689 to Mother de Saumaise; admirable letters, in some of which the reader may detect a certain solemnity, and in others a certain impatience and fear of not being understood. They are like the last scene of the grand drama that so graphically depicts the manifestations of the Heart of Jesus.

The first letter bears date February 23, 1689, and is written to Mother de Saumaise to thank her for what she had done toward promoting devotion to the Sacred Heart. In it we see broached, though in vague words, the social and national side of that sublime devotion. "Ah, what happiness for you," she says, "and for those that contribute to it; for they draw upon themselves the friendship and eternal benedictions of this amiable Heart, and a *powerful protection on our country. It will not be less effectual to turn away the vengeance and severity of the just anger of God for so many crimes committed against it.*" She adds: " But I hope the divine Heart will become an inexhaustible source of mercy. It wishes only to establish its reign among us, in order to grant us more abundantly its precious graces of sanctification and salvation."

To show how necessary it is that repentance should begin where sin had begun, she says: " One thing that consoles me much is that I hope, in exchange for the bitterness this divine Heart suffered in the palaces of the great during the ignominies of His Passion, this devotion will in time magnificently flourish therein. Pursue, then, courageously what you have undertaken for His glory in the establishment of His reign. The Sacred Heart will reign in spite of Satan and all that may rise up to oppose it. But now is the time to work and suffer in silence, as He has done for our love."[1]

The second letter, though in a different sense, is much more important. It was written on coming out of ecstasy, on the Feast of the Sacred Heart itself, *Friday after the octave of the Blessed Sacrament,* June 17, 1689. The Spirit of God had rested on the holy Sister, and displayed to her in prophetic light His designs of mercy on France.

There is to the devotion of the Sacred Heart a private and a social side. Margaret Mary begins with the first.

" In fine, my dear Mother," she writes, " are we not all consumed in the burning heat of His pure love ? It will reign, this amiable Heart, in spite of Satan, his imps and his agents. This word transports me with joy. But to be able to express to you the great graces and benedictions it will attract upon all that shall have procured it the most honor and glory is what I cannot do in the way that He has given me to understand it.

[1] Letter of February 23, 1689.

"He has made me see the devotion to His Sacred Heart as a beautiful tree, destined from all eternity to spring up and take root in the midst of our Institute, and to extend its branches into the houses that compose it, so that each may gather from it fruits most pleasing to her liking and taste. But He desires that the daughters of the Visitation should distribute abundantly to all that will eat of it the fruits of this sacred tree. By this means He desires to restore life to many; and, by withdrawing them from the way of perdition, and destroying the empire of Satan in their heart, to establish in them that of His love."

Behold the first design, the supernatural, the special side of devotion to the Sacred Heart, that which regards souls at all times and in all places. Margaret Mary continues: "But He does not wish to stop here. He has *still greater designs*, which can be executed only by His almighty power."

Which are those designs that the Saint calls *the greatest*, and for which she invokes the All-powerful?

"He desires, then, it seems to me, to enter with pomp and magnificence into the palaces of kings and princes, therein to be honored as much as He has been despised, humiliated, and outraged in His Passion. May He receive as much pleasure therein at seeing the great ones of the world abasing and humbling themselves before Him as He once felt bitterness at beholding Himself annihilated at their feet!"

The tone of these words convinces one that Margaret Mary, when uttering them, was in a sort of ecstasy. What follows leaves no room for doubt on the subject.

"Here are," she continues, "the words that I heard on this point: 'MAKE KNOWN TO THE ELDEST SON OF MY HEART,' SPEAKING OF OUR KING, ' THAT AS HIS TEMPORAL BIRTH WAS OBTAINED THROUGH DEVOTION TO THE MERITS OF MY HOLY CHILDHOOD, IN THE SAME MANNER HE WILL OBTAIN HIS BIRTH OF GRACE AND ETERNAL GLORY BY THE

CONSECRATION THAT HE WILL MAKE OF HIMSELF TO MY ADORABLE HEART, which wishes to triumph over his heart, and by his mediation over those of the great ones of the world. IT WISHES TO REIGN IN HIS PALACE, TO BE PAINTED ON HIS STANDARDS AND ENGRAVEN ON HIS ARMS, IN ORDER TO RENDER HIM VICTORIOUS OVER ALL HIS ENEMIES.' "

Margaret Mary spoke only of the king, because, in the spirit of those times, the king and France were one. The king personified all the souls of France living and breathing in one single soul.

To comprehend Almighty God's request with regard to the standard, we must recall that, from the earliest ages, France had always had a sacred standard, one that was not borne to vulgar combats ; one that rested in the sanctuary of St. Denis under the shadow of the country's holy protectors. It was removed from its sacred shrine only when the monarch headed the army, when it was solemnly sought in the hour of greatest danger, or when it was to be carried afar to the holy wars. It symbolized the religious soul of France, and floated like a sacred prayer amid the nation's banners. It was a standard of this kind that God had given to Joan of Arc. He had prescribed its form and emblems, and communicated to it the secret virtue that roused exhausted France to unhoped-for triumphs. To-day, through the lips of the virgin of Paray, God asked of the king of France something of the same kind, a sacred standard which was to symbolize an act of faith. It was to be borne side by side with the nation's flag, and, in a voice that could be distinctly heard above the proverbial bravado of her enemies, proclaim that France places her trust in the blessing of God.

Mother de Saumaise was probably rather surprised by so serious a communication and one that tallied so little with what she knew of Margaret Mary's humility. She made no reply, and our sweet and humble *Mar-*

guerite became anxious at her silence. Were her letters lost? Would Mother de Saumaise, until then so courageous for the interests of the Heart of Jesus, hesitate before this new perspective? Again she wrote to her, August 12, 1689 : " I declare to you, my dear Mother, that your silence regarding the two long letters that I have had the honor to write you has given me a little pain. I know not to what to attribute it, except that perhaps I have set down my thoughts too freely and simply. I should perhaps have kept them concealed under an humble silence. You have only to tell me this, and I assure you that it will greatly gratify my inclination never to speak of these things, but to bury them in the secret of the Sacred Heart of my Divine Master. He is witness of the violence that I must do myself to speak of them. I should never have resolved to do so, *had He not made known to me that it is for the interest of His glory;* and for that I should cheerfully sacrifice millions of lives, if I had them, through my great desire to make Him known, loved, and adored. But perhaps you have not received my letters, *and that would be still more afflicting to me.*" [1]   It was perhaps in the fear that these letters were lost, and that in the event of her death her secret might not descend with her into the tomb, that Margaret Mary reduced to writing the following. It was in the month of August, some days after the 12th, perhaps the 25th, the feast of St. Louis. It is less a letter than a sort of declaration, throughout which reign unaccountable solemnity and majesty :

" Live ✚ Jesus !

"August, 1689.

" The Eternal Father, wishing to repair the bitterness and agony that the Adorable Heart of His Divine Son endured in the palaces of earthly princes, amidst the humiliations and outrages of His Passion, wishes to establish His empire in the heart of our great monarch,

[1] Letter of August 12, 1689.

of whom He desires to make use in the execution of His design, which is *to have an edifice erected in which shall be a picture of His divine Heart, to receive the consecration and homage of the king and all the court.*

" Moreover, this divine Heart wishes to make itself the defender of the sacred person of the king, his protector against all his enemies. Therefore has it chosen him as its faithful friend, to have the Mass authorized by the Holy Apostolic See, and to obtain all the other privileges that ought to accompany devotion to this divine Heart.

" It is by this divine Heart that God wishes to dispense the treasures of His graces of sanctification and salvation, by bestowing His benediction on the king's undertakings, according a happy success to his arms, and making him triumph over the malice of his enemies."

A consecration of the nation to the Heart of Jesus, a national temple raised to the Heart of Jesus, an inscription to the Heart of Jesus on the national standard— this is what Our Lord asked of the blessed Sister. Under this condition He will render the king, that is, France, victorious over all her enemies, and will give her an eternal reign of honor and glory.

Saint Margaret Mary then goes on to recount the best means for realizing this plan ; the best means for reaching the ears of Louis XIV. She mentions Père de la Chaise, the king's confessor, who at this time enjoyed great favor. " If the goodness of God," says she, " inspires this great servant of the Divine Majesty to employ the power He has given him, he may rest assured that he has never done an action more useful to God's glory, more salutary to his own soul, nor for which he will be better recompensed.

" It will be very difficult, on account of the great obstacles Satan purposes putting in the way, as well as of all the other difficulties God will permit in order to

make His power seen. He can effect all that He
pleases, though He does not always do so, not wishing
to do violence to man's will. *For this we must pray much
and get prayers."*

We may have remarked that in all these letters there
breathes a deep and holy enthusiasm. The Heart of
Jesus will reign in spite of its enemies! All that
God wishes from France—that national consecration,
that national temple, that inscription to the Heart of
Jesus on a standard,—all will be accomplished; *but it
will take time, and nothing less than the omnipotence of God
is necessary.* Fearful misfortunes will, moreover, take
place in the mean time.

We have not Mother de Saumaise's answer to this
letter of August, 1689. She who had known how to
reach Rome and arouse the thoughts of the Sovereign
Pontiffs would neglect nothing to reach even Louis
XIV. We know that she had recourse to the Superioress
of the Visitation of Chaillot, the refuge of Mlle. de la
Fayette, where dwelt the queen of England, and which
held, so to say, its door open to the court of Louis
XIV. Might it happen that Père de la Chaise would
not dare to speak of it to the king? Might it happen
that Louis XIV.'s soul would not be sufficiently humble
to comprehend the Christian grandeur of such a thought?
Be that as it may, those tender and magnanimous advances to the Heart of Jesus were not understood, and
Margaret Mary's last admonitions were without avail,
were lost in oblivion. They were, indeed, her last
words, for we are at the close of 1689, and she was nearing her death.

1689! Involuntarily we pause at this date, for it
evokes another, 1789! A century has just rolled by between the epoch in which an humble virgin, hidden in
the depths of a cloister, pointed out to Louis XIV. the
ark of salvation prepared for him by the goodness of
God, and that other epoch in which arose the storm

that was to sweep away the monarchy, and with it all other monarchies. If told in the days of his splendor of the perils in store for France, of the necessity of seeking a remedy, a shelter far above man, yea, even in the Adorable Heart of Jesus, Louis XIV. would have smiled incredulously. And yet this was true. From Louis XIV. France descended to Louis XV., from Louis XV. to Voltaire, from Voltaire to Robespierre and Marat; that is to say, from pride to corruption, from corruption to impiety, and from both the one and the other to a hatred of God and man which was to bring about her universal punishment.

Ah, this was only the beginning of our sorrows ! From 1789 let us go to 1889. There we find a new century, one scarcely less sad than its predecessor ; one in which minds are darkened and hearts chilled ; one in which nothing is lasting ; one whose every cycle of fifteen years witnessed a storm that carried away a throne ; one in which man lives amidst constantly recurring political convulsions, in distrust of the present, in uncertainty of the future.

It was for such times that had been providentially prepared, and it was in the midst of such catastrophes, that we see making its way, painfully but surely, devotion to that Heart which is meek and humble, which suited so well the age of Louis XIV.; which is pure, for it was of purity that Louis XV.'s reign had so much need ; which was consumed by love and devotedness, qualities that would not have proved prejudicial to the age of such as Robespierre ; which raises sad hearts and comforts crushed souls ; which suits our own times and all times.

CHAPTER XV.

MARGARET MARY'S MISSION ENDED—SHE IS CON-
SUMED IN THE FLAMES OF DIVINE LOVE—HER HOLY
DEATH.

1690.

" Sicut virgula fumi ex aromatibus thuris."
" As a pillar of smoke of aromatical spices."—*Cant.* iii. 6.

MARGARET MARY had finished her mission. It
now remained for her only to die ; or rather,
she must die that her mission may be accomplished. Those admirable revelations of God, of which
we know so much to-day, were known in the time of
Margaret Mary to only a few, and only three or four
knew them in detail. Many had only a vague notion
of them, and, through delicacy and respect for Margaret
Mary, no one dared speak of them. " I must die," said
she, " for I am an obstacle to this sweet devotion." [1]
Again: " I shall assuredly die this year, in order not to
prevent the great fruits that my Divine Saviour expects
to reap from a book *of devotion to the Sacred Heart of
Jesus,*" [2]—words that very much surprised Father Croiset, who was working at this book, but who had not yet
spoken of it to any one.

When Margaret Mary finished this first work, she
ended a second, one more personal but not less admirable : she had finished moulding her soul to the image
of the Sacred Heart. In the fire of suffering and of
voluntary sacrifice, what was human and imperfect in
her had been gradually consumed; all that was left
was purely celestial. As in all great fires, when everything has been devoured, the flames sink and gradually

[1] Letter XCIX.　　　　[2] Contemp., p. 294.

die out for want of fuel ; thus the sufferings, physical
and mental, that for so many years had overwhelmed
the saint one by one disappeared.   Hence she concluded that she was soon to die.   "I shall certainly die
this year," she exclaimed, "since I have nothing more
to suffer." [1]

The sacrifice was, in reality, nearing its consummation.
To the criticisms, the discussions, of which she had
been the object, succeeded a sort of deep and discreet
enthusiasm.   Not only were the Sisters daily witnesses
of her virtues ; not only the little boarders, who clipped
relics from her habit ; but priests and religious began
to make journeys to Paray, to have the happiness of
conversing with her.   On leaving the parlor they were
often heard to say :   "We came to see the saint !"
There was no one, not even the laborers in the convent,
that did not watch for her at the recreation hour, and
say to one another :   "Let us try to see the saint of the
house." [2]   "The women who did the washing never
called her anything else." [3]   On feast-days when the
grate was open, one could not prevent pious souls from
crowding against the bars in order " to catch a glimpse
of the saint."   The aureola of holiness was definitively
placed upon her brow ; and all contemplated with respectful admiration the victim approaching the consummation of her sacrifice on the altar.

Among the many virtues that excited admiration at
that last hour, what was most astonishing was her love
for the hidden life, carried almost to passion.   Ordinarily, when God calls a soul to a public mission, He
puts into it a sort of chivalric enthusiasm, a holy boldness that renders it capable of any undertaking.   Witness the pure and ardent St. Catharine of Siena, who,
in spite of the ruling powers, led the Pope back to
Rome after an exile of seventy years.   But in Margaret

[1] Contemp., p. 294.   [2] Process of 1715, p. 69.
[3] Vie et œuvres, tom. i. p. 201.

Mary we see nothing of the kind. From her cradle to her tomb, she thought but of hiding herself ; she never found a solitude sufficiently retired. The more brilliant became her graces, the more her craving after forget-fulness, contempt, and humiliation increased. Her greatest desire, a desire that on her deathbed amounted to a torment, was to destroy all that she had ever written, thus to prevent any word from ever being spoken of her. " It would be very sweet to me, my dear Mother, if you would assure me, as your charity has promised, that you will burn everything without exception ; that nothing may ever be seen or known ; for my desire to remain buried in contempt and forget-fulness after death is not less than that which I have had during life." [1] " How grateful I should be to you, my good Mother, if you would do me the favor of burn-ing all the writings that you have belonging to me." [2] " I pray and implore you to burn all my writings, for I do not wish that there should survive so wicked a sin-ner anything that could preserve her remembrance after death. I wish to be buried, annihilated in eternal oblivion." [3]

Her thirst for contempt and humiliation increased with her reputation. She wished to write no more letters, to appear no more in the parlor. " Tell me what I must do, for the number of letters written to me makes me suffer a most painful species of martyrdom, seeing that, though not wishing it, I have so deceived people. I think nothing can better undeceive them than my silence. I feel so strongly attracted to that course that, without extreme violence, I can no longer resist, whether for the parlor or for letters. If obedience did not constrain me, I should neither go to the one nor re-ply to the other. The only consolation that I have in this is that it is to me a cross, and the cross is good at

[1] Letter IX.   [2] Letter X.   [3] Letter XXXII.

all times and in all places." [1]   " Alas ! if you knew how criminal my life is, and how little conformed to my words, you would see that like a miserable sinner who, without willing it, has deceived others, it is most just for me to desire to be buried in eternal contempt and oblivion." [2]

She went to the parlor only when constrained by obedience, and whilst there kept herself so recollected, so abyssed in God, and so humble, that all gazed at her in admiration. "The great difficulty I have to speak," she said, " would prevent my ever doing so if obedience did not require it. It seems to me that, seeing myself so very wicked, contemptible, and despicable, I commit a great crime in speaking of myself. I am often aston- ished that the earth does not open under my feet and swallow me, on account of my great sins. Ask, I conjure you, the Sacred Heart to grant me the grace to die with it on the cross, poor, unknown, despised, for gotten by all creatures, overwhelmed by all sorts of suf- ferings ; but all according to His choice, His desire, not mine." [3]

The last words show us a second characteristic of Margaret Mary's inclinations. We do not think that any creature has ever loved suffering more, nor plunged into it with greater enthusiasm. " To tell you in a word of the delights with which His goodness has, up to the present, favored me, I cannot better express it than by saying that in mind and in body I am on the cross. I cannot complain of it, nor do I desire any other consola- tion than that of never having any in the world, and of living entirely hidden in Jesus Christ crucified, unknown in my sufferings. I wish no creature to have compassion on me, none to remember me, excepting to increase my torment." [4]

" I consider the hours that I have spent without suffer-

---

[1] Letter LXXX.   [2] Letter XCVI
[3] Letter LXXXV.   [4] Letter I.

ing as lost. Indeed, I assure you, my good Mother, that I do not wish to live longer unless I may have the happiness to suffer." [1]

The more Margaret's pain increased, the more her soul thrilled with joy. "As to myself, my dear Mother, alas! what can I say, excepting that it pleases the Lord to keep me in a state of continual suffering, my strength so exhausted that it is with extreme difficulty I carry my miserable body of sin. When I behold my sufferings, it seems to me that I feel the same joy that the most avaricious and ambitious do in seeing their treasures multiply." [2]

Every instant we meet similar utterances: "I know of nothing that so sweetens the prolongation of life as constant suffering in loving. Let us then suffer lovingly and uncomplainingly, esteeming as lost the moments passed without suffering." [3] "Who can hinder us from being saints, since we have a heart to love and a body to suffer?" [4] "Although I suffer as a criminal, it is that, however, which makes the prolongation of life endurable ; for in it there can be found no pleasure, excepting that of loving God and suffering in His love." [5] We may page through her letters, peruse her Mémoire, but in each we shall see that never was deeper passion expressed in cries more touching, never was it revealed in darts more penetrating. When we recall these words of Mother Greyfié: "The scourge had to be snatched from her hand ; for had we let her, she would have disciplined herself to blood,"—one involuntarily pauses in presence of one of the greatest examples of love of the Cross and passion for suffering that hagiology presents to the admiration of Christians.

There is no need to say whence arose in her virtues so elevated above nature. They came from the only source that can produce them : a love of God of which she

[1] Letter XI.   [2] Letter XXXIX.   [3] Letter LXXXVI.
[4] Letter XCII.   [5] Letter VIII.

herself was not able to note the beginning ; which was awakened in her crib ; and which, carefully cultivated, increased with age, arrived at its culminating point, and there consumed her life. There were, she said, three tyrants installed in her heart, which left her no longer mistress of any movement : the first was love of contempt ; the second, love of suffering ; the third, and the most insatiable of all, love of Jesus Christ. " God has put into my soul three persecutors that cruelly torment me : the first, which produces the other two, is so great a desire of loving Him that it seems to me that whatever I see ought to be changed into flames of love." [1] Her great motto was : " Love, suffer through love, and be silent. This is the secret of the lovers of the Beloved." [2]

Writing to a friend a short time before her death, " Love," she said, " and do what you please, for he that has love has all. Do all through love, in love, and for love ; for it is love that gives value to everything. Love wishes not a divided heart. It calls for all or none. Give, then, love for love, and never forget Him whom love has put to death for you. You will love Him only inasmuch as you know how to suffer in silence and to prefer Him to creatures." [3]

Under the empire of these three tyrants, where could there be room for the most imperceptible regard for creatures ? Although Margaret Mary had a very tender heart, its purity was charming. Her chastity was that of an angel. She herself has acknowledged that, except the day on which she was sent to take the place of Louis XIV. before the Blessed Sacrament, she never had even the shadow of a temptation. She had preserved her baptismal innocence. There was in her countenance something angelic, something ineffably pure ; though, at the same time, her eyes were so clear and her gaze so penetrating that one might have been embar-

[1] Letter XII.   [2] Letter LXXXIV.   [3] Letter LIII.

rassed under her holy glance, had it not been tempered by extreme sweetness and modesty. She possessed the secret of reading hearts. By a word, a glance, a sweet and delicate allusion, she frequently revealed to her novices that she knew their interior dispositions. One look, for example, sufficed to show her that one of the Misses de Vichy-Chamron was not, like her sister, intended for the Visitation ; and the importunity of her family, no more than the persecution her refusal to receive her excited, could make Margaret Mary yield. To another who ardently desired to enter the Visitation she said that God did not call her there; that He wished her to go to the Ursulines, where she would do great good. This happened, indeed, to the surprise of the whole Community. On another occasion she was in the parlor with a cousin, very young and gay, recently received among the Dominicans. Another relative present wished to check the young monk's gayety. " Let him laugh," said Margaret Mary; " these are his last joys, for he has not much longer to live." The young man died suddenly a few days after.

Margaret's vision extended beyond the most distant horizon. " Do you think, then," said she, smiling, to a lady who asked of her news of her deceased relatives, " that I know what passes in purgatory ?" But the facts disabused her words, and no one would have thought of putting such a question to her, had not some exact and striking revelations on several occasions declared her gift of prophecy.

To it she joined the gift of miracles. It happened one day that a good domestic Sister, whilst splitting wood, wounded herself with the axe. Fearing that this accident might cause her to be sent away, she tried at first to conceal it. But the wound increased, and, like the poor woman of the Gospel, she said to herself : *If I shall touch only her garment, I shall be healed.*[1] Follow-

[1] St. Matt. ix. 21.

ing out her good thought, she touched her wounded
limb to the hem of Margaret's garment, and she was
almost overcome with joy on perceiving the next morning no trace of her wound.

Thus did Margaret rise day by day to the summit of
sanctity. After having run through the elementary degrees so rapidly, she had arrived at that high pinnacle
upon which the heart of man unites itself to the Heart of
God, and has no longer any other than divine thoughts,
desires, and aspirations. But she had now gone a step
farther. She was elevated to that sublime state in
which the weakness of man, as says the Holy Scripture,
enters into the power of God, reigns like Him, sees into
the future, penetrates the secrets of souls, and sovereign-
ly commands the elements.

It must be added that, " although Margaret Mary
shone brilliantly in all the virtues, yet her sanctity entirely resolved itself into that love with which she so
ardently burned for the Heart of Jesus, and that amaz-
ing zeal which led her to draw all hearts to render Him
love for love." [1] We can say that this devotion was the
summary as well as the living and vivifying source of
all her virtues.

It was for the Sacred Heart that God had created
her, and it was by the Sacred Heart that He had conducted her to the summit of perfection. Thence came
her faith, her humility, her virginal modesty, her angelic purity ; and if, as a little one in the bosom of her
family, in the streets of the village of Vérosvres, people
said, on seeing her pass, " She is an angel," it was
because, though unknown to her, the Sacred Heart had
already darted upon her a first ray of love. Thence,
too, came her love for God and man, her apostolic
spirit, her zeal, her spirit of prayer, and her long contemplations from which she drew her grand, prophetic
lights on the Church, on consciences, and on the most

[1] Décret de Béatification.

hidden events.   Many of those lights had some connection with the mission she had received.   Thence also
her frightful sufferings, the trials that assailed her, the
doubts, the humiliations that God permitted, in order
that the heart of the humble virgin might be broken
and wounded like that of her celestial Spouse.   Thence,
in fine, came in the last years of her life that aureola of
sanctity which attracted the eyes of all.   In proportion
as she ascended above the horizon, the Sacred Heart
darted its rays upon her.   He who was so soon going to
inundate her with light allowed its reflection to shine
upon her forehead.

Heaven itself delighted to make it seen.   One day, a
good Sister, hearing holiness spoken of in the Community, said to herself: "Oh, how I should love to see a
saint!"   Instantly she heard a voice in the depths of
her heart: "Look at Sister Margaret Mary!"   She
raised her eyes to Margaret's face glowing with celestial
light from her recollection and union with God.

What Heaven thus showed to an humble religious
was not concealed from others.   The last mists were
slowly clearing away, and God's glory was appearing
on the countenance of His servant.   This could not
last.   It was a new martyrdom, more cruel than all
others, and absolutely above her strength.   She must
of necessity die.   It was necessary for her, and it was
needful for the exaltation of the Heart of Jesus, whose
grand revelations could no longer remain unknown.

There is no doubt that, from the beginning of 1690,
Sister Margaret Mary had of her approaching death the
most vivid light.   She spoke of it incessantly.   Vainly
did the Superioress, the Sisters, the physician smile on
hearing her proclaim her end as so near.   She sweetly
and humbly maintained that it would be "this year."
She told them how it would take place, and at a time
in which the Community was least expecting it.   She
even named the two Sisters in whose arms she was to

breathe her last sigh. "Dear Sister," said she to young
Sister Rosalie Verchère, who had never assisted at a
deathbed, and who very likely would be terrified at the
sight, "you greatly fear witnessing a death. Ah! very
well, depend upon it, I shall die in your arms and those
of Sister Péronne-Rosalie de Farges." [1]

July 22d, a little less than three months before her
death, she heard more distinctly than ever the call of
the Spouse. Although in good health, and only forty-
three years old, she solicited with so much importunity
the favor of making a forty days' retreat to prepare herself for death, that her Superioress could not refuse her.
She committed to paper some of the thoughts that then
occupied her, and which permit us to contemplate for
the last time the perfect beauty of her great soul.

"On the first day of my retreat my chief care was to
think whence could come to me this great longing for
death, since it is not usual for criminals, such as I am
before God, to be so easy about appearing before their
judge, and a judge the sanctity of whose justice penetrates even to the marrow of the bones. How, then
my soul, canst thou feel so great joy at its approach?
Thou thinkest only of ending thy exile, and thou art
enraptured at the idea of soon going forth from thy
prison. But, alas! take care that temporal joy, which
perhaps proceeds only from the blindness of ignorance,
plunge thee not into eternal sadness, and that from this
mortal and perishable prison thou fallest not into those
eternal dungeons where there will be no more room to
hope. Let us, then, O my soul, leave this joy and these
desires to die to holy and fervent souls for whom great
rewards are prepared. For us whose works leave us
nothing but chastisements to hope for, if God is not
more good in our regard than just, let us think what
will be our fate. Canst thou, my soul, endure for all
eternity the absence of Him whose presence fills thee

[1] Année Sainte, vol. ix. p. 214.

with desires so ardent, and whose absence causes thee pains so cruel?

" My God, how difficult it is for me to render this account! I feel it impossible to nerve myself up to it, and, in my impotence, I know not to whom to address myself unless to my Adorable Master. I have remitted to Him all the points on which I shall be judged, namely, my Rules, Constitutions, and Directory. It is on them I shall be justified or condemned. After confiding to Him all my interests, I felt admirable peace *under* His feet, where He held me for a long time abyssed, as it were, in my own nothingness, and there expecting that He would judge me, a miserable criminal."

Later on, having measured " the immensity of her malice," she adds: " I am insolvent. Thou seest it well, my Divine Master. Put me in prison. I consent, provided it be in Thy Sacred Heart. There keep me fast captive, bound by the chains of Thy love, until I shall have paid Thee all that I owe Thee; and as I shall never be able to do that, I shall never come forth from that prison."

We ask the most severe judges, could there be words more beautiful than these?

In this elevation of thought, this humility so true, this depth of sentiment, this peace and calm already heavenly, do they not recognize a great soul soaring to the loftiest heights? And when, overwhelmed with the remembrance of her sins, the blessed Sister asks, on the verge of the tomb, to be hidden in the Heart of Jesus, may we not find in that an indirect, though very high, proof of the perfect sincerity of her rare mind and noble heart?

In these sentiments Margaret Mary awaited death. Autumn came, the season in which the religious of the Visitation make their annual retreat. Now the eve of the day on which she was to begin hers, for that of the

month of July did not dispense her from the one prescribed by the Rule, she was taken with a slight increase
of fever. A Sister having asked her whether she could
enter her retreat, she replied: "Yes, but it will be into
the *great* retreat." The physician, Dr. Billiet, was called.
He venerated her as a saint, and used to say that her
maladies proceeded from divine love. He saw nothing
serious in her indisposition, and declared she would not
die of it. Margaret Mary, on the contrary, looking at
him smilingly, said: "After all, it is less culpable for a
secular than for a religious to tell a lie."

After a short interval she asked for little Sister Marie-
Nicole de la Faige des Claines, whom she called her St.
Louis de Gonzaga, wishing, as she said, to have her by
her when she died. "Come see me, my dear Sister,"
she said, as soon as she perceived her, "for I shall die
of this illness. We shall not have a long time to be
together." [1]

It was the eve of her death, though none suspected
it. The physician reassured the Sisters. The countenance of the invalid confirmed his words and dis-
pelled every trace of apprehension. However, toward
evening little Sister des Claines, who never left her,
observed that she suffered much, though from interior
pains, the nature and cause of which it was difficult
to divine. "You suffer," said she to her. "Oh, not so
much," the saint earnestly replied, and relapsed into
silence. A little later, toward the beginning of the night,
she called the little Sister, and spoke to her of the ardent
desire that consumed her of seeing God in heaven; adding that she would nevertheless prefer to remain on
earth till the last judgment if such were His good
pleasure.

The next day, October 16th, eve of her death, she
implored from early morning to have holy Viaticum
given her. As she was positively refused, her condition

inspiring no fears, she asked at least to be allowed to communicate, since she was still fasting. Her importunity was at last victorious. When she saw her Well-beloved entering, she opened wide her arms, and, with a vehemence that the witnesses declared themselves incapable of describing, thanked Him for coming to her. This was the last time she received her God on earth. She knew that it was to be so, and after the ceremony she told little Sister des Claines that she had communicated as Viaticum, because the end was near.

All who approached her on this last day admired the extraordinary joy depicted on her face. She was in continual outbursts: "Ah! what happiness to love God! Let us love Him, let us love Him! But let it be perfectly!" For one instant only the thought of divine justice crossed her mind. She trembled, then humbly and ardently kissed her crucifix. "Mercy, my God! Mercy!" she exclaimed. But this trouble was only passing. The next moment she plunged into the Heart of Jesus, and on her brow appeared a radiant serenity that was never more to leave it.

Once, after having said with great fervor: "What do I desire in heaven, and what can I wish on earth, except Thee alone, O my God!" she called her little infirmarian to her, and inquired: "Shall I last much longer?" The latter answered that it was the doctor's opinion she would not die. Then Margaret Mary cried out: "Ah, Lord! when wilt Thou recall me from this place of exile?" and asked Marie-Nicole to recite the Litanies of the Sacred Heart of Jesus and those of the Blessed Virgin. After that she desired her assistants to invoke St. Joseph, St. Francis de Sales, and her guardian angel to come to her aid; and then relapsed into a silence of several hours.

In the evening a last thought of humility, of love for the hidden life, began to preoccupy her. She called Sister de Farges, and asked her to burn all that remained of her writings, and particularly the Mémoire drawn up by order of Father Rollin. The Sister, seeing the peril, gently insinuated that it would be more perfect to remit herself into the hands of Superiors and abandon everything to holy obedience. At these words the patient ceased to insist. As Sister de Farges showed distress at seeing Margaret Mary so convinced of her approaching death, the saint repeated to her what she had several times said, namely, that her death was necessary for the glory of the Heart of Jesus.

Thus passed the day and the night of October 16th. On the morning of the 17th, whose eve she was not to see, being attacked by some slight fainting spells, she asked for holy Viaticum. The physician was called in haste. He again declared that there was nothing urgent in the case, and that she would not die. " You will see!" said the saint. When he left, she said to Sister de Farges, in allusion to the holy Viaticum just refused her: "Happily, I foresaw that. I doubted as to whether they would believe me so ill, and so I communicated yesterday for this intention." This last decision of the physician having reassured the Community, the Sisters dispersed to their various duties. Sister de Farges alone remained with Margaret Mary, who conversed with her upon the ineffable excess of God's love. Her words were few but inflamed. Towards seven in the evening, a slight convulsion having passed over the invalid, Sister des Claines ran to call the Superioress. At this moment Sister de Farges re-entered, and, thinking it only a passing crisis, tried to stop her. " Let her go," said Margaret Mary, "it is time."

The Superioress came, and wished to send for the doctor. "Mother," said Margaret Mary, "I no longer need any one but God alone, and to be buried in the Heart of Jesus."

In an instant all the Sisters, notified that she was in her last agony, hurried in and prostrated in tears at the foot of her bed. Margaret Mary collected her remaining strength to conjure them to love God, but without division, without reserve, and then warned them that it was time to give her Extreme Unction.

The priest entered and began the ceremony, the saint being recollected and absorbed in prayer. Suddenly she raised herself, to present her members for the last unction. At this moment two Sisters, impelled solely by their affection for her, threw themselves forward to support her in their arms. These two Sisters who rose so spontaneously were, to the right, Sister Péronne-Rosalie Verchère and, to the left, Sister de Farges—the same to whom the saint had foretold that she would die in their arms. They had lost sight of her words at the moment. They remembered the prediction only afterward, and affirmed the incident under oath. At the anointing of the Fourth Sense, Margaret Mary sweetly expired in their arms, pronouncing the Holy Name of Jesus, October 17, 1690, at seven o'clock in the evening. She was aged forty-three years two months and four days.

When the saint, consumed by seraphic ardor, was going to enjoy the sweet embraces of the Heart of Jesus,[1] an unknown beauty spread over her face; her features, so delicate and so pure, assumed a heavenly expression. The two young Sisters that supported her in their arms received such an electric current of divine love that one of them, Sister Verchère, scarcely twenty-four years old, made a vow the next day to do always what was most perfect; the other, Sister de Farges, vowed herself to that extraordinary life of sanctity which surnamed her a second Margaret Mary. The physician was kneeling at the foot of the bed. On recovering from his astonishment, he said that he was not surprised that Margaret Mary, having lived by love, had died of love. But one cry was heard throughout the house:

[1] Décret de Béatification.

The Convent of Paray-le-Monial, in which occurred the chief events of St. Margaret Mary's life: her novitiate, profession, revelations and death.

Chapel in Novitiate of Paray-le-Monial in which
St. Margaret Mary began her religious life.

St. Margaret Mary Alacoque,
Religious of the Order of the Visitation.

Autographed Record of St. Margaret Mary's reception of the habit,
reading in part as follows:

I, Margaret Alacoque, daughter of M. Claude Alacoque and Mlle. Philiberte Lamyn, having with their
consent lived for two months at this Convent, considered its rules and exercises and voluntarily petitioned
for the habit of a choir sister of this Congregation,
have, by the grace of God, obtained same together with
the name of Margaret Mary, this 25th day of August,
1671.

Sister Margaret Mary Alacoque.

Courtyard in which the Sacred Heart of Jesus, surrounded by
Seraphim, appeared to St. Margaret Mary.

Interior of Chapel of Visitation Convent at Paray-le-Monial in which the apparitions took place.

288-6

Picture of the Sacred Heart of Jesus as originally painted at
the Novitiate of Paray-le-Monial in 1685, and presented in
1738 to the Convent at Turin, where it is still preserved.

Altar in the room in which St. Margaret Mary died,
since transformed into an oratory.

Infirmary of the Convent, with the room in which St. Margaret Mary died indicated by + .

288-9

Shrine of St. Margaret Mary in the sanctuary of the chapel
in which the apparitions took place.

Beautiful hand-wrought reliquary in the form of a heart at
Paray-le-Monial, containing relics of St. Margaret Mary.

St. Margaret Mary Alacoque, 1647-1690.
This portrait is considered to be the best likeness of her.

"The saint is dead!" And that cry having crossed the grate, in an instant the whole town was in the parlors asking to see her for the last time. When taken to the choir, two entire days were spent in touching her virginal remains with chaplets, medals, and crucifixes. The witnesses at the process of canonization knew not how to describe the eagerness of the crowd, the enthusiastic veneration, the touching recollection, and the sweet odor of sanctity exhaled from the virginal remains. The sacrifice was ended; but the incense was still smoking and embalming the church.

On the afternoon of the second day after her death, a number of the clergy met for the funeral rites. They buried the illustrious virgin under one of the choir flags, near the spot upon which she was kneeling when the Lord appeared to her. The first part of the grand drama of the Sacred Heart, the private part, was ended; the second was about to begin.

CHAPTER XVI.

DEVOTION TO THE HEART OF JESUS BEGINS IN THE WORLD—ANGER OF SOME, ENTHUSIASM OF OTHERS.

'' Quare fremuerunt gentes, et populi meditati sunt inania ?''
'' Why have the Gentiles raged, and the people devised vain things ?''
—*Psalm* ii. 1.
'' Venient, et adorabunt.''
'' They shall come and adore.''—*Psalm* ixxxv. o.

THE saint is dead! There is no longer any obstacle to the glory of the Heart of Jesus! The pure alabaster vase is shattered, but its perfume spreads abroad! This the saint had predicted; this really happened. Hardly had the virgin closed her eyes, when the secrets hidden in the depths of the convents of Paray, Dijon, Moulins, Semur, escaped. Father Croiset published the "Abridged Life" of the saint; her incomparable Mémoire saw the light; and, in a flash, the report of the sublime revelations of the Sacred Heart filled France and the whole Church.

It seems that, even if such a revelation were not enthusiastically welcomed by all, it could nowhere meet with opposition; for what is more natural than devotion to the Heart of Jesus? What more luminous has ever sprung from Christianity or from humanity than devotion to the Sacred Heart? Everywhere and always has the heart of man been *honored:* why, then, be astonished that we should *adore* the Heart of the Man-God?

The heart is the organ of love. Scarcely come into the world, even before putting his hand on his forehead to say, "I think," man puts his hand on his heart and says, "I love!" Is this God's inspiration? is it innate impulse? is it instinctive movement? Whatever it may be, from it man has not varied for six thousand years. Take the greatest geniuses of antiquity: Moses,[1] Job,[2] David,[3] Solomon,[4] Isaias;[5] take Homer,[6] Euripides,[7] Theocrites,[8] Ovid,[9] Plautus:[10] to them, as to St. Augustine, Dante, Tasso, Shakespeare, Corneille, Bossuet, Racine; to all authors, sacred and profane, the heart is the seat of the strongest affections. It is expanded in happiness, it is contracted in sadness; it palpitates more quickly in enthusiasm; and sometimes, like those musical instruments that utter strains so brilliant under the passionate touch of some great artist, it breaks with love.

There is nothing more divine in the natural order of things than the union of our soul and body. If our

---

[1] " Diliges Dominum Deum tuum ex toto corde tuo." *Deut.* vi. 5, x. 12, xi. 13, xxx. 2. " Cor meum diligit principes."—*Jud.* v. 9.

[2] Job xxix. 13, xxxi. 9.

[3] " Defecit caro mea et cor meum. Deus cordis mei, et pars mea, Deus, in æternum."—*Psalm* lxxii. 26.

[4] " Vulnerasti cor meum, soror mea, sponsa, in uno crine colli tui."—*Cant.* iv. 9. " Ego dormio, et cor meum vigilat."—*Cant.* v. 2. " Præbe, fili mi, cor tuum mihi."—*Prov.* xxiii. 26.

[5] *Passim*, in more than ten places.

[6] Hom., *Iliad*, 206; *Odyssey*.

[7] Eur., *Hipp.*, 26.

[8] Theocr. xxix. 4, et Aristoph., *Nab.* 86.

[9] " Virginibus cordi, grataque forma sua est."—Ov. *Medic. fac.*, 32.
    " Molle, cupidineis nec inexpugnabile telis
       Cor mihi, quodque levis causa moveret, erat."
                                        Ov. *Trist.*, iv. 10, 65.

[10] " Corde amore inter se."
                                        Plaut. *Capt.*, ii. 3, 60.
    " Meum mel, meum cor, mea colostra."
                                        Id., *Pœn.*, i. 2, 154.
    " Nunc denum sum liber, meum corculum."
                                        Id., *Cas.*, iv. 4, 14.

Expressions usual among all Latin authors : " *Cordi esse;*" " *Corde habere.*" See Forcellini, *Lexicon totius latinitatis.*

means of investigation were more perfect, we should see in the slightest turnings and windings of the brain the revelation of the most imperceptible thoughts of our mind. In like manner, if a delicate hand, the hand of an angel for example, were laid on our breast, we should discern the slightest emotion of love, whether good, elevated, pure and noble, indifferent or bad, that momentarily causes our heart to beat.

Thus, in all times and under all skies, when an emblem of love is needed, men represent it by a heart. This remark does not apply so much, as we know, to antiquity; for then men loved with the senses, and these, alas! were what they made use of as symbols. Our words hold good for Christian times, because in them man loves with his heart.

Antiquity, however, though almost submerged in the sensual, was not wholly ignorant of pure, ideal love; and the representation of a heart was not altogether unknown. But it is rarely found among the frivolous Greeks, excepting engraved as souvenirs and emblems [1] on rings and medals. The Egyptians, on the contrary, those deep thinkers, deemed the heart everything in man's home; and in the divine scarabee, which the Egyptians wore upon their breast, there is a special mention of the heart, that grand power of man. [2] It

---

[1] Heart. "This form is very ancient in the arts. We find it in the medals *de Cardia* in the peninsula of Thrace. It is a sign indicative of the name of the city, which signifies heart."—*Dictionnaire des beaux-arts*, par Millin, membre de l'Institut (Paris, 1838). "I recollect," writes the learned archæologist of Autun, M. Bulliot, "to have formerly seen a ring (in the Jaubert collection at Moulins-Engilbert) bearing a heart with a Greek legend. The collection has been scattered, unfortunately, without hope of ever again being collected." See, also, a mirror in bronze, in M. Dobrée's collection at Nantes, representing Eolus in the midst of the Alcyones, framed with a border of hearts.

[2] Thanks are due to the kindness of M. François Lenormand. It is one of the new proofs that science furnishes of the long relations of the Jewish people with the Egyptians; for we know that in the Holy Scrip-

was the same with the Romans, and even with the
Etruscans, called by Cicero "the most religious of all
nations." They hung around the neck of their children jewels frequently in the form of a heart, to remind
them, says a pagan author, that without the heart man
is nothing.[1] And even in their infancy, as if fearing
that the lesson might come too late, mothers fastened it
to the curls of their first-born.[2] The Gauls, so good, so
ardent, so tender, and, Tacitus says, so chaste, were not
strangers to this great doctrine. We have reason to
believe that their wives wore a heart suspended from
the neck,[3] and that the husbands wore on their

tures the heart is very frequently mentioned. Whoever wishes to measure the extent and truth of this remark needs only to open a concord-
ance at the word *Cor.*

[1] " Nonnulli credunt ingenuis pueris attributum, ut *cordis figuram
in bulla ante pectus annecterent,* quam aspicientes, ita demum se homi-
nes cogitarent, si corde præstarent."—Macrob., *Saturn.,* i. 6. "Others
believed that to children of free condition the right was accorded to
wear on the breast *an ornament in the shape of a heart,* that the sight
of it might awaken the thought that man is truly a man only by reason
of his heart."—*Traduction de C. de Rosoy* (Paris, Didot, 1827). According to others, " *this ball in the shape of a heart* that free children wore
on the breast," etc.—*Traduct. nouvelle par Henri Decamps* (Paris,
Panckoucke, editor, 1845). " These balls," says Montfauçon, " were
hollow in order to contain an amulet, according to Macrobe. He
found *numbers* heart-shaped, others round." (Montfauç., *Antiquités
expliquées,* t. iii.) The Montfauçon engravings give two balls on
which the heart is engraved, and three that have the form of it (Pl.,
XXXVII). Casale in his work *De Veterum christian. Ritibus* (Rom.,
1644, p. 265) cites a marble statue of a young pagan who wore a heart
on the gold ball. See Caylus also, " *Recueil d'Antiquités,*" t. iv.
Balls in the form of the heart: Pl. XLIX., No. 1; Pl. L., No. ; Pl.
XC., No. 1.

[2] " They gave it to little children also, but fastened it on the forehead."—Montfauçon, *Antiquités expliquées supplém.* 46.

[3] See, at the Besançon museum, a heart found in a tomb Gallo-
Roman d'Eternoz (Doubs). This heart is formed of a sort of paste,
surrounded by silver filigree very finely wrought, with a ring to suspend
it from the neck. This magnificent Gallo-Roman jewel was found
with bracelets, swords, cutlasses, clasps, etc. See, also, at the museum

finger a ring on which were engraven two hearts united.[1]

What was only a germ in antiquity soon expanded under the more genial warmth of the Gospel. The golden balls, filled with charms and worn by young pagans around the neck, were now refilled with relics of the saints and martyrs, the image of whom was sometimes engraven on them, and the balls themselves gradually assumed the form of a heart.[2] This form or representation of a heart became very popular. We find it engraven on the pedestals of sacred vessels,[3] and on

of Saint-Germain-en-Laye, in that portion called the *Merovingian Hall*, another heart like this, similar in material and size, but wrought with less taste and delicacy. See, in the Orleans museum, a little gold medal, round in form, whereon is engraven a heart. There is a little ring to it, which proves that it was worn from the neck. These three very precious jewels are Gallo-Roman ; but it is difficult to fix their precise epoch. See, in fine, a heart in bronze of great antiquity, found in the forest of Compiègne (Museum of Saint-Germain, Hall of Mars).

[1] Rings in gold or silver found at Veillois (Poitou) closed by two united hearts, changing in color and made of a transparent paste engraved. The Gallo-Roman rings are very numerous. We have seen three at the museum of Nantes, in the private collection of M. Parenteau. Are these rings pagan or Christian? It is hard to say, the subjects engraven on the paste being but ill-preserved.

[2] From this usage sprang that of the Christians wearing on the breast *Agnus Dei* made from paschal wax in the form of a heart. See the great work of Fanciroli (*La Bulla d'oro de' fanciulli romani*, Romæ, 1732, p. 14). Museum of Cluny, jewels found in the Seine, quay of the goldsmiths. See also nine specimens of hearts worn on the neck, twelfth and thirteenth centuries. Very often the heart is hollow, and in it is the statuette of a saint.

[3] The most remarkable vase from this point of view is what they call the Gourdon chalice (at the Museum of Medals in Paris). It is not a chalice, but very probably a holy-oil vase for Confirmation. On the base is found a Latin cross, the corners ornamented by four hearts, one in garnets, the others in turquoise. The little vase is itself ornamented with a garland of hearts. This precious memorial was found with some gold coin of the sixth century, from 518 to 527, under the reign of the Emperor Justin.

the crowns of kings.[1] They painted and embroidered
it on the most precious textures of the Middle Ages;[2]
we are pleased to find it even in the games and relaxa-
tions of life;[3] above all, they engraved it on marriage-
rings.[4] It was suspended from altars, and placed on
tombs as a souvenir, a symbol of affection that survives
death.[5]

Soon chivalry arose. As it had need of a mysterious
sign to hide and, at the same time, reveal the face beneath the casque, heraldry was invented. And now the
heart appeared sparkling under a thousand various
forms in the armorial bearings of the oldest families of
England, Germany, France, Italy, Belgium, etc. It was
a heart wounded or inflamed; again two hearts united;
or a heart crowned; a heart pierced with an arrow, etc.,

[1] Not having seen the original and knowing only one design of it, we
merely repeat the words of others when we say that on the celebrated
iron crown at Monza, a crown of the Byzantine style ornamented with
diamonds, there are four hearts set in the four corners. (Du Som-
merard, *Les Arts au Moyen Age*, Album, X. série, planche XIV., No.6.)

[2] See the rich silk stuffs preserved at Aix-la-Chapelle. On one of
these Byzantine stuffs, of solid green and red, we see swans facing each
other, and on the border a series of hearts, also facing each other.
(*Mélanges d'archéologie*, par les PP. Charles Cahier et Arthur Martin.
Paris, Poussielgue, 1851. Tome II., Pl. XII.) See, also, at Fontevrault, the statue of Isabella d'Angoulême, wife of John Lackland,
died in 1218. On the corsage of her robe are three hearts reversed.
(*Annales archéol.*, v. p. 281.)

[3] This is not the place to enter into a dissertation on the game of
cards. We know its antiquity, and the part that the heart plays in it.

[4] See records of marriages at the close of the fourteenth and the
fifteenth centuries. There are numbers of them, and the wedding-rings
are always two hearts united together with an infinite variety of most
delicate devices.

[5] See some of the primitive churches, the "Marble of St. Agnes"
cemetery (V. Boldetti, *Osservationi supra i cimiteri*, Roma, 1720,
p. 373), where three hearts, perfectly formed, surround a little grated
opening destined, according to all appearances, to let the eye penetrate
into the interior of a tomb.—*Diction. des antiq. chrétiennes*, par
l'Abbé Martigny: Cœur.

ingenious revelation of the heart, sensitive, loving, wounded, or sad, that beat under the corselet of steel.[1]

But they were not to pause here. Homages grander, more striking, were to demonstrate man's idea of the human heart. These representations of the heart in gold, silver, or precious stones were, after all, very cold! Why is it that when a great man, a hero, a bene-factor, a saint dies, his fellow-men respectfully open his breast? Why do they draw out his heart, that sacred relic of love, and, embalming it in the per-fumes of gratitude, preserve it as a souvenir? This is done everywhere. Everywhere is preserved man's heart; it is even borne in triumphal procession; it is given an

---

[1] In France, for example, the families of :

> LEMIN DE BRANSAC—*three silver hearts*, engraved two at the head, the other at the point, of the shield.
>
> DU GARREAU (in Limousin and in Perigord)—field of sky-blue with a stripe of gold, at the base *a heart of the same*, having a cross also of gold.
>
> DE LESTANG (in Berri)—*two hearts* opposite to the base of the shield.
>
> D'ARNOULT—a stripe of red on a field of silver, with *three hearts* placed two at the base, the other at the apex, of the shield.
>
> DE CUERS DE GOZOLIN—azure on a field of gold, with *three hearts* of the same, two at the base, and the third at the apex, of the shield.
>
> DE CURSAI—on a field of silver *a fiery-red heart*, supported by cross-pieces, also red.
>
> LEMERCIER DE MAISONCELLE—azure on a field of silver, with two golden stars at the base of the shield and a *heart of gold* at the apex.

In England, see the families of :

> CATHCART—a hand holding a *crowned heart* above the coat-of-arms, in the centre of which is a *heart* uncrowned.
>
> COCKBURN—*a heart* in the centre of the coat-of-arms.
>
> DOUGLAS—*two hearts crowned.*
>
> JOHNSTONE—*a single heart crowned.*
>
> MORTON—*two hearts crowned.*
>
> QUEENSBERRY—*two hearts crowned.*
>
> TORPHICHEN—*four hearts crowned.*

exceptional burial ; and there is not one of our cathedrals that does not contain some example touching the sublime veneration of man for the heart of man.[1]

Soon a still more delicate thought was evoked. On the brink of the tomb, when searching for what was most precious to bequeath the tenderly loved, disdaining gold and silver, fit only to reward inferior services, man conceived the idea of leaving his heart to his dearest ones. This under a symbolical form was the legacy of that love with which it had been consumed. Cremation had deprived the ancients of this touching and sublime legacy. In Christian times it became universal. Kings, queens, princes, bishops, even the saints made such donations. When wandering through our ancient basilicas and abbeys, Saint-Denis for example, or Fontevrault, we meet at every step urns of marble, alabaster, or bronze, containing the heart of a king, a queen, or a prince. Though possessing immense lands, they declared that what they could leave most precious to those whom they loved was their heart.[2]

[1] See, among others, at Saint-Denis : An urn of white marble, sculptured by John Goujon, containing in the days of yore the heart of Francis I. A spiral column surmounted by a bronze urn, on which three cupids support a heart: in the urn was once inclosed the heart of Henry III. Another sculptured column, surmounted by an urn, once contained the heart of Francis II. See, at Nantes, the magnificent jewel set in gold, in which was inclosed the heart of Queen Anne of Brittany, wife of King Louis XII., etc.

[2] For example, Richard Cœur-de-Lion, who, dying (1199), bequeathed his body to Fontevrault, *his heart to Rouen.* In like manner, John Lackland's heart was deposited at Fontevrault (1216) in a golden cup near the tomb of Henry II., King of England, deceased in 1189. At Fontevrault the tomb of Isabella d'Angoulême (1218) contained a golden vase inclosing the heart of King Henry III., her son. Again, Henry IV. gave the Jesuits his castle of La Flèche in which to establish a college, and there he wished his heart to be preserved. (Duruy, *Hist. de France*, ch. li. § 5.) St. Chantal gave her heart to the Visitation of Paris, etc., etc. There are thousands of examples of this custom.

[Mgr. Bougaud's own heart now rests in the Sacred Heart chapel of the Visitation Convent at Orleans. It is sealed in a leaden box inclosed

This is the history of humanity. Right or wrong, foi six thousand years, it has been thought that, if there is anything of value on this poor earth, it is love ; and that the sanctuary of love, its tabernacle, its consecrated ciborium, is the heart. It has despised all else. Love alone was esteemed, love alone was borne in triumph. Not the dust of man's sword, nor of his sceptre, nor even that of his genius has been honored ; but on the whole face of the globe, has been carried in triumph only the dust of his heart. Moreover, let that heart have been a beneficent one, noble, elevated, pure,—a heart that beat for others instead of itself,—and with more reason are exceptional honors paid it. Is it, then, astonishing that when a heart that surpassed all hearts appeared, unprecedented enthusiasm was felt for it ? Had it been only the heart of a man, it might have been carried in triumph: but it was the Heart of the Man-God ! Homage, therefore, could not suffice ; adoration was necessary.

Here we are shocked by one of those problems of which there are millions in the history of our poor nature. As long as there was question of loving, honoring, exalting *man's* heart, not one objection was raised ; but as soon as there was question of the Heart of Jesus, it became the object of outrageous abuse.

in a casket of oak. The following is the inscription at the base of the monument :

"Here rests in the peace of the Lord
The heart of the most Reverend and Illustrious
L. V. E. Bougaud,
Bishop of Laval,
Former Vicar-General of the Diocese of Orleans,
Who deserved well
Of the Visitation of Holy Mary
For writing in an able manner
The Life of St. J. F. de Chantal
And that of Blessed Margaret Mary,
And who was, by his numerous Writings
And Discourses, the Signal Defender of the Church."
—*Translator's Note.*]

Strange ! The grandest and most legitimate ideas, the most touching of all that religion consecrates, are scornfully rejected. What is there more beautiful, more manifest to the eyes of the heart than the unity of the human species; the brotherhood of all men and all peoples ? Suppose that the Bible taught the contrary, with what indignation, with what efforts of science would men affirm the fact that we are all brethren ! But no ; because the Bible thus declares, they expend the treasures of mind, wit, and learning to prove, first, that we have nothing in common with the negro race ; and secondly, by way of retaliation, that we are the children of lower animals, of apes and baboons. A similar thing happened when there was question of the Heart of Jesus. Hardly had this sweet and august sign begun to rise above the world than commenced universal revolt and conspiracy. Jansenists, rationalists, wits, scholars, priests, and, alas! even bishops, seized the pen, and left untried no species of raillery and contempt in their effort to destroy tender and deep devotion to the Sacred Heart.

One called it *a new devotion*. As if the Church interdicted, or ever could interdict, new devotions ! A devotion is not a dogma ; it is an act of love. To ask the Church not to have new devotions is to ask a glowing furnace not to dart its flames heavenward ; it is to ask a heart that loves to hide within itself every manifestation of tenderness, never to grow young again by a new expression of the unchangeable love that forms the depths of its soul. It is over eighteen hundred years since Jesus Christ died on the cross, over eighteen hundred years since the Church at His feet adored and loved Him ; but imagine not that at all times that love and adoration were testified in the same way. There were periods in which she kissed in preference His sacred feet wearied in seeking us ; and others in which His brow crowned with thorns, His face furrowed with tears, most deeply touched her soul. To-day we rise to His breast, we press our lips to His Sacred Heart in eager desire to warm and inflame our own cold heart. Strange people that ye are, ye that attack the Church! If we Catholics do not advance, if we intrench ourselves in our immutable doctrines, ye say that we are mummies. And if we do advance, if we display the love that is in us, ye say that we are inventors of novelties. Ye ignore and blaspheme the double, the sublime character of the Church, the immutability of faith, and the progress of love!

Others called the devotion absurd. What! absurd to honor a father's heart! To love, to venerate, to preserve with filial piety a mother's heart! So incensed were some minds at seeing the Heart of the Man-God receiving Christian adoration that they began forthwith to deny that man has a heart. In order to be able to combat this noble organ even in the breast of the Man-God, they preferred giving the brutal lie to the manifest consent of mankind which has always made the heart the seat of the affections. They called man's heart *a little morsel of flesh* [1] — *a muscle;* [2] and in the picture of the Sacred Heart they only saw *a great shining liver,* [3] clearly evidencing by their fury that a decisive stroke was hurled against it.

Others, again, they of the fastidious class, found the devotion too material. " Adore matter! Adore flesh!" they said. " What a degradation!" As if it had just entered man's mind that the material Heart of Jesus Christ was to be separated from the sacred fire of His love to which we offer our homage and veneration! As if the Heart of Jesus Christ were more material than were His feet and His hands, which we kiss ; His crown of thorns, which we carry in triumph ; His cross of wood, which He stained with His blood and before

---

[1] Lettre pastorale de Scipien Ricci, évêque de Pistoie.

[2] Histoire des sectes religieuses, t. ii. p. 246.   [3] Ibid., p. 269.

which, for that reason, we cast ourselves on our knees!
No; what they refused to adore was not flesh! The
time was approaching in which these vainly scrupulous
souls would adore flesh, living and defiled, in the profaned sanctuary of Notre Dame. What frightened
them was the suffering, the wounded flesh of their Redeemer! They pretended that to adore it was degradation; though at heart they knew well that the adoration of the wounded flesh of Jesus Christ is the condemnation of concupiscence in our own flesh, the apotheosis
of pure love, the glorification of sacrifice; that is to
say, honor rendered to what is greatest, noblest, most
intellectual, and most divine in the heart.

Happily, there is humanity higher than man. Higher
than the narrow, violent, superficial portion that vanishes like the waves of passion, like the storms of wrath,
there is a calm, tranquil humanity that listens to false
reasoning with a smile, and then passes on.

This was what happened in the present case. Corre-
sponding to the deepest wants of the human soul, sweetly
and efficaciously responding to the sad wounds of this
epoch, the devotion to the Heart of Jesus began its triumphal march from the day of Saint Margaret Mary's
death. The Visitation Order gave the signal. Paray,
Dijon, Semur, had already set up the banner of the Sacred
Heart. The following years saw all the other convents
rallying around it: in 1690, Marseilles, Montbrison,
Nantes; in 1691, Autun, the first convent of Lyons, that
of Fribourg, and the second of Rennes; in 1692, Besan-
çon, Blois, Loudun; in 1693, Aix, Bordeaux, Bourges,
Farcalquier, Langres, the second of Lyons, Nevers,
Valence, Toulouse; in 1694, Dieppe, Thonon, the second
of Marseilles, Salins; in 1695, Chaillot, Périgueux,
Pont-à-Mousson, Montargis; in 1696, Nancy, Aurillac,
Romans, Naples; in 1697, the first of Rouen, Rumilly,
Arone, Caen, Condrieux; in 1698, the second of Paris,
Orléans, Mamers, Vannes; 1699, Montferrand; in 1700,

Troyes, Metz, Saint-Etienne, and shortly after Amiens, Auxerre, etc. The seventeenth century is nearly ended. Only ten years had passed since Margaret Mary died, and already the Visitation houses, one after another, had risen to consecrate themselves to the Heart of Jesus. We would be interminable did we undertake to relate all the touching, beautiful, and sublime facts, all the charming episodes that marked the triumphal march of the devotion of the love of Jesus throughout the Visitation. Its convents drew from it strength to remain fervent amid the defections of the eighteenth century, and tenderly loving in face of the cold sophisms of Jansenism. This sacred fire, so carefully guarded by the Visitation, though sad were the times, shone through her grates. Each Community became the centre of a Confraternity of the Sacred Heart, by means of which the whole neighboring country grew warm again. To cite only one fact : in 1698, eight years after Margaret Mary's death, the Confraternity of Dijon numbered from twelve to thirteen thousand associates, not only in Burgundy, France, but in Spain, England, and Germany.

Such a movement would not have been possible if the French bishops, the Superiors of the Visitation convents, had not approved it. But we find them everywhere blessing chapels, erecting Confraternities, and presiding at those first feasts of the Heart of Jesus, so private, so recollected, and so sweet, in the interior of the convents.

Soon, however, they opened to it their cathedrals. In 1688, Charles de Brienne, Bishop of Coutances, established in his diocese the feast of the Sacred Heart of Jesus. In 1694, Antoine Pierre de Grammont, Archbishop of Besançon, ordered that it should be celebrated in his metropolitan see. In 1719, François Villeroy, Archbishop of Lyons, published an admirable pastoral in favor of devotion to the Sacred Heart, which he also established himself in all the churches of his diocese. Every year saw similar things. But though triumphant, the march of the devotion of love was still slow and timid, until, all at once, in 1720, thirty years after the death of Margaret Mary, an extraordinary fact occurred to hurry it on.

The pestilence from the East burst upon the city of Marseilles, and in a short time reaped a harvest of forty thousand souls. The silence of death fell on the streets and public places encumbered by dead bodies. In vain had the survivors recourse to penance and prayer. Nothing could disarm the divine anger. At last the saintly prelate of Marseilles, Mgr. de Belzunce, received a heavenly inspiration. It came to him from a religious of the Visitation, Sister Anne-Madeleine Rémusat, to whom he frequently had recourse to strengthen his heart and rouse his courage, and who never ceased to exhort him to place his hope in the Adorable Heart of Jesus. One day, therefore, November 2, 1720, like another Borromeo, the prelate, barefooted, a cord around his neck, a cross in his arms, left his palace accompanied by all his religious and priests, and many other holy souls. When the procession reached the principal square of Marseilles the bishop knelt, and, amid silence broken only by the sobs and groans of the assembly, solemnly consecrated his diocese to the Heart of Jesus. From that moment, as if by enchantment, the pestilence ceased : not another interment took place at Marseilles.

The municipal body, however, had taken no part in the public demonstration ; two years later, therefore, the plague reappeared. Repenting their fault, the authorities vowed to go yearly, on the feast of the Sacred Heart, to communicate in the Church of the Visitation, there offer a white wax taper ornamented with the city escutcheon, and take part on that same day in a public procession. As soon as the proceedings were drawn up and signed by all the officials, the scourge ceased with the same suddenness as on the first occasion. It is from this event that the city of Marseilles dates devotion to the Sacred Heart, so productive of good during the horrors of the Revolution, and which in our own day has played so brilliant a part in the sanctification of souls.

Such events could not overrun a country so Christian as was Provence at that time without shedding their radiance everywhere. After the example of the illustrious Henry de Belzunce, the Archbishops of Aix, Arles, Avignon, as well as the bishops of Toulon and Carpentras, hastened to issue orders for the establishment of the feast in their respective dioceses. Soon the whole south proclaimed devotion to the Sacred Heart.

Shortly after, and under circumstances most favorable, the long-expected history of **Saint Margaret Mary** appeared. Its author was Mgr. Languet, formerly vicar-general of Autun, Superior of the Visitation of Paray, and at that moment Archbishop of Sens. No one was more capable of knowing Margaret Mary than he, for he had been in daily communication with herself, her contemporaries, and her disciples. Unfortunately, the gloomy spirit of the eighteenth century had slightly impressed upon him its mark ; and besides, the violent attacks of the rationalists and the impious had rather hampered his piety. Instead of narrating he discusses. He tries to explain what he should have enthusiastically contemplated. The eighteenth century was not made to understand such a figure, nor was he the man to paint it ; therefore his work, cold and incomplete, timid and indiscreet, added fury to the tempest that it should have stilled.

They who have had occasion to page through the writings of the eighteenth century, pamphlets, journals, light poetry, ecclesiastical leaves, all so infected with venom, may form some idea of the rage, contempt, and

raillery roused against Margaret Mary and the Sacred
Heart. We have had in our hands at Dijon a collection
of manuscripts in which are found the verses of Piron,
the Christmas carols, satirical ballads of la Monnaye,
letters of President Bouhier, and sonnets from the
various Burgundian wits of the eighteenth century.
One cannot conceive the insipidity, the sottish pleasantry roused by the name of Alacoque, the surname of
Margaret Mary, the stupid play upon words connected
with devotion to the Sacred Heart, the sarcasm launched
against Mgr. Languet. But these times have long
passed. France has indeed still many wounds ; but more
than a hundred years separate us from such an epoch.
Before long the society of the nineteenth century will
appear to be bound and strongly welded to the great
society of the seventeenth, of whom she is the legitimate daughter. The miserable interval between them
will no longer be reckoned. It is like a lovely morn
and a balmy evening forming one beautiful summer
day, though its noon has been darkened by a storm
whose last traces may be floating far off on the edge of
the horizon.

Whilst the wits spent their arrows against devotion to
the Sacred Heart, it continued its march, exciting anger
and arousing enthusiasm, wounding and captivating the
hearts of men. It had already left France, and spread
along the shores of the Mediterranean. In 1733 it was
established at Constantinople ; in 1740, at Aleppo and
Damascus, in Lebanon. The Life of **Saint** Margaret
Mary, translated into Arabic and published at Antora,
a city of Anti-Lebanon, spread through the vast plains
of Cœle-Syria, from the great Hermon to the Baltic.
It even extended further. After 1709, we find two Confraternities of the Sacred Heart at Macao, another at
Pekin ; and in 1743 a third was erected in the very
heart of the imperial palace.

Rome is, however, always slow to sanction novelties

in devotion. In 1726 Frederick Augustus, King of Poland, vainly addressed a most pressing supplication to Benedict XIII.; in vain had the French bishops in 1728 conjured the See of St. Peter to recognize the feast of the Sacred Heart; in vain did the King of Spain, Philip V., and shortly after the prelates of Poland, formulate a similar request. Rome would not yield. The Congregation of Rites even issued a decree, by which, July 30, 1729, on the decision of him who was, some time after, to become Benedict XIV., it absolutely refused to authorize the demand. And lo, the Jansenists clapped their hands with joy! What was there, however, astonishing in the hesitancy of the Holy See? There was question of a private revelation not yet canonically examined; of a religious who died, it is true, in the odor of sanctity, whose process of canonization, begun in 1715, was still under the official seals; of a devotion, in fine, that touched the most profound mysteries of Christianity, but of which the first theologians or historians had spoken in so inexact a way that one of the chief and most pious works respecting it had been put on the Index. The devotion, on the other hand, bordered so closely upon the physiological question of the functions of the heart in the human organism that, as the Jansenists said, they could not decide the one without the other. The question was, then, to be considered more closely before giving a definite solution. Instead of censuring the Holy See, its prudence makes us admire it.

Thirty-six years more, 1729–1765, were employed in letting the question mature in the minds of theologians, in the disputations of the schools, in the hearts of Christians, in the intuitions of saints, until one appeared whom Providence had chosen solemnly to inaugurate the devotion to the Sacred Heart throughout the Church. Scarcely was the illustrious Clement XIII. seated on the chair of St. Peter than, prompted thereto by the ever-increasing intrigues of the Jansenists and the incessant solicitations of the prelates, particularly those of Poland, the question was again agitated, and decided amidst the applause of the Church. A decree, dated 1765, granted to the prelates of Poland and the Roman Archconfraternity permission to celebrate with Mass and proper Office the feast of the Sacred Heart of Jesus. Liberty was left to other prelates to solicit the same for their respective dioceses. Hardly had this decree been issued, when the clergy assembled at Paris hastened, at the importunity of the pious Queen Marie Leczinska, to subscribe to it; and it was decided that the devotion to the Heart of Jesus should be established in all the dioceses of France. Thus did God, on the eve of their great misfortunes, reunite Poland and France, that they might work together at the spread of devotion to the Heart of Jesus in the Church. We may believe that this Heart, the most faithful of all hearts, will one day return all that it has received.

Thus stood affairs in 1765. Less than a century after Margaret Mary's death, the first part of her mission was realized—the devotion to the Heart of Jesus was officially established in the Church. And if the solemn feast demanded by the Lord for the Friday after the octave of the Blessed Sacrament is not yet of obligation, it is at least authorized by the Sovereign Pontiff. The rest is only a matter of time.

As to the second part of our saint's mission, that which regarded France and the king, it was in a less advanced state. Louis XIV. died too blinded by his passions and, when they were chilled by age, too enervated by his pride, to have any suspicion of the abyss into which his errors and disorders were about to precipitate France. Louis XV., who succeeded him, saw the danger, for from year to year the gulf widened; but the sight affected him little. The monarchy would last as long as he, and the future mattered not to this voluptuous egotist. For a greater reason, neither the one nor the other dreamed of the supernatural remedy God had made known to Margaret Mary. We may even believe, seeing how little they interested themselves in it, that the second revelation never reached them.

However, when looking at it more closely, we are persuaded that the mission confided by Margaret Mary to Mother de Saumaise had been fulfilled, and that Louis XIV. knew exactly what God desired of him. Sad indeed as might be that court of Versailles, it was full of the Sacred Heart. It was that Heart that there consoled the afflicted queens, the deserted wives, souls agitated by sad presentiments. We even think we can perceive in those more nearly related to Louis XIV. and Louis XV. certain delicate, indefinable efforts to supply for what those monarchs should have done and which they did not do. If, for example, the first convent of the Visitation at Paris undertook to build, in 1694, on the Mansart plan, a handsome chapel to the Heart of Jesus, it was the Queen of England, Henrietta Maria of France, aunt of Louis XIV., who laid the first stone, and who wished to be inscribed first on the register of the Confraternity.[1] A little after, the third convent of Paris, that of Chaillot, decided to establish, every first Friday of the month, a solemn Benediction with an Act of Reparation to the Heart of Jesus. The Duchess of Orléans was frequently perceived assisting at it. Kneeling on the ground among the crowd, she was seen trying to hide herself, her tears, and her painful anxiety of heart.[2] At the same time, the grand personages of the court pressed around Sister Marie-Eléonore, Princess of Lorraine, a poor and humble religious of the Visitation of Paris, supplicating her to inscribe them on the

---

[1] Circular of the second convent of Paris, May 25, 1698.
[2] Circular of the convent of Chaillot, November 26, 1739.

register of the Confraternity of the Sacret Heart.[1] A little later, at the court of Louis XV., the devotion increased still more. By the side of those salons in which were enthroned the Pompadours and the Du Barrys, there were humble oratories in which the most admirable royal family in tears took refuge: the pious queen, Marie Leczinska; her four daughters, one of whom was Madame Louise of France; the Dauphin, father of Louis XVI., and his young and saintly wife. Never before were witnessed scandals so closely allied with virtues so angelic. In the whole royal family devotion to the Heart of Jesus was alive. It betrayed itself in so marked a manner that it is impossible to believe that the revelation to the saint relative to the king of France was not known at the court. It was the queen, the pious and admirable wife of Louis XV., Marie Leczinska, who solicited and obtained from the bishops of France, summoned to Paris for the assembly of 1765, that the public worship of the Sacred Heart should, "according to her ardent desire," be established in all the dioceses of France.[2] She and her daughters, amid ineffable private sorrows, and apprehensions of inevitable public misfortunes, found no other consolation than in devotion to the Heart of Jesus. The Dauphin went further. He caused to be erected in the very palace of Versailles, as a place of refuge for them all, a chapel to the Sacred Heart.[3] It was thence came forth one day, beautiful and pure, to shut herself up among the Carmelites, the daughter of Louis XV., Madame Louise of France, whom the Church has already declared Venerable, and who is going to be raised to her altars. If the sacrifice of an unspotted dove were in proportion to our crimes, France would have been saved;

---

[1] Circular of the second convent of Paris, May 25, 1698. Année Sainte, Life of Sister Marie-Eléonore de Lorraine, vol. iii. p. 128.

[2] Procès-verbaux du clergé, t. viii. p. 1440.

[3] Life of the Dauphin, Father of Louis XVI.

but it had been ordained in the adorable designs of God that even the immolation of the king should not suffice, and that France should be saved only by the Sacred Heart.

The son of him who had erected an oratory to the Heart of Jesus in the palace of Versailles, Louis XVI., had not yet mounted the throne when the tempest burst forth. Its progress was terrible. Every year saw an anchor break away, and soon it became evident that no human hand could stay the rudder. Then it was that the unfortunate Louis XVI. decided, though too late, to perform an action which, had it come in time, would perhaps have averted the danger. Cast from the throne into prison ; overwhelmed, not by his own misfortunes (for he had a soul magnanimous enough to rise above them), but by the misfortunes of France ; seeing no resources on any side, he thought of Saint Margaret Mary, and of the secret that had been confided to his grandfather. He resolved to accomplish the consecration of France to the Heart of Jesus, which God had asked of his fathers, but which had not been effected. With that hand and heart with which, so shortly after, were to be written those sublime pages called the "Last Will of Louis XVI.," he himself drew up the act of consecration of his person and his kingdom to the Heart of Jesus.

We give this act, in which are found the very terms of our saint, the precise things that God had asked of her ; and which, coming to us through the tears, the anguish of Louis XVI. in prison, has something solemn and tragic in it, like the last cries of a shipwrecked voyager still vainly striving to save his loved ones.

"Thou seest, O my God, the wounds that rend my heart, the depth of the abyss into which I am fallen, and the innumerable evils that encompass me on all sides ! To my own frightful misfortunes and those of my family are joined, to overwhelm my soul, those that sweep over the face of my kingdom. The cries of the unfortunate, the groans of oppressed religious sound in my ears. An interior voice again warns me that perhaps Thy justice reproaches me with all these calamities, because in the days of my power I did not repress their principal sources, namely, the license of the people and irreligion; because I myself have furnished triumphant heresy with arms by favoring it with laws which have increased its strength and rendered it audacious.

"O Jesus Christ, Divine Redeemer of all our iniquities, it is into Thy Adorable Heart that I desire to pour out my afflicted soul. I call to my aid the tender heart of Mary, my august protectress and my mother, and the assistance of St. Louis, my patron and the most illustrious of my ancestors! Open, O Adorable Heart, and from the pure hands of my powerful intercessors receive graciously the satisfactory vows my confidence inspires me to make, and which I offer Thee as the simple expression of my sentiments.

"If, by an effect of Thy infinite goodness, O God, I regain my liberty, my crown, and my royal power, I solemnly promise:

"1. To revoke as soon as possible all the laws that shall be pointed out to me, whether by the Pope, or by a council, or by four bishops chosen among the most virtuous and enlightened of my kingdom, as contrary to integrity and purity of faith, to the discipline and spiritual jurisdiction of the Holy Roman, Catholic, Apostolic Church, and *notably* the civil *Constitution of the Clergy.*

"2. Within a year to take, with the Pope and bishops of my kingdom, all necessary measures to establish in canonical form a SOLEMN FEAST IN HONOR OF THE SACRED HEART OF JESUS, which shall be celebrated to perpetuity throughout France on the FIRST FRIDAY AFTER THE OCTAVE OF THE BLESSED SACRAMENT. This shall always be followed by a public procession, to repair the outrages and profanations committed in the holy temples by schismatics, heretics, and bad Christians, during the time of our troubles.

" 3. Within three months, counting from the day of my deliverance, to go in person to the church of Notre Dame in Paris, or to any other principal church of the place in which I may be, and on a Sunday or feast, at the foot of the main altar, after the Offertory of the Mass, and in the hands of the celebrant, pronounce A SOLEMN ACT OF CONSECRATION OF MY PERSON, FAMILY, AND KINGDOM TO THE SACRED HEART OF JESUS, with the promise to give my subjects an example of the honor and love due this Adorable Heart.

" 4. During the course of a year, counting from the day of my deliverance, TO ERECT AND DECORATE AT MY OWN EXPENSE, in the church that I shall choose for that purpose, A CHAPEL IN WHICH AN ALTAR SHALL BE DEDI-CATED TO THE SACRED HEART OF JESUS, and which shall serve as an eternal monument of my gratitude, and of my unlimited confidence in the infinite merits and the inexhaustible treasures of grace inclosed in that Heart.

" 5. Lastly, I resolve TO RENEW EVERY YEAR, wherever I may be, on the day upon which the feast of the Sacred Heart is celebrated, the ACT OF CONSECRATION CONTAINED IN THE THIRD ARTICLE, and to assist at the public procession that shall follow the Mass of that day.

" To-day I can pronounce this engagement only in secret, but I am willing, if necessary, to sign it with my blood. The most beautiful day of my life will be that on which I shall be able to publish it aloud in the church.

" O ADORABLE HEART OF MY SAVIOUR : may my right hand be forgotten, and may I myself be forgotten, if ever I forget Thy benefits and my promises, if ever I cease to love Thee and to place in Thee my confidence and consolation !"

Behold the consecration of France to the Heart of Jesus by the lips, or rather by the heart, of the martyr-king! Who does not feel that the words of the saintly Sister really reached Louis XIV., and that they were transmitted as a secret hope for the hour of peril? All that Margaret had asked is indeed done : a consecration of France to the Heart of Jesus ; a national temple erected by the king, as an eternal monument of this consecration ; and, lastly, a feast and a solemn procession the Friday after the octave of the Blessed Sacrament. Whence would we derive all these facts, did we not know the revelation made by God to Saint Margaret Mary, and, until the present, hidden in the archives of the Visitation of Paray? Now, all this the king knew ; and he promised in his own name, in the name of the royal family, in the name of France. Will there not some day be found a soul to do honor to such a signature?

After writing this consecration with his own hand, Louis XVI. gave it to Père Hébert, his confessor, Superior-General of the Eudistes. The latter, fearing that so important a document might be lost, immediately made several copies of it, one of which he always carried about him. When himself condemned to death, he hid it at the moment of setting out for the scaffold in a chink of the stones of his prison. The other copies were scattered, though with a thousand perils, in the midst of Christian families. At the same time began to be distributed from hand to hand, from dungeon to dungeon, little images of the Sacred Heart, the rallying sign, the gleam of hope. Soon even they were hoisted on the battle-field of the Vendée. Had these images come from the Temple, and did they know of the consecration of Louis XVI.? or rather, had they in them only the revelation to Margaret Mary, and did they obey the same inspiration as the martyr-king? However that may be, when they rose up in arms, Henri de la Rochejaquelin, Lescure, Charette, Cathelineau, bore the Heart of Jesus on their breast. This was the last thing that God had asked of

Margaret Mary. The Vendeans finished the work of Louis XVI.

Why did not Almighty God accept such a consecration of France from hands so pure, from a heart so worthy of being heard? one feels tempted to ask in amazement. But we soon learn the reason. It was because Louis XVI. *was not king,—he was only a captive.* The Vendeans were *the giants, the mighty ones,*—but *they were not France!* France, instead of proclaiming the consecration of Louis XVI., dragged the king to the scaffold ; and instead of uniting with the Vendeans, shot them. The national homage demanded by God did not yet exist.

Thus ended the eighteenth century. When standing at a distance in order to see best, we perceive, as it were, a double France : the first suffering, the second inflicting the pain ; the France of the victims, and the France of the executioners. On the victims, to support and console them, beamed the Adorable Heart of Jesus. As to the executioners, they also adored a heart. In the threatening shadow in which they hid, or under the sinister glare that enlightened them, we see some carrying in triumph the heart of Voltaire, and others kneeling before the heart of Marat.

The Heart of Jesus, or the heart of Marat! This was the cry at the close of the eighteenth century. It would be well for it, sooner or later, to receive an answer!

CHAPTER XVII.

THE FIRST-FRUITS OF DEVOTION TO THE SACRED
HEART—THE CHURCH OF FRANCE VIVIFIED IN THE
RAYS OF THE SACRED HEART—BEATIFICATION OF
SAINT MARGARET MARY.

" Jam hiems transiit ; imber abiit, et recessit.   Flores apparuerunt
in terra nostra ; vox turturis audita est in terra nostra; vineæ florentes
dederunt odorem suum.   Surge, amica mea, speciosa mea, et veni."
" For winter is now past, the rain is over and gone.   The flowers
have appeared in our land, the time of pruning is come : the voice of
the turtle is heard in our land : the vines in flower yield their sweet
smell.   Arise, my love, my beautiful one, and come."—*Cant.* ii. 11-13.

AINT MARGARET MARY gradually came
forth from obscurity.   She rose slowly in glory,
leaning on her Beloved.[1]   As long as the devotion
to the Heart of Jesus had not been approved at Rome
the humble Margaret remained in obscurity.   But it
was now time for her to rise to our altars, that the glory
of the *revelatrix* might show forth resplendently the
beauty of the *revelation.*

The eighteenth century closed, however, without
Margaret Mary's being declared *Venerable.*   Her process
of canonization had been begun in 1715; and although,
in its brevity, it felt the effects of the sad times through
which it was passing, though it had neither religious
grandeur nor the precision and abundance of details
that characterize similar grand acts of the sixteenth
century, enough had been heard from contemporary
witnesses, and too many admirable facts had been col·
lected, to allow any doubt as to the success of the cause.
But the acts of the process of 1715 were sleeping in the

[1] *Cant.* vii. 5.

episcopal archives of Autun, and were not sent to Rome till 1820—that is, after an interval of one hundred and five years. Pilgrimages began to the chapel of Paray; and the years 1745 and '46, periods of fearful epidemics, saw the pilgrims multiply. The name of Margaret could not, however, be mingled with public prayers, and her body rested, without other glory than the faithful rememberance of her Sisters, under the choir slab where it had been laid in 1690. One hundred years had flown, and nothing was yet changed in her regard.

The Revolution swept like an impious whirlwind over France, uprooting thrones, overthrowing altars, suppressing convents. That of Paray was closed like the others, and the religious driven out. Must they, then, abandon that cherished sanctuary of the Sacred Heart, that sanctuary redolent with holy memories of our Lord, that garden in which He had appeared, those hallowed spots upon which they had so often kissed His footsteps? At least they would not leave without taking their treasure with them, the humble wooden casket that contained the bones of their saintly Sister. They laid them in a safe place, then changed their dress and separated, some to their own families, others to small houses that they rented in the city, and there remained faithful in secret to their God, whom they were no longer permitted to adore in public. There they lay concealed until the Revolution passed. They were like travellers surprised by a storm and seeking refuge in some cave until the clouds should roll away and sunshine return.

As soon as liberty was restored to them, they took active measures to regain possession of their convent. But, alas! it had been sold as public property, shared among several proprietors,—and the Sisters were poor! More than twenty years were spent in fruitless efforts. At the close of 1817, seeing that their exertions amounted to nothing; that death was diminishing their number without their having resumed the religious life to which

they had been consecrated in their youth,—a house having been offered them at Charité-sur-Loire, they decided
to go there. As we have seen the monks of the Middle
Ages shouldering the relics of their saints and fleeing
before the incursions of the Normans, so, on quitting
Paray, the Sisters determined to carry with them the
humble coffin that contained the precious remains of
Margaret Mary. But hardly had their determination
become known in the city, than it excited extraordinary
commotion, and the magistrates interfered to oppose
the departure. The mayor even went so far as to have
the city seals affixed to the wooden casket, and, as in
the Ages of Faith, they set a guard around it. Things
remained thus till June 16, 1823, when, under the pres-
sure of public opinion, and with charitable assistance,
the Sisters were enabled, at a cost of fifty thousand
francs, to regain possession of their old home. The Revolution, that had demolished so many abbeys and illustrious convents, had respected this one. It was standing, old and battered indeed, but still complete. The
entire city conducted processionally the aged religious
carrying in their arms the remains of Margaret Mary.
No painter's brush could portray the emotion of those
venerable religious on again beholding that chapel,
those grates, the witnesses of our Lord's apparitions;
the little cell in which Margaret Mary died; the stair-
case of the seraphim; the novitiate oratory; the grove
of hazels, which had blossomed and was actually bloom-
ing as if there had not been a revolution; the chapel
of the Sacred Heart in the middle of the garden,
closed and locked by the religious at the time of their
departure, and into which, as if our Lord wished to
preserve from sacrilegious contact the sanctuary of His
Adorable Heart, no one during the whole period of the
Revolution had entered. All was as on the first day;
all was redolent of piety, all was venerable, full of ineffaceable traces of Jesus Christ and His servant. The

Sisters mingled their tears with their kisses, and forgot in a pious rapture their thirty years of exile and suffering.

One of the places that had most suffered was the chapel. The arched roof was full of cracks, and the pictures of the Heart of Jesus on the walls were cut in a thousand places. An architect proposed demolishing the old building, which was threatened with ruin, and presented the religious a plan for a grand chapel in its stead. But the bare idea inspired them with horror, and, thanks to the good old nuns, the sanctuary of the communications of the Heart of Jesus, more fortunate than the church of Vérosvres, was preserved to the veneration of the faithful.

Reinstalled in their convent, the Sisters had but one thought: that of resuming as quickly as possible the cause of the canonization of their holy Sister. God blessed their endeavors, for in the course of the year, March 30, 1824, Leo XII. signed the commission for the introduction of the cause, and the servant of God was declared *Venerable*. Six years after, during the year of 1830, the Commissaries Apostolic arrived in France, delegated by the Holy See to inquire into the heroic virtues of Margaret Mary. They held their sessions during five entire months at Paray; then went to Autun, convoked witnesses; followed religiously the least traces of the saint; and, before returning to Rome, wished to proceed to the opening of the tomb and the authentic recognition of the relics. The diocesan bishop, Mgr. d'Héricourt, presided at this ceremony, at which a large number of priests and religious assisted. Four physicians were present. The coffin-lid was raised, and all that remained of the virginal envelope of the favored Sister—only some bones exhaling the aroma of immortality—was disclosed to the reverent gaze of the bystanders. With deep emotion they contemplated that head which our Lord had one day pressed to His breast;

those large cavities whose eyes once saw Him resplendent on the altar; that, also, of the heart into which our Lord once put His hand, and kindled by His sacred touch the divine fire which consumed the saint. This was all that remained of the mortal temple in which the great soul had dwelt. An unlooked-for circumstance suddenly raised the general emotion to the highest degree. The bones were dried up and the flesh consumed. The head alone was intact. Wonderful prodigy! It had resisted the corruption of the grave. That portion of the human body so tender, so delicate, which dissolves so quickly, which is always the first to see corruption,—there it was, after one hundred and forty years, in all its freshness! One could not believe his eyes. The miracle was most brilliant. Four physicians attested it, and great was the amazement at the procès-verbal. Thus this humble though great religious, whom the eighteenth century had overwhelmed with raillery, whom the Jansenists treated as a fool, a poor maniac, a deranged head, was, from a scientific and medical standpoint, proved to have possessed a head that was the best constructed part of her whole frame, since it was the part that best resisted the action of death and time.

Two extraordinary cures, one of which was submitted to the examination of the Sacred Congregation and was declared miraculous, filled all hearts with holy joy.

A poor, sick Sister, given up by the physicians, Marie-Thérèse Pitit, had been confined for three months to a bed of pain, and in such a state of weakness and exhaustion that, even by putting the ear to her mouth, her words could with difficulty be caught. Learning that Margaret Mary's tomb was to be opened, she rallied her strength in the ardor of her faith, placed on her breast some linen that had been around the holy relics, and on the instant felt in the region of her heart some wonderful change. Entirely cured, she rose at once and went to kneel, happy and grateful, at the tomb of her benefactress. This miracle is mentioned in the *Decree of the Miracles.*

The same day a poor, infirm workwoman arrived at the tomb, brought thither from Lyons by a charitable person. As she could not walk, she had to be carried. The decay consequent upon a certain accident had attacked her bones, and made such progress that the physicians, having removed part of the tibia, declared amputation necessary. Her friends bore her to the holy tomb, where she at once arose, knelt without pain, and then stood erect. She had become so strong that they who had brought her weak and helpless now took pleasure in letting her walk.

It was under the lively impression of all these events that the Apostolic Notaries finished their visit. After the procès-verbal had been drawn up by the physicians, and the surgeons sworn, they inclosed the holy relics in a new casket, sealed it with the bishop's arms, and respectfully deposited it under a slab at one of the corners of the cloister; for they thought the hour near in which they should bring her forth again with glory, to be exposed on the altar for public veneration.

That day was, indeed, to come. If prodigies that every day attested her sanctity were brilliant, what were they beside another miracle greater still, one which for over thirty years was accomplished under the eyes of the astonished nineteenth century! The great proof of Margaret's sanctity lay not in the cure of the sick. It is best seen in the Church of France itself, rewarmed, revivified through her by rays from the Sacred Heart. Thus are her prophecies realized; thus is the ice of these latter times melted. It is the Heart of Jesus triumphing over all obstacles, reigning in spite of Satan and his agents. It is the marvellous renaissance of faith, of piety, of the purest love of God, of the most enthusiastic devotedness to the Church in France of Louis XV., of Voltaire, of Robespierre, and of Marat.

Yes, Catholic France, born again in the nineteenth century, has expanded under the beams of the Sacred Heart. All that was good in her she has resuscitated and developed, she has displayed in flowers more beautiful than ever, in fruits more sweet and luscious. Behold, for instance, her missionaries, her apostles! At what epoch have they been more numerous, more poor, more pure, more fruitful than in the nineteenth century? We travel very fast to-day. We have invented steam, railroads, the telegraph; but there is one that travels more quickly still, and that one is the apostle. When our soldiers push on to the very extremities of the world, even to the walls of Pekin, there is found one awaiting them, one to receive them with the chant of the *Te Deum!* When they touch upon those countries at which the Englishman himself, the commercial Englishman, pauses for want of courage to carry further his traffic, there is found one that does not stop, one that presses on, one that ever advances: it is the French missionary, reanimated, rewarmed in the nineteenth century by the Sacred Heart of Jesus Christ.

And whilst all around our frontiers this army of apostles is drawn up, who here in France does not feel himself likewise rekindled?

The priest's heart! Ah! compare the priest of 1770 with the priest of 1870, with our incomparable French clergy who, under the fire of incessant publicity and evil-mindedness, have forced admiration from even their enemies.

The virgin's heart! France knows that there are to-day on French soil more than one hundred thousand maidens who have left all; who in the flower of youth and beauty, in the hour of sweetest hopes, have left all to consecrate themselves to the love and adoration of Jesus Christ! One hundred thousand young girls, pure, chaste, vowed to the sole love of God and mankind, in an age like ours! Who does not see here the impression of the Heart of Jesus Christ on the heart of the Church?

The heart of the mother! Ah! it, too, will be sensibly warmed. Never at any epoch, if we except the first ages of Christianity, have mothers been more jealous of the beauty of their children's soul, more holily eager for their salvation; never have they better transformed their maternity into the priesthood, and their love into an apostolate. Our century is undoubtedly very depraved; but the mother's heart beats too sublimely for us not to hope all things from it. Let us not doubt the age of the Augustines will be redeemed and transfigured by the age of the Monicas!

The hearts of our young men! Will they not also be rekindled? Is it not by young men that the admirable society of St. Vincent de Paul, which to-day extends over the whole world, was founded? And the works of St. Francis Regis, of St. Francis Xavier, of St. Joseph—who supports them? who maintains them? Is it not Christian youth inflamed by the greater love of Jesus Christ? Oh, the French youth! They shine in the nineteenth century with a double and glorious aureola, for they have given their heart to the poor and their blood to the Pope!

All, then, are warmed: the heart of the apostle and the priest, the heart of the virgin and the mother, the heart of the young man. All Christian hearts are now beating in unison; and the sacred flame is the flame of immolation of sacrifice, of love. In what are they all occupied, these young people, these virgins, these Christian women, these men of the world? In visiting the poor, protecting children, consoling the afflicted, spreading faith and hope in every place in which detestable doctrines once sowed irritation and despair. Tell me of some disease, and I shall tell you what sacred battalion is employed in tending and consoling the sufferer. And as the old theologians taught that there is in heaven for each star a choir of angels to direct and inhabit it, even so there is to-day for every misery a choir of virgins, of young men, or Christian women, charged to beguile it into hope and embalm it with charity.

But how greatly admiration increases when we behold at the cost of what sacrifices, in what poverty, in spite of what laws and malevolence, are established and re-established all those apostolic works of charity! Enemies had sold all, proscribed all, destroyed all: these champions of Christ have redeemed all, re-established all. If Louis XIV. could be born again, he would find nothing of his old monarchy. He would, we may well believe, return sad enough to his royal tomb, unwilling to live in the midst of a society no longer known to him. If, on the contrary, saintly Margaret Mary should reappear, she would behold nothing changed in the Church. "See," she would say, "that holy Society of Jesus, in which I found Père de la Colombière, Père Croiset, Père de Gallifet, all those venerable men who were the first servers and adorers of the Heart of Jesus. Behold them, those pious Benedictines, in the grand church overshadowing the little convent of Paray; behold them born again over the whole face of France, renewed and transformed in Burgundy by that venerable Père Muard who, after resuscitating the Order of St. Benedict, to rewarm it placed on his breast the Sacred Heart of Jesus. Behold those Dominicans—they, too, regenerated by a man who was a saint before being a renowned orator; those Capuchins, those Oratorians, all those religious men and women; all those works that then existed, though slightly languishing. All have found new strength, power, youth, vigor, such as they never possessed in the old society. They have now something that renders them more apostolic, more able to conquer, more fruitful, more holily passionate for God and for the Church."

What rouses our greatest admiration in this renaissance of Catholic works in the nineteenth century is that all have lived in misery, yet all have lived in liberty.

They have lived in misery! They were robbed of their wealth, and forbidden to acquire more; they held out their hands to beg—they knew not to-day on what they were to subsist to-morrow: and yet they lived.

They lived in liberty! The eighteenth century proclaimed on every possible key that it was the religious grates, the laws, and decisions of parliament that protected vows. They said: "Destroy the grates, repeal the laws, and you will see the religious life perish miserably." Ah, well! The laws were abolished, parliaments destroyed the grates: the inmates may now clear them when they please and as they please; every facility is offered them. But never has the religious life been more pure, more redolent of virtue. Whilst the enemies of the Church tore down the grates and opened the convent doors, though without succeeding in making the religious leave their seclusion, the Church, more daring still, took the virgin from her cloister, and sent her into the cities and the villages, into hospitals, schools, and workshops, yes, even into prisons. And these religious, so free, so identified with the crowd, do you know what kind of vows the Church allows them to make? Very simple ones; and the greater number of them make those vows for only one year at a time. There is one day in every year, November 21st, upon which nearly one hundred thousand religious are free, for their vows expired the preceding midnight. Can you imagine such a spectacle? One hundred thousand religious freed yearly to return to the world, to marry if it seems good to them. And yet the next morning, at the Mass of seven o'clock, all voluntarily and generously resume the chains that had fallen off, yes, that it was even theirs to unbind. I ask the detractors of religious Orders, do they know of many oaths that could bear to be submitted to a similar test?

In the midst of this vast display of active love, this grand multiplication of apostolic works, contemplation suffers not. Do you know that there are to-day more Carmelite convents than there were in the time of Louis XIV.? Do you know that the Visitation is as fervent, as humble, as contemplative as when directed by St. Francis de Sales or St. Vincent de Paul? Do you know that the sons of St. Bernard are more numerous, more austere in their Trappist homes, than they were in De Rancé's time? Do you know that the spirit of prayer has been revived in families, among maidens, wives, mothers, women of the world? Do you know that self-discipline has become a part of Catholic morals, and that there is no day, no night, in which a multitude of Christians, of husbands, wives, and mothers, even of young girls, do not voluntarily imprint upon themselves the bloody stigmata of the Passion of Jesus Christ? Every day throws some new light on the mysteries of contemplation and penance buried in the heart of our own century. Only yesterday I read an admirable book in which the greatest Christian orator we have had since Bossuet, namely, Père Lacordaire, was shown me all wounded by penitential blows. Causing himself, on leaving the pulpit of Notre Dame, to be tied to a pillar and beaten with scourges until he fainted, he equals and even surpasses the most austere penitents, though still unable to satisfy the thirst for immolation and sacrifice that devoured him.[1] And yet all is not told of him nor of others. When the secrets of lives shall be revealed on the last day, we shall understand why this age, so agitated and so guilty, has not been sunk in the depths of the abyss; and we shall bless the Church for having redeemed it by forcing it to suffer and to immolate itself for Christ.

[1] Le P. Lacordaire, Sa Vie Intime, par le R. P. Chocarne. 1 vol. octavo.

Now, what is the source of all these wonders? Manifestly, all spring from the Heart of Jesus, known, adored, loved, casting its beneficent rays over the whole world. The old fear has departed, the cold breath of Jansenism has vanished; under the fire of love, the ice has everywhere melted. The holy table is more frequented; daily is the Lord more tenderly received, and by a greater number. This is the hidden source, the wellspring of all these marvels. It is thence comes to the Church of the nineteenth century her beauty, her fruitfulness, her invincible strength. The Heart of Jesus has darted its rays upon her. It has vivified her, warmed her, transfigured her, and rendered her all beautiful. And here we behold Margaret Mary's great miracle. She knew it in advance, she predicted it, she trembled with joy at the thought of it. In her humility, she asked to die that she might not be an obstacle to it, that she might not for one moment delay the glorification of the Heart of Jesus, and the universal rekindling of love in hearts. It was this movement daily becoming more brilliant and more irresistible that pleaded her cause at Rome, and advanced it in spite of a thousand obstacles.

From the departure of the Apostolic Notaries for Paray in 1830, forty years were necessary to examine the virtues and writings of the saintly Sister. Everything was analyzed, studied, and discussed with that exactitude, that maturity, which characterizes the irrevocable acts of the Roman court. The Congregation of Rites had just pronounced favorably on the heroicity of our saint's virtues, when Gregory XVI. died, leaving to Pius IX. the glory and joy of proclaiming them. It was one of the first acts of his illustrious pontificate. Scarcely seated on the Chair of St. Peter, Pius IX. raised his eyes to the Heart of Jesus; and one morning in the month of July, 1846, saw him going on foot to the Quirinal, to the Visitation, there to say Mass, and to announce to the Sisters, trembling with emotion, that the hour was come to promote, at one and the same time, devotion to the Sacred Heart and the glory of its servant. The decree appeared in the month following, August 23, 1846, during the octave of the feast of St. Chantal, the foundress of the Visitation. A delicate thought had decided the choice of this day, and it again brought the Pope into the midst of the daughters of St. Francis de Sales, to break to them the happy news of the future glorification of their holy Sister.

All was now thought to be ended. Alas! twenty-four years were still to elapse before the last and solemn Decree of Beatification, April 24, 1864. The delay had, however, no other effect than to excite the impatience of the Christian people, and to prepare for Margaret Mary a triumph worthy of her.

It began at Paray by a new opening of the tomb, with a view to recognize definitely the holy relics. They were not to be returned to their resting-place, and from them was to be taken the special relic which, on the altar of St. Peter, was to receive the first homage of the Pope and the Church. Although very private, this opening of the tomb had in it something triumphal; for no public demonstrations of joy and devotion were as yet permitted. But the humble cloister in which Margaret rested, and in which her feast was to be celebrated, saw its poor walls hidden under ornamentation the most brilliant. Oriflambs, escutcheons, pictures, devices in verse and prose, everywhere met the gaze. All was bright, elegant, devout, and pleasing. All was like unto the spirit of St. Francis de Sales; and, let us add,—for this was what touched us most,—all was in a high degree Catholic and French. In the solitude of the little convent, shut in on all sides, whose inmates the votaries of the world imagined knew only how to raise toward heaven an egotistical eye, was felt the great soul of France palpitating, of that France which had not abdicated her baptism and which, in the midst of all her sadness and misfortunes, still hoped on. The oriflambs streaming from the windows all along the galleries were ablaze with emblems and devices; loud cries of love for the Church and the Holy Father, for France and Paray, for the whole nation, cries of love for their home in heaven and for that of earth, united on all the escutcheons as they did in all hearts.

Mgr. de Marguerie, Bishop of Autun, who had taken the most pious and intelligent interest in the cause of the Beatification, presided at this private ceremony. After forming a jury for the recognition of the relics, and receiving the oath on the holy Gospels of all about to help at the opening of the coffin, priests, physicians, workmen, he went to the humble tomb containing the remains of the venerable Sister. They were laid in one of the corners of the cloister, under a simple stone, upon which was inscribed merely her name. As if to make amends for its poverty, there were seen all around on the wall hearts of gold or silver suspended as tokens of the veneration that embalmed her memory, and the favors obtained by her intercession. The tombstone being carefully raised, in an excavation sufficiently deep was disclosed the wooden coffin that contained the bones of the saintly Sister. Without opening it, and after having permitted some few to kiss it, a rich pall was thrown over it, and the honor of carrying it was left to the tender and loving hands of her Sisters. It was borne processionally through the cloister to the room in which the relics were to be examined. The Visitandines, with lighted tapers, and chanting the Office of Virgins, walked before the casket; and over three hundred priests, accompanied by the chief magistrates and inhabitants of the city, followed the holy relics in silence. The countenance of all, recollected or beaming with joy, proclaimed better than words the sentiments that filled their heart.

Thus came forth from her tomb, never again to enter it, this illustrious virgin of God! Thus, after two centuries, did she traverse again, in triumphant recollection, and hidden as was her life, those cloisters that she had once filled with the perfume of her humility! In spite of a revolution that had crushed empires and scattered royal races, the religious of the Visitation were still there to form the cortège, to carry their Sister's blessed remains, to make glad her path by their songs of joy, their prayers, and their tears!

Arrived at the assembly-room, the procession paused, and all bowed low in veneration of the precious wood that inclosed the virginal body of one of the purest of God's creatures. Then they opened the coffin and exposed to view all that remained in this world of her to whom our Lord had so frequently appeared. Admirable fact! Skeletons inspire horror, but not so those of the saints. The mouldering bones, the shreds of flesh gone to dust found in the depths of a tomb and for which no language has a name, whether once animated by a mighty genius, whether once transfigured by glory and beauty,—all creates fear. But if the love of God, the heroism of sanctity, cling around those remains, behold, they live forever! To touch them, to kiss them, was the desire of the crowd. It was actually necessary to drive them from the church, to prevent their throwing themselves on the sacred body, pressing to it their lips, and distributing its remains. Death was conquered, and life was felt triumphantly circulating through the dry bones.

During the examination and veneration of the relics occurred one most impressive moment. Deep anxiety filled all hearts. The head, which up to 1830 had been preserved from corruption,—in what state would it now be found? Would God allow a sign of life still to reside in the dry bones? The bishop raised the cranium. Behold the august sign! Vainly had the past thirty-four years rolled by! Vainly had the casket been opened and the head exposed to the air! It has continued the same, intact, living! We prostrate, we admire, we adore! We relate analogous facts, and all hearts beat with holy enthusiasm. When, for example, Mary Magdalen died, and time had gradually dried up all her bones, there was in her, also, a morsel of flesh that resisted corruption. It was that which the Lord had touched when she approached Him after His resurrection. With the words, "Noli me tangere," He laid His finger on her forehead to keep her at a distance. Twelve hundred years after, on that spot of the forehead, the flesh appeared quick and living, as if to show us human flesh, even the most profaned, after the transfiguring finger of God has touched it to purify it. In like manner, when St. John Nepomucene was martyred for not revealing the secrets of the confessional, his tongue was spared, although his whole body had become the prey of death. Three hundred years after his death, it was found fresh and living, an eternal witness to the divinity of the confessional. Again, when St. Chantal died, nothing could dry up her heart. It still seemed to live. At certain moments it was seen to swell with sorrow or love, as if to teach the world not to doubt the ardor with which it beat when living. In Margaret Mary's case it was the head that resisted death, because it was of the head the world doubted. God preserved it intact, in order to render venerable the thoughts that emanated from it. Let us add faith in the sublime inventions of which it was the organ.

Ah! long years must pass before we shall forget our emotion when the head of Margaret Mary, entire and intact, was given us to hold in our hands. We were almost alone, for the crowd had been forced to retire, that the physicians might have more liberty to recognize the relics, to contemplate at leisure what remained of her body, and in that study to form some conjecture of what the holy soul had been. Those delicate bones, those well-proportioned curves, the beauty of the forehead, the breadth of the temples, the incorruptibility of the cranium, the fine lines of the face,—all these remains of the mortal vase that once inclosed so beautiful a soul afforded us, as it were, a glimpse of the saint such it might seem she was two hundred years ago, in the days of her earthly pilgrimage. She was of medium height, though rather tall than short, of a fragile and delicate constitution, as God makes souls whom He has destined for great sufferings ; of exquisite sensibility, as is fitting to those who are to love much. She added to this great intelligence, perfect good sense, judgment proof against every species of delusion, as was requisite in order not to mingle the imagination and human ideas with what God deigned to reveal to her. To complete the picture, she was possessed of a gentle but unshaken will ; a soul patient but immovable, which recoiled before no opposition ; of love so ardent and such power of devotedness that no sacrifice could ever satisfy. She possessed, moreover, elevation and delicacy of sentiment, and a depth of heart which rendered her capable of understanding the Heart of her Divine Master, of divining its sublime inventions, of presenting them to a cold and railing world, and of leading it to their acceptance in preparation for its own regeneration.

Behold the illustrious Margaret Mary, such as her soul appeared to us whilst, with respectful hand and agitated heart, we replaced one by one in a rich casket of silver-gilt the remains of her virginal body ! That done, the religious again took it up joyously, and we carried it in triumph to the interior choir, where it was placed on the throne prepared for it. Above it were two figures of angels holding a virgin's crown. There the precious relics were to remain until the solemn day of Beatification, which took place in Rome, September 4, 1864. From early dawn on that memorable day, the

cannon of St. Angelo announced in joyous boomings
that the lover of the Heart of Jesus was about to be
proclaimed Blessed. On the evening of the same day,
Pius IX., attended by a numerous cortège, in which we
remarked over two hundred French priests, knelt before her picture. The bishop of the diocese to which
the saintly Sister belonged approached the Father of
the Faithful and, together with his allegiance and that
of the Church of France, offered him some simple gifts,
among them a bouquet of flowers, emblematic of the
virtues that his diocese had seen flourish in the humble
Visitandine parterre of Paray, and whose perfume was
now about to embalm the whole Church. The year
following, the feast of the Beatification was celebrated
in every convent of the Visitation. At Paray it lasted
three days with extraordinary brilliancy, over a hundred
thousand persons being in attendance. His Eminence
the Cardinal-Archbishop of Besançon presided, assisted
by the prelates of Autun, Bourges, Dijon, Nîmes,
Évreux, Annecy, and Hébron ; the mitred abbots of
Sept-Fonds, d'Aiguebelles, of Mount Olives, of Sainte-
Marie-du-Mont, of Grâce-de-Dieu ; over four hundred
priests and a multitude of religious belonging to various Orders. The holy relics were removed from their
humble wooden casket and placed in a magnificent one
of silver-gilt set with precious stones, amethysts, and
topaz, and enamelled in the style of the Middle Ages.
For three days the relics were carried in triumph through
the parish streets of Paray, on the shoulders of twenty-
four priests robed in dalmatics. Nothing could exceed
the beauty of these processions, which recalled the
splendor of those of the Middle Ages. But what
would be still more difficult to describe is their triumphal character, the joy depicted on all faces, the enthusiasm that swelled all hearts. One felt himself at the
last act of a sublime drama, of which he recalled the
humble beginning and the sorrowful progress with its

hard trials. We now touch as with the hand the magnificent denouement. God's promises were then realized. The Church of France was there before the eyes of all, living, fervent, rejuvenated, warmed by the beams of the Sacred Heart. Margaret Mary ascended the altars. The Heart of Jesus reigned, in spite of all its enemies, and illumined the wide world.

After three days of holy inebriation, the virginal body was carried again into the chapel of the Visitation. There our humble Margaret Mary now rests. They have laid her in a splendid casket beneath the white marble altar, under the very spot upon which our Lord appeared to her. Fifty-three lamps cast their radiant light upon this altar, now become a sepulchre. They burn day and night in honor of the Divine Spouse and His humble servant. The pilgrim on his arrival pauses, involuntarily moved. The sweet mysteries accomplished in this place : on the one side, virginity, tenderness, thirst for immolation, heavenly detachment ; on the other, condescension, mercy, infinite love ; and the divine effects, touching and sublime, of the drama enacted on this altar,—all that speaks to the soul. He forgets himself for hours in mute contemplation. There have been places more highly venerated on this earth, but there are very few more august or more sweet.

CHAPTER XVIII.

UNEXPECTED AND MARVELLOUS SPREAD OF DEVO-
TION TO THE HEART OF JESUS AMID THE MISFOR-
TUNES OF FRANCE—THE SECOND PART OF THE
MISSION CONFIDED TO **SAINT** MARGARET MARY
APPROACHES ITS ACCOMPLISHMENT.

1870–1874.

ABNER. " The holy Ark is silent and gives no more oracles."
JOAD. " Ah! what time was ever more fruitful in miracles!
Shall we, then, always have eyes and see not ?"
Racine, "Athalie."

THE first part of the mission confided to Saint
Margaret Mary was ended, but not so the second.
The words spoken for the Pope and the Church
had been realized; those spoken for the king and
France had been despised. Neither Louis XIV. nor
Louis XV. had deigned to notice them; and the lamenta-
tions of the captive Louis XVI. were drowned in the
blasphemies of the Revolution. Thus, whilst the Church
in France opened to the nineteenth century under the
sweet and genial rays of the Sacred Heart, and produced unrelaxingly and unwearingly the most savory
fruits of faith, charity, and purity, of the apostolate and
of martyrdom, society, civil and political, strayed further
and further toward destruction. In vain had God
given France of the nineteenth century gifts the most
beautiful: gifts of genius, eloquence, science, glory; gifts
greater than at any other epoch. Like a sick man refusing the only remedy that contains a cure for him,
she saw her evils increase every day. Torn by a utopian
and impious revolution from her old national and
Christian constitutions, fruit of the experience of fifteen

centuries, she has since been unable to find her centre. She has tried in turn the republic, the empire, and constitutional royalty. She returned to the republic, then to the empire, and back again to the republic. Ever agitated, disquieted, and ill at ease, she finally went so far as to abandon all her constitutions, and, not knowing which to choose, she ended in a futile attempt to rest on the provisional pillow, thus showing to the world in her own person the greatest political incapacity yet recorded in history.

At the same time France felt in her bosom the mutterings of most awful passions. Shamefully hidden in the folds of guilty hearts were pride, envy, covetousness. Kept in check hitherto by the power of Christian conscience, they now publicly showed themselves, united, and became an army. The cannon of civil war, unheard in France since the time of Henry IV., which had sounded neither in the seventeenth nor even in the eighteenth century, began to boom in the nineteenth. During three days of 1830, at two different intervals of '48, and for six whole months in '70, its ominous tones burst forth. Every fifteen years the fratricidal war assumed vaster and more odious proportions, whilst opulent France danced on the volcano and stirred its flames. Her great writers, Lamartine, Thiers, Michelet, Victor Hugo, glorified Robespierre, acquitted Marat, palliated Louis XVI.'s execution, and even hailed it as a grand, patriotic act. Her savants employed their learning, their discoveries, and even the resources of the state to assert that there is no God, no soul, no living and immortal mind; that all will one day be reduced to vile matter; and that the ideas of vice, virtue, liberty, responsibility, are good old words, but, like those that taught them to us, worthy only of contempt. Her industries, her great proprietors, the directors of her public works, neglected no means to snatch God and every idea of religion from the heart of the mechanic, the laborer, and

the poor. Ah, that was not the most excellent means
to render them upright, honest, chaste, and religious observers of the rights and property of others! The poets,
the novelists, the dramatists of France labored day and
night to make the theatre a hell. Her high-born ladies
seemed to regret the happy days of Mme. de Montespan,
of Mme. de Pompadour, of Mme. du Barry ; and, no
longer having under their eyes models so illustrious,
they set to work to imitate the allurements, the cos-
tumes, the walk, even the language of their sisters of
the demi-monde. Morals became corrupted, minds ob-
scured, character weakened, health destroyed; physical
and moral deformity invaded every circle. Meanwhile
our grave statesmen were occupied only in watching
that God and religion might not gain too much influence.

Then came the barbarians! Their hour sounded.

History will long record their deeds, though not
knowing how to describe the Queen of Nations, accustomed to conquer, always victorious, rising twenty times
to a degree of heroism that her conquerors had never
known, and yet falling as often into the dust. Her
counsels were reversed, her chiefs paralyzed; the very
elements turned against her, the better to mark whence
came defeat. In seven months of struggle France
found again neither one flash of her genius nor one ray
of her happiness.

As everything connected with this nation must be extraordinary, so, too, with her misfortunes. At the close
of this fearful war, when the sword should have been
sheathed, behold Paris suddenly fired with fratricidal
flames! Our monuments, our palaces, our libraries, our
museums destroyed by French hands! Bands of savage
beasts in human form, by the glare of the incendiary,
pillaged and profaned her churches, shot her bishops,
priests, magistrates, and soldiers; and on the heights
bordering upon Mont Valérien Vanves, Saint-Denis,

behold the long-sighted Prussians clapping their hands at seeing in flames the magnificent city that had resisted all their assaults ! This is what history shall long contemplate, and, as in another Rome, recognize in it the finger of God.

But soon from this scene of grandeur, already so tragical, it will rise to a spectacle still higher and more solemn. France, conquered, wounded, laid low on twenty battle-fields, will be seen to divide into two kingdoms : one frivolous and always full of self, seeking in political combinations, in recriminations and condemnations, if not a remedy, at least a solace for her evils, and trying to prove that she is not guilty; the other, striking her breast, asks pardon, raises her eyes to heaven, and to be more sure of averting God's anger, instead of kissing His feet and bedewing them with tears, rises higher, even to His Heart.

Admirable thing! This recourse to the Heart of Jesus, which in 1793 was spontaneously and as if instinctively offered to the victims, is also presented in 1870 to the vanquished. This thought that slept for sixty years in the heart of France, is awakened by the bloody glare of her simultaneous defeats at so many points, and with so little opposition that it is impossible not to see in it the hand of God. He is a good and tender Father who recalls to His sick child the thought of the grand remedy.

The first fact that we are going to relate will alone suffice to show the merciful hand of God. Toward the close of 1870, at the time in which all our regular army was paralyzed or destroyed under the walls of Metz and Paris, bands of volunteers were seen to rise at the same time in a thousand places. They were called by different names, and they bore different standards; but what of that ? The hour of exclusiveness was past. The appeal to voluntary sacrifice was general: and the Pontifical Zouaves were the first to offer their swords to

France. The Vendeans arose under Cathelineau; the Bretons organized as skirmishers; and, without preliminary or preamble, the various troops placed on their breasts the badge of the Heart of Jesus: those, because it was the emblem that Pius IX. had blest and given them at Mentana; and these, too, in memory of their fathers, Henri de la Rochejaquelein, Lescure, Bonchamps, Charette; and all in remembrance of the consoling and prophetic revelations of Paray. The sequel will show whether or not the Heart of Jesus on the soldier's heart made him fight less valiantly.

Some days after, on a cold night, December 1, 1870, two superior officers turned their steps toward Paray, whither they were going to spend the next day in amusement before setting out from France. One was General de Sonis, commandant of the 17th corps of the army; the other, Colonel de Charette, who was at the head of the Zouaves. Both were deeply impressed with the gravity of the times through which they were passing, and the evident fact that, without the manifest assistance of God, all was over with France. The cold was intense. It was impossible to proceed on horseback; therefore the General and the Colonel dismounted, and continued their journey on foot. Whilst walking along, the General expressed his regret to Colonel Charette at not seeing on his own banner an emblem more religiously characteristic. "General," replied the Colonel, "I can give you what you desire." Then he told the General that the same day on which he had received authorization from the French Government to fight along with the Zouaves, on condition that they should take the title of "Western Volunteers," there had arrived from a distance a flag on which was painted the Sacred Heart. It had come under this address: "To the Defenders' of the West." He learned later that the banner had been embroidered at Paray by the religious; that it was sent first to Paris and then to Tours, with the request that it should appear on the battle-field. General de Sonis regarded it as an inspiration of God, and the banner of the Sacred Heart was immediately chosen as the labarum, the oriflamb, of the Zouaves. To prevent opposition, it was decided not to unfurl it until it could receive the baptism of fire; and that France should see it only when it would be, so to say, tinged with French blood. They felt sure that, after the battle, this banner, victorious or conquered, would command such respect that no French army would allow it to pass without inclining to it their swords.

The next day, December 2, 1870, first Friday of the month, a day consecrated to the Sacred Heart, Mass was celebrated at three o'clock in the morning. General de Sonis, Colonel de Charette, the greater part of the officers, and a number of soldiers approached the holy table, to learn from the Heart of Jesus how to suffer, how to sacrifice themselves. The battle began at once, and, in spite of numerical disproportion, remained undecided until half-past two in the afternoon. The enemies' reinforcements continued to pour in, and it was easy to foresee the moment in which, without some heroic and successful effort, the Zouaves would be obliged to retreat. General Sonis took his resolution. Gathering together a column for attack, he tried to hurl it upon the village de Loigny; but two of the regiments threw themselves on the ground and refused to advance. At this juncture, the General hesitated no longer. Pressing forward with his Zouaves, he cried: " Gentlemen, behold the hour to show that you know how to conduct yourselves as Frenchmen and Christians! Forward!" An enthusiastic cry was the only response. Sergeant Henri de Verthamon at the head of his battalion darted forward fifty steps, and displayed the standard of the Sacred Heart. All rushed after him with the cry: " Long live Pius IX.! Long live France !" A considerable distance had to be cleared under a fearful discharge of musketry. The Zouaves, without one shot, crossed bravely and in good order. Arrived in front of the little wood, they opened fire, presented bayonets, tore up the wood, gave chase to the Germans, reached the village, amid a cloud, not of *incense,* but of *powder,* and placed in position the banner of the Sacred Heart.

The enemy, now perceiving the smallness of the number by which they had been routed, in surprise called forth·their reserve. The masses ranged. After astonishing the Prussians by their assault, they were now going to astonish them by their heroism Generals de Charette, de Sonis, Troussures fell at the side of the banner of the Sacred Heart, become the target of all projectiles. De Verthamon, who held it, died purpling it with his blood. Count de Bouille instantly raised it again. He, too, was soon struck with death. He passed it to his son, Count James de Bouille, who, after bearing it aloft for some time, fell in his turn. Parment, who succeeded him, had his hand broken. He was, consequently, obliged to relinquish the sacred standard, now stained with blood and rent in several places, to Sergeant Landeau. Most of the Zouaves were conquered where they wished to die. They fell in the Heart of Jesus, and their death shed on the battle-field a ray of pure glory like unto that of the Crusades.

Next day Orléans was taken, and the remnant of the Zouaves went to be hacked to pieces at Manns, in order to cover the retreat of Chanzy. Five months later Paris surrendered, the war was over, and the Zouaves free. Before separating they wished to take leave of their banner, to offer it supreme ovation, and accomplish an action suggested by the events that had just transpired.

They met in a church at Rennes. There during the Holy Sacrifice, at the moment of holy Communion, the banner of the Sacred Heart was solemnly borne in and placed at the foot of the altar. General de Charette and his officers grouped around it. The almoner-in-chief, Mgr. Daniel, read on his knees an Act of Consecration to the Sacred Heart, composed and sent by General Sonis, who was detained at a distance by his wound. After that General de Charette pronounced in a sonorous voice the following words: "Under the shadow of this flag stained with the blood of our dearest victims, I, General Baron de Charette, who had the signal honor of commanding you, consecrate the legion of the Western Volunteers, the Pontifical Zouaves, to the Sacred Heart of Jesus; and with my soldierly faith, I say with all my soul, and I ask you all to say with me: 'Heart of Jesus, save France!'" A unanimous cry, spontaneous, awe-inspiring, responded: "Heart of Jesus, save France!"

Thus ended this heroic episode of our sad war. It was only the second time since the oriflamb of the Crusades that a religious flag had appeared on the battle-field. The first had been carried by Joan of Arc; the second by the Pontifical Zouaves.

Whilst these things were passing on the battle-field, and in a manner so wonderful, though so little foreseen, the words of the Lord to Margaret Mary, "I desire that the image of My Heart be engraven on the French standard," were being accomplished, another word of the Lord was realized still more unexpectedly. In the midst of Paris, then occupied by the Prussians and isolated from the rest of France, some pious and eminent laics were recounting their country's misfortunes and seeking for means to come to its assistance. Suddenly they were inspired to make a solemn vow to erect in the heart of Paris a church consecrated to the Heart of Jesus. The vow was drawn up in due form. In it are read these words:

"In view of the misfortunes that are now afflicting

France, and of the still greater evils that perhaps yet threaten her;

" In view of the sacrilegious outrages committed in Rome against the rights of the Church, of the Holy See, and the sacred person of the Vicar of Jesus Christ;

" To make honorable atonement for our sins, to receive pardon through the merciful intervention of the Sacred Heart of our Lord Jesus Christ, and to obtain by this same intervention the extraordinary assistance that alone can deliver the Sovereign Pontiff from his captivity, put an end to the misfortunes of France, and lead to its social and religious restoration,—

" We promise, when these graces shall have been granted, to contribute according to our means to the erection in Paris of a church consecrated to the Sacred Heart of Jesus, permission for the erection of which will be asked of proper ecclesiastical authority."

Did the signers of this act think of the revelations made to Saint Margaret Mary? No more, perhaps, than the Vendeans on the battle-field, or the " Western Volunteers " at Paray. But there was One that thought for them.

The war ended, their vow was not forgotten. The first step of those that had taken it was to address themselves to the Archbishop of Paris, submit to him their project, and ask his blessing for its accomplishment. The see of St. Denis was then occupied by Mgr. Guibert, successor of the illustrious victim of the Commune, Mgr. Darboy. The prelate, in his piety and intelligence, understood the Christian grandeur of such conceptions; and not satisfied with granting the authorization asked of him, he determined to devote to its realization his authority, his exalted position, his influence, and his whole heart. He addressed, in consequence, all the bishops of his diocese, and begged them to come to his aid. The work had already assumed, and as if of itself, large proportions. What was originally to have been a chapel, or a small church (the result of an initiative movement on the part of a few) was now to become a national church, built with the funds, the concurrence, and the heart of all France.

It remained to choose a suitable locality. When we glance at the map of Paris, we perceive on the north a mountain celebrated not only for the geological treasures that it incloses in its depths; not only because, by its mysterious composition in the midst of the vast basin of the Seine, it is an inexplicable wonder yet to science; but celebrated, above all, because from remote ages it has always been a holy place, a sanctuary venerated and visited from afar. It is there that St. Denis, come to evangelize the Gauls, met their most famous idols and hurled them down; there, succumbing to the fury of the pagans, he consecrated and transfigured this mountain by the shedding of his blood; and there it was that, on the very spot of his sufferings, arose that illustrious church, built and rebuilt from age to age, consecrated in the thirteenth century by Innocent III., and whither flock in pilgrimage all that Paris has ever possessed of eminent holiness and sanctity. It was there that St. Ignatius and his companions laid the foundation of the Society of Jesus. It is there that are met in the same faith and the same memories Cardinal de Bérulle, M. Olier, Père de Condren, Bossuet, St. Vincent de Paul. Montmartre is the holy place of Paris. The people, who best preserve the grand traditions of holy things, have never ceased to love and visit Montmartre.

No position could, then, be better suited. Encouraged as the work progressed, they resolved to build on this mountain, whence it could look down upon all Paris, a temple which, by the immensity of its proportions, the beauty of its sublime outlines, the splendor and richness of its ornaments, would be truly a national temple consecrated by all France to the Heart of

Jesus. And in order to note well of what inspiration it was born, they agreed to engrave upon the portal the words:

CHRISTO EJUSQUE SACRATISSIMO CORDI
GALLIA PŒNITENS ET DEVOTA.

To realize so gigantic an enterprise, it was necessary to expropriate a certain number of houses built on the summit of the mountain. This brought the matter before the National Assembly—that is to say, since France is a republic, before the sovereign. It was an occasion that the goodness of God offered France to accomplish what Louis XIV. had not done, but what Louis XVI., enlightened by misfortune, had promised God in prison. If the National Assembly allowed this providential occasion to escape, it performed at least one important act, one that will be to its eternal honor. On the plea of public utility, it voted the expropriation; that is to say, it declared it to be a public utility that repentant France should erect a temple to the Sacred Heart. This church not having been asked for under the title of a parish church, nor exacted by the needs of worship, the vote of the Assembly could be interpreted only in this sense, as even the enemies of the project remarked. France herself understood it in this way; and the idea of a national church on the summit of Montmartre, an idea popular from the very outset, received new impulse. Subscriptions were opened in all the dioceses; committees were formed to excite and sustain zeal; and soon some intelligent and delicate initiative measures were begun. The army asked to build and ornament a chapel at its own expense. The working-men, also, offered shortly after to build one that should be consecrated to "Jesus as a Workman." The movement went on. Christian mothers desired to erect a church to St. Monica; the children would also consecrate one to the Child Jesus; the priests, one to " Jesus as Priest;" and bishops,

to " Jesus as Pontiff." The virgins could not be forgotten
by their Divine Spouse. And thus the temple built with
the gold and silver of France shall ever be a monument of the sweetest inspirations of her piety and
heart. But who will lay the first stone? Above all,
who will make the solemn consecration? No one
knows. Let us trust that God will descend among the
workmen, and make Himself known by strokes most
unexpected.

He had said to Saint Margaret Mary: "I desire
that a temple be dedicated to My divine Heart." He
will, then, assist in the building; and, as it is said of
several of our old cathedrals that on the day of their
consecration angelic voices were heard filling the air
with sweetest songs, so we may believe that on this day
there will descend upon kneeling France celestial words,
words of love and pardon.

It is in this temple will be made by the mouth of her
sovereign, whoever he may be at the time, the consecration of France to the divine Heart of Jesus. That
day will be a great one in our history. The old alliance
will be renewed, and God will again become the God of
France. Can we credit the facts just narrated—the
banner of the Sacred Heart on our battle-fields, and
the erection in Paris of a national church to the Heart
of Jesus? Can these two events, so extraordinary, be
surpassed? Yes, and they will be. The month of June,
1873, witnessed a fact which, whether we consider
the time in which it occurred or the manner in which
it was accomplished, the gigantic proportions with
which it was clothed bear all the appearance of a miracle.

Shortly after the close of the war, the day after the
horrors of the Commune, toward the autumn of '71 and
during the year of '72, we felt an unusual breath pass
over France. The celebrated sanctuaries were more frequented; pilgrimages began, though timidly at first,

like the distant prognostics that precede or foretell a
storm. In 1873, Catholic France was agitated by an
impulse it had not felt for over six centuries. National
pilgrimages began to Lourdes, Salette, Chartres, Four-
vières, Pontmain, Puy, and France threw herself into
them suppliantly. On one day Lourdes saw one hundred thousand kneeling men gathered round her shrine.
Then came the local pilgrimages. Each diocese had its
own, and in it were sometimes seen thirty thousand pilgrims. Had we the exact statistics of these pilgrimages, we should indeed be astonished.

Among them all, that of Paray holds a rank apart. It
was estimated that one day would suffice for all the
others; but that of Paray required a month. One felt
that all France was coming. Marseilles, the city of the
Sacred Heart, opened the march and arrived the first.
It was followed every day by two, three, four, five dioceses, each with its own banner. June 25th, Friday
after the octave of Corpus Christi, they numbered
twenty-five thousand men ! A month was not enough
for the procession, which daily received new increase.
The pilgrimage had to be prolonged until the end of
July. Then, when the concourse of the French began
to subside, English, Dutch, and Belgian pilgrims arrived. They who could not yet come (not the Ameri-
cans, for they were coming), the Scots, the Poles, the
Russians, sent their banners to represent them. The
invisible Lover, until then hidden in the secret of the
cloister, had been brought to light. He attracted all
hearts. "Hundreds of banners, hearts, ex votos, letters
were sent to us from all corners of France," wrote the
religious of Paray. "All the parish churches, all the
Communities, all the institutions of the capital, though
ever so little religious, sent their souvenirs. . . . It was
an unheard-of assemblage. . . . We at first thought
that we should be able to keep an account of the ex
votos; but at the end of three days we found that to

number them would be impossible. Our choir-grate was not large enough to hold them, for we found them everywhere. All these manifestations may be summed up in these words inscribed some thousand times on the ex votos: 'France to the Sacred Heart of Jesus!'" [1]

But it was not only its duration and the number that composed the pilgrimage that gave to it its miraculous character; it was the manner in which it was performed that rendered it truly surprising. The same was re-marked everywhere. Such a movement was opposed to French habits,—so opposed, in fact, that one asks him-self how it could have taken place so spontaneously and unanimously. This is the plan they followed. The pil-grims set out in procession from some church and went to the railway station. There they set up their banner, placed on their breast the picture of the Heart of Jesus, and, at the first sound of the whistle, began their chants.

Almost every age, to express its sentiments or give soul to the emotions it has aroused, produces a popular chant or song. Who is the author? Whence did it come? Who put it one day, fiery or terrible, on the lips of the people? Neither the Greeks in the time of Tyrtæus; nor our own ancestors, the old Gauls, in their forests; nor France at the epoch of her grandest crises, could say. No one has written it, but every one sings it. It springs from the soul of the people. In the same manner came forth the hymn that then resounded for the first time, ardent and sad, supplicating and tender, bathing in tears the sorrows of the Church of France, and uttering at each refrain a cry of hope and a cry for pardon. Very different from the savage clamors of the revolutionists, it appealed to the tenderness of Heaven and not to the anger of earth; instead of exciting souls to hatred, it appeased them by repentance.

Giving our soul up to a sort of pious joy and recol-

[1] Circular letter of Paray upon the pilgrimage of the montb of June, 1873.

lection as if in a private chapel, we sang the whole length of the journey. When the train slackened its speed, the singing was heard to proceed from each car; and the sound, so unusual and so sweet, brought tears to the eyes.

Sometimes it happened that two trains met at the same station. The pilgrims, taking their stand in the doorway of their several cars, sang in choir. We shall never forget our emotion on a certain occasion of this kind. Our train had to stop at a station to let two special trains from Paris pass. One of them, speeding along like lightning, hurled at us this verse of the canticle:

> " Mercy, my God, for on a new Calvary
> The Head of Thy Church is groaning in tears!"

In an instant we were on our feet with the spontaneous, unanimous cry: "Long live Pius IX.! Long live France!"

The morning of the great feast, June 20, 1873, the sun rose in splendor, and all the rest of the month the processions were not delayed a single day by rain. As was formerly said "the sun of Austerlitz," was now said "the sun of the Sacred Heart."

As we neared Paray, the stations assumed an unusual appearance. Crowds of pilgrims were huddled around them long before the time: priests, religious, swarms of young girls dressed in white, gay as birds, and wearing on their breast the Heart of Jesus; vehicles of all kinds, grand equipages, and common carts, laden and overladen with passengers, coming at triple speed, in their fear of losing a place which they foresaw would be difficult to find. In the midst of all this concourse of people reigned a calm and joyous serenity. Of these thousands of men, women, and young girls, all prepared to approach the holy table. They preserved, even in their eagerness, and notwithstanding the astonishment excited by so unusual a scene, the recollection which, in Christian homes, always precedes such an action. Spectacles such as these France does not see often enough. Her profoundly religious nature, her heart so sympathetic with all that is elevated and sincere, would find it hard to resist such influence.

Nothing for many a day will equal in this respect June 20th at Paray. It was the Friday after the octave of the feast of Corpus Christi, the day of which the Lord had said to His humble lover: "*I wish the Friday after the octave of Corpus Christi to be dedicated as a solemn feast in honor of My divine Heart.*" From midnight, Masses were being said on the altars everywhere improvised. They were not sufficient, despite their great numbers. This was the only regret of the day. There should have been a hundred altars more. In the Visitation chapel, between the altar upon which our Lord appeared and the grate behind which she knelt, reposed Saint Margaret Mary. Her splendid casket had been raised on a throne surrounded with myriads of lights, and covered with hearts, crowns, petitions, ex votos of all sorts. At the head of the throne, like the banner of Joan of Arc, which, after having waved at the stake, was one day, to the honor of the country, to shade with its folds the altar of coronation, was seen the banner of the Zouaves, pierced by Prussian bullets and stained with blood. It was waving above the casket. The faithful kissed it in passing; mothers approached it with their little ones; and we saw soldiers touching it reverently with their naked swords.

At nine o'clock the procession began to move. It was no longer a brilliant triumphal march; it had become official and liturgical like that we had admired in 1865, at the time of the Beatification. There were, however, neither cardinals nor bishops [1] nor mitred abbots, for they were mingled with the people. The liturgical

---

[1] Except the titular bishop, and Mgr. de Marguerie, former bishop of Autun.

chant had given place to one single canticle in French, which incessantly rose to all lips:

> " Save, save France,
> In the name of the Sacred Heart !"

Shall we dare to say that this was not a procession of the Church ? It was a procession of France humbled, repentant, striking her breast, and crying: " Mercy, my God!"

Each diocese ranged under its own banner, as did the various institutions, colleges, and Communities. There were over three hundred banners, each richer than its neighbor, each symbolical and eloquent, each displaying mottoes and legends and words that pierced the soul like a dart. The people applauded as they were borne along. Their enthusiastic cries of joy or of sorrow, mingling with the chants of those that formed the cortège to the banners, produced an indefinable impression on the soul.

An unexpected event happened at the very outset, which was well calculated to rouse and excite the multitude. Some banners had already passed, wending their way toward a little hill that overlooked the town. There an altar had been erected for Mass in the open air. All at once, through a cross street, a group arrived a little late, and took its place in the cortège. It was the Alsatian banner, pure white, but enveloped in folds of crape. The cords were held on one side by a simple soldier, maimed and decorated, crape on his arm; on the other, by a noble lady in black and covered in a veil of the deepest mourning. On the banner we read:

> " Heart of Jesus, restore to us our country!"

Who could gaze upon such a sight unmoved ? The procession paused, the songs ceased, and the Alsatians cried out: " Long live France!" And we replied: " Long live Alsace!" We embraced, we mingled our tears. Eight days after, the emotion of those that had witnessed this incident was still so lively that to speak of it brought tears to the eyes.

Loud shouts were heard some moments after, and the excitement became great. It was caused by the approach of the banner of Metz, which was entirely black, as if to attest the deepest despair. Metz, the Virgin City, the thoroughly French city! Ah, the tears that flowed as its banner was borne along! How can we think that prayers so elevated, so heart-felt, can remain unheard by Him who has made nations curable?

After that of Metz, the Parisian standard was most touching. Around it was grouped all that survived of the most ancient and illustrious of the French nobility. All those noble ladies wore the same costume, a black dress and veil. We mentally called them by name, and found among them the most famous of our history, those that were the glory and sometimes, alas! the peril of the seventeenth and the eighteenth centuries. We said: " 'Tis the beginning of the reparation. After the expiation on the scaffold, this is much better: repentance and recourse to the Sacred Heart."

We were roused from these reflections by songs full of manly ardor. They proceeded from the Pontifical Zouaves. In a spirit of prudence, they had left the banner of Paray near the holy casket, and carried hither only a fac-simile of it. General Sonis held one of the cords, General Charette the other. All the officers followed. One felt, whilst listening to their chants, something of the enthusiasm that had animated them when fighting at Loigny. A heart of stone would have thrilled at such a spectacle. Along the whole route we heard a thousand cries of "Long live Charette! Long live Sonis! Long live the Zouaves! Long live France! Long live Pius IX." Or rather, we heard only one cry, for all signified the same at heart. An unexpected incident crowned the emotion. In the evening the procession defiled to cross the convent garden. At

the very moment that they were passing the little clump
of hazel-trees under which the Lord had appeared to
Margaret Mary and first' explained to her the bloody
mystery of the Cross, the Alsatian banner with its
drapery of crape clung to a branch. Whilst an effort
was being made to disengage it, a sudden blast of wind
carried away the crape. The lookers-on trembled, and
in all eyes glistened tears of joy and hope.

We cannot forget you in this feast, noble banner of
Orléans, which we had the happiness to bear to this pilgrimage, as a messenger bears to sorrowing friends a
word of consolation! On a rich white ground appeared a beautiful picture of Joan of Arc, her drawn
sword above her heart, in the noble position, so humble
and yet so resolute, given her by a royal princess. When
the people perceived it, they pointed with their finger :
" Joan of Arc ! Joan of Arc !" and the enthusiasm became great. It was the resurrection of France that
they hailed in this standard.

Thus, at every step we made, the true character of the
pilgrimage was proclaimed. We had under our eyes
France mutilated and bleeding. We could not pray
for self ; we prayed for her. We forgot our own miseries. We cried : " Save, save France, through Thy
Sacred Heart !" To give its true character to this day,
a last ceremony was to be performed. When the sun
was setting, and the first shades of evening falling on
the city, blessed tapers were lighted, and Paray saw
pass through it a procession of from three to four thousand men carrying flambeaux and singing the *Miserere.*
The ceremony ended at the chapel, at the foot of the
altar of the Sacred Heart, and before the shrine, by an
Act of Reparation. Profound emotion filled every soul.
The adorers pressed hands in silence, for hearts were
overflowing.

The great regret of the day, one felt by all, was that
there was no deputation, no representatives of the Na-

tional Assembly, at that moment the sovereign of France. They came nine days after, June 29th, the feast of St. Peter. But they were too few in number. One hundred and fifty, so said their banner, had given their names; but all were not grouped around it.

" SACRATISSIMO CORDE JESU
E LEGATES AD NATIONALEM GALLIÆ CŒTUM
CL VOVERUNT."

It was, however, a manifestation not less grand and touching. Arrived at the terminus, they put the Heart of Jesus on their breast, unfurled their standard, and, in the midst of the shouting crowd, reached the Visitation chapel, where they received from the bishop's hand the God who loves the French.

At this moment a voice arose in the name of all: [1]

"Most Sacred Heart of Jesus, we come to consecrate to Thee ourselves and our colleagues united with us in sentiment.

" We ask Thee to pardon the evil we have committed, and also all those that live separated from Thee.

"Inasmuch as it is in our power, and as far as it belongs to us, we consecrate to Thee, with all the ardor of our soul, France, our well-beloved country, with all her provinces, her works of faith and charity. We ask Thee to reign over her by Thy all-powerful grace and holy love. And we ourselves, pilgrims of Thy Sacred Heart, adorers and partakers of Thy great Sacrament, most faithful disciples of the infallible See of St. Peter, whose feast we are happy to celebrate to-day, consecrate ourselves to Thy service, O Lord and Saviour Jesus Christ, humbly asking of Thee the grace to belong entirely to Thee in this world and in eternity! Amen!"

Deep emotion filled every heart during the reading of this act. But it was not yet that consecration of France which the saintly Sister had demanded, which

---

[1] M. de Belcastel, Deputy of the Haute-Garonne.

France alone can make, and which Almighty God exacts.

Such was the pilgrimage to Paray. To complete the picture, we ought to speak of its fruits, relate the outbursts of faith and piety, of grand simplicity, that recalled the best ages of the Church ; the crowd contending for the least relic of the saint, even the leaves of the hazel-trees, even the earth and stones of the garden ; those nights passed in prayer before the shrine ; those Communions so numerous that the altars did not suffice for them, that the arms of the priests fell from fatigue, and the religious of Paray " no longer knew how to procure enough hosts *for the multitude famishing for Jesus !*" [1]

Yes, the finger of God is here ! Who can deny it ? The Heart of Jesus is regenerating us. Since our fearful disasters, marked by a character of chastisement so pronounced ; since the horrors of the Commune, whose torch lighted with an ominous glare the abyss into which they were about to ingulf what remained of France ; since the blood of the hostages accepted by God in expiation, a new France has arisen. She it was that unfurled at Paray the standard of the Sacred Heart ; she it is who is about to construct at Paris the Church of the Sacred Heart ; [2] she who during two months pressed around the foot of the altar upon which Jesus had said : *"Behold the Heart that has so loved men !"*

The miracle is there, or it is nowhere. It is as sublime as it was unexpected ; and the rapture of such a spectacle is all the more sweet as we have reason to think that it is only the beginning of future graces.

[1] Circular of Paray, November 6, 1873.

[2] This grand basilica is now an accomplished fact ; and in it hangs a bell, the joint offering of the Visitation houses from all parts of the world. It is, as its inscription tells, a " Monument of piety to the divine Heart, to chant from the summit of the Holy Mountain, to the city, to the nation, to the whole world, the legend of the Visitation Order : VIVAT ✠ JESUS !"—*Translator's note.*

O Margaret Mary, Virgin of Paray, finish thy work! Thou hast sown these beautiful seeds; help them to ripen under the rays of the Sacred Heart. Extend thy aid to all souls that have not had our happy privilege. One day, in one of thy most private communications with Heaven, thou didst hear thy Lord saying to thee : "*I shall make thee forever the heiress of all the treasures of My divine Heart.*" Enjoy them forever, O Virgin, but be not avaricious of them! Share them with us!

And Thou, O Jesus, place Thy Heart on the heart of France! Thou knowest of what elements it is made. To be good, she must be loved. When enthusiasm sways her, she is sublime. O Divine Enchanter, captivate her by Thy beauty! Pierce her with darts so sharp that she may be forced to surrender. They were so grand, this people, when love held them suspended at Thy pierced hands and feet : what will they be when they rise to Thy Heart! Then all our evils will be ended. We shall again behold that ancient France so loved by the Church, contemplated with a noble jealousy by all Europe ; whose sword, genius, and heart were at the service of every good cause; and which, finally, released from the fearful poison that consumes her, will, for the happiness of all, resume her rank at the head of the nations.

CHAPTER XIX.

MONTMARTRE—THE WISH OF ST. FRANCIS DE SALES
—THE VISITATION ORDER AND JANSENISM—THE
VISITANDINES AS REFORMERS AND FOUNDERS—
THE VISITANDINES IN THE REVOLUTION—THE
SCAPULAR OF THE SACRED HEART IN THE
REIGN OF TERROR—THE GUARD OF HONOR OF
THE SACRED HEART—THE CONSECRATION OF
THE WORLD TO THE SACRED HEART.

IT is told of Julian the Apostate that when he represented the Roman Cæsars at Lutetia, he would
night after night go to the roof of his palace to gaze
up at the stars, wherein he thought to read the downfall
of Christianity. If he had really read the future he was
so anxious to foresee, well might he have exclaimed, as
the heights of Mons Martys caught his eye—"Thou hast
conquered, Galilean!"

No fitter site could have been chosen for the great
Basilica of the Sacred Heart, raised by France as a temple
of expiation and praise, than the hill of Montmartre, of
which it is the glory. The associations of the mount
with France stretch back to the earliest history of the
country. In the river Seine, after its junction with the
famous Marne, lie seven islands, the largest of which was
in ancient times the haunt and refuge of an insignificant
tribe of Gauls known as the Parises. They were no
people of villages or towns, and left not a mark save their
name behind when the Romans came down upon them,
swept them into oblivion and founded on their island the
town of Lutetia, the embryo of the Paris of to-day,
named in remembrance of the original possessors of the
soil. On the slope of the hill that rose above their new

settlement, the conquering Romans raised a temple to the God of War, where now the Prince ᴏ̃ Peace reigns triumphant, and gave to it the name of Mons Martys in his honor. Later on, an attempt was made to change the name to Mons Mercurii, who, as leader of those who help themselves to other people's property, was quite as appropriate a patron for the Roman nation as the fiery Mars. The statue of Mercury was placed alongside of the first diety's, but the original name remained until the dawn of Christianity. Dionysius, the first Bishop of Lutetia, came hither in the third century with his ardent companions, preaching the Gospel of Christ. On Mons Martys, just below the temple of the pagan god, he built a chapel to the Mother of the true God, and on this hill he and his companions, Rusticus and Eleutherius, received the palm of martyrdom. Tradition says that after his execution, Dionysius arose from the ground on which his lifeless body had fallen, and raising the severed head in both his hands, carried it from Montmartre, to where the famous Abbey of St. Denis, named in his honor and the necropolis of the French kings, now stands. When Christianity finally triumphed over Gaul and Roman, a chapel was raised in his honor on the spot where he had laid down his life for Christ, and as the centuries rolled away, a stately basilica arose, to which came pilgrims from every clime. Among those who knelt at his shrine were Genevieve, the wonderful maiden Saint, whose prayers drove back the haughty Attila, Scourge of God, from the gates of Paris; Clotilde, the wife of Clovis, the "true apostle" of France, as she has been styled; Bernard of Clairvaux, Peter of Cluny, St. Francis de Sales, Ignatius of Loyola, with that first band of followers who here made their vows, and many others, famous in our day as in their own. Numerous religious communities, in the course of time, took root and flourished on the hill, no longer Mons Martys, but Mons Martyrum, in commemoration of Dionysius and his companions. Their relics were discovered in the church dedicated to their honor as late as 1611. "A wonderful mount, indeed," writes the Jesuit, Father Charles Croonberghs; "a chosen battleground, as it were, whereon decisive struggles have been waged between the powers of hell and the all-conquering love of Christ."

Montmartre has played, time and time again, a conspicuous part in French history, through civil strife and war. It has more than once been the defense of the city of Paris, its commanding height serving well for such purpose. Henry of Navarre and the first Napoleon are prominent among the rulers who have seized on its natural advantages. But further back still, an old chronicle gravely tells us, "Otho II., emperor of Germany, at war with Lothaire of France in the year 978, did cause an Alleluia to be sung from the hill of Mons Martyrum by the monks thereon, with such power of lung as terrified all Paris." This record speaks well for both the purity of the atmosphere of Montmartre and the vim of the singers.

The first public praise ever offered the Heart of Jesus was sung in a chapel erected on Montmartre and dedicated to it in the year 1670. This was afterwards destroyed, at the time of the Revolution. In blasphemous contrast, that makes one wonder at the forbearance of Heaven, the name of the hill was now changed to Mont Marat and a creature received the homage of incense in its chapel. Near the close of this terrible epoch of history, when the skies were just showing signs of clearing, the Vicomte de Bonald prepared plans for a temple of expiation for the crimes so lately committed against God. Napoleon, then at war in Spain, approved, and sent orders that public subscription should be started for the erection of a temple of peace on Montmartre. His orders, however, were never carried out. Years after, at the time

of the sudden revolution that put Louis Philippe upon
the throne of France, the scheme of a mad artist drew
the attention of the nation for a time. He proposed to
cut the rock of Montmartre into an immense head of
Liberty "or of some emperor"—the personality, evidently,
of small moment. His project was not warmly received
and the rock is still unsculptured.

Three memorials to the Sacred Heart arose on Montmartre in the reign of Napoleon III.—a chapel, a church
and a temple. It was not until the year 1872, however,
that the initiative of a formal dedication of the mount,
as a symbol of France, had birth. A French gentleman
detained in Poitiers during the siege of Paris, conceived,
in this time of deadly anxiety and suspense, the idea of
an expiatory monument to be erected on Montmartre for
the deliverance and salvation of France. He at first
thought of putting this under the patronage of Our Lady
of Deliverance; but the claims of the Sacred Heart and
the promise of Its protection, made to Saint Margaret
Mary, two centuries before, carried the day.

Full of his purpose, he went to Father Henry Ra-
miére, the founder of the Messenger of the Sacred Heart.
The latter, well pleased, at once took up the project, and
enlisted prominent people of the day in its success. Then
came the horrors of the Commune, when Montmartre was
drenched in the blood of victims. When peace was
again restored, Cardinal Guibert, Archbishop of Paris,
espoused the cause with ardor; all the French bishops
united with him in the plan, and it spread with incredible
rapidity, assisted spiritually and materially by Pope Pius
IX. In 1873, the permission of the Government was
solicited for the building of the proposed memorial; this
was not only accorded by the National Assembly under
President MacMahon, in a vote of 382 to 138, but it did
not hesitate to declare that the proposed basilica was a
work of public utility, established by the Archbishop of

Paris in honor of the Sacred Heart, for the purpose of drawing down upon France, and especially Paris, the merciful protection of God. "A miracle in itself," remarked a contemporary.

Architects from all parts of the world sent in their plans. The erection of the basilica proved a work of immense difficulty and was a triumph of engineering, for the soft crumbling stone of the hill was undermined with abandoned and forgotten quarries, necessitating the digging of the foundations at a depth of 75 feet below the cornerstone. This was finally laid, with great ceremony, in 1875. The date originally assigned for the purpose was delayed more than once by circumstances, and it is a coincidence worthy of note that the event was at last accomplished on June 16, 1875, the 200th anniversary of the revelation of the First Friday devotion, June 16, 1675.

"In July, 1914, at the close of the Eucharistic Congress at Lourdes, the Papal Delegate, in the presence of ten cardinals, two hundred bishops, two thousand priests and an immense throng of people, announced that the consecration of the Basilica of Montmartre to the Sacred Heart would take place on the coming October 17th, the feast of Saint Margaret Mary. One week later, the great World War broke out, and the ceremony had to be postponed. But by the express wish of Pius X the Bishop of Autun on that day read in the chapel of the Visitation at Paray-le-Monial, the convent where Saint Margaret Mary spent her cloistered life, and in the basilica of that town, a solemn act of consecration, repeated by the people, imploring the Sacred Heart to establish its reign over France." (Life of Margaret Mary, by Sister Mary Philip, of Bar Convent, York).

The solemn consecration of France to the Sacred Heart, so long delayed, took place in 1919, one year after the closing of the war, and a few months before the canonization of Saint Margaret Mary.

"I will reign in spite of all who oppose Me," said Our Lord Himself to His handmaid. It is a far cry indeed from the first humble altar in the noviciate of Paray-le-Monial, hardly more than a chair, with its small picture of the Sacred Heart and its few flowers and lights, to the magnificent Basilica of Montmartre, on which the wealth of human genius has been expended, and its Perpetual Adoration, with its daily and nightly crowd of earnest worshippers.

In the convent of Annecy, the cradle of the Visitation Order, is still preserved the book in which, for thirty-one years, St. Jane Frances de Chantal wrote the annual renewal of her vows; and every nun of this community, from her time up to the present day, has followed her precedent and yearly inscribed afresh her name and vow. Besides these names are many others, some well-known to the world, for kings and queens, statesmen, soldiers, ecclesiastics, artists, writers, as well as people from all ranks of life, have placed their names upon its pages in the hope of obtaining the fulfilment of the wish of St. Francis, written upon the first leaf in his own hand.

"Yea, Lord Jesus, graciously hear the exclamation of my heart in behalf of Thy spouses. Be this book inscribed by Thine own self, and suffer not any one of them to set her name in it except through Thy inspiration and motion, so that this little volume may cover my shoulders as a mantle of honor, and my head as a crown of glory; and that in all my aspirations towards Thee, I may mentally pronounce, in a canticle of joy and praise, every name that shall be recorded in it, offering the list as a posy of sweetness to Thy Divine Providence. O Jesus, sweet and holy Love of our souls, grant the year in which every Sister shall write her vows and oblations in this book be to her a year of sanctification, the day a day of salvation, the hour an hour of never ceasing benediction. Grant that the hearts Thou hast aggregated to Thy name and that of Thy dear Mother be never dispersed; that what Thou hast assembled be never divided, and that what Thou hast joined be never separated. Rather say, that the names inscribed in these perishable pages shall forever be written in the Book of Life with the just who reign with Thee in immortal bliss. Amen, Amen.

"History shows us the heresy of Jansenism, the principle of so many evils, seeking to insinuate itself by every means into the cloister," says Father J. B. Lemius, in his "Mission of the Order of the Visitation" (1911). "Alas! it was sometimes but too successful! But as to the Order of the Visitation, the Cardinal of York said: 'It is enough to be a daughter of St. Francis de Sales to be likewise a true daughter of the Apostolic and Roman faith.' The superiors everywhere displayed the greatest vigilance. Every confessor who showed the slightest leaning to this error was immediately replaced. The parlors were closed to every person suspected of the heresy. But a peculiar danger threatened the nuns from their very virtue—the perfect obedience the Visitation has always shown to the bishops, their superiors. What reader of French history is ignorant of this—the supreme trial of the Church in France? In the episcopate of the 18th century, there were bishops who endeavored, no matter at what cost, to introduce the poison into the monasteries. Among these was the Bishop of Auxerre,— or at least he was accused in the matter. Now Auxerre possessed a convent of the Order, and this convent became an impregnable fortress of the faith. With respect united to invincible firmness, it resisted and triumphed. Humbly but energetically, the Superioress refused a Jansenist confessor. This enraged many, gained over to the sect, who had formerly been friends; relatives of the Sisters, Jansenists also, became inflamed with passion. But nothing could daunt the courage of the Visitandines. They chose rather to submit to an order forbidding the reception of any new members and to gradually die out, martyrs to the faith. But eleven religious remained in the cloister when the Jansenist bishop was himself called to appear before God.

"At Mâcon, a splendid resistance was made. The city was infested with heresy, and the monastery was promptly attacked. Mother du Bousquet called her community together, and put them under the protection of the Blessed Virgin by a fervent act of consecration. In season and out, she impressed upon them the necessity of perfect regularity in their observances, of a real union of hearts and of submission to the Pope. When the bishop of the city put himself at the head of the sectarians, she called a chapter, proclaimed the obedience due the Holy See, and on her knees made the profession of faith in her own name and that of all the community.

Trials and want came upon the convent, but it boldly fronted the storm. 'The kingdom of God first!' cried the valiant Mother.

"The story of the monastery of Caen is pitiful. What made things worse was that Mother du Beaumanoir was allied to the family of Mgr. de Bayeux, Prince of Lorraine. The six years of her incumbency were one continuous struggle. The Bishop used his power to the utmost—the nuns were deprived of the sacraments, elections were hindered or thwarted, their officers were deposed, an attempt was made to modify the rules, the reception of new members was forbidden. Faithful to God, Mother du Beaumanoir never failed to show the respect due to episcopal dignity; but she recoiled before no humiliation or suffering, nor lost any opportunity to defend the constitutional rights of the Order, the liberty of election— above all, the purity of the faith. From this stand, nothing could move her. There were, it is true, a few breaches—such as that of Castellane.[1] But in this case, one might even say 'Felix culpa!' for it but served to show how vigorously the Order could repair an evil and cast out the venom that sought the life of its spirit."

"Although the Visitation Order was on the whole loyal

[1The instance of the convent at Castellane, of which Father Lemius speaks, is here drawn from a Visitandine source. The Life of Ven. Anne Madeleine Remusat, by the Visitation Sisters of Harrow, 1920.]

during the Jansenist heresy, it, too, suffered by the assaults made upon every institution in the Church . . . Jansenism appears to have been, of all heresies, one of the most insidious. No Jansenist would admit that he was not a Catholic, for to remain in external communication with the Church was essential to his aim . . .Madame de Sévigné, granddaughter, as is well-known of St. Jane Frances de Chantal, speaks in one of her letters of giving the 'Treatise on Frequent Communion,' by Arnauld (a book discountenancing frequent Communion) to the nuns of a certain convent which she was in the habit of visiting. They were charmed with it, she says, but the perusal of this book by them must be kept a great secret. Notwithstanding, this very community later on became conspicuous for its opposition to Jansenism and its loyalty to the Holy See. The two convents of Nevers and Castellane unhappily became infected to a large extent with the disease, and all the other houses of the Order offered unceasing prayer to God for them. It is remarkable that neither of these houses encouraged devotion to the Sacred Heart, and that coincidently with its adoption at Nevers, the sisters turned at once from their error and became true children of the Church again. Castellane, however, was completely under the influence of the Bishop, Jean Soanen, who used all the eloquence for which he was noted to imbue his daughters with Jansenistic doctrine. At the age of eighty, he was suspended and sent to a monastery, where he died, contumacious, at the age of ninety-three. The condemnation of their bishop seems to have simply urged the Visitandines of Castellane on to further rebellion. Not the Pope nor the whole Church, they declared, should make them change their opinions. Threatened with excommunication, they declared they gloried in suffering for justice' sake!

"The unhappy nuns continued in open rebellion till they

drew upon themselves the condemnation of the Church, and the king (Louis XV.) ordered, by *lettres de cachet,* eleven of them to leave Castellane and go to various religious houses instead.

"This step and the charity and kindness with which they were received by their sisters in religion, at last opened their eyes. Hearing of the happy result, M. de la Motte, the priest who had replaced their former Jansenistic chaplain, obtained permission for them to return to their own convent again.

"A singular obstacle presented itself. Twenty of the less rebellious nuns had been allowed to remain at Castellane. When the exiles sought admittance again, they were refused and called *apostates* by their unrepentant sisters. Admission had to be gained by force, and the trouble became a scandal. Each party went its own way, sharing nothing in common. The prayers of the entire Order were offered for the recalcitrants, and finally the tact and gentleness of Father de la Motte and the sweetness and firmness of a Superior sent them from the Convent of Embrun won them all back, with the exception of four sisters, who died before peace was made, and who were styled martyrs on the roll of the Jansenists."

"At first glance, the work of the Visitandines as Reformers and Founders would seem entirely opposed to the spirit of an Order which its saintly Founder said was to be as an humble violet in the garden of the Church. Yet one of the greatest glories of the Order, that which its modesty has striven hard to conceal, is the part it has played in the reformation of relaxed monasteries and it is an indisputable fact that every house which accepted the good offices of the Visitation returned to its original spirit. Such houses did not change old rules— they simply regained old fervor. Not only this, but the Visitation has more than once cast seed into the field of religion which has borne a hundredfold in new orders, distinct from itself. The Order of the Sacred Heart is one of these magnificent fruits. At Paris, Marseilles, Lyons, Grenoble, Montpellier and a number of other places, Visitation superioresses were called on by the bishop to take charge of Magdalen Refuges. Mother Patin, at Caen, was, in fact, co-foundress with Blessed John Eudes of the Congregation of Our Lady of Charity, the mother-house of all the Refuges which claim Blessed Eudes as their founder, and the admirable Congregation of the Good Shepherd of Angers, which to-day has so many branches throughout the world.

"Mother Patin, putting her hand to the plough, did not look back; she triumphed over every obstacle, she effected miracles, so to speak, in the maintenance of her charges, she drew novices to the new Order, wrote its Constitutions and its directions, and even selected its dress. Then she devoted herself, successfully, to obtaining approval of it at Rome.

"The Bernardines of Clermont, the Clares of Tarascon and of Avignon, the Augustines of Toulouse, the Ursulines of Brive and many others, received with gratitude the aid of the Visitandines. Mother du Houx, of the monastery of Cacé, was called by the bishop of Rennes, at the express desire of the Abbess herself, to the Abbaye de la Joie, brought almost to ruin by internal dissensions. In two months, she had reconciled the belligerents, and went back to her cloister leaving the Abbaye in profound peace and calm. Her work had just begun. The bishop of Tréguier next invoked her aid in his troubles with four different Ursuline convents. Successful again in this undertaking, she was a third time withdrawn from her convent to the same work of reformation in Brittany. Twenty-five years afterwards, she completed her extraordinary ministry by a masterpiece of spiritual accomplishment. Father Huby had inaugurated a series of retreats

at Varennes, believing this to be the best method of pre-
serving the faith in Brittany. But to insure the perma-
nency of this work, it was found necessary to have the
services of an Institute entirely devoted to it. Mother
du Houx was called upon to head the enterprise. For
two years, she trained the Foundresses in the spirit of
St. Francis de Sales, and thus created one of the most
solid and meritorious congregations in Brittany.

"Mother Duret was called on to reform a convent where
a heretic priest had sown bad seed. 'All the universities
in the world,' said the good mother, 'could never have
converted these poor souls—but the grace of our Blessed
Mother and the mildness of St. Francis de Sales triumphed over their obstinacy, and the monastery returned
to its old faith and fervor.'

"The greatest achievement of the Visitation Order, in
the eyes of the world, was doubtless that of the royal
foundation of St. Cyr, in 1692. When there was question of the training of the Dames de St. Louis in the
religious life, Madame de Maintenon was emphatic in
her declaration that a Visitandine alone could give the
proper direction. Louis XIV. upheld her views, having
a great admiration for the work of Mother de Lorges
in the Refuges of Paris. Mother de Priolo, of the monastery of Chaillot, was obliged by the order of the Archbishop of Paris to leave her cell and devote herself to
this mission. This remarkable superioress labored to in-
still the spirit of St. Francis into the minds and hearts
of her charges, and so successfully that she went back to
her cloister overwhelmed with the felicitations of the
king and Madame de Maintenon, who said: 'To the Visitation is owing all the good that has been and ever will
be done at Saint Cyr.' In our own day, Mother Sera-
phine Fournier, at the desire of the Archbishop of Paris,
aided in the foundation of the Blind Sisters of St. Paul,
a triumph of religious charity and zeal. 'What has not

St. Francis de Sales done,' she said, 'to help these dear blind sisters to consecrate themselves to God, notwithstanding their affliction, he who wished that in his Visitation he could gather all the afflicted of the earth!'

"How is it that the Visitation Order, vowed to a life hidden, par excellence, has thus come forward in the world, in spite of itself, and taken so prominent a part in works that have carried its name to all the winds? It is because the spirit of St. Francis never dies in the hearts of his daughters." (J. B. Lemius, Mission of Visitation Order.)

"I love my veil as you do your sword," said Sister de Montmarin to her soldier brother. This was the spirit of all the daughters of St. Francis de Sales when the storm of the Revolution broke over France. "A heroic courage in hearts united to God, the practice of observances in the midst of a perverse world and upon ground deluged with blood, a smile in the very face of the scaffold, testified that outside the cloisters from which they had been torn, as within them, the nuns of the Visitation lived in the Sacred Heart of Jesus." The National Assembly abolished all vows in 1789. The unanimous response of the Visitandines to this was—Rather die than leave our monasteries! A second decree proclaimed the restoration of "liberty" to all persons living in religious communities, and a delegate was sent to all the convents with this piece of news. "So be it," was the response, "respect that liberty then, and leave us in peace!" Some made even more spirited rejoinder—"If we had not already made our vows, we would go this instant to the house tops and proclaim them to the world!"

But soon came threatening crowds outside their walls; men rushed through their cloisters brandishing swords red with the blood of faithful priests. Then came the dissolution of all monasteries, a return into the world convulsed in revolutionary throes. At Annecy, where Fran-

cis de Sales and Jane Frances de Chantal were awaiting
the call of resurrection, there was profound anxiety.
What would become of these precious relics in the hands
of monsters who cared for neither God nor man? The
courage and presence of mind of a friendly official saved
them from profanation, and restored them to their children in happier times. At Lyons, where the heart of
St. Francis was preserved, a veritable miracle snatched
it out of unhallowed hands and brought it in safety to
Venice. Reading the history of the Order in that dread-
ful time, one finds natural emotion, it is true, at the ruin
of "the fair land of France;" but the predominant thought
in every breast was how to keep the Rules, the daily
observances of religious life? The poor exiles clung together, wherever possible, united in the chanting of the
Divine praises, strove to keep up their relations with their
Superiors and even held chapters, from time to time.
Some drew for themselves, in the privacy of the homes to
which they had returned, or the lodging places they were
forced to seek, limits that they regarded as cloister and
which they never passed except to assist at some stealthily
said Mass. Bitter poverty was the lot of many—yet they
cried "Vive la Pauvreté!" "I suffer," wrote one of the
nuns, "but it is from excess of happiness. Privations,
torments, prisons, the scaffold—ah, what consolations!"
In the daily hearing of that terrible roll of the drum
which announced crime upon crime, assassination upon
assassination—"Nothing," declared another, "gives me
a quicker beat of the heart."

The oath was unanimously refused. "I am a child of
the Roman Catholic and Apostolic Church, and I am
ready to die for my faith!" Such was the brave response
upon every lip. "Live Jesus! *This* is my oath." Many
of the nuns were brought before the Tribunal and sen-
tenced to transportation or the guillotine. But by a
special protection of God, though all were ready to lay

down their lives, the majority escaped death,—and this
is the explanation. "You are rather too ready," said the
executioner to one: "you can wait till to-morrow, then!"
To another—"Since you are so joyful about it, wait
awhile longer!"

These delays practically meant deliverance. They
were the work of the Sacred Heart, protecting those It
had chosen for Its apostolate. "Hidden in the world,
they become to those around them so many centres of
prayer, of reparation and of confidence in God, at the
very time that the Sacred Heart of Jesus was being
mocked and insulted in Paris. After the storm the
Order rose anew, fresh and full of vigor. "Thy youth
shall be renewed like the eagle's."

A story not told in the histories, but strange enough,
is that of the part played by the Scapular of the Sacred
Heart of Jesus during the Reign of Terror. In 1771 the
Parliament of Paris, a party of Jansenists and "philoso-
phers," prohibited the devotion to the Sacred Heart in
France. This decree was by no means as effectual as
they vainly hoped to make it, and the faithful of the
nation were but little affected by it. When the rumblings
of the storm that later on overwhelmed the unhappy land
began to be heard, and popular suspense and anxiety commenced to become almost unendurable, it was to the
Heart of Jesus that France instinctively turned for help.
"You cannot imagine how fervent souls are redoubling
their zeal—surely Heaven cannot be deaf to so many
prayers, offered with such trustfulness," wrote Madame
Elizabeth, the "Genevieve" of the royal family, to the
Abbé de Lubersac, then in Rome, during the dark days
of 1791. "It is from the Heart of Jesus that they seem
to await the favors of which they are in need; the fervor
of this devotion appears to redouble; the more our woes
are increased, the more these prayers are offered up."
The scapular of the Sacred Heart was eagerly sought,

its wearing deemed a protection, and the Visitandines had all they could do to supply the demand. The ways of God are not ours. With these scapulars on their breasts the Carmelite martyrs were immolated, many other victims mounted the scaffold, and the King of France himself laid his head beneath the axe." Louis XVI and all his family were devout wearers of this scapular, even in the times when the dark future of the kingdom was undreamed of. Those they used were of cloth of gold, on which was embroidered the Heart, pierced with two arrows, with the words "miserere nobis!" beneath. The meaning of these scapulars was without doubt perfectly familiar to the Revolutionists; but when on searching numerous prisoners they found the same emblem, it was assumed that these little pieces of cloth, marked with the Heart of a Savior Whom they no longer acknowledged, were in reality evidences of a wide-spread plot against "public safety." Then began a systematic search on the persons of all suspects and prisoners, and thousands of victims were executed for no other offense. In spite of this, the brave Vendéans went into battle with the powers of evil that were crushing France with the scapular of the Sacred Heart openly displayed upon their breasts; to that Heart they attributed the successes they made, and falling on the field, vanquished but unconquered, they died in a faith and confidence that made them martyrs.

One of the royal treasures confiscated in the Temple was the scapular of the Sacred Heart worn by Marie Thérèse, the young daughter of Louis and Marie Antoinette. "They took from my mother the address of a shop," she wrote, "from my aunt Elizabeth a stick of sealing-wax, and from me a Sacred Heart of Jesus and a Prayer for France." St. Beuve, commenting on this, says: "That Sacred Heart of Jesus and that Prayer for France were closer bound together than would seem at first; and perhaps she needed all her faith in the one to be able at that moment to pray for the other."

The beautiful prayer that her aunt, the courageous and noble Madame Elizabeth, gave to her friend the Marquise de Raigecourt, is still preserved in the Bibliothèque Nationale, in her own handwriting:

"Adorable Heart of Jesus, sanctuary of the love that led God to make Himself man, to sacrifice His life for our salvation, and to make of His body the food of our souls: in gratitude for that infinite charity, I give You my heart, and with it all that I possess in this world, all that I am, all that I shall do, all that I shall suffer. But, my God, may this heart, I implore You, be no longer unworthy of You; make it like unto Yourself; surround it with Your thorns and close its entrance to all ill-regulated affections; set there Your cross, make it feel its worth, make it willing to love it. Kindle it with Your divine flame. May it burn for Your glory; may it be all Yours, when You have done what You will with it. You are its consolation in its troubles, the remedy of its ills, its strength and refuge in temptation, its hope during life, its haven in death. I ask You, O Heart so loving, the same favor for my companions. Amen."

"The monastery of the Visitation in Bourg was one of the first to be re-established after the French Revolution, in the year 1806. In 1824 new quarters were selected—the Hotel of the Meillonas family, in the Rue Teynière. It is said that a certain pious woman of Bourg never passed this mansion, before its occupancy by the Visitandines, without the sign of the cross. Asked why she did this, she answered: 'Our Lord has made known to me that He will one day be greatly glorified in this place.'

"In fact, it was here that in 1825 the first confraternity of the Sacred Heart was established, and a chapel erected in 1834, in which the entire month of June was consecrated to Its honor with public services. An association of more than 300 women was formed for this purpose, and visible marks of heavenly favor followed. These associates selected one hour each month for adoration and worship; or rather, without neglecting their ordinary occupations, they kept one hour of recollection and prayer in honor of the Sacred Heart of Jesus. This was the nucleus of the Guard of Honor. In 1862, the community of this house proclaimed the Sacred Heart as King of their monastery. They later learned that at the same time the monasteries of Annecy and Paray-le-Monial, unknown to each other or to Bourg, had done the same thing. 'Find some new means of glorifying the Heart of Jesus!' cried the nuns of Bourg, turning to Sister Marie of the Sacred Heart, one of their number. The commission could not have been placed in better hands. On January 1, 1863, Sister Marie of the Sacred Heart put before the community a formal protestation of devotion to the greater glory of the Sacred Heart, of fervent desire to console It and to obtain through It the salvation of poor sinners. This was signed by every Sister and deposited on the altar during Mass.

"On the 6th of January, the proclamation of the Royalty of the Sacred Heart was again made and the question of forming Its court, as it were, considered. During recreation, various plans were suggested. The thought of changing the monthly hour to a daily one, and that of a dial on which each hour should be placed under the patronage of the angels and saints, and the names of each member inscribed, came to the mind of Sister Marie of the Sacred Heart. And it was she, likewise, who gave to the band the name of the 'Guard of Honor,' and adopted for its watchword—'Glory, Love, Reparation and Zeal.' In her soul was, deep down, the conviction that the Guard of Honor would be a source of abundant graces for the Church and for sinners' conversion and salvation. Moreover, she believed that it would eventually spread over the whole world—a belief entirely justified.

"The priest of the parish and the chaplain of the convent were the first to inscribe their names, and it was not long before the whole city of Bourg accepted the devotion with enthusiasm. But there was one source of disquiet. How would Annecy and Paray, the two Holy Mounts—the one, centre of the Apostolate of the Sacred Heart, the other the fountain-head of the Order, regard the new movement? From both came unequivocal approval and a warmth of encouragement beyond expectation. The Superioress of Annecy happened at the time to be ill and suffering greatly. Hardly had the Dial of the Guard of Honor been brought into her room, that she might see its arrangement, than she rose from her bed cured. Asking for a pen she wrote: 'This practice is simply a more perfect observance of the Rule during the hour of guard.' In 1864 she wrote to Sister Marie— 'I love to think with what complacency our holy founders must look at you from heaven, watching you work thus for the glory of the Heart of Jesus.'

"At the monastery of Paray, it was even better. The person charged with showing the Dial to the Superioress felt great embarrassment in so doing, for at this very moment Paray was occupied with a promotion of the Communion of Reparation, and would naturally find rather strange the request to assist in the promulgation of another novelty in the religious world, issuing too, as if in rivalry, from a sister-house so near! However, taking her courage in her hands, the messenger made a casual allusion to the Dial of the Guard of Honor. 'A dial?' said the Superioress. 'Show it to me at once!' After examining it with attention, she said, with some emotion, 'Come with me, my child.' And she took her into the community room, where there had just been hung another Dial, exactly similar, down to the very protectors of each hour—a coincidence absolutely above suspicion of any collusion. The whole body of sisters put down their names on the Dial of the Guard of Honor, as those of Annecy had previously done.

The movement proved irresistible. The Pontifical Zouaves, through their chaplain, a native of Bourg, enrolled themselves to a man. The Dials journeyed in every direction, not only through France, but to England, Austria, Italy, Switzerland—and at the present day are to be found in every country of the world.

Pope Pius IX was deeply interested in the Association. He revised the prayer himself, gave his sanction, enriched the Archconfraternity with numerous indulgences and inscribed his name as the First Guard of Honor. His successors have all followed his example.

A new inquietude now took possession of the Visitandines of Bourg. It was not for them, they thought, of whom their Foundress, St. Jane de Chantal said: "The glory of the Sisters of the Visitation is to have no glory, and their greatness is their weakness," to stand forth to the world as the "callers to the flag," even if the flag be that of Christ. Where would be their obscurity, their annihilation in the sight of men, if they should thus become so prominent? Time was to show, however, that the mission of the Visitation is the Apostolate of the Sacred Heart, and that it was of the Visitation Order, that the Sacred Heart demanded this apostolate.

At the foundation of the devotion, the Visitandines of Bourg applied to the Jesuits to take charge of the work, but Father Beckx, the General of the Order, refused their request, saying with a touch of humor: 'The name, Guard of Honor, is a trifle military. Now the idea of the General of the Jesuits leading on a Guard of Honor would certainly give rise to an interpretation but little desired!' Then the Sisters begged the Fathers of the Sacred Heart at Issodoun to assume direction. This request also was refused. Later on, the bishop of the diocese, seeing the immense expansion of the Guard of Honor, and the onerous labor it involved, began to fear that the spirit of the monastery might become weakened by so much outside distraction, He therefore built a chapel in Bourg, with the intention of making it the headquarters of the devotion. The work immediately declined; it was not until it was placed again in the hands of the Visitandines that it took on new life and vigor. It is plainly to this Order that the Sacred Heart itself has willed the apostolate of Its honor.

"I think that in heaven the Sacred Heart will call in review before It all the works of this, His Institute, each monastery presenting to Its view the part it has taken in the distribution of Its treasures, and that each will receive its own particular glory in recompense. But it seems to me that when Sister Marie of the Sacred Heart appears, with her banner of the Guard of Honor, Jesus Himself will incline His Head to her, that Mary, His Mother, will smile upon her; that Francis de Sales, addressing Mother de Chantal and all his Visitation children, will say: 'Behold a true daughter of the Visitation! She has raised immense armies of guard around the royal Heart of Jesus—blessed be she forever!'" (Father J. B. Lemius, Mission of the Visitation Order.)

Mother Mary of the Divine Heart, a holy Good Shepherd nun of Oporto, in the world Mary Droste zu Vischering, of a noble German Catholic family, made known to Pope Leo XIII in 1898 that she had received from Our Lord a command that she should tell him He desired a formal consecration of the whole world, Christian and pagan, to his Sacred Heart. This was done by Pope Leo on June 9, 1899, after a solemn triduum, held throughout the world. He himself pronounced the words of dedication. "How his voice trembled," says one who was present, "when he besought Christ Our Lord, to be, indeed, the Supreme King of all mankind—of Catholics, whether faithful or not, of heretics and schismatics, and of the poor heathens; when he besought liberty for the Church and peace for nations, his soul, great as the world which he then embraced, seemed to overflow in the ardor of its accents. The two hundred privileged witnesses of this sublime act did not attempt to conceal the tears which the touching scene drew from their eyes." His concluding words were: "From pole to pole let but one voice resound—Praise to the Divine Heart which has given us salvation; to It be honor and glory forever and ever!" Afterwards he said—"This is the greatest act of my pontificate!" He likewise sent a letter to all the bishops of the Church, urging them to spread devotion to the Sacred Heart by every means in their power. A short while before, receiving the Count and Countess Droste zu Vischering, parents of Mother Mary of the Divine Heart, in private audience, he said to them: "Tell your daughter that the consecration to the Sacred Heart she has asked of me will be made in every cathedral and church of the world, and tell her clearly that this is in consequence of what she made known to me; and that I expect from it the greatest graces for the whole world." Mother Mary of the Divine Heart was then at the point of death and passed away shortly after, at the early age of thirty-six.

CHAPTER XX.

ENTHRONEMENT OF THE SACRED HEART—SOME
AMERICAN ASSOCIATIONS—THE WORDS OF POPE
BENEDICT XV., AND THE DECREE OF CANONIZA-
TION OF SAINT MARGARET MARY ALACOQUE,
PROFESSED RELIGIOUS OF THE ORDER OF THE
VISITATION OF THE BLESSED VIRGIN MARY OF
THE DIOCESE OF AUTUN.

IN the year 1907, Father Matthew Crawley-Boevey of
the Congregation of the Sacred Hearts of Jesus and
Mary, from Chili, though of English birth, was kneeling in the chapel at Paray-le-Monial, the scene of the apparitions of Our Lord to Saint Margaret Mary. This
priest was, according to the doctors, suffering from an in-
curable disease of the heart. While praying before the
tabernacle, he suddenly felt his strength return to him,
and realized that he was cured. At the same moment, an
overpowering desire seized upon him to draw every
household in the world to the Sacred Heart, and the
conviction took possession of him that for this end was
his vigor restored to him. A few days later, he was in
Rome, kneeling before Pope Pius X, begging his approbation and blessing for the task he felt impelled to undertake. "I give you no *permission* for a work as magnificent as this," the Pope answered him, smiling; "I command you, instead, to devote yourself to it." Father
Crawley-Boevey began his mission without delay. The
spread of the devotion was remarkable. Two years
afterward, Pope Pius X gave it his special blessing, and
to all priests who should become its apostles. Ten years
after its conception, Father Crawley-Boevey writes:

"The Enthronement of the Heart of Jesus as King has

been made in the palaces of kings and princes, in the homes of thousands of workmen and of the poor; it has been carried out in Parliaments; hearth by hearth, amid Arctic snows and in the centre of Africa; from the archipelagos of Oceania to the distant lands of Tibet and China, and to all the countries of Europe and America. There have been Enthronements of rare beauty, performed in the seclusion of the cloister, in brilliant gatherings held in the halls of Catholic clubs; Enthronements full of divine poetry, carried out in convent schools, homes and orphanages, hospitals—even in prisons; the homages of bishops and priests, of shepherds and their families to the Shepherd-King; the leper settlement of Molokai; it has penetrated into the Congo, Ethiopia, Alaska and the Fiji Islands."

Mother Mary Philip of the Bar Convent, York, England, says in her interesting Life of Saint Margaret Mary:

"We have seen how the first ceremony of the Enthronement of the Sacred Heart took place in the novitiate of the convent of Paray-le-Monial; this present devotion differs in no way from the devotion practiced by the humble Mistress of the novices and her subjects." Cardinal Billot writes in 1915 to Father Crawley-Boevey as follows:

"The work is the pure, simple and unalloyed devotion to the Sacred Heart handed down to us in the revelations of Blessed Margaret Mary. It is nothing more, nothing less. To introduce or set up in the place of honor in each household a representation of the Sacred Heart, in recognition of the supreme rights of Jesus Christ over the family as a whole, and over each of its members; to recite family prayers each evening before it, and to renew each night, by the lips of the father or mother, the consecration made on the first day; to be faithful to the practice of Holy Communion, and as far as possible to that of the Holy Hour, on the eve of the First Friday of the month; to meditate upon the lessons and examples given us by the Sacred Heart; to have recourse to this Fount of all graces in the family joys as well as the family sorrows, in good and evil days, in sufferings, in reverses, in partings, amid the tears shed at the grave and the smiles bestowed upon the cradle—in a word, amidst all the events that interrupt the normal and regular course of the family life . . . . .One has but to read in the life of Blessed Margaret Mary the description of the First Enthronement, carried out with closed doors in the novitiate . . . . .if the book of the future had been opened to her at the page entitled the *Enthronement of the Sacred Heart of Jesus in the Home,* she would have recognized in it the expansion of the acts so delicately outlined by her little novices."

In January, 1918, Pope Benedict XV, put the seal of approval on the devotion of the Enthronement in these forcible words:

"If from the canonization of Blessed Margaret Mary there results a more complete diffusion of the worship of the Sacred Heart, who would not by desire and deed thus hasten the spread of so excellent a devotion as that of the Enthronement of the Sacred Heart in families and their consecration to It? The dawn gives us an idea of what the midday will be like, and we, who in this praiseworthy consecration of families to the Sacred Heart recognize the dawn of that much-desired day when the sovereignty of Jesus Christ shall be acknowledged on all sides, repeat with confident joy the words of St. Paul: *Opportet illum regnare*—He must reign."

While the devotion to the Sacred Heart spread rapidly throughout Europe, and numerous chapels were everywhere erected in Its honor, there was, strange to say, no formal consecration of a church in Its name for a century after the death of Saint Margaret Mary. The wishes of

Our Lord, expressed through her medium to Louis XIV, that France should raise a temple to His Heart; that there should be a solemn consecration of king, court and the whole nation to It, and that Its image should be placed upon the standards of France and engraved upon her arms, and so be victorious over her enemies, were disregarded. Louis XV, in his turn, failed of response. Marie Leczinska, his amiable and long-suffering wife, of whom he was entirely unworthy, became deeply interested; she obtained from the council of the bishops of France, assembled in Paris in 1765, that the worship of the Sacred Heart should be, "according to my most ardent desire," established in every diocese in France. One of her daughters embroidered the image of the Heart of Jesus on a set of splendid hangings meant for one of the French churches; Louis' son, the Dauphin, raised a chapel at Versailles himself in Its honor; but he died, too early for France and his people. Louis XVI, a prisoner in the Temple, remembered the Divine promises, and made a vow to erect the Church of the Sacred Heart when he recovered his liberty—but this was not to be.

It is claimed that this first church was that attached to the Convent of Notre Dame des Oiseaux, in Paris, by some French writers, but this is incorrect, as the date of this edifice is 1837, a claim long antedated by the dedication to the Sacred Heart of the Royal Basilica of Lisbon, in 1790, during the reign of Queen Maria I. There is a third claim, even better substantiated. To the United States of America belongs, beyond question, the honor of having first dedicated a church to the Sacred Heart of Jesus, humble and poor as was the first altar of Annecy, and, like it, the nucleus of a magnificent development. In the little Pennsylvania town of Conewago, 10 miles to the southeast of the famous battlefield of Gettysburg, there still stands a little wooden structure, whose date is three years earlier than that of the Lisbon basilica. Father James Pellentz, a Jesuit priest in charge of the mission, was its builder. The year of its foundation—1787—is cut into a stone inserted near the roof, and below this is an oblong slab of marble bearing a Heart encircled with a crown of thorns and surmounted by a cross.

America has still another claim as a client of the Sacred Heart. It is said to contain at the present time more churches bearing the name of the Sacred Heart of Jesus than any other country on the globe. Three great lamps hang in the chapel of Paray-le-Monial before the tabernacle above which Our Lord appeared to Saint Margaret Mary, and of the three the largest and most beautiful is from our country. It is of massive silver, exquisitely wrought, and bears testimony, night and day, of the homage and devotion of America to the Sacred Heart of Jesus.

The Words of His Holiness, Pope Benedict XV Concerning the Canonization of Saint Margaret Mary.

"We thank the Lord for the opportunity afforded us to-day of giving new proof of our benevolence towards the French nation, of which Margaret Mary Alacoque is a shining glory and will be a loving protector. Equally grateful to Him are we for the opportunity of holding up to public esteem the Religious Institute in which the spirit of St. Francis of Sales ever lives . . . . Engraved on our heart, beloved children, is the record of the hope that we expressed on the day of the publication of the Decree on the two miracles attributed to the intercession of Blessed Alacoque. On that memorable occasion there rose to our lips, spontaneously, because it was formed in our heart, the hope that the solemn recognition of the prodigies wrought by God at the intercession of Margaret Mary Alacoque might serve to spread ever more the devotion to the Sacred Heart of Jesus, because the pious daughter of St. Francis of Sales received from Jesus Christ Himself the mission of making known the riches of His Divine Heart that men might come to Him as a Fount of graces and a model of virtue. We should praise God that there is such evident connection between the prodigies attributed to Blessed Alacoque and the devotion to the Sacred Heart that there followed from that, universal agreement on the necessity of helping in every way the apostolate of the pious virgin of Paray-le-Monial. It gives us special pleasure to be able thus to bear witness publicly to our satisfaction in hearing of the further development of the work of the consecration of families to the Sacred Heart of Jesus. In the sadness in which our pontificate must go on, as it was born, more and more does the Lord make us feel His hand—of a father, and we wish that all the members of the Christian family may praise and thank Him for it.

"But to-day's Decree, which brings to its conclusion the Cause of the Canonization of Blessed Alacoque is far more eloquent than that on the miracles. To-day, too, we must turn our ear and hear the word of God, Who shall determine *if and when* the humble inmate of the cloister of Paray-le-Monial shall be raised to the honor of the altars. Nevertheless, the historian may say that to-day her story is completed; the theologian and the canonist have carried their researches and examinations to the full length; in the hands of even the most critical the arms are broken and not even any outside circumstance hinders the sentence, that now it is possible to go on with security to the Canonization of Margaret Mary Alacoque. So this happy event may be greeted as imminent by those, too, who do not allow themselves to be guided by a too warm imagination. But does not he who knows that he is close to his goal hasten and move more quickly? So should all those devoted to Blessed Alacoque hasten and perfect themselves in the devotion to the Sacred Heart of Jesus in proportion to their present hope for the approach of the Canonization of the heroine, the efficacy of whose apostolate has grown ever since the day of the approval of the miracles attributed to her; indeed by the means of that approval.

"We said on another occasion that all the faithful should help forward that apostolate by welcoming and making their own all the holy activities suggested by devotion towards the Divine Heart of the Savior . . . . May the blessing of God descend copiously on France, cradle of Blessed Alacoque, and bring about that from the place whence came the first ray of devotion to the Sacred Heart may come ever the example of constancy and fervor in this beautiful devotion, to rejoice not only the Salesian cloisters, but the entire Christian family." (February 6, 1918.)

The Canonization of Blessed Margaret Mary, owing to the war raging at the time of these words, it was found necessary to defer awhile longer; but on May 13, 1920, Feast of the Ascension, the Apostle of the Sacred Heart of Jesus received the honors of the Church, under the name of Saint Margaret Mary Alacoque.

Translation of Decree of Canonization of Blessed Margaret Mary Alacoque, Virgin, Professed Religious of the order of the Visitation of the Blessed Virgin Mary, of the Diocese of Autun, in response to the question: What is to be thought of the miracles wrought after her Beatification and of the evidence for them, both in the event and afterwards?

Amid the social disorder, bloodshed and fratricidal strife of the time, we can easily imagine the overwhelming joy which filled the hearts of all loving children of Holy Church, when the announcement was made that the cause of the Canonization of Blessed Margaret Mary Alacoque had been brought to the long-desired issue. Anyone who considers, even for a moment, the intimate connection between Blessed Margaret Mary Alacoque and the devotion to the Sacred Heart, must instantly recognize that this happy event will bring about a great increase in that devotion, ever peculiarly appealing to man's heart, ever most rich in good, never more needed than now.

For men today, more perhaps than ever before, are prone to forget, if they do not indeed openly ridicule, any detail of life which transcends the natural order; an attitude of mind which grows daily worse. As a natural result of the lust for wealth and power which long since displaced the pursuit of the higher things of life, mankind utterly forgot God, and hence were sowed the seeds of that mutual hatred in which nation has risen against nation and kingdom against kingdom. But even while this world war rages fiercely, a divine voice has spoken, has spoken all the clearer for the tumult through which it must be heard: "I have come to cast fire upon the earth, and what will I but that it be enkindled," (Luke, XII, 49) the voice of our Lord Himself, opposing to the devouring flames of unbridled human passion the fire of divine charity, recalling men to the sweet concord of brotherly love, and proposing Himself as their divine model. "Learn of Me because I am meek and humble of heart, and you shall find rest for your souls." (Matt. XI, 29).

Nothing, clearly, can so readily conduce to the realization of this ideal as devotion to the Sacred Heart. Once before, the love of God had waned in many hearts through the spread of Jansenism, which portrayed the Divine Majesty as unconcerned with the welfare of mankind; then did the all-merciful God, in accordance with

His promise never to fail His Church in her hour of need, a promise so wondrously fulfilled throughout the ages, once more supply a sovereign remedy for the peculiar needs of the age, by disclosing the infinite treasures of His singular love for man, making the visible symbol thereof the most Sacred Heart of Christ, which, from the Incarnation to Calvary, had given numberless unmistakable proofs of the ardent love for souls by which It was consumed.

In regard to the form in which devotion to the Sacred Heart was to be practiced, the part played by Sister Margaret Mary Alacoque is known to all. Inspired by the Heavenly vision, she well understood the importance of the work given to her to do, and devoted to it all the energy of her being, under the wise direction of the Venerable Servant of God, Claude de la Colombiere. Not only did he witness and bear testimony to the sanctity of his daughter in Christ, but emulated it to such a degree that the virtues of the Venerable Claude have long since been acknowledged by the solemn pronouncement of the Holy See to be heroic. Throughout her life Sister Margaret Mary with ardent zeal labored incessantly to arouse in the hearts of the faithful true love and veneration for the divine Heart of our Lord and Savior; and, after her holy death, this same great work was carried on no less effectively by the cause of her Beatification which was immediately introduced in due form. As was only to be expected, the strength of her cause kept equal pace with the growth of the devotion to the Sacred Heart; together they met and conquered opposition, until, in 1864, her cause having been crowned by the solemn rites of Beatification, and the feast of the Sacred Heart raised to a double of the first class for the universal church, this devotion, so consoling to humanity, spread far and wide in a manner truly miraculous. And as experience soon proved how eminently profitable and fruitful this devotion was for the whole church, the cause of her Canonization, introduced within two years after her Beatification, was greatly fostered, and, with several Bishops taking the lead, earnest prayers and petitions were presented to the Holy See that it might be brought to a happy conclusion. God Himself deigned to put the seal of His approval upon these pious desires by various signs and prodigies, from among which two cures were proposed for consideration, and found, after due investigation, to have been real miracles and wrought by God through the intercession of the Blessed Margaret Mary Alacoque.

The evidence was discussed first in an introductory meeting, then on two separate occasions in subsequent preliminary meeting, and, finally, on the fourth of last December, in a general meeting, held in the presence of our Most Holy Father, Pope Benedict XV, in which His Eminence Cardinal Vico, the Promoter of the cause, introduced the following question for deliberation: "What is to be thought of the miracles wrought after her Beatification and of the evidence for them, both in the event and afterwards?" Their Eminences the Cardinals, and the Reverend Consultors, then expressed their opinions, which were carefully considered by the Holy Father. He, however, according to custom, postponed his final decision, asking those present to offer meanwhile their earnest prayers to God.

Today, however, a most auspicious day as that on which the three Wise Men came to adore the Infant Savior, after devoutly celebrating the Sacred Mysteries, he summoned to the Vatican His Eminence Cardinal Antonio Vico, Bishop of Porto and Santa Rufina, Pro-Prefect of the Sacred Congregation of Rites, and Promoter of the cause, together with Reverend Angelo Mariani, Promoter of the Faith, and myself, the undersigned secretary, and, in our presence, solemnly declared that each of the proposed cures were true miracles: the first, the instantaneous and complete cure of Aloysia Agostini Coleschi of chronic inflammation of the spinal chord in the region of the loins, the other, the instantaneous and complete cure of the Countess Antonio Astorri of Pavesi of a cancer in the right breast.

This Decree is declared of public record and inscribed in the "Acta" of the Sacred Congregation of Rites, January 6th, 1918.

ANTONIO CARDINAL VICO, Pro- Pref.
ALEXANDER VERDE, Sec.